STANLEY G. PAYNE

The Collapse of the Spanish Republic, 1933–1936

ORIGINS OF THE CIVIL WAR

YALE UNIVERSITY PRESS   NEW HAVEN & LONDON

Set in FontShop Scala by Duke & Company, Devon, Pennsylvania.
Printed in the United States of America.

Library of Congress Cataloging-in-Publication Data
Payne, Stanley G.
The collapse of the Spanish Republic, 1933–1936 : origins of the Civil War /
Stanley G. Payne.
p.   cm.
Includes bibliographical references and index.
ISBN-13: 978-0-300-11065-4 (alk. paper)
ISBN-10: 0-300-11065-0 (alk. paper)
1. Spain—History—Republic, 1931–1939. 2. Representative government and
representation—Spain—History—20th century. I. Title.
DP254.P37 2006
946.081′1—dc22
2005023407

A catalogue record for this book is available from the British Library.

The paper in this book meets the guidelines for permanence and durability of the Committee on Production Guidelines for Book Longevity of the Council on Library Resources.

10 9 8 7 6 5 4 3 2 1

To Adolfo Suárez and the leaders and members of Unión de Centro Democrático, who demonstrated how to construct a democracy in Spain.

Their history was brief, but glorious.

CONTENTS

Preface   ix

Introduction: The Problem of Representative Government
in Spain   1

1 The Republican Project   8

2 The Turning Point of the Republic: 1933   26

3 The Revolutionary Insurrection of 1934   52

4 A Conservative Republic? 1934–1935   96

5 Frustration of the Parliamentary System   118

6 Toward the Popular Front   140

7 The Elections of February 1936   170

8 The Left Returns to Power: February–March 1936   185

9 The Left Consolidates Power: March–May 1936   215

10 Breaking Down: May–June 1936   248

11 Competing Utopias: The Revolutionary Movements in the Spring of 1936   273

12 The Final Phase: May–July 1936   294

13 The Military Conspiracy   308

14 The Assassination of Calvo Sotelo   319

Conclusion: Could the Breakdown Have Been Avoided?   339

Notes   369

Index   411

PREFACE

BY COMPARISON WITH THE vast bibliography on the Spanish Civil War, there has been surprisingly little attention to its origin in the collapse of the Republic. This book is an attempt to compensate for that lack and to open a new discussion of the implosion of democratic politics in Spain from 1933 into 1936. Though it builds on the second half of my earlier history of the Second Republic, it is not merely a revision of that book, but a new and greatly expanded study.

What this inquiry reveals, above all, is the need for much more research on the six months preceding the Civil War. Particularly necessary is careful investigation of the state of the economy and the effects of the new socioeconomic changes, the role of the several sectors of the Socialist movement and the rivalry between them, the internal debate (such as it was) within the government, the activities and internal debate of the left Republicans, the government's security policy and the role of the police, the use of revolutionary *delegados*, the extensive disorder in the southern countryside, the assault on the Church, the closure of Catholic schools and the seizure or arson of Church property, and any number of other problems. Historians have preferred to concentrate more on hopeful early years of the Republic than on its convulsive ending.

My thanks, as ever, to Juan Linz for his reading of the manuscript and for his valuable suggestions.

Introduction

HISTORIANS HAVE RECOGNIZED THAT the advent of the Second Republic in Spain in 1931 was a unique event, the only major new step toward democracy in Europe during a decade of economic and political crisis. Spain was indeed "different," but only in the most exemplary way. At that point the country seemed to be resuming the role it had played a century earlier, when Spain had introduced the word "liberal" to the modern lexicon and had provided inspiration to progressives throughout Europe. First it had been Spain's war of independence against Napoleon—the only true "people's war" of the era—which had aroused the admiration of a continent and had popularized the term "guerrilla." Equally important had been the Constitution of 1812, Europe's first nineteenth-century liberal constitution, which inspired liberals for an entire generation in southern and central Europe, in Latin America, and in the Russia of the Decembrists.

The drama of liberal government in nineteenth-century Spain lay especially in the fact that no other country in the world made such persistent efforts to introduce such advanced political forms amid similar conditions of social and economic underdevelopment. Such premature liberalism had seemed destined to fail.

One reason was that Spain never experienced the "long peace" enjoyed by most of nineteenth-century Europe; rather, it spent a greater proportion

1

of that time engaged in war of one sort or another than any other country. Continual turmoil arose both from the legacy of empire and from incessant efforts to introduce more advanced liberalism. Spain was the only country for which the century began and ended with major international conflicts—the war of independence against Napoleon from 1808 to 1814 and the Cuban-American war of 1895–1898—with the Moroccan war of 1859 in between. As if this were not enough, Spain became the classic arena of civil war, beginning with the limited liberal-traditionalist conflict of 1822–23 (ended by French military intervention), followed by the Catalan peasant insurrection of 1827 (Guerra dels Agraviats), the devastating First Carlist War of 1833–1840 (in which well over one percent of Spain's population died in military action), a minor Carlist insurrection in Catalonia from 1846 to 1849, the major Second Carlist War of 1873–1876, and the Republican cantonalist revolt of 1873. To these were added numerous brief civilian-military *pronunciamientos,* several of which involved serious fighting, as well as large-scale campaigns to repress Hispano-American independence movements, first in the decade 1815–1825 and later in the Ten Years' War in Cuba (1868–1878), which in turn was quickly followed by the brief "Guerra Chiquita" (1879–80). To all these might be added a campaign in the Philippines and another in Morocco in 1894, as well as the struggle to regain Santo Domingo and the naval conflicts on the west coast of South America during the 1860s. The two main Cuban campaigns would cost the Spanish army a combined total of more than 100,000 fatalities. No other nineteenth-century European state proportionately lost so much life and treasure in its colonial campaigns, and yet at the end Spain had nothing to show for it, whereas nearly all other European colonial empires, even that of Portugal, had greatly expanded.

It was first of all major war and foreign invasion that destabilized the Old Regime in Spain, giving liberalism its initial opportunity, but one for which the country was not prepared. Liberal politics would emerge through a series of seven convulsions, in each of which the liberal or radical initiative would seek to push Spanish institutions further to the left than the society was prepared or willing to sustain. The political history of most of the nineteenth and twentieth centuries can thus be divided into a set of seven subperiods in which a rapid and precocious liberal or radical breakthrough was followed by a longer period of conservatism or reaction, until a consensual democracy was finally achieved after 1977.

A major threat to stability arose with the emergence of an extreme left in 1821. Many of the leading *doceañistas* (men of the year twelve) who had written the Constitution of 1812 had moderated their politics when they had a chance to return to power in 1820, but they found themselves outflanked by a new minority generation of radical liberals, the *exaltados*, who took power in 1821. The exaltados imposed a centralized Jacobin regime that flouted some of its own liberal laws in favor of coercive government, which drew little popular support and was soon overthrown by French military intervention. Despite the failure of their policies, however, they established a Spanish exaltado tradition that resurfaced in five successive generations, each time culminating in equivalent or worse disaster as the extreme left sought to undermine the broader left-liberal cause. Its avatars continued to champion the seizure of power, the rejection of moderation, and the use of violence and coercive government—a tendency overcome only temporarily by the moderate liberal generation of 1876 and, it is to be hoped, more permanently by the democratic generation of 1976.

Table 1

Sequences in Modern Spanish Politics

LEFT-LIBERAL INITIATIVES	CONSERVATIVE OR RIGHTIST REACTIONS
1808–1814	1814–1820
1820–1823	1823–1833
1835–1838	1839–1854
1854–1856	1856–1868
1868–1873	1874–1917
1917–1923	1923–1931
1931–1939	1939–1975

Nineteenth-century Spanish liberalism was personalistic and sectarian, generally tending toward fragmentation. For more than a century, through the Civil War of 1936, the political elite struggled with a long, slow transition from the culture of the Old Regime to modernization, often exhibiting the same egotism and rivalry shown by aristocratic cliques under the traditional monarchy. A kind of psychological cultural deficit persisted, even stronger in leftist than in rightist groups, for among the former it was further stimulated by the introduction of modern radical doctrines.

The first long era of liberal convulsion and military pronunciamientos lasted for six decades, until 1874. The restored Bourbon monarchy led by Antonio Cánovas del Castillo managed to establish a stable parliamentary regime for the first time, and was generally successful until the crisis of World War I, which brought turmoil to most of Europe. Cánovas was the greatest statesman of modern Spain, not only achieving stability but also overcoming the great defect of Spain's liberal movements and regimes, namely their exclusivism and denial of access. The liberals had insisted on imposing their own versions of liberalism and radicalism, denying reasonable representation or equal participation to their rivals. By contrast, the restored parliamentary monarchy was based on what Carlos Dardé has called "la aceptación del adversario,"[1] permitting access and representation to rival forces willing to accept the new constitution and the framework of legality it established. Cánovas declared an end to what he called the politics of *la bolsa o la vida* (your purse or your life). The Restoration system did not install universal male suffrage until 1890. Elections were controlled largely by the governing parties and by established local elites, a system that reflected the level of social and cultural development existing in late-nineteenth century Spain. The possibility of a genuine democracy did not exist until the beginning of the second quarter of the twentieth century, at the earliest. As it was, the Restoration system represented a major civic achievement, creating stability, stimulating economic growth and modernization, and permitting the evolution of liberal institutions toward greater reformism and greater inclusiveness. This made it possible to exclude the military from politics, for military intervention had stemmed above all from the absence or weaknesses and divisions of civilian power, rather than from inherent military ambition. At the same time, like most nineteenth-century regimes, the Restoration system suffered from notable limitations, which by the early twentieth century could not readily be overcome.[2]

By the beginning of the twentieth century Spain had one of the longest "modern" political histories in the world, dating from the time that it had become only the second large continental European country to adopt independently a modern liberal constitution in 1812. Development accelerated after 1900,[3] and World War I brought both new prosperity and new tensions, with pressure for democratization and also, for the first time, for worker revolution. The Restoration system, like all nineteenth-century systems of elitist liberalism, had to reform itself in order to survive. More than half the countries of Europe failed to make a successful transition to democratization. The Spanish system did reform itself sufficiently to permit a degree of electoral semidemocracy in the larger cities, but the essentially feudal cacique system persisted in most of the country. Moreover, the limited decentralization achieved between 1907 and 1923 was inadequate to satisfy the demands of the new peripheral nationalisms and of other autonomist movements. As the "social question" moved nearer the center of public debate, revolutionary anarchosyndicalist domination of the only mass trade union, the Confederación Nacional del Trabajo (National Confederation of Labor; CNT), after 1917 produced escalating violence that eventually threatened the stability of Spain's political system.

The Restoration system was not, however, an economic failure; it achieved accelerated economic development, particularly in the era of World War I. The problem with accelerated development had to do with its late arrival, after the demonstration effect of more advanced economies and social structures in northwestern Europe had begun to take hold in Spanish psychology. The inflation accompanying the war created genuine hardship and heightened labor demands, especially in view of the greatly expanded profits enjoyed by owners. Added to this was the absence of a relatively strong and moderate Socialist movement of the sort that had taken hold in most west European countries. Thus a combination of factors, which included the rather harsh mentality of Spanish employers, had emerged after World War I to create an explosive labor situation, one that would not be constructively resolved for many decades.

By the early 1920s there was a strong sense that the established political elites still had such a stranglehold on the system that it could hardly be reformed. Though some progress was made, there was no breakthrough to democratization—whether or not that was truly feasible—and increasing fragmentation made responsible government ever more difficult. Nonetheless, the system would not have been overthrown in 1923 had it not been for the stalemated colonial war in the newly established Moroccan Protectorate, which created further pressure for more decisive leadership.

The peaceful imposition of what was universally perceived as a temporary, "Cincinnatian" dictatorship by Lieutenant General Miguel Primo de

Rivera in 1923 was at first welcomed by many informed political thinkers, including many liberals. The dictatorship was seen as cutting the Gordian knot that made political reform unlikely or impossible, and to some extent that perception may have been valid. Martial law facilitated control of political violence, and in 1924–25 the dictatorship was able to seize a new opportunity to achieve pacification of the Moroccan Protectorate in collaboration with France.

A truly "Cincinnatian" dictatorship may have had some limited justification. That justification, however, ceased by the end of 1925 with the full restoration of order, a realignment of administration, and resolution of the Moroccan crisis. Had the dictatorship been terminated then, Primo de Rivera might have gone down in Spanish history as a benign and even salvific dictator. In 1926, however, he instituted a "civil dictatorship," with regular civilian ministers, signaling an intention of making the arrangement at least semipermanent. Not long afterward he tried in vain to revise the constitution in a permanently authoritarian direction. Despite his failure by 1930, in the process he put an end to the parliamentary system of the Restoration, creating what became a decisive hiatus in constitutional government. Although Alfonso XIII had not conspired to install the temporary dictatorship, his acceptance and tacit support fatally identified the Bourbon monarchy with the overthrow of the constitutional system. The fact that it had been one of the most benign dictatorships of the century was, in terms of its long-range effects, irrelevant.

Had Primo de Rivera stepped down in 1926, allowing space for electoral reform under a restored Alfonso XIII, a democratized constitutional monarchy could have maintained the continuity of institutions that was probably necessary for a new system of democracy to succeed. As it was, the dictatorship created a decisive break with constitutional progress, ended the parliamentary evolution of the most progressive regime in Spanish history, fatally compromised the monarchy, and left behind it a radicalized political climate that rejected the resumption of moderate reform.

Even so, the prospects for constructive reform were perhaps not entirely hopeless when Primo de Rivera resigned at the close of January 1930. The situation in Morocco was stable, the economy had expanded enormously, and domestic subversion had been extinguished. But the next fifteen months were wasted by timid and inept government, political division, and lack of leadership. The old monarchist parties had largely vanished and could not easily be reassembled. The most accomplished remaining monarchist politician, Francesc Cambó, was stricken with throat cancer and unavailable. The government repeated the mistake of the Russian Provisional Government in 1917 by delaying new elections, the only way to achieve a legitimate administration; and whereas the Russians delayed only nine months, the leadership in Madrid postponed balloting for fifteen, a fatal mistake. With each month that arbitrary rule was extended, the tide of alienation and republicanism rose higher. When elections were finally held in April 1931, another major mistake was made: municipal elections were to be followed by provincial contests and only later by national elections. This arrangement overlooked the fact that the left always did better at the local than the national level, and guaranteed a maximal vote for the republican opposition in the first elections held, which the opposition then artificially converted into a sort of plebiscite, which technically they were not at all. By that point the monarchy seemed to have lost public support, and it handed power very abruptly to the new republican leadership.[4]

Thus, instead of being introduced under the stabilizing guidance of established institutions, the new democracy began as a quasi-revolutionary regime, building its institutions and political practices *ab ovo*. The dictatorial interlude thus had the effect of returning Spain to the era of pronunciamientos and convulsions. Though the Second Republic was not inevitably doomed to failure, a democratic system would have stood a better chance had it been associated with more historic and conservative institutions, which might have served to arbitrate and channel new mass democratic forces. There was of course no guarantee that a democratized constitutional monarchy would have enjoyed greater success under the radical pressures of the 1930s than did the Republic, but it would probably have enjoyed greater success in avoiding total polarization. Once Spain's only liberal regime of tolerance and progressive evolution had been overturned between 1923 and 1931, such a system would not be regained for nearly half a century.[5]

CHAPTER ONE

The Republican Project

THE INTRODUCTION OF THE Republic and the manner of its birth reflected the widespread transformation of Spanish society and culture during the preceding generation. Throughout the 1920s Spain achieved one of the highest economic growth rates in the world, and during the decades 1910–1930 it experienced the most rapid proportionate expansion of the urban population and industrial labor force in the country's history to that time. Industrial employment almost doubled, from 15.8 percent of the labor force to 26.5 percent, a figure that in fact slightly exceeded the proportionate shift to industrial employment during the next great boom decade of the 1960s. Though agriculture remained the largest single sector, despite the rapid growth of the labor force by 1930 the share of the active population engaged in agriculture and fishing had dropped to less than half for the first time, shrinking from 66 percent in 1910 to 45.5 percent in 1930. The growth in service employment was even more rapid than in industry, increasing from 20.8 percent in 1920 to 28 percent in 1930. Of an active labor force of approximately 8,773,000, some 2,325,000 were industrial workers and nearly 2,500,000 were engaged in services. Though about 1,900,000 were landless farm laborers, Spain was no longer the overwhelmingly rural, agrarian land that it had been as recently as 1910.[1]

Adult illiteracy dropped by almost 9 percent during the 1920s, apparently the most rapid improvement within a ten-year period in Spanish history. Opportunities for women expanded: their presence in the labor force grew by nearly 9 percent during the 1920s, while the percentage of women university students nearly doubled, from 4.79 to 8.3 in the years 1923–1927. Indeed, the absolute number of university students doubled between 1923 and 1930.[2]

The result was the beginning of a fundamental social and cultural transformation, which produced the most fundamental of revolutions—the psychological revolution of rising expectations. By 1930 millions of Spaniards for the first time expected rapid continuation and even expansion of major improvements in social and political affairs. Unless the magnitude of the recent expansion and its attendant sociopsychological changes are taken into account, Spanish society in the 1930s cannot be understood. The radical demands that followed did not stem from the fact that Spain had earlier failed to make progress, but precisely from the fact that in many areas it had been making rapid progress. As millions experienced rapid improvement in their lives, they and others would be determined to demand even more.

This transformation created a potential basis for democratization, though at this stage not one that could guarantee success. The republican forces that suddenly seized power in April 1931 were for the most part new formations. The original republican movement of the 1860s had produced the disastrous experience of the First Republic of 1873–74, when the country nearly fell apart. For two generations republicanism had been discredited as anarchic, and during the early twentieth century it expanded only slowly. What gave republicanism a new lease on life was not merely the accelerated modernization of Spain but also the disastrous failure of the dictatorship, which seemed to show that the monarchy itself was corrupt and authoritarian, and that democratization could be achieved only under a republic.

The Second Republic was inaugurated amid a dramatic explosion of popular enthusiasm in the larger cities, a mood of expectation and euphoria that constituted a Spanish variant of the yearning for some kind of new human order that was so widespread and intense in Europe during the generation following World War I. Its bloodless introduction—in contrast to the civic turmoils and military pronunciamientos of the preceding century—argued a new civic maturity. Comparisons with the French

Revolution were sometimes heard, but to the advantage of a new Spanish regime that had been born without violence. Such a favorable comparison, of course, betrayed more than a little confusion. The French Revolution had degenerated into repression and violence only after three years, so that any Spanish parallel with its phase of maximum conflict could be expected only later, a phase that did in fact afflict Spain. A more exact historical parallel might have been the French Third Republic, which from 1871 through its first decade took a very conservative form that reinforced stability.

The difficulty that Spain faced in consolidating a new democracy may be better understood through some comparative examples. In terms of civic culture, literacy rates, and economic development, it might be judged that Spain in 1931 was approximately at the level of Britain and France toward the end of the nineteenth century. During that earlier time neither northern country had had to face such severe political and social tests as those undergone by Spain in the 1930s. Victorian England had one of the most dynamic economies in the world and the longest of all parliamentary traditions but still had not introduced universal male suffrage, much less the female vote. The nascent French Third Republic had been faced with a quasi-revolutionary revolt in Paris, which it repressed with a ferocity that equaled anything seen in the Spanish Civil War of 1936. It then proceeded on a markedly conservative basis, for the working-class movement long remained rather weak in France. In contrast, Spanish society would soon be subjected to severe pressures of multiple and conflicting mass mobilizations.

Moreover, by 1931 the general European era of postwar democratization had already ended, and political currents both in the advanced countries of central Europe and in the underdeveloped ones of eastern and southern Europe were flowing strongly in the direction of radicalization and authoritarianism, not democratization. Once again, as a century earlier, Spanish political forces were seeking to play a unique role by inaugurating a new phase of progressivism. Republican leaders were conscious of this role, and some of them declared that the democratization of Spain would start a trend of rolling back fascism throughout the continent. Yet more than a century earlier Spanish progressivists had failed, and their failure had been most complete during the decade 1814–1823, when not merely was Spanish society unprepared but the international climate was hostile, as well.

Thus in 1931 Spain inhabited a dangerous "frontier zone" in which its new political institutions would attempt to approximate those of advanced northern Europe but in which its society and culture, despite recent rapid progress, had still not achieved levels equivalent to those of the northern countries. Accelerated development had helped to make possible the breakthrough of 1931, but the danger remained that it might have promoted a kind of developmental trap, stimulating major new demands and mobilization without having yet achieved the means to satisfy them.

Though the Republican coalition claimed to represent a new kind of politics, it had first attempted to overthrow the monarchy through an old-fashioned and abortive military pronunciamiento in December 1930. It gained power bloodlessly in April 1931, even though monarchists won most of the seats in the municipal contests, because the monarchists refused to engage in civil conflict. The Republic was thus initiated through a kind of political understanding. Despite the patriotic and self-abnegatory attitude of the crown and the monarchist politicians, the new coalition initiated a politics of vengeance toward the crown and the ministers of the fallen dictatorship through a series of political prosecutions that served no constructive purpose. Given the participation of the Socialists in some of the institutions of the dictatorship, they were also hypocritical. The new coalition took the attitude, which proved to be entirely mistaken, that conservative and Catholic opinion had been reduced to hopelessly minoritarian status and need no longer be considered in the political equation.

The Republican coalition rested on an alliance among three sectors: the Republican left (often termed *la izquierda burguesa*—the bourgeois left), the Republican center-right, and the Socialists, their initial cooperation masking the fact that each sector conceived of the Republican project in quite different terms. The Republican center-right was led by former monarchists such as the Catholics Niceto Alcalá Zamora and Miguel Maura, each of whom led very small new parties, and more substantially by Alejandro Lerroux's Radical Republican Party, which had moved from onetime radicalism to centrist moderation. The Republican center-right stood for the development of liberal democracy—the rules and practice of parliamentary constitutionalism—with only limited institutional and social reform. To the Republican center-right, the essence of the system would simply be civil rights and the constitutional rules of democratic fair play.

The coalition's fulcrum, however, was the parties of the Republican left, for it was they, rather than the Radical Party, who stood for a radical Republicanism and the revival of the exaltado tradition. Their concept of the Republican project was based on the cultural revolution of the nineteenth century, as well as a certain amount of social reform. This last concern was at first represented among the left Republicans, especially by the new Radical Socialist Republican Party, whose name was derived, as was customary, from French nomenclature, but which would be condemned to a short life because of its internal contradictions. It was much less socialist than its name indicated.

The most substantial sector of the Republican left was Acción Republicana, led by the writer and state functionary Manuel Azaña. This group also recognized the need for social reform, but placed uppermost the cultural revolution of republicanism, which would require creation of a strong modern state completely separated from religion, a series of fundamental institutional changes and reforms, and the construction of a modern secular educational system, to which Catholic education would be completely subordinated. According to Azaña, the failure of nineteenth-century Spanish liberalism had lain in its moderation, and the weakness of the past two generations of republicans lay in their willingness to compromise and collaborate with nonrepublican forces. In speeches in 1930 and 1931, Azaña proclaimed his republican intransigence, describing his stance as "radical" and "sectarian." Thus, from the point of view of the Republican left, the democratic Republic was not intended to be a democracy tolerant of equal rights for all but a radical reform project enjoying total hegemony over Spanish life. As Nigel Townson has put it, their goal was not to achieve a "consensual framework" for all Spanish society but rather "to give substance to secular and modernizing ideals,"[3] which, as José Manuel Macarro Vera observed, "was not initially identified with democracy, but with social, economic, or political reform."[4]

The left Republicans ignored the example of the neighboring Portuguese republic, which had governed disastrously from 1910 to 1926. As one of its leading historians, Rui Ramos, has described it, the Portuguese "First Republic was not a liberal democracy. It was a state ruled by a revolutionary movement, the Portuguese Republican Party (PRP). The PRP disfranchised most of the electorate and, although it allowed other forces to be represented in parliament, it never allowed any peaceful rotation in power. . . . Only the army was able to defeat the PRP."[5] The Portuguese Republic had represented a continuation of nineteenth-century radicalism, rather than a breakthrough to twentieth-century democracy.

The left Republicans also intended to exclude the right permanently from government, but believed that their position would be consistent with democracy because they were convinced that the governing Republican coalition represented a strong majority of Spanish opinion. This conclusion at first glance was borne out by its overwhelming victory in the parliamentary elections of June 1931. The rightist opposition was confused and disorganized, as well as leaderless and intimidated, and was very weakly represented in the first Republican parliament, the Cortes.

The Republican left formed only the left-center of the new governing alliance, whose left wing was the Socialist Party. Founded in 1879, the Spanish Socialist Workers Party (PSOE) was a classic movement of the Second International that for decades had been one of the weakest Socialist parties in Europe. When its first leader, Pablo Iglesias, had first been elected to parliament in 1910, in his maiden speech he launched a vicious attack on the reformist Canalejas government, Spain's most progressive administration in more than two decades, while declaring legitimate the assassination of the leader of the Conservative Party. In conjunction with the anarchosyndicalists, the Socialists had launched a revolutionary general strike in 1917 to install a constituent republic, which resulted in 71 dead and hundreds injured. Always treated leniently by the Spanish government, the Socialists had on most occasions followed more moderate policies, participating in elections and slowly building a trade union base. The profound structural changes of the 1920s and the coming of democracy enabled the Socialist trade union, the Unión General de Trabajadores (General Union of Workers; UGT), to expand into a mass movement, reaching more than a million members by 1932. The Second Republic offered the Socialists their first opportunity to participate in a government—something that the French Socialists had not yet done—an opportunity that they accepted without having fully resolved the issues of reformism versus revolutionism in their doctrine. The dominant tendency was to take the position that the Republic would produce decisive changes, opening the way peacefully for a Socialist system to be achieved without revolutionary violence. The UGT leader Francisco Largo Caballero declared at the outset of the new regime that as a result violent revolution "would never put down roots in Spain." The Socialists also viewed the Spanish changes within a larger context as a new tide of democracy and progressivism that would roll back the trend toward fascism initiated by Mussolini a decade earlier.

With the exception of the chief moderates, Alcalá Zamora and Lerroux, the new Republican leaders had little practical political experience. From their point of view, this sharp rupture with the older elites of the preceding parliamentary system was an advantage, leaving them uncorrupted with the "old politics," but their inexperience and doctrinaire approach, combined with their misreading of national sentiment in general, deprived them of contact with large moderate and conservative sectors of the middle classes.

The broad alliance in fact lasted less than a year. By the close of 1931, with completion of the new constitution and the elevation of Alcalá Zamora to the presidency, the Radicals demanded that the Socialists leave the government so that an all-Republican coalition could rule. This demand was perfectly feasible, given the Radicals' parliamentary strength. The Radicals argued that continued participation by the Socialists was a contradiction, since the Republican parties and the constitution were based on private property. The broad alliance was denounced as unnatural, skewing Spanish affairs to the left.

This assessment overestimated the moderation of the Republican left. To the new prime minister, Manuel Azaña, and to most of his party associates, alliance with the Socialists was necessary first to guarantee the strength of the new system, giving it a base among the workers, and secondly to guarantee the specifically leftist, radically reformist character of the Republic. The left Republicans clearly preferred the Socialists to the Radicals, and thus until September 1933 Azaña would preside over a leftist coalition from which the democratic Republican center had already withdrawn.

Azaña would remain the key leader of the left until the collapse of the Republic, and even after that he would serve as a valuable figurehead. His greatest talent was rhetorical; none of the other leftist leaders could equal his eloquent and lapidary definitions of Republican policy or his clarity and vigor in defining the priorities of the new regime. This gift, together with his aloof and dominating personality, gave him an unmatched authority not merely among the Republican left but among some of the Socialists, as well. His approach was doctrinaire and anticonsensual. Azaña had little capacity for empirical analysis, his orientation resting more on the rejection of Spanish conservatism and tradition than on a careful study of the existing character of Spanish society. It was symptomatic that his only extended political analysis had been of French rather than Spanish military policy, and even that study was incomplete. His basic formation was subjective and esthetic, as he himself admitted, and he had very little capacity for political self-criticism. Though he had been known in the literary and cultural life of Madrid for some time, he had never published a truly major work, and his writings had attracted only limited interest, so that he himself admitted that he had been "an author without readers."[6]

Azaña's aloof, acerbic, and arrogant personality was both a strength and a weakness. His more moderate colleague Miguel Maura later wrote, "The Azaña that I knew in 1930 lacked the most elemental human touch," demonstrating "disdain for everything and everyone, born of the conviction that possessed him of being a neglected and misunderstood genius . . . pitiless in his judgments of others and their actions; in a word, insufferable."[7] His lack of practical political experience was also a limitation, and he did not develop greater tact or wisdom as the years passed under the Republic.

His strength lay in clear, firm ideas that crystallized the goals of the moderate left, in a willingness to lead without a hint of serious compromise or any whiff of corruption, and in his compelling oratorical ability. His tongue and intellect made him both respected and feared, though his rhetoric was sometimes counterproductive. As Maura observed, "His famous lapidary and scalding phrases contributed more than a little to the hatred that the right came to feel for him. . . . He offered them with genuine delight and, knowing their effect, like a real masochist with regard to the enmity and hatred they created."[8] But like many intellectuals in politics, Azaña was also characterized by a profound ambivalence. Physically timid and constitutionally averse to violence, he yet was determined never to compromise. His undeniably great political energy and ambition were not boundless, for he lacked the patience, tolerance, and stamina for petty politics necessary during a long period of leadership, and he periodically suffered from deep moods of alienation and a yearning for withdrawal. On the morrow of electoral defeat in 1933, one follower was scandalized to come upon Azaña placidly reading an esoteric history of the Byzantine empire, a millennium removed in time and place.

THE REPUBLICAN REFORMS OF 1931–1933

For the left Republicans and the Socialists, the Republic was not to consist solely of a democratic political system open to the representation of all social and cultural interests, but was rather the institutional matrix for a series of far-reaching reforms, even though the two sectors disagreed, sometimes profoundly, about the character and extent of these reforms. Those approved between 1931 and 1933 primarily involved seven areas: church and state, educational expansion, the military, regional autonomy, labor relations, agrarian reform, and expansion of public works.

For several generations the animus of the Spanish left had been directed increasingly against the Catholic Church, as much as or more than against conservative political and economic interests. In completing the cultural revolution of the nineteenth century, the chief aims of the left Republicans were laicization and a certain concept of cultural modernization, which held that Spain could never become truly modern and harmonious without thoroughly subordinating all influence of the Church.

As secularization increased, anticlericalism became the principal common denominator of the left. By the 1930s Spain had become a partially secularized country and thus had entered the "danger zone" of cultural change in which religious conflict would become most intense. A generally secularized society no longer quarrels very much about the role of traditional religion, while in a society of only limited secularization, as in nineteenth-century Spain, secular and anticlerical interests could present only a limited challenge. As it was, the wars of religion, which had never afflicted sixteenth- and seventeenth-century Spain, arrived in modern form in the 1930s with a vengeance. Probably in no other country have so many different ideologies seriously entered into direct political and cultural competition at one time as in Spain during that decade. The more radical secular ideologies themselves functioned, if not as "political religions," at least in many cases as politico-ideological substitutes for religion.

Only as a kind of religious warfare can the intensity of the clerical-anticlerical conflict in Spain be understood. Much of anticlerical doctrine came from France,[9] and condemned Catholicism for every manner of ills: excessive possession of wealth of various kinds, oppression of the poor, maintaining an authoritarian internal structure, a supposedly overweening political influence, preaching political doctrines in church, sexual abuse and perversion, chaining the common people to ignorance and poverty. The Church was also blamed for historical abuses and the failures of Spain and of its empire.

The anticlericals seemed to present a mirror image of what they denounced, exhibiting extreme intolerance and desire for domination, which might be expected to stimulate an equivalent response in Catholics. Anticlericalism also showed a pronounced tendency to replace the sacrificial and liturgical role of the Church, inverting the Passion of Christ in anticlerical rituals, while the worker left advanced its own concepts of the sacrificial, redemptive role of the common people.[10]

In fact, in the early twentieth century the Vatican did not hold the Spanish Church, despite its fidelity, in particularly high regard. It was always more impressed with whatever was written about Catholic doctrine or theology in French, and in Spain was willing to accept the formal separation of church and state so long as there existed a quid pro quo acceptance of the principle of a free church in a free state. This the anticlericals were in no way willing to concede, arguing that separation would leave the Church with too much power and influence. They rejected "negative secularism," which would leave all religions and ideologies uncontrolled, in favor of "positive secularism" as an alternative faith that required the subordination of religion. The anticlericals made no effort to restrict ordinary religious freedom within Church confines, but insisted on the importance of controlling and restricting all aspects of its public expression, especially in education. Legislation would eventually be passed to deny all clergy the right to teach—one of the most fundamental violations of religious freedom and civil rights. Azaña recognized that the persecution of Catholic interests was illiberal and undemocratic, but declared it a vital issue of "public health." Certain other restrictions were placed on Church economic activity, and public demonstrations of religion were also banned. The Society of Jesus was dissolved, priests were occasionally fined for delivering "political sermons," and some of the more zealous city councils even fined Catholic women for wearing crosses around their necks. Very early in the life of the new government, Catholic churches and buildings became targets of arson and mob destruction in the famous *quema de conventos* of 11–12 May 1931, in which more than 100 buildings were torched and sacked in Madrid and several cities of the south and east, destroying also priceless libraries and art. The authorities then gave the first example of the left Republican habit of "blaming the victim" by acting to arrest monarchists and conservatives rather than the authors of the destruction. Later, during the spring of 1936, illegal seizures of Church buildings and properties would often simply be winked at by the Azaña–Casares Quiroga governments then in power. At no time did any of the leftist parties take the position that Church interests and properties merited the full protection of a state of law.

The Spanish left was obsessed with the conviction that it represented the irresistible march of history and that the correlation of political forces had shifted decisively in its favor. The left did not deny that conservative sectors of society still existed, but it deemed them to have fallen into a hopelessly minoritarian status that merited no recognition in the legislation and administration of Spain. While it was true that by this time those political groups overtly supporting Catholicism had dropped to less than half the total vote, they nonetheless amounted to a very large minority of the population. This latter fact was held by the left to be irrelevant on the grounds that Catholic opinion would not be able to mobilize and play a major role in public affairs, when faced with the power of the left.

The new administration meanwhile embarked on the greatest expansion of school facilities in Spanish history, with the goal of providing free public education for all children within a decade or less. But planned elimination of most Catholic education would in the short term only increase the existing deficit, requiring even greater expansion of state facilities in the future.

As minister of war in the new government, Azaña initiated the most serious reform of the army in two centuries, with the twin goals of technical modernization and of political reform or "Republicanization." The main target was the hypertrophy of the officer corps, whose 21,000 members resulted in the highest officer/soldier ratio in Europe. Azaña extended a generous offer of immediate retirement at full pay, accepted by some 8,000 officers. Thus the size of the officer corps was significantly reduced for the first time in more than a century, but at great cost, leaving little money for technical reform, where the achievements were limited. Scarcely more was gained in "Republicanization," for from the beginning the acerbic Azaña maintained an adversarial relationship with the military, whom he preferred to berate and insult on public occasions, awakening a strong sense of antipathy among a group that had earlier refused to take up arms on behalf of the monarchy.

A statute of regional autonomy was approved for Catalonia in September 1932, providing for broad self-government but stopping short of complete autonomy. Basque and Galician nationalists began to prepare similar projects, but internal division in the Basque Country and limited support in Galicia frustrated these initiatives.

The eight laws that composed the labor reform led by Francisco Largo Caballero, the Socialist minister of labor, were far-reaching. The most important were initiation of a national system of *jurados mixtos* (joint arbitration committees) under the state to negotiate labor contracts, new technical regulations for contracts that were highly favorable to organized labor, efforts to stimulate new employment, and new measures to promote worker insurance and social security. These were the most successful of the Republic's social democratic reforms, and over the next year or two resulted in an approximate 10 percent increase in wages, despite the international depression and a somewhat deflationary price structure. The downside, of course, was that sudden wage increases tended to intensify unemployment, worsening the effects of the depression.

New public works were devoted especially to dam construction and hydroelectric expansion and to improvement of railroads, which remained under private ownership. Funding was nonetheless severely curtailed by the depression and by the fact that the debt inherited from the dictatorship was technically the largest in Spanish history (in absolute numbers if not in proportionate size). The Republic nonetheless succeeded in launching the most extensive program of dam construction to that date in Spanish history.

The agrarian reform was one of the most controversial Republican programs. For more than a generation opinion had been growing that the existence of what had become nearly two million landless farm laborers, concentrated mainly in the southern half of the country, was Spain's most serious social problem. Yet there was no agreement on how to remedy this. Socialists demanded a sweeping reform to create agrarian collectives, left Republicans sought more moderate changes, and Republican moderates preferred a comparatively limited reform. Conservative opinion opposed state intervention and looked instead to expansion of the urban economy and general modernization to remedy the situation.

The result was a remarkably complicated compromise that displeased most political and social groups. The final reform law of September 1932 made large amounts of land potentially liable to expropriation, even in the case of some smaller properties. The great majority of the 80,000 landowners potentially subject to partial or nearly total expropriation were medium- and smallholders, while, through technicalities, much of the property of some of the largest owners was allowed to escape. Nearly all seizure was to be compensated according to a complex sliding scale, but so little money was available that only a small amount of land would change hands in any given year. Moreover, there was very little funding for technical development, so that much of the new reform would amount to little more than the redistribution of poverty.

In general, the reforms in labor, public works, regional autonomy, and educational expansion were impressive, though employers complained that the new labor arbitration system was one-sided and increased costs exorbitantly. Parts of the military reform were both generous and well conceived, though Azaña's remarkably hostile and adversarial style of administration had the effect of alienating much of the officer corps. The church-state reform turned out to be a civic disaster, restricting civil rights for Catholics and encouraging a strong right-wing Catholic reaction against the Republic. The agrarian reform antagonized both left and right, intensifying the climate of political hostility.

CHALLENGES TO THE REPUBLIC

The new system was first challenged by enemies on the extreme left, with the main assault launched by the anarchosyndicalist CNT. Mass anarcho-syndicalism was perhaps the most anomalous force of early twentieth-century Spain. Anarchism had earlier exerted some appeal in Italy and Russia, where it had played a role in the revolutions of 1905 and 1917. Only in Spain, however, did it come to constitute the chief force of the revolutionary left, at least before 1934. Some observers have calculated that its mass support, cast on the side of revolution, was the single main obstacle to the consolidation of democracy and social democracy in Spain.

Chagrined Marxists attributed the strength of anarchosyndicalism to Spanish backwardness and the small-shop structure of Spanish industry, which did not generate such dense concentrations of workers as in more advanced countries or even as in underdeveloped Russia. Yet since Marx-ism gained mass adherence in certain countries more backward than Spain, and since anarchosyndicalism was nowhere else as successful in other societies no more advanced than Spain, the argument from sheer backwardness is too simplistic. In eastern Europe, for example, anarchists gained the greater share of their support from Ukrainian peasants and from Jewish workers and artisans, both resident in small towns and villages, but also representative of some of the more individualistic sectors of society. Lenin apparently feared that Russia anarchists were expanding their following on the eve of the Bolshevik takeover.

During the nineteenth and early twentieth centuries, the Spanish state was weak, indeed more so than in some other underdeveloped countries. Moreover, the stance of neutrality in World War I had discouraged the growth of state administration and economic regulation to the same degree as in most European countries and did not foster the "nationalization" of workers to the same extent as elsewhere. The Spanish state's lack of penetration made it all the easier for anarchists to conceive of the state as a null or negative factor, and the more readily dispensed with, a source neither of progress nor even of decisive power. In addition, Spanish society had a long history of localism and particularism, pactist and confederal on the national level while often enjoying de facto self-governance on the local level. Anarchosyndicalism developed roots in both the backward agrarian south and in modernizing, industrializing Catalonia. In each case the process was probably encouraged by the broader ambience. In western Andalusia, where anarchism gained considerable backing, the lower middle classes and workers of the towns had from the mid-nineteenth century been attracted to a radical republicanism that was highly individualistic, egalitarian, and anticlerical, creating an environment propitious for a libertarian movement among the working classes. Moreover, Andalusian anarchists did not appeal merely to the most immiserated but also to a somewhat broader cross-section of society. Early twentieth-century Catalonia was rife with individualism and with political particularism on the bourgeois level, a situation perhaps not totally unassociated with the growing libertarianism of workers.

In Spain anarchosyndicalist success had been partly predicated on Socialist failure. The latter's UGT was originally founded in Barcelona, but the Madrid Socialist leadership soon moved it to the Spanish capital. By comparison, the anarchists proved more imaginative and flexible, developing a broad network of propaganda that drew support from more than a few intellectuals early in the century. They paid much more attention to peasants while simultaneously finding a formula to more easily mobilize urban workers. While the UGT held to a restrictive craft union principle, the CNT in 1919 adopted the strategy of the *sindicato único* (industrial union), maximizing its organizational potential. Whereas the UGT maintained structural rigidity, the CNT's emphasis on flexibility enabled it to go underground and also to reconstitute itself after periods of repression. Its fanatical anti-Catholicism also found a popular response in newly secularized and alienated sectors of the lower classes, which resented the identification of the Church with the established order.

Finally, the anarchosyndicalists gained mass support partly because they were simply more radical, and also more violent, even practicing violence against workers who refused to join them. Anarchosyndicalist violence and revolutionism became self-perpetuating, creating a self-radicalization of industrial relations that frequently provoked a polarization that could never have taken the same form through peaceful trade unionism, such as that normally practiced by the Socialists. Anarchosyndicalism thus demonstrated a capacity for revolutionary self-generation that the more moderate and disciplined Socialists had heretofore lacked. It was the main source of political violence in early twentieth-century Spain,[11] its so-called *pistolerismo* (gunmanism) becoming one of the factors that helped to precipitate dictatorship in 1923, as the Socialists correctly charged.

To maintain a consistent revolutionary focus, militants had organized a Federación Anarquista Ibérica (FAI) in 1927, which was to serve as a revolutionary vanguard. During the final phase of the monarchy and the first year of the Republic the CNT was able to reconstitute itself, once more gaining possibly a million members. Now, however, it was no larger than the UGT, which the anarchists charged with having created the jurados mixtos as a state monopoly. Anarchist militants vowed never to be forced to participate in state institutions to negotiate labor contracts, and declared that the Republic had become more coercive than the monarchy. By the close of 1931 the CNT was under the domination of revolutionary militants who preached a doctrine of violent insurrection to achieve a utopia of *comunismo libertario*. The FAI-CNT promoted hundreds of strikes, sometimes without much interest in practical solutions, and launched three revolutionary insurrections, the so-called *tres ochos* (three eights), revolts beginning on 18 January 1932, 8 January, and 8 December 1933. Each involved attempts at revolutionary general strikes and violent insurrections in several regions, but especially in Catalonia and Andalusia. Each failed to mobilize a broader revolt and was soon put down, each time costing scores of lives and bringing severe repression of the CNT.

The other violent revolutionary movement to contest the Republic was the small Spanish Communist Party (Partido Comunista de España; PCE), a minuscule force until 1936. It pursued the standard Comintern line of the "united front," a futile strategy that called on all workers to support the Communists in overthrowing the bourgeois Republic and forming "soviets." Though the Communists sometimes seconded anarchist efforts, they were too weak to unleash a revolutionary offensive of their own.

The so-called Spanish Communist Party was in fact the Soviet Communist Party in Spain, ruthlessly controlled from Moscow. The nearest thing to a genuine independent Spanish Communist party was Joaquín Maurín's tiny Bloque Obrero y Campesino (Worker-Peasant Bloc; BOC), centered in Barcelona. Members of the BOC considered themselves true Marxist-Leninists, uncorrupted by Stalinism. Denounced by the Comintern, their dream was to win over the CNT to revolutionary Marxism-Leninism.

Monarchist groups also began to conspire against the new regime, though the *alfonsino* monarchists tended to divide between moderates and those who had moved to the authoritarian radical right. By the end of 1931 the latter had begun to publish a new journal, *Acción Española,* devoted to propagating a new doctrine of the future installation, not mere restoration, of a new-style authoritarian and centralized Catholic monarchy. Carlist traditionalists reorganized themselves as the Comunión Tradicionalista and soon started to train their own militia in the northern province of Navarra.

The only rightist revolt, however, was the so-called *sanjurjada* of 10 August 1932. This took the form of an abortive pronunciamiento by a handful of army officers in Madrid and Seville, encouraged by monarchists and other elements. Only in Seville did the revolt succeed for a few hours, the retired General José Sanjurjo briefly seizing control of the garrison and city before he was forced to flee. This revolt was even weaker than any of the anarchist insurrections and was easily suppressed. Ten people were killed. Sanjurjo was quickly arrested, tried, and sentenced to a long prison term.

The Republican government dealt vigorously with any opposition, passing a draconian Law for the Defense of the Republic, which provided for three different categories of suspension of constitutional rights, the most severe being the *estado de guerra* (martial law). It provided for preventive arrest without accusation, arbitrary closing of publications, and deportation to the colonies. Mindful of complaints that the special national constabulary, the Civil Guard, was armed only with Mauser rifles and not trained for modern crowd control, the Republican authorities set about organizing a new urban constabulary armed with clubs and pistols, theoretically prepared for more humane crowd control. Its very name, Guardias de Asalto, indicated the vigorous policy espoused by the Republican regime. Incidents proliferated as strikes, demonstrations, and insurrections produced considerable violence, which in turn prompted harsh repression from the Civil Guard and the Assault Guard. After two and a half years, there had been nearly 500 fatalities in such confrontations, the majority of the victims being anarchosyndicalists, and suspension of civil guarantees had become more frequent than under the constitutional monarchy before 1923.

Press censorship was so severe that on 19 February 1932 Miguel de Unamuno and several other moderate deputies requested in the Cortes that the government simply return to the old Liberal Party monarchist press law of 1883, which provided some guarantees against incendiary journalism and libel but more freedom than the draconian new Republican regulations. Azaña replied stiffly (and somewhat misleadingly) that "press policy is one of complete freedom. Everyone can say whatever he wants, so long as he does not attack the Republic in the terms defined by law," a formula that most dictatorships might have been willing to subscribe.[12] Azaña sounded more like Salazar in Lisbon than the prime minister of a democratic regime in Madrid. Subsequently, on 9 March, Lerroux, Unamuno, and others urged that at least newspapers that had not been convicted by a specific judicial finding not be suspended arbitrarily by the government, as had been the practice. Azaña admitted that the latter's power was "extraordinary" but as usual blamed all government excesses on the preceding regime, the standard excuse of Spanish government down to the Constitution of 1978. The government, he claimed, was only defending liberty, adding his oft-quoted and scornful motto, "They bark—therefore we ride on." This was the sort of gesture that had led Mussolini on one occasion to declare, with his customary extravagance, that in Spain the only analogue to Fascism was Azaña, because of his firm leadership. The coerciveness of the new Republican state was compared to that of Italian Fascism on several occasions, particularly by the Catholic opposition during 1931–32.

By 1932 the latter had begun to create a mass-based Catholic political movement for the first time in Spanish history. This emerged as the Confederación Española de Derechas Autónomas (Spanish Confederation of Autonomous Rightist Groups; CEDA), which would soon become the largest political party in the country. Unlike the revolutionary left and the radical right, it was pledged to legality and parliamentarianism in the interest of a drastic reform of Spanish political institutions to protect Catholic and other conservative interests. It sought to use peaceful political mobilization to transform the regime into a Catholic and corporative republic instead of a competitive multiparty parliamentary system, rather like the corporative and authoritarian "New State" republic then being constructed by Salazar in Portugal. The young law professor José Ma. Gil Robles provided eloquent and energetic leadership as the CEDA incorporated a sizable part of the Catholic population, by the next election outdistancing any other single party.[13]

This was a fateful development, for, though the CEDA was legalistic, evolutionary, and opposed to violence, it also represented the turn away from Christian democracy taken by Catholic parties in some countries during recent years. Antiliberal corporatism had become the dominant Catholic political creed in a large part of the continent, encouraged by the papacy itself. Had the CEDA been a Christian democratic party, it might have been able to stabilize Republican democracy, but its own Christian democratic minority was too weak to lead the organization.

The CEDA thus became in some respects an opposite twin of the PSOE. Down to 1934 the Socialists were likewise committed to legal and parliamentary tactics, but with the goal of converting the system into a socialist regime. Each of the two largest national parties—the Socialists on the left, the CEDA on the right—thus had ulterior motives, and were profoundly distrusted by most of the rest of Spain's political society. Both supported legalism for the time being—the Socialists until 1934, the CEDA until 1936—but neither was committed to Republican democracy as an ultimate goal and value. The most extreme left and right could be held at bay, but the ambiguous stance of the two largest parliamentary parties boded ill for the stability of the new regime.

CHAPTER TWO

The Turning Point of the Republic

1933

THE BEGINNING OF THE breakdown of the Second Republic is conventionally dated from the revolutionary insurrection of 1934, which marked the start of total polarization between left and right. This approach has a certain persuasive logic, but it overlooks the fact that the initial turning point of the Republic, the emergence of the polarization and the beginning of systematic interference with parliament and the political process, all commenced in 1933.

The left Republican-Socialist alliance under Azaña had governed since the end of 1931, when Alcalá Zamora, the first prime minister, was elevated to the presidency of the Republic. The Azaña government had the opportunity to enforce the new constitution during 1932 and to continue to develop legislation promoting the Republican reforms, which would not be completed until June 1933, at the earliest.

The leftist alliance employed the Law for the Defense of the Republic vigorously, not least against insurrectionary anarchosyndicalists. Many hundreds were arrested and some deported to serve their sentences in prisons in the African colonies. Yet the policy of *mano dura* (harsh hand) blew up in the face of the government during the insurrection of January 1933, when overworked Assault Guards summarily executed a dozen peasants in the hamlet of Casas Viejas in Cádiz. This was exactly the sort of police atrocity that the creation of the Assault Guards had been designed to prevent, and it occasioned a great political outcry from conservatives, moderates, and the extreme left, for the first time seriously weakening the prestige of the Azaña government.

More serious damage was inflicted by special municipal elections, held in April in northern provinces that had been governed for two years by special administrations appointed from Madrid. These resulted in the government's first clear-cut defeat, nearly three-quarters of the seats being won by centrist liberal Republicans and by the right. This setback was accompanied by the public alienation of some of the leading intellectuals who had strongly supported the new regime, such as Unamuno and José Ortega y Gasset. During the spring Ortega delivered a number of speeches criticizing the government and calling for a more moderate and constructive policy.

The Azaña administration nonetheless continued on course, passing in May the Law on Religious Congregations, which specified restrictions on their activities and prohibited them from teaching. This legislation formalized and completed the left's religious policy initiated in 1931, and was accompanied by new outbreaks of arson against Church buildings in more than a score of localities in May and June.

The law was signed on 2 June by a reluctant President Alcalá Zamora, who had been convinced since the autumn of 1931 that the Republican alliance had veered too far to the left and that it was necessary to introduce changes to "center the Republic." The president was highly critical of the constitution for technical defects and sectarianism, writing that it "encouraged civil war." In a 1936 book titled *Los defectos de la Constitución de 1931* he declared that the Republican parliament elected in 1931 "suffered from a grave defect, in that it completely failed to coincide with stable, true, and permanent Spanish opinion" in its rejection of consensus or even tolerance of opposing political viewpoints. He sought to take advantage of the first opportunity to try to change the government, moving its balance toward the center. This opportunity came in the spring of 1933 with the weakening of the governing alliance, signs of divergence between the left Republicans and the Socialists, and especially the internal splintering and divergence of the largest left Republican grouping, the so-called Radical Socialists. After some experience in government, many of the latter had begun to repent their initial radicalism. As they moved more toward the center, some of them began to demand an all-Republican alliance, insisting that the time had come for the Socialists to leave the government. This demand was strongly resisted by Azaña, whose sectarian policy required complete rejection of centrist Republicanism.

At this point, however, Azaña's government was temporarily brought to an abrupt end by authority of the president. Alcalá Zamora enjoyed exceptional power to interfere in the political process under article 75 of the constitution, which built upon the prerogatives of the crown and gave the president somewhat greater authority than in many other constitutional parliamentary systems. He held the power to appoint and to depose prime ministers, as well as other government ministers, though dismissal of the latter had first to be proposed by the prime minister. He was specifically required to dismiss any cabinet that was denied a vote of confidence by the Cortes, but his power to dismiss was not necessarily bound by that requirement alone. The Second Republic was thus governed by "a semi-presidential system in which the president was free to appoint and dismiss prime ministers without the need for parliamentary approval,"[1] at least initially, though no prime minister could remain in power very long without parliamentary approval. Presidential prerogative would become the dominant factor in Spanish government between June 1933 and February 1936, and the way in which Alcalá Zamora used that authority worked to the profound detriment of the parliamentary system.

The president first found an opportunity to interfere immediately after the passage of the Law on Religious Congregations, when Azaña had to replace his finance minister, Jaume Carner, who was dying of cancer. Despite the dissidence of some Radical Socialists, Azaña still enjoyed a parliamentary majority as well as a coherent cabinet that was willing to continue. Rather than allowing him to appoint a new finance minister, however, Alcalá Zamora seized on the vacancy as though it were a government crisis—which it definitely was not—and opened a round of consultations about forming a new government.

Alcalá Zamora's intention was to "center the Republic" with a more moderate governing coalition that would modify the existing sectarian policies. Though the goal was laudable, the means chosen were arbitrary and twisted the procedures of parliamentary government. Such arbitrary manipulation would eventually result in the disastrously polarized elections of 1936. The president was correct that the sectarian legislation of 1931–1933 was sharply dividing Spain, but it would have been preferable to allow the working majority to continue so long as its mandate lasted, rather than to interfere in the functioning of the parliamentary majority. A democratic Republic could not achieve stability and maintain legitimacy unless the procedures of parliamentary government were followed fairly.

The Azaña government did not want to force a constitutional crisis and meekly submitted to the president, all its members resigning. It might have been wiser to contest Alcalá's position and clarify the use of his powers, but at this point nearly all the parties sought to foster the stability of the new system and accepted the president's authority.

Alcalá Zamora did not yet dare dissolve parliament, where there was a working majority whose legislative mandate had not altogether been completed, but at the very least he sought to draw the Radicals and other Republican moderates into a new government that would automatically become more conservative. This might take the form of restoring the broad coalition of 1931, even if that might require leadership by a Socialist. Therefore among those whom the president consulted about leading a new government was the public works minister, Indalecio Prieto, the most flexible of the top Socialists. Alcalá Zamora made it clear to Prieto that his charge would be to form a broad coalition. Azaña, who cooperated readily with Prieto, agreed to participate, but the Radicals refused to cooperate with the Socialists, while other Socialist leaders vetoed participation with the Radicals.

There appeared to be no alternative to Azaña, but the president insisted that in forming a new government Azaña must restore the broad alliance of 1931. His effort to do so quickly drew the double veto just encountered by Prieto, so that Alcalá Zamora finally had no alternative but to authorize the same majority coalition of left Republicans and Socialists that he had just forced to resign.

Even though the president's goal had been a desirable one, the whole maneuver was a foretaste of worse to come. At this point restoration of the alliance of 1931 would have been in the best interests of the country, for the Radicals would have moderated official policy. The obstacle was the gulf that had opened between the Republican center and the Socialists. Moreover, the Radicals grasped that by holding out for new elections, they might well emerge in a more moderate climate as the dominant Republican party, able to capitalize on resentment among the moderate sectors of the middle classes and the business interests. This had been their goal since the end of 1931, when they realized that the longer new elections for a regular parliament were postponed, the more time conservative forces would have to reorganize themselves effectively, as indeed proved to be the case. Yet more at fault were the Socialists in refusing to moderate their own position. They were determined to maintain the all-left Republic, which would remain their fixed goal, even though they were not strong enough to do so by democratic means.

Azaña's own position in June 1933 was more moderate than it would be in subsequent years. He believed that his own administration should continue for another year or so, to complete its program of legislation and to consolidate the new regime. He was willing to work with the Radicals, and even pledged to overcome Socialist refusal to do so. At this point he was not completely bound by the *socialazañismo* (pro-Socialist posture) that from 1934 would become his fixed policy, but accepted that the Socialists would eventually leave the government after the task of this initial administration had been ended, following which Spain would be probably governed by an alliance of all the Republican parties.[2]

THE AMBIVALENCE OF THE SOCIALISTS

The commitment of the Socialist leadership to the Azaña coalition government increased during 1932 and 1933, but not the commitment to the concept of the Republic then held by Azaña, much less to that of Republican moderates. Though the attitude of part of the party might be described as social democratic, the party had never adopted a merely reformist program. It remained an officially Marxist party, a position that would not be renounced until 1979. The party was committed to collaborating only with an all-left Republic that would encourage rapid progress on the path to socialism. At the Thirteenth Party Congress in October 1932, the committee charged with short-term policy reported that "the revolutionary cycle characterized by Socialist collaboration is rapidly drawing to a close. The time for ending ministerial collaboration is coming nigh and is desirable, without setting a fixed date but without any further delay than may be required by the life of the regime. . . . Once the Republic is established, the Socialist Party will dedicate itself to categorically anticapitalist action . . . and will direct its efforts to the full conquest of power to inaugurate socialism."[3] In practice, however, the party leaders were in no hurry to see the phase of government collaboration come to an end.

The dissident left wing was represented primarily by the Socialist Youth, whose own congress in February 1932 had endorsed virtual elimination of the national defense budget, withdrawal of all troops from Morocco, and drastic reduction of the armed forces. The Socialist Youth also petitioned the party leadership to begin formation of Socialist paragovernment organs that could later replace the ministries of the existing "bourgeois regime." As late as the first part of 1933, however, no large sector of the Socialist movement had any concrete recommendation on how exactly to move from the parliamentary Republic to a Socialist regime. Tactics depended on the further evolution of the Republican system.

Nonetheless, by the beginning of 1933 the revolution of rising expectations that had accompanied inauguration of the Republic was turning in some Socialist sectors to disillusionment and even to bitterness and anger, under the joint impact of the economic depression and employer resistance. The former, together with rising labor costs, increased unemployment, though this was not generally as severe as in more industrialized countries, and in the Spanish countryside by the latter part of 1932 there were growing complaints that the jurado system was not benefiting labor as much as had been expected. Wages were higher, but less land was being sown, there were fewer jobs, and it was proving difficult to enforce some of the new regulations. On the local level, Socialists were well represented in municipal councils, though all the provincial governors were middle-class Republicans. The latter were in charge of administering the new laws, and it was on the local and provincial levels that tensions rose between the two sectors. Even at the top party leaders began to hedge their position, with Largo Caballero stipulating that the PSOE "is not [purely] reformist, nor is the spirit of its members. And one has only to look at the history of the party to see that legality has been broken whenever that fits our ideas. . . . No one is trying to revise our doctrine. The only question is one of tactics."[4] Even at the apex of the left Republican-Socialist alliance, part of the Socialist leadership made clear its limited commitment to the democratic Republic itself, depending on whether it served Socialist interests and seemed to be leading to socialism.

Though about two-thirds of the new agreements negotiated by the jurados mixtos in 1933 were still categorized by the Ministry of Labor as favorable to workers,[5] strike activity increased markedly. That year the total doubled, to 1,127 (compared with 681 in 1932), and the number of workers on strike rose from 269,104 to 843,303. The Patronal (employers' association) reported that during the first half of 1933 strikes and political conflicts had resulted in 102 deaths, with 14.5 million workdays lost.[6] Socialist collaboration in government and significant reform legislation seemingly had led only to greater labor unrest. One problem was that a large proportion of the new contracts negotiated in 1931 were two-year agreements, up for renegotiation in 1933. Another was constant incitement by the CNT, determined not to allow the collaborationist Socialists to increase their strength. Hence the paradox that the depression and increasing unemployment had the opposite effect in Spain from that in most other countries. Whereas these conditions generally discouraged labor activity elsewhere, in Spain the increased power of organized labor stimulated by the Republic brought acceleration of militant labor action, and the number of workdays lost to strikes increased by more than 400 percent in 1933.

The dilemma facing Spanish industrial relations in general and the Socialists in particular was illustrated by the radicalization of labor in Madrid during 1933. Unemployment in the construction industry, one of the largest economic sectors in the capital, had reached 30 percent or more. For the first time the CNT made a major effort to organize construction workers in Madrid, appealing especially to unemployed laborers who had recently immigrated from the countryside. In September the CNT's Sindicato Único de Construcción launched a strike of 5,000 workers that spread rapidly and lasted three weeks, despite energetic UGT efforts to break it. The Republican jurado system had heretofore achieved major gains in salaries and benefits for Madrid construction workers, but the depression had forced so many layoffs that thousands were ripe for radicalization. The CNT managed to achieve equal bargaining rights with the UGT while bypassing the official jurado, demonstrating that the UGT's legalist, reformist tactics could be outflanked by anarchosyndicalist direct action. Now there was strong pressure from young UGT workers and shop-floor leaders to emulate these tactics, with the result that the jurado arbitration system in the capital never fully recovered.[7]

The Socialists' role in government became largely defensive during that year, seeking primarily to sustain the existing situation. To the venerable Julián Besteiro, the philosophy professor who was perhaps the only serious Marxist theorist in the party and leader of what would soon be called the "Socialist right," this frustration meant that the time had come to withdraw from the government and to expand and strengthen the movement in opposition. To the more pragmatic and non-Marxist Indalecio Prieto, this meant that the party must follow an even more practical policy in power and continue to support the existing coalition. To Largo Caballero and important elements within the UGT, however, this meant a more ambiguous approach, one of supporting the coalition in power as long as possible while also being willing to adopt a policy of opposition and revolutionism if future circumstances so indicated. In a major speech in Madrid on 23 July, Largo insisted once more that "the Socialist Party is moving toward the conquest of power under the Constitution and the laws of the state," but also warned of the danger of "fascism"—meaning the growth of the power of the right, a major concern in 1933, as it had not been two years earlier. This trend might make it necessary to seize power by violent means. He reminded his audience that Marx had declared categorically that the dictatorship of the proletariat was inevitable in consolidating a socialist society and that, even though it would probably still be possible to win control of the government by parliamentary means, liberal democracy alone would never completely suffice. The ultimate dictatorship of the proletariat should be achieved with as little violence as possible, but the amount of violence would depend on the degree of resistance.[8]

In August the top Socialist leaders had an opportunity to define their policy preferences in addresses before the Socialist Youth summer school at Torrelodones. Besteiro spoke first and was coldly received. In July he had blamed Italian and German Socialists for provoking the bourgeoisie of their countries into fascism through the premature use of Socialist power, even though in Germany this had taken the form of parliamentary government participation. Worse yet, the introduction of a Socialist regime in Spain through Bolshevik-style violence and dictatorship would simply inaugurate a bloodbath, "the most sanguinary Republic known to contemporary history."[9] Besteiro's Cassandra-like predictions were uncannily accurate, and this was no exception: in the Republican Zone during the first six months of the Civil War in 1936, the rate of political executions would considerably exceed that of the Bolsheviks during the Russian civil war. At Torrelodones he once more warned of the folly of extremism, the results of which would be quite different from what its advocates imagined: "If a general staff dispatches its army to fight in unfavorable conditions, it becomes totally responsible for the subsequent defeat and demoralization," adding that "often it is more revolutionary to resist collective madness than to be carried away by it."[10]

Prieto was less challenging but also warned that there were definite limits to what Spanish Socialism could achieve at the present level of development and given the changing relations of political forces both in Europe and in Spain. He too stressed the fallacy of the facile comparisons being made by the left wing of the movement between Russia in 1917 and Spain in 1933. In Russia key institutions had already collapsed before the Communist takeover; in Spain the government, Church, and armed forces were intact, while the bourgeoisie was stronger than in Russia.

Since the closing months of 1932 Largo had been increasingly aware of the radicalization of worker sentiment, but at Torrelodones he once more defended government participation, which he termed orthodox Marxism. Largo referred to a letter from Engels to Karl Kautsky in 1875 stressing that a democratic republic was the specific form that would lead to the dictatorship of the proletariat. "I myself have had a reputation of being conservative and reformist, but this is mistaken," he declared, stressing that "I am convinced today it is impossible to carry out a socialist project within bourgeois democracy." Largo added, "Let us suppose that the time has come to install our own regime. Not only outside our ranks, but even within them, there are those who fear the need to establish a dictatorship. If that happened, what should our policy be? Because we cannot renounce our goals or do anything to impede the achievement of our aspirations." He cited Marx once more to the effect that the ultimate transition to socialism could not be carried out by means other than the dictatorship of the proletariat. With regard to the only existing model, the Soviet Union, he declared that he did not agree with Soviet foreign policy but that he fully agreed with Soviet domestic policy.[11] All this was said at the height of the genocidal campaign against the Soviet peasantry, revealing that Largo was probably quite ignorant of what he was talking about. The old trade union leader had now entered heavy political waters that he could not readily navigate, but he told the young militants what they wanted to hear, and at this point the first cries of "Long live the Spanish Lenin!" were supposedly heard.[12]

THE END OF THE AZAÑA GOVERNMENT

Survival of the reorganized Azaña government became increasingly dependent on the declining support of the Radical Socialists. At a crucial Radical
Socialist Party congress in June, one of its major figures, Félix Gordón
Ordás, publicly referred to Azaña as a "dictator," though for the moment
the party still gave his government its support. The Radical Socialists eventually split into three different parties—left, right, and center—while the
tiny Federal Republican Party also split into three. The Socialists insisted
on full speed ahead, but the Radical Party pressed for the government's
resignation, and the left Republicans themselves seemed increasingly
uncertain. In the balloting for the fifteen members of the new Tribunal
of Constitution Guarantees, to be elected at large in September, the government parties won only a third of the seats. Conservatives similarly
won new elections to key professional institutions such as the College of
Lawyers, the Academy of Jurisprudence, and the College of Physicians.

Neither the left Republicans nor the Socialists wanted to abandon the
coalition, for the inevitable result would be a more conservative government and/or new elections whose results would be likely to weaken the
left. The government therefore asked for and obtained a vote of confidence
in the Cortes, even though many of the Radical Socialists seemed near the
point of withdrawing support. Despite the reaffirmation of a temporary
working majority, Alcalá Zamora decided to interfere, when according to
custom he should for the moment have done nothing. On 7 September
he asked the government to resign and authorized the Radical chief, Lerroux, to form an all-Republican coalition, which he was able to do within
five days. This move prompted the Socialist executive commission to announce a complete break with all the Republican parties.

The Lerroux all-Republican government lasted only three weeks.
When the new prime minister first appeared before parliament on 2 October, it became clear that he had obtained from Alcalá Zamora a pledge
for new elections rather than for a regular government. Azaña's Acción
Republicana immediately withdrew its confidence, automatically bringing the new government down. It had been willing to support a broad
coalition government under Lerroux, but would not accept his presiding
over new elections. More dramatically, Prieto declared in the same Cortes
session: "In the name of the Socialist parliamentary group and absolutely
certain of interpreting the judgment of the Spanish Socialist Workers

Party, I declare that the collaboration of the Socialist Party in Republican governments, whatever their characteristics, shade, and tendency, has definitively ended," a rupture that he declared "indestructible and inviolable." Azaña's strategy had run its course, and not even an all-Republican coalition government was possible any longer, because of the Radicals' insistence on elections. All three formulas—the grand alliance of 1931, the left Republican–Socialist alliance of 1932–33, and now the all-Republican alliance—had been attempted, and none was any longer viable. In a final attempt, Azaña urged formation of a grand alliance once more to preside over elections, but this was not possible, either. After the veto against Lerroux, Alcalá Zamora appointed a new caretaker administration under Diego Martínez Barrio, the most liberal of the top Radical leaders, to preside over elections. Martínez Barrio attempted to convert this into an all-Republican alliance, but Azaña would participate only if the Socialists did too, a scenario that was also impossible.

The simplest alternative would have been the broad centrist all-Republican coalition, which could have continued to govern for some time on the basis of the existing parliament. There is no certainty that a center coalition would have endured, but it had much to recommend it, for it might have introduced more moderate policies and attempted to conciliate Catholic and conservative opinion. Such a course would have been very complicated, requiring much tact and cooperation. Perhaps such an arrangement would simply have exceeded the capacity of the ambitious, vain, highly personalistic middle-class Republican politicians, who in some ways exhibited in an exaggerated form the traditional vices of nineteenth-century Spanish politics rather than the new politics that they invoked with rhetorical regularity. However slim its chance of success, such an alternative might have been the best hope of consolidating a liberal democratic system during the depression decade.[13]

As Ángel Alcalá Galve observes,[14] one of the striking features of the new regime was the manner in which it quickly reproduced key weaknesses of the old monarchist system, demonstrating that the problem was not really one of monarchy versus Republic but of the Spanish political culture of the early twentieth century, which was proving intractable. Just as a revolutionary worker left had pressured the monarchy, so now it attempted multiple violent insurrections against the Republic. Just as the old "Dynastic Left" had sought to appease republicans who rejected the established system, so the left Republicans preferred to govern primarily with Socialists who refused to accept a democratic Republic as their ultimate norm. Whereas the old system had been threatened by an extreme left, the new system was threatened with subversion and violence by both an extreme right and an extreme left. Just as the monarchist parties had become too internally divided to govern, this internal division now threatened the Republican parties. The Socialists had attempted a revolutionary general strike against the monarchy in 1917; in 1934 they would attempt one against the Republic.

Azaña would later write during the Civil War that "the internal division of the middle class and, in general, of the bourgeoisie, constituted the true origin of the civil war,"[15] and to some extent this assessment was correct. The middle classes were fragmenting into a Catholic right, a liberal center, and a Republican left. What Azaña failed to add—with typical self-justification—was that the main forces of the Catholic right and liberal center were willing to collaborate in a center-right coalition, whereas after 1933 Azaña's left Republicans would tend increasingly to reject a center-left coalition, until by 1935 they were willing to ally only with the revolutionary left, facilitating subversion of the very system that they had done so much to create. Eventually the gulf between liberal and left Republicans would become unbridgeable. The increasing split in the Republican parties, with only the liberals willing to accept the logic and rules of a liberal democratic system, placed the future of the new regime in doubt. If all the Republican parties did not accept their own system, there was even less to expect from the non-Republican parties.

THE ELECTIONS OF NOVEMBER 1933

New elections, eagerly sought by the right and by much of the center, were convened by President Alcalá Zamora as part of his continuing effort to "center the Republic." The president was in many ways sorely disappointed in the new regime and its constitution. His concept of the Republic was a liberal democracy with equal rights for all, not just equal rights for anticlericals. He strongly endorsed goals such as laicization of the state and the creation of a democratic system that would deal with pressing social problems, but envisioned the Republic above all as a state based on an objective rule of law not subject to arbitrary political whims. He supported separation of church and state, but as a sincere liberal and practicing Catholic he believed that a democratic laic state would endure only as a democracy guaranteeing equality to all, and not least for Catholics and the Church. He had resigned as the initial prime minister of the Republic after the passage of the first legislation limiting Catholic rights, but had accepted the presidency with the goal of reforming the new system and encouraging a more liberal political orientation among Catholics in support of a genuinely democratic Republic.

Alcalá Zamora also criticized other features of the new constitution, such as the absence of a second chamber in the Republican legislature, contrary to most democratic systems. He was equally critical of the heavily disproportionate electoral law, which gave strongly weighted premiums to the plurality or majority in each district and severely and undemocratically underrepresented minorities, with the potential for creating artificial majorities and immense pendular shifts in representation. More broadly, he believed that much of the constitution had simply been drafted hastily and had been poorly thought out, and paid inadequate attention to economic issues. Alcalá Zamora was himself a distinguished jurist and also a legal scholar, and his criticisms were shared by some of the country's leading intellectuals, such as Ortega y Gasset, Unamuno, Gregorio Marañón, Salvador de Madariaga, and Ramón Menéndez Pidal.

Alcalá Zamora was equally worried about the great rise in social conflict, political violence, and common crime. The return to more liberal police policies in 1930 had permitted a great increase in crime, most notably armed robberies, and the situation had deteriorated further under the Republic. The hope was that a more moderate and responsible government might be able to reduce this trend.

The constituent process had been initiated by a badly skewed Cortes in which most conservative opinion had not been represented. This dearth resulted both from the enthusiasm and political pressure generated by the governing parties during the campaign of 1931 and from the disorganization and partial abstention of rightist sectors, which in many cases had made little serious effort to participate. The Cortes of 1931–1933 had constituted a kind of leftist convention, giving the impression that the change of regime stemmed inevitably from the overwhelming power of the left. In fact, the Republic had been inaugurated rapidly and peacefully because of the acquiescence and cooperation of the right, which had refused to put up a struggle for the monarchy, had cooperated with the new government, and in some cases had even voted for Republican candidates in April 1931.

Opposition had also been weakened by the fact that the center was divided by faction and personality, the only large center party being the Radicals. The small center groups, led by Miguel Maura, Melquiades Álvarez, Alcalá Zamora himself, and a few others, held few seats and sometimes refused to cooperate among themselves. Similarly, the most moderate and responsible of the Socialist leaders, Julián Besteiro, had dropped out of active party leadership to serve as president of the Cortes.

During 1933 a crescendo of criticism about the political situation had been building in the press, its tone ranging from liberal to conservative to extreme rightist. A lengthy series of books had appeared in the course of the year presenting complaints and accusations of all sorts, from the reasonable to the unfair, ranging from detailed analyses of the various perquisites and emoluments enjoyed by Cortes deputies to categorical ideological diatribes.

The elections would be held under the Republican electoral law that was based in part on the Italian Fascist Acerbo Law of 1923. In July 1933 the second Azaña government had passed an amendment making the law even more heavily disproportionate in the hope of facilitating the victory of the left in the next contest. Thus in each district plurality lists would receive 67 percent of the seats no matter how weak the plurality, while a list drawing a majority was guaranteed 80 percent of the seats in that district. The liberal Ángel Ossorio y Gallardo not unreasonably termed the electoral law "Mussolinian," while the CEDA leader Gil Robles observed that with such a law Hitler might have won power in Germany as early as 1930.

In the elections of 1933 the law had a boomerang effect, because the Socialist veto on collaboration with the "bourgeois" left Republicans made another broad alliance impossible. Since centrist liberals also refused to ally with left Republicans, the latter would suffer most of all. The campaign was marred by greater violence, coming especially from the Socialists, than in the preceding contest, and the two major ambiguous, "semiloyal" parties, the Socialists and the CEDA, both used strong language. The Socialists sometimes invoked revolution, while CEDA leaders sometimes spoke of the need for "a strong state" and "a totalitarian policy." There were also outbursts of anticlerical violence and a number of church burnings, as was de rigueur under the Republic.

The worst violence of all came not from the Socialists but from the Republic Union Party (PURA) of Valencia, earlier built up by the novelist Vicente Blasco Ibáñez and now led by his son, Sigfrido, which was closely allied with the Radicals. Alarmed by the rise of the CEDA in Valencia, PURA militants killed two *cedistas* during the campaign, and then murdered a CEDA electoral official on election day. There were a number of other assaults, as well as widespread violent interference with the balloting.[16]

Election day was generally calm, except in the Valencia region, though several killings were reported, of which only three can be substantiated. The conditions of balloting were generally the freest and fairest in Spanish history to that date. By the time the *segunda vuelta,* or second round, was over, the big winners were the CEDA and the Radicals, who had often formed alliances for the second round. The CEDA, capitalizing on the lower-middle-class Catholic vote (which had partially abstained in the preceding elections), emerged as the largest single party, with 115 deputies, while the Radicals, who had played the game most effectively, were the proportionately most overrepresented party, with 104 seats. The Socialists, in isolation, dropped to 60 seats, though they retained most of their popular vote. The biggest losers were the left Republicans, who were nearly wiped out except in Catalonia.

Clearly, there had been some shift of opinion toward the center and center-right, together with a much more intense mobilization of the rightist vote; yet the actual change of opinion was less than the drastically altered composition of parliament made it appear. The overall abstention rate was 32 percent, not far from the average of the three Republican elections. This was well above the west European norm, but not necessarily surprising for a country still with 25 percent adult illiteracy and a large anarchosyndicalist movement that promoted abstention. Altogether, centrist Republicans had drawn more than 2.5 million votes, the moderate right more than 2 million, the Socialists nearly 1.7 million, and left Republicans fewer than 1.2 million, concentrated in Catalonia. The extreme right garnered nearly 800,000 votes, the Communists and other parties of the extreme left less than 200,000.[17]

The electoral law had effected a pendular swing. A basic adjustment in representation was inevitable, given the artificial results of 1931, but the shift would have been considerably less with a more responsible system. Moreover, the discontinuity in parliamentary experience that had been so marked in the Constituent Cortes would continue. In 1931 only 64 deputies had sat in a preceding parliament, while 55.6 percent of all deputies elected that year would never participate in a second. Forty-six percent of the deputies elected in 1933 were equally bereft of experience, while the percentage of newcomers in the Cortes of 1936 would be almost as high. Of the 115 CEDA deputies, only 10 had previous parliamentary experience.[18]

The potentially most constructive feature of the new Cortes was the increased strength of the democratic center, which, among all broad sectors, had drawn a plurality of votes. Radicals almost equaled cedistas in number, while the Progressive Republicans of Alcalá Zamora and the Conservative Republicans of Miguel Maura had retained most of their seats (though dropping from a combined total of twenty-eight to twenty-one), and the Liberal Democrats of Melquiades Álvarez rose from two to eight.

The elections had generally been fair, though subsequently the results were impugned in several provinces, especially in Andalusia. There fraud was committed by both left and right, though perhaps most marked in the case of rightist fraud in Granada province, where the left had behaved equally badly in 1931.[19]

THE LEFTIST ATTEMPT TO ANNUL THE ELECTORAL RESULTS
The defeated left reacted with rage, fearing that a more conservative government would undo many of the Republican reforms. They were much less disposed than the right in 1931 to accept temporary defeat, even though they themselves had drafted a highly gimmicky electoral law calculated to serve their own interests. The initial response of the left was not to prepare to act as a loyal opposition but to attempt to gain cancellation of the electoral results. To the surprise of Alcalá Zamora, this was first proposed to him by none other than the incumbent minister of justice, Juan Botella Asensi. When he saw that the center-right was about to win the segunda vuelta, Botella urged the president to cancel the electoral process even before the second round was concluded. Soon afterward a similar proposal was made by Gordón Ordás, the incumbent minister of industry.[20]

The next effort was made not by incumbent left-liberal cabinet ministers but by Azaña himself. On 4 December, the day after completion of the second round, he met with the caretaker prime minister, Martínez

Barrio, to maintain that the results should be cancelled because they were so disproportionate to the actual vote totals, ignoring the fact that Azaña and his allies had written this unrepresentative electoral law precisely in order to guarantee disproportionate benefits for themselves. Martínez Barrio, like the president, rejected Azaña's proposal for a *pronunciamiento civil*, but Azaña was not easily discouraged in his efforts to subvert the constitutional process. The following day he repeated his proposal in a letter that was also signed by Marcelino Domingo and Santiago Casares Quiroga (former minister of the interior and a top leader of Galician left Republicans). Azaña urged the prime minister to seize the initiative by organizing a new all-leftist coalition government immediately, so as to place all power in the hands of the left before the new parliament had an opportunity to meet. Such a government could avoid convening the latter by holding another round of elections as soon as possible.[21]

The most bizarre of these proposals to subvert constitutional process came from the Socialists, who sent the physiology professor and Madrid Socialist Juan Negrín to intercede with Alcalá Zamora. Speaking on behalf, he declared, of Fernando de los Ríos and the Socialist parliamentary delegation, Negrín urged the president to cancel the electoral results immediately and to form a new government led by left Republicans that would prepare a new electoral law. Since the latter had failed in their first attempt to write an unrepresentative electoral law that would favor the left, it was now proposed that they should try to write a second set of regulations that this time would be guaranteed to favor only the left. Since under this scheme there would temporarily be no parliament, the artificially rigged new law could be given a dubious legality by reconvening the Diputación Permanente (Permanent Caucus) of the old parliament, after which there would be a new round of balloting. The president rejected this preposterous proposal out of hand, writing later that first the left would not accept a bicameral legislature and now rejected an honest unicameral legislature.[22]

This whole dismal maneuver revealed what had become the permanent position of the left under the Republic: they would accept only the permanent government of the left. Any election or government not dominated by the left was neither "Republican" nor "democratic," a position that might well have the effect of making a democratic Republic impossible. Down to September 1933 the left had governed through legal means, partly by means of its draconian Law for the Defense of the Republic, replicated in the equally stringent Law of Public Order of July 1933, which made it easy to restrict the civil rights of opponents. When even its own tendentious and unfair regulations were inadequate to give it electoral victory in 1933, the left chose to ignore the very constitution it had been instrumental in writing. From this time forward, the left would flout legality ever more systematically, eventually reducing the legal order to shambles and setting the stage for civil war.

THE ANARCHOSYNDICALIST INSURRECTION OF DECEMBER 1933

While the moderate left sought to subvert the legal order through political manipulation, the revolutionary left attacked it with violence and arson. The year 1933 had been a time of decline for the CNT, but its leadership calculated that the time had come for a major revolutionary spasm before the new parliament could convene. The last of the tres ochos, this insurrection enjoyed considerably more organization than its two predecessors of January 1932 and January 1933, and indeed was the only one to enjoy the official endorsement of the national leadership of the CNT. Though it proved to be yet more of the typically anarchist "playing at revolution," the notion was that, with the CNT weakening in Barcelona, the initiative would be taken in Aragon and in other regions, somehow sparking an all-Spanish insurrection.[23]

On 1 December two large bombs went off in Barcelona. One day later, after a request from the autonomous Catalan government, Madrid declared an *estado de prevención* throughout Catalonia and forty-eight hours later throughout Spain. The police began to close down CNT centers and, for good measure, those of the Carlists and the new fascist party Falange on the right. The main insurrection broke out on 8 December, with explosions and outbursts in eight cities. By the next morning a state of alarm had been declared throughout the country. The main fighting took place in the provinces of Zaragoza and Barcelona, but there were violent incidents in nine other provinces in the north, east, and south, including acts of indiscriminate terrorism. Several trains were derailed; the blowing up of a bridge in Valencia produced a wreck in which between sixteen and twenty passengers were killed, depending on reports. The most spectacular episode occurred in the town of Villanueva de la Serena (Badajoz), where the sergeant in charge of a local army recruitment post mutinied, together with several other soldiers and fifteen civilian anarchists. Troops were called in to storm the building the next morning, killing seven rebels, including the sergeant.

The insurrection was most vigorous in Zaragoza, where it spread to four neighboring provinces. The FAI-CNT momentarily took over several small towns in Huesca, Alava, and Logroño, officially declaring "libertarian communism," burning records, and abolishing money. By 12 December the authorities had largely regained control. The Ministry of the Interior announced a month later that the insurrection had cost the lives of eleven Civil Guards, three other policemen, and seventy-five civilians, in statistics which were probably incomplete. Hundreds of CNT activists were arrested.[24]

In three years there had been six efforts to subvert the legal order in Spain: the abortive Republican military pronunciamiento of December 1930, three revolutionary insurrections by the CNT, the failed rightist military pronunciamiento of August 1932, and the failed leftist pronunciamiento civil of November–December 1933. After late 1933, full constitutional normalcy and civil rights were comparatively rare. A state of either alarm or prevention continued, a state of alarm being restored for most of March. April 1934 began with a state of prevention, raised to a state of alarm on 17 April, and accompanied by press censorship until the end of May. A state of prevention was then restored before the close of June, and so on.[25] Republicanism had opened a new era of convulsion, and nearly all the convulsions stemmed from the left, as the list above indicates.

RULE BY MINORITY GOVERNMENT: ALCALÁ ZAMORA THWARTS THE PARLIAMENT

The government had thwarted subversion by the left, but the question remained whether the democratically elected parliament would be allowed to form a normal majority government led by the largest party, the CEDA. Now it was the president himself, Alcalá Zamora, who chose to flout the regular parliamentary system. Whereas in 1933 he had worked to undercut the left, in the new year he would continue to pursue his goal of "centering the Republic" by denying access to the legally elected right.

Under normal parliamentary practice, Gil Robles, leader of the largest parliamentary party, would have been offered the opportunity to form a coalition majority government. Though the CEDA had made clear its determination to obey the law scrupulously, it had never declared itself "Republican." Like all the Spanish political forces, it was internally divided. A left minority was Christian democratic and sought to convert the Republic to true liberal democracy.[26] A larger right wing looked to Catholic corporatism and hence a corporatist, no longer fully parliamentary, Republic, similar to the new Catholic regimes being constructed in Austria and Portugal. Gil Robles and most of the top leaders declared themselves "accidentalists," willing to work with the Republic in order to reform it drastically, presumably along corporatist lines. Alcalá Zamora therefore believed that he had both a moral and political duty to keep the largest parliamentary party out of government, however much such a veto might conflict with normal democratic practice. Gil Robles had the presumed constitutional right to ask to be allowed to form a governing coalition, but for some time chose not to exercise that right. He initially took the position that as a very new party, scarcely more than a year old, the CEDA needed a little more time to consolidate itself and to prepare to govern, though it would be happy to participate in a broader coalition. This was perhaps a tactical mistake, for it began by conceding a principle that could never be fully reclaimed. The CEDA was arguably in its strongest position when flush with electoral victory, before it had begun to accept exclusion. At the same time, Gil Robles recognized that Spanish voters had not voted against the Republic but against the policies of the left, and further that the moderate, cooperative approach of the CEDA had probably been a significant factor in gaining it so much support.

Alcalá Zamora was determined to keep the CEDA out of office, at least until it had become more mature and reliable, and deemed his best alternative to be the Radicals, the number two party in the new parliament, now more than ever the main force of the liberal democratic center. The Radicals brought their own liabilities. Theirs was the oldest of the main Republican parties, and also the largest, but one that had gained a reputation for opportunism and corruption when it dominated Barcelona city government earlier in the century. It had become a broad middle-class liberal party under the new regime, appealing to a cross-section of secular and progressivist but moderate liberals attracted to pragmatism and the defense of middle-class interests, and to a Republicanism that would not give in to the Socialists. The Radicals had always been opportunistic and personalistic and had incorporated many new adherents, some of them relatively conservative but eager to get ahead under the Republic. They had developed out of many years of opposition as a localist or "municipal" party strongly oriented toward clientelism. Such clientelism characterized nearly all Spanish parties to some degree, but as a broadly pragmatic group the Radicals had developed clientelism to a high level.

Lerroux had adopted the attractive slogan of "a Republic for all Span- iards," but he was in his seventieth year and his energies were declining. In theory, the Radicals' practical liberal democracy and philosophy of "live and let live" ought to have been attractive in a new democracy subject to severe polarization, but this was true only to a limited extent. Amid the growing polarization, the Radicals cultivated more than a little program- matic ambiguity, which appeared to both the left and right as amoral opportunism. A banner of mere democracy did not have such broad ap- peal in an increasingly ideologically charged atmosphere in which broad sectors of the left and right had little interest in democracy per se, depend- ing on whose interests they perceived to be favored by it. During the first round of the recent elections the Radicals had allied themselves with the small moderate Republican parties, but when they saw the opportunity for major advances through association with the large conservative vote in the second round, this once virulently anticlerical party allied itself with the CEDA and gained numerous seats. In the process, it had failed to present a fully defined program on all issues, though momentarily this silence may have been a source of strength. The caliber of the Radical leadership was uncertain at best, and they seemed to lack strong, experienced, and energetic spokesmen able to confront major problems. Theirs remained a very localist party, made up of diverse groups, held together by Lerroux. One CEDA deputy observed, "This Radical minority reminds me of a ship voyage: persons of every age and condition, brought together solely to make the trip."[27] Yet the diversity of the Radicals might also be a source of strength. They had become in some ways the major force in Spain's local life by the end of 1933, including in their ranks many mayors and presidents of provincial assemblies (*diputaciones*), especially in the Levant and the south. Though some of the more liberal Radicals were leery of working with the CEDA, Lerroux announced the Radicals' goals to be "broadening the base of the Republic," domesticating the main force of the right, and thus stabilizing "a democratic and liberal Republic."[28]

Lerroux presented his new government to the Cortes on 19 December. It consisted of seven Radicals (including himself), two Republican independents, and a member each from Alcalá Zamora's Progressive Republicans, the Liberal Democrats of Melquiades Álvarez,[29] and the more conservative Agrarians. The new administration promised to uphold the Republican constitution and the positive reforms of the first biennium, while correcting previous abuses and providing equal government for all—something that could hardly be said of the Azaña government. The problem was that the coalition parties represented scarcely a third of the votes in the chamber and could not survive without the acquiescence of the CEDA. This Gil Robles was willing to provide, despite his sometimes aggressive and menacing speeches.

That same day Gil Robles presented to the Cortes the CEDA's own legislative program, which included a full amnesty for political prisoners (even though in most cases convicted of objective crimes against the constitution and against society), revision of the religious legislation, and the annulment of certain economic reforms. He attacked jurados mixtos, as well as the program to require more extensive cultivation and expanded hiring of farm laborers, and pressed for a reduction in the amount of land subject to expropriation under the agrarian reform. At the same time Gil Robles declared the need for stronger action against unemployment and for expanded public works, to be paid for by tax increases. He differed publicly with the Falangist leader Primo de Rivera on the issue of national dictatorship, saying that "the deification of the state and the annulment of individual personality" were against his principles. Gil Robles began to use terms like "in deference to," "willingness to work within," and "respect for" the Republic.[30] Meanwhile the Agrarians went further, reorganizing themselves under the banner of official recognition of the Republic, though this provoked the resignation of five of their most conservative deputies.

Lerroux was convinced that the Radicals were accomplishing a major patriotic service by beginning the domestication of the right within the Republic. The most immediate payoff for the CEDA was that the new administration ignored the Law of Congregations passed six months earlier, allowing Catholic schools to continue to operate normally. In January 1934 the new foreign minister, Leandro Pita Romero, was sent to Rome to begin negotiations for a new concordat, and on 4 April a law was passed authorizing the government to continue to pay the salaries of priests more than forty years of age in small towns at two-thirds the rate of 1931. That spring Holy Week ceremonies were performed fully for the first time in three years, and old-line anticlerical Radicals were disgusted to see the new Radical minister of the interior walking in a religious procession in Seville.

This center-right compromise—under the immediate circumstances the only viable option—produced new tensions on both left and right. Martínez Barrio, the number two figure in the Radical Party and head of the recent caretaker government, showed increasing distress over his party's turn toward the right. As grand master of the Spanish Masonic Grand Orient he was also the leader of Masonic anticlerical liberalism. He declared in a published interview on 4 February that he was "a man of the left," and at the end of that month he resigned his portfolio as war minister, joined by the Radical finance minister. Two and a half months later he would abandon the party altogether, followed by a number of the more leftist Radical deputies and a sector of the party in Valencia, one of its strongholds.[31] This departure required reorganization of the Lerroux government after only two months, but it was reformed on the same basis.

Conversely, the CEDA's willingness to support a center-right government enraged its former electoral allies of the extreme right, who moved to a fully subversive position. Spanish monarchists sought direct backing from Mussolini's Fascist regime in Rome, negotiating Italian support for a violent overthrow of the Republic. Representatives of Renovación Española and the Carlist Comunión Tradicionalista met in Rome on 31 March with the Italian air minister Italo Balbo and signed a secret agreement that promised the Spanish rebels 1,500,000 pesetas in financial support, 10,000 rifles, 200 machine guns, and other forms of aid, including the opportunity to train volunteers in Libya.[32] The first half million pesetas were paid the next day, and soon some fifty Carlist volunteers journeyed to Libya. The entire arrangement nevertheless soon became a dead letter because the monarchists failed to build the strength and unity to take advantage of it. No arms were ever sent to Spain, and the whole project was cancelled by Mussolini a year later after the monarchists had shown few signs of life.[33] Spanish publications of the extreme right nonetheless began to discuss openly the doctrine of justified armed insurrection,[34] and in May the Carlists moved even further to the right. Their existing junta, which had been willing to cooperate with *alfonsino* monarchists, was dissolved, and a new secretary general, Manuel Fal Conde, appointed. Fal Conde sought to promote a Carlist restoration by force and encouraged the drilling of Carlist militiamen.

The several governments led by Radical prime ministers during 1934 were pledged to maintain nearly all the Republican reforms, with the exception of the legislation discriminating against Catholics. In their administration of the social and economic reforms, however, these governments failed to enforce all the new regulations, so that even though their overall policy was centrist and in that sense the fairest of any period of the Republic, the effect of their economic administration was more conservative and had an adverse effect on labor interests, heightening the already severe social tensions.

The government fulfilled its pledge to introduce amnesty legislation, presented by the justice minister, Ramón Álvarez Valdés of the Liberal Democrats, on 23 March. Álvarez Valdés quickly got into trouble by declaring that he was opposed to all efforts to seize power by force, whether by rightists in 1932 or by anarchosyndicalists in 1933. The crafty Prieto, seeing an opening through which the government might be weakened, then demanded to know if Álvarez Valdés also repudiated the Republican military rebels of December 1930. To his credit, the justice minister maintained a consistent position, stressing that the legitimate Republic had been introduced by the elections of April 1931. His refusal to endorse Galán and García Hernández, the executed pro-Republican military rebels of 1930, provoked a firestorm of protest from the leftist deputies, who claimed that Álvarez Valdés had slandered sacred martyrs of the Republic. The hapless minister, whose personal position was in fact irreproachable, soon resigned, to be replaced on 17 April by Madariaga, who temporarily occupied two ministries. Madariaga believed that it was vital to go to considerable lengths to achieve national reconciliation before polarization became too extreme. When Socialists objected that the new bill granted amnesty only for acts committed through 3 December 1933, and so would exclude the many hundreds of *cenetistas* arrested after their most recent insurrection, the date was extended to 14 April 1934, the third anniversary of the founding of the Republic. It carried on 20 April by a vote of 269 to one.

An impasse quickly developed at the presidential level. Alcalá Zamora opposed the law for weakening the Republic by placing its enemies at liberty. He preferred to return the bill to parliament for reconsideration, as empowered by article 83 of the constitution, but article 84 required that any such act be cosigned by at least one government minister, and none of the ministers would agree to sign. Lerroux, as was his wont, proposed a compromise. Two additional decrees would be promulgated with the amnesty, one specifying that none of the land expropriated from high aristocrats in 1932 or any of those convicted of involvement in the sanjurjada would be returned, the second that none of the military officers being amnestied would be allowed to return to the active list. The amnesty, dated 20 April, was officially published on 2 May. Offices of the monarchist Acción Española were allowed to reopen for the first time since August 1932, and the monarchist leader José Calvo Sotelo (under indictment for having participated in the government of the dictatorship) returned to Spain two days later.

Alcalá Zamora then deliberately provoked an artificial crisis, attaching with his signature of the new bill a pedantic memorandum of several pages in the form of a message to the Cortes detailing all his juridical and political arguments against it.[35] Gil Robles pledged CEDA votes to Lerroux for a parliamentary vote of confidence, but the latter resigned on the twenty-fifth. The next day rumors spread that the Radicals and their friends in the military, several of whom held high rank, were preparing a coup. A state of alarm was declared throughout Spain, while Azaña and many other left Republicans passed the night on alert, relieved that the president had in effect vetoed Lerroux's continuation as prime minister.

On the following day Alcalá Zamora asked one of Lerroux's chief lieutenants, Ricardo Samper, to form a government. A bald, homely man with a long face, Samper was a veteran Radical from Valencia and a former follower of the novelist Blasco Ibáñez, from the more liberal side of the party. Though the president's de facto veto of Lerroux infuriated many Radicals, they were the party of compromise par excellence, and Lerroux advised them to cooperate. Samper's new cabinet was composed of eight Radicals, one member each from the Agrarians, Progressive Republicans, and Liberal Democrats, and one independent, with Madariaga (who was not a deputy) returning to his diplomatic responsibilities at the League of Nations. The general impression that this was a cabinet of nonentities manipulated by the president was essentially correct. Azaña observed tongue in cheek that it was such a collection of mediocrities that he would prefer to be governed by the monarchy.

The crisis exposed the major problem of Republican government for the next two years: a general refusal to allow the constitutional and parliamentary system to function normally. Once more, the crisis had been a personal and artificial one created by the president himself, who had vetoed the leaders of both of the two largest parliamentary parties as prime minister. To that extent, his interference and manipulation had become more extreme than that imputed to the former king, who had very rarely sought to bypass the established leadership of the major parties. In 1934 Spain would probably have enjoyed more regular parliamentary government if Alfonso XIII had still been reigning in Madrid. Alcalá Zamora now saw Lerroux as a corrupt and dangerous rival, who he was convinced had been informed of, though not a direct part of, the abortive Sanjurjo pronunciamiento. The president would seek increasingly to replace Lerroux as the real leader of the democratic center in Spain, yet, lacking a major party of his own, he could try to do so only by repeated interference and manipulation in the normal processes of government. By this course he would manage to alienate almost everyone. He had been unable to block the generous amnesty bill of the center and right, who were increasingly angry with him, while the left insisted on much more—a kind of presidential pronunciamiento to block constitutional processes and give them an immediate opportunity to return to power. Alcalá Zamora would repeat these maneuvers any number of times in the two years that followed, on each occasion to the further discredit and weakening of the parliamentary system, until he finally achieved the exact opposite of what he sought, and was faced with total polarization of the polity.

CHAPTER THREE

The Revolutionary Insurrection of 1934

SOME HISTORIANS HAVE ARGUED that the most decisive single development in the history of the Republic before July 1936 was the shift in Socialist policy during 1933–34, though there is no agreement concerning the causes of the change. Various commentators ascribe this to the danger from the right, as a result of the rise of the CEDA. Others point to the influence of events in central Europe after the consolidation of the Hitler regime and the imposition of a rightist dictatorship in Austria, marking the defeat of the two strongest Socialist movements in Europe. The deepening of the depression during 1932–33 is also sometimes cited. Still others point to the beginning of Socialist radicalization in the summer of 1933, a phenomenon not directly related to the chronology of either foreign affairs or domestic electoral defeat, but which apparently stemmed from the weakening of the Socialist–left Republican coalition, the increasing frustration met by Republican reform initiatives, and the threatened loss of government power.[1]

Not the least factor was persistent competition with a mass revolutionary anarchosyndicalist movement, which always outflanked the Socialists to the left and sought to draw away their labor support. To this was added the profound weakness of Spanish Communism, which otherwise might have been able to draw a sharp Marxist-Leninist boundary to the left of the Socialists. As it was, there was mounting temptation for the latter to play a revolutionary role. Santos Juliá has written: "In fact, as soon as they had lost their place in the government, the leaders of the UGT took up the practice of the revolutionary general strike, whose manifest goal was no longer simply obtaining improvements for the working class but rather the destruction of the Republic and the seizure of power."[2] Juliá explains:

> the first statements by Socialist leaders about the need to take over power or conquer it by whatever means . . . bore no relation to a presumed fear of the fascist menace. Socialists began to elaborate the discourse about the conquest of power as soon as they were excluded from the government, facing the prospect of the Radicals assuming leadership. At that point no one identified Lerroux with fascism and no one, not even Lerroux, thought that within two months he would have to govern with the parliamentary support of the CEDA. It was enough for the Socialists to find themselves excluded from government power to announce their new political intentions: that change, though only incipient, is incomprehensible unless one keeps in mind that they all considered the Republic their own creature and all believed they held the right, prior to any election or popular vote, to govern it.[3]

There was undeniably a rising tide of discontent among UGT workers. Deepening of the depression increased officially registered unemployment from 446,263 in June 1932 to 618,947 in December 1933 and to 703,814 by April 1934.[4] Major economic interests, particularly the larger landowners, had gone over to the offensive during 1933 as the relatively weak Spanish state demonstrated that it lacked the administrative apparatus to enforce all the new reforms, especially in the countryside. Some of the new regulations were becoming a dead letter in certain provinces, and Largo Caballero claimed that during his last months as minister of labor he regularly received delegations of provincial workers who urged the party to take action.[5] The national committee of the UGT had met as early as 18 June 1933 to face the problem of declining membership. By the end of the year, affiliation in some areas had dropped by as much as a third. The farm laborers' federation (Federación Nacional de Trabajadores de la Tierra; FNTT) was claiming that in southern rural provinces wages had declined as much as 60 percent (probably an exaggeration) and that in some areas work was being offered only to laborers who were willing to drop their membership in the union.

It was in this climate that Largo Caballero had hailed the prospect of direct revolution at the Young Socialist summer school in August 1933, sentiments that he repeated, though usually in more discreet or equivocal terms, in a series of speeches during the next year. The Socialist left increased in influence under his de facto leadership, yet it was not clear what new policies would replace collaborationism. The hard-core left of the PSOE had always opposed government participation, but Largo and the other leaders had no clear-cut alternative to propose. Even after the coalition had collapsed, the party heads had given their support to an abortive effort by the moderate left Republican leader Felipe Sánchez Román to reorganize the coalition once more, even if on a more moderate basis.

As indicated in the preceding chapter, their first response to the electoral disaster had been to urge Alcalá Zamora to change the electoral law, dissolve the new parliament, and then hold new elections under conditions much more favorable to the left. This notion was not so much revolutionary as reactionary, a return to the manipulated elections of the nineteenth century. Concurrently, a joint meeting of the executive commissions of the party and the UGT on 25 November agreed that if "reactionary elements" should take power, the Socialists "would have to rebel [*alzarse*] energetically,"[6] though exactly what that meant was unclear. When the FAI-CNT launched its latest mini-insurrection on 8 December, the executive commission of the party immediately issued a manifesto disclaiming any connection.

Though there was much talk of revolution in some quarters, and increasing nonsense about the similarity to conditions in Russia in 1917, the only strategy that the party leadership could conceive was some sort of undefined initiative to keep the right from forming a government, though the latter had every right to attempt to do so under normal parliamentary rules. Meanwhile the Lerroux government ended the ill-conceived "municipal boundaries" law, which restricted opportunities to hire farm laborers outside of local districts, while the functioning of the jurados mixtos had become much less favorable to organized labor. The reform legislation remained the law, but part of it was no longer being enforced, while unemployment maintained its inexorable rise. The response of the Socialist leadership was provocative yet contradictory. Since a growing sector of the movement had begun to embrace for the first time a process of revolutionary activism that it called *bolchevización*, Largo Caballero had declared in a widely distributed speech of 31 December that, with regard to the Communists, "the difference between them and ourselves is no more than terminology."[7] On 3 January *El Socialista* thundered: "Harmony? No! Class war! Hatred to the death for the criminal bourgeoisie!" Yet five days later a delegation from the FNTT visited the minister of labor to urge him to continue to enforce the existing legislation. The CEDA, however, announced plans to alter drastically the existing labor and land norms and also to seek an increase in the Civil Guard to control dissidence.

Azaña himself expressed alarm at the "bolshevization" of the Socialists, noting in his diary on 2 January that talk of revolution was absurd and that "an electoral defeat with its disastrous consequences ought to be repaired by the same means." Though the Lerroux government had clearly rejected any further reforms and was not even enforcing all those that had been enacted, it was not a government of stark reaction and did not justify "a violent response." As Azaña put it succinctly, "The country will not support an insurrection, because four-fifths of it is not Socialist," accurately proportioning the amount of the vote that the Socialists had received. A revolutionary Socialist government would have no legitimacy save force: "Its power would extend as far as the range of its pistols. Such a situation, insupportable in my political thought and unsustainable in reality, would provide the excuse for a frightful reaction," a prophecy that would prove entirely correct.[8]

Julián Besteiro and part of the veteran leadership of the UGT still opposed radicalization. Besteiro had a much clearer grasp of the situation than most of his colleagues. First, he had realized that the initial left-liberal coalition would probably not at present be in a position to maintain permanent hegemony over Republican politics, and hence had urged his fellow Socialists to temper their ambitions. Second, he grasped that Spanish society had entered a kind of danger zone between mere underdevelopment on the one hand and mature conditions for a prosperous and peaceful socialism on the other. He had stated in a major address the preceding summer that Spanish workers still exhibited much of the destructive reaction against early stages of industrialization, rejecting discipline and moderation, yet at the same time the Spanish economy had achieved a sufficiently complex level of development that it could not readily be "conquered" by revolutionary Socialists. He warned correctly that in somewhat similar circumstances in Italy in 1920 the occupation of the factories by Socialist trade unionists had constituted but a prelude to a triumphant Fascist reaction. Spanish society was not yet prepared for a true Socialist hegemony, which in Besteiro's definition would have to be a democratic one. His unalterable conclusion was that once a democracy based on universal suffrage for both sexes existed, as in Spain, the "dictatorship of the proletariat" was an outmoded and totally destructive concept. By early January there were meetings between the party and UGT leaders to decide on a course of action. Besteiro attempted delaying tactics, insisting that any drastic initiative should be approved by a full national congress of the UGT and should be completely clear about its goals. To meet this objection, the party executive commission approved on 13 January a ten-point program drawn up by Prieto. It called for:

1. Nationalization of the land
2. Major priority for irrigation projects
3. Radical reform of education
4. Dissolution of all religious orders, with seizure of their wealth and expulsion of those considered dangerous
5. Dissolution of the army, to be replaced by a democratic militia
6. Dissolution of the Civil Guard
7. Reform of the bureaucracy and a purge of anti-Republicans
8. Improvement of the condition of industrial workers but no nationalization of industry
9. Tax reform, with introduction of an inheritance tax
10. All these changes, initiated by decree, to be ratified by a democratically elected new legislature

To this program Largo Caballero added five tactical points, with the new government to be composed of all the forces that collaborated in bringing it to power. Besteiro and the executive commission of the UGT responded with a long program of their own, calling for establishment of a special national corporative assembly to initiate a major program against unemployment and begin a carefully planned, long-range nationalization of industry.[9] They grasped that, with the CNT clearly in decline, the UGT might well expand its proportionate trade union base among Spanish labor by emphasizing practical and constructive trade union policies, rather than political violence, and develop a peaceful social democratic hegemony. UGT activists, however, angrily rejected such an orientation.

The elderly official leadership of the UGT was losing touch with the lower-level leaders and much of the rank and file, who were increasingly influenced by the new militancy. When the UGT's national committee convened on 27 January it voted by a sizable majority to accept the more radical party proposal, prompting immediate resignation of Besteiro and his fellow moderates in the leadership. The national committee then elected a new executive commission dominated by *caballeristas*,[10] and Largo felt free to assume actively the post of secretary general of the UGT, to which he had been elected in 1932 but which he had refused to accept so long as *besteiristas* were predominant. He had been president of the party for more than five years and now headed the union organization, as well. *Caballeristas* already led a number of individual UGT federations and on the following day took command of the farmworkers' FNTT, largest of all, followed by assumption of leadership in the key Madrid branch of the party.[11] At the beginning of February a Revolutionary Liaison Committee was set up under Largo's personal leadership, its ten members representing the party, the UGT, and the Socialist Youth organization. News from abroad only made them more determined: on 6 February twenty demonstrators died in a Paris riot unleashed by the radical right, which ended with Senegalese troops patrolling the French capital.

The revolutionary committee had responsibility for the technical organization and financing of an insurrection and also for conducting negotiations with possible collaborators. In the Spanish tradition, Prieto was to undertake contacts with whatever sympathetic elements might be found in the military. The committee declared that its insurrection must have "all the characteristics of a civil war,"[12] its success depending on "the breadth it achieves and the violence unleashed."[13] The map of Madrid was organized by neighborhoods, with key points targeted and lists of people to be arrested drawn up. The committee planned to use thousands of militia in the capital, with the complicity of some Assault Guards and Civil Guards, some of the insurrectionists to wear Civil Guard uniforms. The committee made use of the handbook earlier prepared by Marshal Tukhachevsky and other officers of the Red Army, which had been published in Spanish and other languages in 1932 as part of the Comintern's "Third Period" revolutionary policy, under the pseudonym of "A. Neuberg" as *La insurrección armada.* The Socialist Youth, who held three of the ten seats on the committee, were to play a leading role in what became one of the most elaborately, if not efficiently, organized insurrections to take place in interwar Europe, with responsibility for organizing much of the Socialist militia. Their leaders were more directly influenced by readings in the Bolshevik revolution and thought more in terms of organized violence than did the older leaders. They were also more attracted to the small but revolutionary Communist groups in Spain, hitherto shunned by the main party leaders as much for their extremism as for their insignificance.[14]

In these circumstances came news of an attempted revolt by Austrian Socialists against the new authoritarian regime in Vienna, a revolt that was completely crushed. This outcome was hailed by the Catholic press in Spain and made a strong negative impression on the left, particularly on the Socialists, touching off a brief UGT sympathy strike in Asturias.

Declining membership in the two major national syndical federations did not so much bring a reduction in strike activity as a feverish concern to counter the decline by an increase in activism. The most intense work stoppage was the CNT's general strike in Zaragoza, which lasted six weeks and featured the sending of 18,000 children of workers to Barcelona to be fed by comrades there. When a printers' strike in Madrid closed down the major rightist newspapers for about ten days, the government declared another state of alarm. The long construction strike in Madrid was finally settled on 20 March by the Ministry of Labor, which reduced the work week to forty-four hours but retained the equivalent of forty-eight hours' pay. A metallurgy strike continued in Madrid until 1 June and then was settled on much the same basis—scarcely draconian terms for labor. Yet these had been bitter disputes attended by more than a little disorder. Moreover, there was an increasing tendency in some areas for *ugetistas* and *cenetistas* to make common cause.

The initiative to organize a broader united revolutionary left had already been taken in Barcelona by Joaquín Maurín and his independent Marxist-Leninist Bloque Obrero y Campesino (BOC), centered in Catalonia. The BOC was a development of the old Federación Comunista Catalano-Balear, the Catalan section of the original Spanish Communist Party (PCE), which had been expelled from the party in 1928 after it had rejected the Moscow line. At one point it had contained nearly half the membership of the PCE and in March 1931, on the eve of the Republic, had merged with the Partit Comunista Català, a tiny dissident Catalan Communist group, to form the BOC. Maurín's position had paralleled that of the PCE in its rejection of the Republic and parliamentary reformism. He was the nearest thing to an original revolutionary Marxist theorist in Spain and had forcefully argued that the entire original political posture of the Socialists had been mistaken, for the Republic per se had not constituted the beginning of a complete bourgeois democratic revolution. A bourgeois capitalist revolution of sorts had taken place in nineteenth-century Spain under a weak and incompetent bourgeoisie without bringing democracy. By the 1930s the Spanish bourgeoisie was played out, no longer progressive but actively reactionary. The middle classes alone could neither complete the democratic revolution nor serve as effective allies in moving toward the socialist revolution, and thus the Socialist policy had been totally misconceived. Spain had, however, developed a sufficiently advanced society to have crystallized around two social forces—the rightist bourgeoisie and the leftist workers. It was up to the latter to complete the democratic revolution but also to move directly toward a socialist revolution, with the dual goals of carrying out, in Maurín's unique formulation, a "democratic-socialist revolution" almost simultaneously. The Socialists were rejected for compromise and reformism, and the small Communist group for Stalinism and Soviet domination, but meanwhile the dissident Marxists formed little more than sects.

A new initiative had been taken early in 1933, soon after Hitler came to power in Germany, when the BOC joined with the small Catalanist Socialist party the Unió Socialista de Catalunya (USC), to form an Alianza Obrera Antifascista (Antifascist Worker Alliance; AOA), using the terminology of the Alleanza del Lavoro, an antifascist alliance of much of the Italian left in 1922.[15] The goals of the AOA, which later changed its name to Alianza Obrera (AO), tout court were threefold: to defend the gains of the working class, to defeat fascism in Spain, and to prepare the revolution that would create a federal socialist republic. The BOC and the USC were later joined by the Treintistas, who had split from the CNT, by the Unió de Rabassaires of Catalan sharecroppers, by Andreu Nin's tiny Trotskyist Izquierda Comunista de España (Communist Left of Spain; ICE), and (in December 1933) by the Catalan sections of the Socialist Party and the UGT.[16]

Maurín and the Barcelona leaders of the AO hoped to expand it into

an all-Spanish organization. He met with Largo Caballero and other Socialist figures in Madrid in January 1934, and Largo returned the visit in
Barcelona the following month. A fundamental divergence nonetheless
existed: Maurín intended that the Alianza Obrera become the vehicle
of a large new revolutionary Marxist-Leninist force of a new type; Largo
and the Socialist leaders conceived it simply as an umbrella organization
for an insurrection in which the dominant role would be played by the
Socialist Party.

The chronic dilemma for any proposal of united action by the worker
left was collaboration between the CNT and the UGT. As usual, the CNT
decided in the negative at a sizable meeting of regional representatives
at Barcelona on 10 February. The party refused to join any revolutionary
action not aimed directly at achieving the anarchist goal of libertarian
communism. A different situation prevailed only in Asturias, where the
severe depression of the mining industry and other problems had helped
produce proportionately the highest rate of strikes in all Spain. There
Socialists and anarchosyndicalists had first collaborated in the general
strike of 1917 and had participated in a number of joint actions under
the Republic. Thus the Asturian sections of the CNT and UGT signed an
unusual alliance on 31 March that created a joint "Alianza Revolucionaria"
to promote "a regime of economic, political and social equality founded
on federal socialist principles," a unique attempt to synthesize the revolutionary aspirations of Socialists and anarchosyndicalists.[17]

On 5 May El Socialista announced formation of the Alianza Obrera in
Madrid for "the struggle against fascism in all its forms and the preparation of the working-class movement for the establishment of a federal
social republic." This statement repeated exactly the formula of the AOA
in Barcelona over a year earlier. Under the AO, each member organization was free to carry on its own activity and propaganda independently,
but there were to be regional committees in each area for mutual coordination, and these would ultimately choose a national committee. The
abstention of the CNT everywhere but in Asturias, however, meant that
the AO would basically consist of the Socialists and a number of small
allies, whose significance was mostly limited to parts of Catalonia. After a
time the Catalan USC, a cofounder of the alliance, abandoned it in protest
against domination by the Madrid-based Socialists.

During the spring of 1934 the most active role in labor affairs was taken by the UGT's farmworker federation, the FNTT, centered in Extremadura and Andalusia. Whereas conditions for urban workers had deteriorated only slightly, there was a growing sense of desperation among rural laborers, who had suffered an increase of more than 50 percent in unemployment during the past two years. The new deal offered by the Republic seemed to be fading away as landowners became increasingly obdurate and often found all manner of ways of getting around, or in some cases simply ignoring, the reform legislation of 1931–1933. With no unemployment benefits or other resources to fall back on, empty-handed laborers were sometimes told to "Comed República!" (Eat Republic). There was a growing feeling that the government had become the friend of the employer and the enemy of the laborer, even if the facts did not entirely bear this out. Some of the more excessive regulations had been repealed, but the government tried to maintain most of the new regulations and administer the labor jurados with an even hand. Workers still won some of the negotiations, and in fact the Radical government was more nearly neutral in such matters than its predecessor. Moreover, during the ten months from December 1933 to September 1934 land was distributed to more rural families than during the last ten months of the Azaña administration. By the spring of 1934 some of the organized economic interests that had backed the Radicals' electoral campaign were claiming to have been betrayed. The decline in wages that farm laborers protested was still comparatively limited,[18] though unemployment continued to spread and some of the earlier devices to curtail it were not being rigorously enforced.

The new *caballerista* leadership of the FNTT headlined its first declaration in *El Obrero de la Tierra* on 3 February: "We Declare Ourselves in Favor of Revolution!" It called for full socialization and praised Soviet collectivization, seemingly oblivious to the fact that the latter had created mass famine and resulted in millions of deaths. At the same time, however, the FNTT leadership also bombarded the Ministry of Labor with practical appeals and frequently petitioned the Ministry of the Interior for greater police intervention to enforce labor regulations and work agreements, and to reverse recent closures of Casas del Pueblo (Socialist centers) in several districts. The FNTT claimed that hundreds of appeals on nonpayment of wages had gone unanswered (which may well have been true) and that 500 workers had been imprisoned in the province of Badajoz alone. The

Socialist press was full of horror stories about the arbitrary lowering of wages (possibly true in individual instances but not necessarily true of employers as a whole) and of drastic police intervention, including four laborers shot dead during a farm strike.

The new Samper administration, though handpicked by Alcalá Zamora, seemed to move in some respects further to the right than the preceding Lerroux government. A decree of 4 May annulled the original provisions of the agrarian reform for direct confiscation, guaranteeing compensation for all expropriation. On 24 May the Cortes voted 254 to 44 to abolish the municipal boundaries law, which had restricted hiring of nonlocal laborers, at the same time stipulating that there could be no unilateral reduction of wages. The new interior minister, Rafael Salazar Alonso, was a hard-liner. Whereas Azaña's interior minister, Casares Quiroga, had intervened to replace a total of 270 local mayors or municipal councils over a period of two years, Salazar Alonso used the highly centralized Spanish system to suspend 193 in less than seven months, particularly, he claimed, in order to eliminate entrenched Socialist favoritism, especially in the provinces of Badajoz, Cáceres, Alicante, and Jaén.[19]

After a final appeal to the minister of labor on 28 April, the national committee of the FNTT met on 11–12 May to consider a national farm-workers' strike. The idea got no support from the national UGT leadership, which declared an agrarian strike a bad idea, for it would be extremely awkward to coordinate; under present conditions, such a strike would be considered provocative and would be forcibly repressed. Largo Caballero's revolutionary committee wanted to reserve any general strike for the moment of maximal political crisis. Thus the UGT told the FNTT not to count on urban labor cooperation. The FNTT's national committee issued a list of ten demands, which were far-reaching but not truly revolutionary. They included the *turno rigoroso* (hiring in strict order from the labor list provided by the syndicate), the outlawing of harvest machinery in many areas, creation of supervisory committees of farmworkers in all districts to guarantee fulfillment of contracts, and other changes to tip the balance of labor relations in favor of workers in the countryside. There was no demand for a change in property ownership.[20]

The Ministry of Agriculture remained conciliatory, and on 24 May the government ordered field inspectors from the Ministry of Labor to prevent discrimination in hiring and urged the rural arbitration boards to agree quickly on harvest contracts favorable to the workers. On 2 June the government made further concessions by strengthening the legislation that obliged owners to hire workers only through local employment offices (though not necessarily in the "rigorous order" the Socialists required) and by authorizing its field inspectors to assign additional workers to each owner in areas where unemployment was severe. Meanwhile the harvest contracts issued by the local arbitration boards established minimum wages that were as high as those that had prevailed during the Azaña era.[21] Clearly, progress was being made, but in the thinking of FNTT leaders that progress was offset by the rigorous police policy carried out by Salazar Alonso, who treated all talk of the strike as intolerable subversion, outlawing many local strike meetings and arresting a considerable number of local leaders. The government had no intention of meeting the ten demands, and over the vigorous objections of Largo Caballero and the national UGT, the FNTT called a national farm strike for 5 June.

Whereas the monthly *Boletín* of the Ministry of Labor had listed ninety-eight agrarian strikes for the first five months of 1934, the general strike of the FNTT was declared in a total of 1,563 rural municipalities involving most major parts of the country. It was particularly effective in latifundist areas; approximately half the districts in Córdoba, Málaga, and Ciudad Real were struck, as were about a quarter of those in Badajoz, Huelva, and Jaén. The strike was also strongly supported by the UGT in Seville province, where it lasted longer and involved more sabotage of property and facilities than anywhere else, only ending on 20 June. In general, behavior was restrained on both sides, and the government did not declare martial law. A total of thirteen were reported killed, not so much in police affrays as in fights between strikers and antistrikers. The police arrested approximately 7,000 participants in what had been designated an illegal strike, but most of these were released in less than a month. Conversely, emergency courts tried and sentenced a number of FNTT leaders to prison terms of four or more years. The strike had been a total failure, leaving the UGT's largest affiliate seriously weakened and dispirited. Many Casas del Pueblo in southern Spain would not reopen until February 1936.[22]

Meanwhile in Madrid and several other parts of the country, a much smaller but proportionately more deadly drama had been unfolding between the Socialist Youth and other leftist activists on one side and the militants of Falange Española on the other. Political violence had of course been endemic to the Republic, to the point that the journal *Historia Contemporánea* has spoken of "the militarization of politics under the Second Republic."[23] It had been begun by anarchists and Communists in 1931, when the CNT exploited the inauguration of the Republic to carry out a lengthy round of revenge killings in Barcelona,[24] and reached its two points of climax in 1934 and 1936.

Militancy in Spanish life was heightened by the influx of the largest generation of young people in all Spanish history to that point. During the five years 1921–1926 the Spanish labor force had incorporated 252,000 young adults. The equivalent figures for 1931–1936, with emigration at an end, were approximately 530,000—more than twice as many.[25] The potential for violent conflict, in the Spanish Republic as in the Weimar Republic of Germany, was only encouraged by the arrival of the largest cohort of young males in the history of the two countries. Thus 1934 became a key year for the expansion of political militias, among Socialists, Communists, Carlists, Falangists, and also among the peripheral nationalist groups of the Catalan Esquerra and the Basque Nationalist Party.

One major focus for political violence was the danger of fascism. By 1933 it had become increasingly common for many different groups to call their opponents fascists. This practice was most indiscriminate among the Communists, who often called Socialists "social fascists" while also labeling the democratic Republic "fascist" or "fascistoid." The liberal democrats of the Radical Party were termed "integral fascists." The CNT repaid the Communists in their own coin, calling Stalinist Communism "fascist," while also sometimes referring to "Republican fascism" and the "social fascism" of the Socialists. Some Catholics, in turn, had called the heavy-handed Azaña government "fascist."

All this raised the question of whether there really were any genuine fascists in Spain, but in fact there were a few. The country's first categorical fascist organization, the Juntas de Offensiva Nacional-Sindicalista (JONS), organized in 1931, had attracted little attention because of its insignificance, but the formation of the larger Falange Española by José Antonio Primo de Rivera (eldest son of the former dictator) in October 1933 drew much more interest. The Spanish Communist Party had been the first leftist organization to try to maximize the political banner of antifascism by launching a Frente Unico Antifascista (United Antifascist

Front). The resulting collection of Communist front groups then initiated the formation of the Milicias Antifascistas Obreras y Campesinas (Worker-Peasant Antifascist Militias; MAOC), which became the basic Communist militia organization. Nonetheless, the Communists were not in a position to initiate direct action in the way the anarchists and Socialists could.

Anarchists and Socialists had carried out a number of killings during the 1933 electoral campaign, and *jonsistas* and Falangists soon became the prime targets. By June 1934 ten jonsistas and Falangists had been slain, primarily but not exclusively by Socialists,[26] who had no intention of allowing the development in Spain of the kind of movement that had crushed Socialist parties in Italy, Germany, and Austria.

Since the Falangists did not at first fight back effectively, rightist publicists ridiculed their organization as more "Franciscan" than "fascist," suggesting that the initials "FE" stood for "Funeraria Española" (Spanish Undertakers) and that its leader should be known as Juan Simón the Gravedigger rather than as José Antonio.[27] Soon, however, Falangists had formed their own death squads. After the killing of the tenth young fascist in Madrid on 10 June 1934, Falangists struck back against a group of Socialist Youth. A young woman, Juanita Rico, was killed, and two others seriously wounded. Rico received a massive funeral and for the next few years was hailed in Socialist memory as "the first victim of fascism in Spain." This claim was correct, for the leftist concern about fascist violence had become a self-fulfilling prophecy, and Rico would not be the last victim. A running fight between Falangists and the left (mainly, but not exclusively, Socialists) would continue for two more years, reaching a climax in the spring and early summer of 1936, when it would provide the final spark that provoked the outbreak of the Civil War. The Socialists sowed the whirlwind and reaped the consequences.

Looking back on the events of 1934 a decade later, Indalecio Prieto would lament: "The hands of the Socialist Youth had been intentionally left free . . . they were able to commit all kinds of excesses, which . . . turned out to be destructive of the goals pursued. No one set limits to [their] outrageous behavior. . . . Moreover, certain deeds which prudence requires me to pass over in silence . . . drew no reproach nor any call to responsibility and no effort to bring them under control."[28]

After the failure of the agrarian strike, which only strengthened the center-right and right, "the revolutionary ardor of Prieto and even of Largo began to cool."[29] In Madrid the Alianza Obrera blocked every proposal of the tiny Trotskyist Izquierda Comunista for revolutionary action during the summer of 1934 on the grounds that the UGT must avoid partial actions. Largo stressed that he wanted no repetition of the abortive general strike of 1917 and would not follow Leninist tactics blindly.[30]

THE CATALAN AND BASQUE CONFLICTS

For Catalanists, the great achievement of the Republic was autonomy, with greater political and administrative freedom and the opportunity to introduce further changes. The downside was social relations, in which left Catalanist leaders at first insisted autonomy would open a completely new chapter. As has been seen, what happened was old rather than new; democracy and autonomy made no impression on the CNT other than to provide them with much greater freedom for direct action. Social relations soon deteriorated to the terms of 1917–1923, the last period in which Catalonia had known parliamentary government. By 1933 Catalans frequently blamed the increase in crime and disorder on the negligence of Madrid-controlled police. There was certainly no enthusiasm among the latter to serve under the autonomous authorities; when the transfer of security functions to the Generalitat took place in April 1934, a large number of police personnel resigned or transferred out. A new Catalan constabulary, the Mossos d'Esquadra, was set up to patrol rural villages and supplement the Civil Guard (now known in Catalonia as the Guardia Nacional Republicana).

Unlike the situation with Basque nationalism, Catalanism was severely divided between its left and right wings. In the national elections of 1933, the conservative Lliga Catalana had taken advantage of the new alliance dynamics to best the ruling Esquerra by twenty-five to nineteen seats. However, in the second Catalan regional elections, held in January 1934, the Esquerra won big, the margin in popular votes between a united left and the Lliga being 162,216 to 132,942. This was the only election won by left Republicans in 1933–34 and soon led to the slogan that recognized Catalonia as the "last bastion" of the original leftist Republic.

Internal dissension within Catalanist ranks had grown during 1932–33 as extremists rebelled against the eclecticism and increasing moderation of the dominant Esquerra. Extremist separatists from Francesc Macià's original Estat Català protested the Generalitat's compromise with the

Spanish government and formed several splinter groups. Rightist separatists formed a very small Partit Nacionalista Català, while leftist separatists adopted an increasingly national socialist and Marxist orientation,
forming the pompously titled Estat Català (Força Separatista d'Extrema
Esquerra) (Catalan State [Separatist Force of the Extreme Left]) and also
the subsequent Partit Català Proletari (later, at the time that the Civil War
began, to merge with the Catalan Communists and others to form a new
Catalan Communist party, the PSUC). The tendency toward splintering
of political Catalanism caused the satirical weekly *Bé Negre* to publish the
sardonic rhyme "D'Estats Catalans / N'hi ha més que dits de les mans"
(There are more Catalan states / Than fingers on the hands).[31]

The most important new force was the Esquerra youth, formed in
conjunction with the ruling party in 1932 as the Joventut d'Esquerra Republicana—Estat Català (Youth of the Republican Left—Catalan State;
JEREC). JEREC militia took the name Escamots, wore olive-green shirts,
and sometimes engaged in strong-arm tactics against the CNT, caus-
ing some to call them "Catalan fascists." Escamot leaders, such as the
policeman and former army officer Miguel Badia and the physician Josep
Dencàs, talked of preparing the way for the Esquerra as the *partit únic*
(single party) of the Catalan state, leading a new "national" and "socialist"
corporative social order, though some commentators thought that their
goals more nearly approximated those of postrevolutionary Mexico or east
European regimes than those of Fascist Italy.[32]

The elderly Macià died of natural causes on Christmas Day 1933 and
was succeeded by the most salient leader of left Catalanism, Lluis Companys.[33] The new president of the Generalitat did not attempt to renew
the close relations that Macià had established with Alcalá Zamora, but
Catalanists expected him to complete the transfers of government services
that had evolved during the preceding year and to foster an active reform
program for development of their region.

Though Catalonia was the largest industrial center in Spain, it also
had a significant agrarian economy. In the countryside the greatest pressure came from the Unió de Rabassaires (UR), an organization of sharecroppers who tended much of the land in wine-producing areas, which
Companys had helped form some fifteen years earlier. Though the UR
became increasingly radical, the goal of most members was to convert
the land they worked into private property.[34]

In April 1934 the Generalitat passed its first important socioeconomic reform, the Law of Cultivation Contracts, designed to give *rabassaire* farmers access to property ownership. It enabled renters and sharecroppers to buy land that they had cultivated directly for at least fifteen years and in this regard was similar to the proposed rental law that had failed to pass the Spanish Cortes in the preceding summer. It also stipulated a six-year minimum for rental contracts.

The Catalan Autonomy Statute gave the Generalitat certain powers to legislate in civil matters, but the constitution reserved social legislation to the jurisdiction of the central government, while the Spanish agrarian reform law reserved to the Spanish parliament jurisdiction over all cultivation contracts. The Lliga and other conservative Catalan forces protested the new legislation as radical, unfair to owners, and unconstitutional. They appealed to the Tribunal of Constitutional Guarantees, which ruled on 10 June that the Law of Cultivation Contracts was unconstitutional.[35]

This result sparked major protests in Barcelona and some other parts of Catalonia. Two days later the Generalitat passed identical legislation in defiance of the tribunal, while the Esquerra and the minuscule Unió Socialista de Catalunya announced their withdrawal from the Cortes. This was similar to the left's response to the electoral outcome of the preceding fall—whenever anything of consequence happened that was opposed to their interests, they responded by attempting to ignore the legal structure that they had just established. Shocked, Prime Minister Samper asked why they had taken such abrupt action without any attempt to discuss the matter and indicated his willingness to reach a compromise.

For the rest of the summer, the Catalan dispute remained the focus of attention. All the left, as well as the Basque Nationalists, stood behind the Esquerra. In a typically extremist address to the Cortes on 21 June, Azaña hailed Catalonia as "the last bastion remaining to the Republic," stressing that "the autonomous power of Catalonia is the last Republican power still standing in Spain."[36] This was dangerous nonsense of the worst kind; rumor had it that Azaña and his followers were talking of withdrawing to Barcelona to set up a new ad hoc provisional government of the Republic. The Lliga leader Francesc Cambó pointed out that it was irrational for the autonomous Catalan administration to ignore the terms of the Autonomy Statute and the Republican constitution as soon as the first problem arose, especially since Azaña and the left were primarily responsible for the terms of the constitution, "so that if the honorable gentleman has anything to complain about, it would be his own acts."[37] He also decried talk of Catalonia as simply the bulwark of leftism, since a democratic Catalonia would have to include and respect all its citizenry. Meanwhile Dr. Josep Dencàs, the main leader of the JEREC and the green-shirted Escamots, was appointed the new councilor of security in the Catalan government and set to work (as it turned out, ineffectively) to develop the means of armed resistance in Barcelona.[38]

On 26 June the cabinet in Madrid voted to consider the latest Catalan cultivation law null and void, since it merely repeated the earlier statute, which had been ruled unconstitutional. After a raucous debate in the Cortes, during which Prieto and several others brandished pistols, the government won a vote of confidence 192 to 62, though less than half the deputies actually voted for it. All the while it continued to cooperate in the transfer of administrative and fiscal authority to Barcelona, handing over further powers of taxation on 12 July.

Just as a solution to the Catalan conflict seemed possible, a new controversy began to develop with the Basque provinces. There the third proposal for an autonomy statute under the Republic had failed late in 1933, as a result of the opposition of the province of Alava. A new conflict was touched off by tax regulations on wine originated by the national government in Madrid, which city councils in the Basque provinces impugned as a violation of the special tax arrangement (*concierto económico*) the provinces had long enjoyed and a serious blow to local government finance. Numerous visits to Madrid failed to produce agreement. Basque spokesmen began to call for provincial elections as soon as possible, since none had been held under the Republic, and laid plans for special elections of their own in mid-August to choose a new all-Basque commission to defend their interests.

On 10 August, the eve of the Basque initiative, the Samper government promised to hold elections for provincial legislatures throughout Spain within three months and pledged to respect the terms of the existing concierto económico. It also announced that the special election of a Basque executive commission by the municipal councils would be illegal and proceeded within the next week or so to arrest twenty-five mayors and thirty municipal councilors in Vizcaya, and fifteen mayors and twenty-three municipal councilors in Guipuzcoa. Nonetheless on 21 August the

Basque Interim Commission, created by the nationalists to supervise special elections, announced that the elections had been carried out. A major
incident that day in San Sebastián led to the arrest of eighty-seven nationalists, including ten more mayors. Samper repeated the government's
promise to find a workable solution. His official note pledged to respect
Basque tax privileges, suspend any collection of income tax in the Basque
provinces, and do all in its power to arrange for Basque representation in
Madrid to negotiate these matters directly as soon as the Cortes reopened.
It plaintively asked: "What more can the government do?"[39]

The Basque nationalists held a special assembly of their newly elected
representatives, together with sympathetic Cortes deputies from the three
provinces, in Zumárraga on 2 September. This meeting decided that all
remaining members of Basque city governments should resign on 7 September, producing a wave of resignations in the two northern Basque
provinces. This was followed by a meeting of representatives of the Basque
nationalists, Socialists, UGT, Communists, and left Republicans in San
Sebastián. The leftist parties for the first time sought a common front with
Basque nationalists, but the latter would promise no more than to oppose
"with all their strength" a monarchist restoration or a rightist dictatorship,
refusing to join forces in a broad subversive conspiracy with the left.

TOWARD RED OCTOBER

The political crisis of the summer and early autumn of 1934 was played
against a background of incipient economic recovery. The harvest that year
was one of the two best in Spanish history to that date, and industrial production was recovering from the low of 1932–33, though unemployment,
as is common early in recoveries, generally continued to increase. This
general improvement did not translate into any significant improvement
in workers' immediate economic condition, but it does underscore the
extent to which the events of September–October 1934 were primarily
political in origin, even though conditioned by a general context of depression. This conclusion, earlier expressed by Vicens Vives and several other
historians, may be applied to most of the sociopolitical conflicts under the
Republic. Though economic circumstances played a role, political rivalry
remained the dominant motivation.

At the beginning of autumn Alcalá Zamora delivered one of his typically florid speeches at a ceremony in Valladolid, in which he intoned that

the Republic would soon have "a sound economy, a balanced budget, little foreign debt, and a political transformation with peace and order to make up for the destruction wrought by our earlier civil wars. With all this within our grasp, in our days Spain sees unfolding a future of greatness and well-being never dreamed of before. . . . In 1935, and even in the remainder of 1934, the horizon of Spain's greatness appears clear and cloudless, so that if we seek it Spain may become one of the relative paradises of the Earth. Impatience and agitation have no justification."[40] Though this was spreading it a bit thick, the president had a profound point. In recent years, Spain had done remarkably well, and on a comparative standard had made as much or more progress as any other country in the world. To gamble it all on an orgy of political violence was delirium. Three days later, as he was about to attend army maneuvers in León, Alcalá Zamora was warned that there were serious rumors that he was about to be kidnapped by either the police or the military. As the president noted in his diary, "I thought I was dreaming or had landed in an insane asylum."[41]

The Socialist revolutionary committee continued its preparations but had no immediate plans to pull the trigger. The predominant idea was that insurrection would be set off by the possible entry of the CEDA into the government, but there is considerable evidence that even Largo Caballero believed that Alcalá Zamora would never permit such a thing to happen. Thus Paul Preston has written that "the Socialists tried to preserve the progressive character of the Republic by threats of revolution, which they hoped never to fulfill."[42]

The broader Socialist justification for violent action was the supposed danger of fascism. Such discourse became especially common by the middle of 1934, but earlier Julián Besteiro had denied—correctly—that there was any serious danger of fascism in Spain. As recently as June 1933 Largo Caballero had told the International Labour Organisation that "in Spain, fortunately, there is no danger of fascism,"[43] correctly pointing out the absence of any significant demobilized army, any great mass of urban unemployed, any strong Spanish nationalism or militarist programs, or potential popular leaders. Similarly, in an article in the April 1934 edition of the American journal *Foreign Affairs,* Luis Araquistain, the chief *caba-llerista* ideologue, wrote that true fascism, Italian or German style, was impossible in Spain for much the same reasons as those adduced by Largo: the absence of large numbers of unemployed veterans or university youth without a future, any huge population of the completely unemployed, support for Spanish nationalism or imperialism, and effective leaders.

All this was true, yet for the left in Spain, the issue was not fascism per se but rather what they interpreted as its functional equivalent, the right in general and, most especially, the CEDA. The Catholic party rejected most Republican reformism and, given the left-radical tinge of so many Republicans, refused to label itself officially "Republican"—which in itself could scarcely be wondered at. Its youth group, Juventudes de Acción Popular (Youth of Acción Popular; JAP), used a language of authoritarian corporatism, and Gil Robles himself gave speeches in which the goal was to "conquer" and to make the parliament "submit." Though the CEDA had not introduced mass politics under the Republic, its broad mobilizations tended to escalate this phenomenon. Thus the concentration of 50,000 young *japistas* at El Escorial on 22 April had much the look of a fascist meeting, replete with slogans like "antiparliamentarianism" and "The Chief [Gil Robles] Is Never Wrong," as did a smaller rally at Covadonga, nominal birthplace of the Spanish nation, on 6 September. Equally or more important, however, was the fact that the CEDA had scrupulously fulfilled its pledge to obey the law, the existing Republican constitution, and democratic political processes and had rejected violence, even though the left not infrequently employed violence against it. To all the left, the CEDA's pacifism was a mere smoke screen, because its growing strength foreshadowed a possible rightist takeover of the Republic. The left simply refused what decades later the Russian political scientist Lilia Shevtsova would define as what "really matters" about a true functioning democracy: "definite rules of the game and uncertain results."[44] The Spanish left insisted on a permanently leftist regime that could ignore the rules of the game but guarantee predictable results, not a functioning democracy.

Though the "fascist menace" was frequently invoked, leaders of the Alianza Obrera made it clear that the goal was revolution, not defense of the Republic, and the rhetoric of the Socialist Youth often outdid that of the JAP. Segundo Serrano Poncela of the FJA wrote in *El Socialista* on 29 June that the Alianza Obrera movement "will not seek objectives for the workers within the boundaries of bourgeois democracy. Its goal is to prepare the insurrection for the conquest of power. . . . The Communists stress the organization of Soviets to conquer and hold power. The Worker Alliances pursue the same thing." He went on to say that the difference between

Russia in 1917 and Spain in 1934 lay in the absence of broad well-organized proletarian parties in the former, which had required the creation of a new organ such as the soviets. In Spain the well-organized Socialists and their Alianza Obrera allies were already prepared for such a role.

In the opening number of his new monthly revolutionary review *Leviatán* (May 1934), Araquistain declared: "The Republic is an accident," adding that "reformist socialism has failed." He exhorted: "We cannot trust parliamentary democracy, even if socialism sometimes wins a majority: if socialism does not employ violence, capitalism will defeat it on other fronts with its formidable economic weapons."

Less frequent were voices such as that of G. Munis (the pseudonym of Manuel Fernández Grandizo), possibly the number-two theorist of the tiny Trotskyist Izquierda Comunista after Andreu Nin, who soon published a pamphlet, *Qué son las Alianzas Obreras?*, which criticized the Socialist thesis as "too optimistic" in maintaining that "the ascendant process of revolution is following its course." Munis stressed more cogently that present-day Spain differed from Russia in 1917 especially in that the Spanish right was much stronger. He urged that the AO first create full unity among all the worker groups and build a unified paramilitary force, but not launch a general insurrection. A much wiser course, said Munis, would be to work for the dissolution of parliament and new general elections to weaken the right, first extending leftist power through political rather than violent means.

Though the Republican left would not endorse the plans of their former Socialist ally for violent insurrection, they reorganized themselves and moved further left so as to more easily maintain contact with the worker groups that Azaña correctly judged would be indispensable to restore an all-left Republic. At a meeting held on 1–2 April, Azaña's Partido de Acción Republicana, the splinter Partido Radical Socialista Independiente, and most of the left Galicianist Organización Regional Gallega Autónoma (ORGA) joined together to form a new united Partido de Izquierda Republicana (Party of the Republican Left). Its economic program called for greater state regulation of credit and finance, control of certain industries by state agencies or even possible nationalization, expansion of public works, prosecution of the agrarian reform, though with clearer exemption of medium and small owners, creation of a National Bank of Agricultural Credit, tariff revision, progressive income tax reform, expansion of social security, and creation of a central government economic council.[45] The program recognized the need to modernize and mechanize agriculture and to expand modern industry. It emphasized the need to strengthen the Republican state, reforming and modernizing its bureaucracy, and even suggested creation of a national corporative chamber to represent productive interests. Later, at the close of June, a newly constituted Juventudes de Izquierda Republicana (Republican Left Youth) held its first congress, proclaiming its members "leftists, democrats, parliamentarians, in that order." More stridently than the parent party, the young people made it clear that, if necessary, leftist goals were predominant over democracy.[46]

In May Diego Martínez Barrio, number-two leader of the Radical Party, who had earlier resigned from the Lerroux government, abandoned the Radicals altogether, forming a splinter Partido Radical Demócrata, to the left of the old party. As grand master of the Spanish Grand Orient, he was able to take about one-third of the considerable number of Masons in the Radical Party with him.[47] Alcalá Zamora apparently urged him not to leave the Radical Party, suggesting that he might be the more liberal leader who would eventually be needed to replace Lerroux and make a more liberal Radical Party "the base of the Republic."[48] During the summer the Radicals suffered other losses as a group of Valencian Radicals went over to Azaña, while others in Alicante followed Joaquín Chapaprieta into a new independent formation. Loss of the left wing of the party weakened the Lerroux government specifically and the democratic center more generally, reducing the Radicals' parliamentary delegation to eighty-five deputies, fewer than it had numbered in the first Republican parliament. Moreover, the fragmentation of the more moderate sectors of left Republicanism continued, for, though Martínez Barrio's new group soon merged with what remained of the Radical Socialist Party to form a new Unión Republicana, the other main figure of the center-left, Felipe Sánchez Román, refused to join them. In July he organized instead his own tiny Partido Nacional Republicano, slightly to the right of Unión Republicana.

Azaña now stood more clearly than ever before on a doctrine of "Republicanism" rather than of democratic practice or strict adherence to the constitution that he had helped to write. In a February speech he advanced the idea that the Republic and its constitution had been legitimated by a "popular impulse," whose hyperlegitimacy was the true basis of the regime and should not be thwarted by legal technicalities. This was a return to the radical democratic discourse of the nineteenth century, still popular in Spain, a residue from the era of pronunciamientos, which claimed a special legitimacy for the left, if necessary apart from constitutionality or electoral support. From April to July, left Republican leaders carried on a series of talks among themselves and also with elements of the Republican center. Azaña hoped to pressure Alcalá Zamora into manipulating the formation of a new left-center coalition to thwart Lerroux and the CEDA, employing a different version of the strategy that the president had used during the preceding summer, when he had worked to undercut Azaña with a new center coalition. What the left Republicans had in mind would be a minority left-center government that Alcalá Zamora could not possibly countenance, because it would lack parliamentary support.[49]

The alternative was to force the president's hand with a sort of pronunciamiento civil. What Azaña seems to have had in mind by the end of June was an entente between the left Republicans, the Esquerra in Barcelona, and the Socialists. This might form an alternative left-center government in Barcelona that, supported by a peaceful Socialist general strike, could convince the president that it must be allowed to take power. Azaña declared again on 1 July that "Catalonia is the only Republican power still standing in the peninsula. . . . We find ourselves with the same situation and attitude with which we faced the Spanish regime in the year 1931. . . . Then a few drops of generous blood watered the soil of the Republic and the Republic flowered. Rather than see the Republic converted into the garb of fascism or monarchism . . . we prefer any catastrophe, even if we lose."[50] According to Azaña's military associate, Major Jesús Pérez Salas, "The plan was to announce to the people that a new government had been formed. Simultaneously, in Madrid and in the rest of Spain a general strike would be called in support of the new government." Nonetheless, "there was not complete agreement among the parties and personalities who would form the government."[51]

The main problem was the reluctance of the Socialists to participate in a "bourgeois" project. At a meeting of the joint executive committees of the PSOE and UGT on 2 July, Prieto and De los Ríos urged support for the left Republican scheme, but the majority demurred. It was decided to dispatch a special commission, led by Largo Caballero, to meet with

Azaña and other left Republican leaders, to learn what sort of regime the latter had in mind.[52]

Meanwhile, playing both sides of the question, Azaña continued to pressure Alcalá Zamora. Martínez Barrio was sent to the president on 7 July to urge the appointment of a left-center government that would prepare for new elections to reverse the results of the preceding year. Otherwise, left Republicans would consider themselves, in Martínez Barrio's words, "free from all solidarity" with Alcalá Zamora's manner of administering the Republic.[53] The president rejected this proposal, observing that there were no grounds for dissolving a parliament that had existed for scarcely more than six months and was providing an adequate government. He would later write that he could not sleep the night after this visit, for he then realized that the Republican left would never accept the normal functioning of their own constitution if that meant their loss of power, and this attitude in turn seemed to make either an armed revolt, governmental breakdown, or both, almost inevitable.[54]

A week later there was a general conference of the left Republican leaders, including one or more representatives of the Esquerra, and Largo Caballero on behalf of the Socialists. Azaña tried to promote once more a broad left-liberal government that might restore the alliance of 1932–33 in its bid for power. The Catalanists were enthusiastic, but the Socialists refused to support another "bourgeois" coalition,[55] rejecting Izquierda Republicana's new economic program as mere reformism.

Socialist preparations for direct action were scarcely a secret. On 6 June Madrid police discovered a cache of 616 pistols and 80,000 cartridges, whose custodians declared was destined for a Socialist deputy in parliament, in whose home another 54 pistols were found. After repressing the agrarian strike, however, the government's only direct measure against the Socialists was more frequent censorship of the increasingly incendiary Socialist press. It tried to maintain an even hand in the escalating violence between Socialists and Falangists. Eighty of the latter were arrested at the Falange's Madrid headquarters on 11 July, followed by a decree from the Ministry of the Interior outlawing any meeting at which either fascist raised-arm or revolutionary clenched-fist salutes were given. Midsummer brought more public marches by the Socialist Youth—which as usual outdid the supposedly fascist JAP in fascist-style behavior—while a statement by the national committee of the UGT on 1 August denounced the hapless Samper administration as "a regime of White Terror." More accurately, it pointed out that of the 315 days of "Lerrouxist government," 222 had been passed under a state of either prevention or alarm, and that only 93 were days of full constitutional normalcy and civil rights (60 of the latter pertaining to the electoral period).[56]

The principal scandal concerning arms discoveries prior to the insurrection took place on the Asturian coast on 10 September. It involved a shipload of arms that the Azaña government had ordered two years earlier as part of its interventionist policy in favor of leftist anti-regime rebels in neighboring Portugal. These had never been delivered, and the Socialist revolutionary committee had finally managed to purchase them from the Republican state Consortium of Military Industries through middlemen. The arms were transferred from a warehouse in the south aboard a ship named *La Turquesa,* which began to unload them by night off the Asturian coast only to be discovered by *carabineros* (customs guards). *La Turquesa* immediately put to sea again with most of the arms still on board and steamed to Bordeaux, where the boat and its cargo were impounded by the Spanish consul. Indalecio Prieto, who was in overall charge of the operation, was near the site but managed to talk his way past police and soon fled to France, where he would remain for the next seventeen months.[57] The Madrid Casa del Pueblo was searched by police on the eleventh, yielding a sizable number of guns, 107 small boxes of ammunition, and thirty-seven packets of hand grenades. Several other small Socialist caches of arms were uncovered in the capital and elsewhere. In a search for arms on the Madrid-León highway a few days later, the Civil Guard mistakenly killed an innocent driver.[58]

The volume of strike activity remained high throughout the summer. There were numerous minor clashes involving gunfire, as well as frequent cases of arson in widely scattered parts of Spain. Four moderates and conservatives were killed, as were a number of workers. The most publicized deaths were the murder of the Falangist provincial chief of Guipuzcoa in San Sebastián, followed by the retaliatory killing the same day of Manuel Andrés Casaus, minister of the interior in the last left Republican government.

Biggest of the summer work stoppages was a general strike called by the UGT in Madrid when a major protest meeting of all the provincial landowners' associations was held in the capital. Altogether six people were killed on this occasion. *El Sol* editorialized on the morrow:

> An arm which is too often employed in inappropriate situations ends up weakening itself to the point where it can no longer be used when the propitious moment arrives, not only because it tires and the edge is dulled, but also because the corresponding reaction grows, perfecting contrary arms, to counteract it.
>
> ... By using all revolutionary means with ill-measured frequency to fight against a fascism which does not exist, except as a pallid imitation, what definitely might happen is to provoke the necessary conditions, the soil, the climate, for the real growth of fascism. Not the gentleman's fascism which we have [in Spain] by reason of style, but the true and fearful one, against which the arms raised by the liberal state are no good. In a not dissimilar manner fascism was engendered in other countries.

Two years earlier the German Socialists had failed to take resolute action when illegally ousted from control of the state of Prussia (two-thirds of Germany), which they had won through democratic elections. That might have been the last chance to challenge arbitrary government in Germany. Now the Spanish Socialists were preparing to commit the opposite mistake, in trying themselves to overthrow a popularly elected regime. They thought they were following the lessons of history, but in fact they were ignoring them.

September brought a new series of minor legal crises between Madrid and Barcelona, climaxed by resolution of the Catalan agrarian dispute. On 13 September the Generalitat published a long series of new regulations slightly modifying the original terms along lines sought by Madrid, and when the Cortes opened for the fall session on 1 October the prime minister announced that this modification amounted to a *refundición* (revision) of the Law of Cultivation Contracts that had the "character and force of law," so that he now judged the legislation to be constitutional, thus finally resolving the dispute.

THE SPANISH COMMUNIST PARTY BREAKS OUT OF ISOLATION

If fascism was new in Spain, Communism was relatively old, the Soviet Comintern having founded the Partido Comunista de España in Madrid in 1920 by provoking a schism in the Socialist Youth. Spanish Communism did not prosper, however, with the possible exception of its small nucleus in Bilbao, and remained a tiny and isolated sect. The most militant and active group, the Barcelona sector led by Joaquín Maurín, was ostracized in 1930–31 and subsequently set up the very small Bloque Obrero y Campesino (BOC), even more exiguous than the PCE. The BOC would claim to be the true Spanish Communist party, since it was independent, exclusively Spanish, and not under orders from Moscow.

The Comintern greeted the founding of the Republic as the unfolding of a new road map to revolution, denouncing Republican democracy as a capitalist fraud manipulated by crypto-monarchists, which would soon result in full fascism unless overthrown by worker revolution. Since 1928 the Comintern had declared the world situation to have entered its Third Period since the Russian Revolution, with the capitalist system soon to face a fatal crisis. Conditions were purportedly propitious for the rapid advance of world revolution. Though in general Spain had been categorized in 1928 along with Japan and other less fully modernized lands as one of a second tier of countries in which the full preconditions for revolution had not yet developed, this analysis was changed after establishment of the Republic. The country was now declared ready for revolution, and the leaders of the PCE were instructed to "form soviets," as in Russia in 1917.

Just how this could be done was not made clear, since worker organization was dominated by the UGT and CNT. Comintern leaders in Moscow and Berlin witnessed the rapid growth in power of the Spanish left in general, and the violent strike waves and armed insurrections launched by the CNT during 1932–33, only to become dissatisfied with the failure of the PCE leaders to make use of this revolutionary potential. They rated the revolutionary quality of Spanish workers as high or higher than that of Russian workers in 1917, and finally purged the PCE leadership in October 1932. The new chieftains appointed by Moscow—José Díaz, Jesús Hernández, Vicente Uribe, Dolores Ibárruri ("Pasionaria"), and others—were more subservient to the Comintern and would lead the party throughout the dramatic years that followed.[59]

Throughout the first half of 1934 the Comintern consistently followed its Third Period strategy, though this had yielded only disaster in Germany, materially assisting the triumph of Hitler. In Spain the PCE continued its revolutionary demands, constant encouragement of strikes, and efforts to set up new "factory and peasant committees" as a prelude to creating soviets. The Communist tactic of the "united front from below" rejected formal alliance with other parties and instead sought to win their members over to cooperation with Communist organizations alone. On 16 May 1934, the Communist Milicias Antifascistas Obreras y Campesinas, initiated on a very modest basis the preceding year, called for the organization of a broad unified worker antifascist militia to prepare for revolution. Yet Third Period revolutionary isolationism had prevented the PCE from joining the Alianza Obrera, so that the Young Socialists, though generally well disposed toward Communists, could accuse the latter of showing interest only in "partial" and "not seriously revolutionary activities." Rhetorically the tables had been turned on the Communists, some of whom were increasingly disturbed by this fact. The PCE leadership continued to denounce what it called the inauthentic "leftization" (*izquierdización*) of the Socialists, who ever since 1928 had been ritually denounced as "socialfascists."[60]

The Comintern line was first altered in France, where the growing strength of the radical right and the Paris riot of 6 February had stimulated interest in unity of action against fascism among Socialists and Communists alike. French Socialists had heretofore never moved quite so far in the direction of reformism as had their Spanish counterparts during 1931–33. As early as 1925 the French leader Léon Blum had defined his theory of the "exercise of power," which rejected participation in a government not led by Socialists, but was willing to accept leadership of a coalition government including non-Socialists. The first such democratic Socialist-led coalition would respect legality and not try to end capitalism but concentrate on major legislation to aid workers. The French party had strong pacifist tendencies, despite its support of the government during World War I, and its leaders were strongly anti-Soviet, with Blum and others convinced that the Soviet regime would even provoke major war to advance its own interests. Nonetheless, both Socialist and Communist leaders increasingly believed that their two parties should work together against fascism and the radical right in France. French Communism was now the most influential national sector of the Comintern (after suppression of the German sector by Hitler), and Comintern bosses were themselves beginning to reveal some doubts about the exclusivist Third Period policy. Consequently French Communist leaders were permitted to negotiate their first agreement with Socialists at the end of June, which finally led to signing of a formal unity pact against fascism on 27 July. However, some of the top French Socialists remained wary of their Communist counterparts. Paul Faure, general secretary of the Socialist Party from 1920 to 1940, detested Communists, whom he considered barbaric, un-French, and "agents of Moscow." Moreover, he accurately informed the press on 13 November that "the fascist peril is perhaps not so real. . . . Fascism in France is in retreat."[61]

By the summer of 1934 the Latin Section of the Comintern was becoming excited about the possibilities opening up in Spain, where the situation was potentially moving further to the left than in France. One source of encouragement was the recent success in penetrating the left-liberal intelligentsia, among whom a variety of front organizations were operating.[62] Even more important, of course, was the militancy of the Socialists and other worker organizations. The Comintern informed PCE leaders on 2 July that the radicalization of Spanish affairs now provided the opportunity to achieve PCE hegemony on the worker left. Though the Alianza Obrera was itself still rejected, the goal was to use pro-Communist elements within the PSOE to persuade the latter to adopt the Communist program; if that should happen, the PCE might then enter the Alianza Obrera as part of its own revolutionary strategy.[63]

On 12 July the PCE leaders proposed to Spanish Socialists an agreement similar to that with their French counterparts, but still rejected membership in the AO, insisting that the Socialists join a separate alliance with the Communists. When the Socialists refused, the Spanish Communists repeated the proposal—their sixth appeal of the year to the Socialists. The AO was stridently denounced as the very opposite of a united front from the base, though in both of their July appeals the Communists publicly called the Socialists "comrades" for the first time.[64]

PCE leaders showed increasing interest in a change in tactics, and Díaz led a delegation that arrived in Moscow on 31 July, remaining in the Soviet capital for twelve days. The Soviet chieftains fretted and fussed but could not bring themselves to accept a basic tactical change in Spain, for which they apparently received no encouragement from Stalin. During August, however, the PCE ceased to attack the AO directly and made few public references to "socialfascism." The funeral in Madrid on 29 August for a Communist central committeeman who had been killed in a skirmish with Falangists became the first major public occasion of fraternization between Communists and Socialists. Some days later the two parties held their first joint rally to protest a new decree from the Ministry of the Interior banning participation of minors in political groups.

A change in tactics was finally decreed by the Comintern in mid-September, and on the fifteenth the PCE announced in Madrid that it was joining the Alianza Obrera. The Comintern's complete message, which arrived the following day, did attach some strings. It insisted that the AO be called "Worker-Peasant Alliances" (following Communist terminology), adopt every point in the PCE program, and employ the slogan "All Power to the Alliance." The PCE was not to renounce the goal of forming soviets as soon as possible, but should participate in any local AO or resulting AO government that accepted its program. These points arrived too late, for type was already set for *Mundo Obrero*, the official PCE mouthpiece, which carried the full announcement on the seventeenth. This did urge the formation of revolutionary soviets, of factory and peasant committees, and of a Worker-Peasant government. Nonetheless, as Antonio Elorza and Marta Bizcarrondo have pointed out, joining the already revolutionary AO did not involve any drastic change in Communist tactics, but simply brought together a new united front from above with standard revolutionary goals.[65] Much the same argument was made by the PCE announcement, which said that the revolutionary movement of the AO would lead directly to the formation of soviets. This statement was accompanied by a large joint meeting of Socialist and Communist Youth in Madrid's Metropolitano Stadium on 16 September to lay the groundwork for a united revolutionary militia.[66]

THE INSURRECTION BEGINS

Before the fall session of the Cortes opened on 1 October, Gil Robles announced on behalf of the CEDA that the Catholic party would no longer support a minority government as it had for nine months, but would demand to form part of a new governing coalition. CEDA leaders were fully aware that this move might trigger the long-threatened insurrection, but calculated that they could combat the latter more effectively if they formed part of the government.[67] Similarly, leaders of the Radical Party met on 29 September and agreed not to give in to further pressure from Alcalá Zamora or the left to keep Lerroux out of the premiership. Thus when Samper opened the new session, the only spokesman to reply to his speech announcing resolution of the Catalan agrarian dispute was Gil Robles, who simply said that there must be a change in government, prompting the immediate resignation of the cabinet.

The president no longer had much choice, since a *cedorradical* coalition led by Lerroux and including, as it turned out, three cedistas was the only formula that could produce a parliamentary majority. The alternative was dissolution, as perpetually demanded by the left, but Alcalá Zamora was understandably reluctant to take so drastic a step. The nascent regime desperately needed stability, the parliament was less than a year old, and it clearly was able to produce a viable majority coalition. Under the normal rules of parliamentary regimes, dissolution was therefore in no way justified. Moreover, the president himself might be subject to parliamentary review and impeachment for having called two elections within a year, as required by the constitution when more than one dissolution took place during a single presidential term. Whether dissolving the Constituent Cortes—which might be regarded as a constitutional convention rather than a regular parliament—should actually count as an ordinary dissolution had never been determined.

The three cedista ministers were carefully chosen from the moderate sectors of the party and were excluded from the most sensitive portfolios, such as the Ministries of War and the Interior. The last major change stemmed from Alcalá Zamora's insistence on replacing the hard-line Salazar Alonso as minister of the interior, a post taken over by the more liberal Eloy Vaquero, an autodidact, teacher, and lawyer from Córdoba and a crony of Lerroux's.[68]

The left were understandably distressed when a large party entered government with the ultimate goal of transforming the Republic into a Catholic corporative regime, but the left Republicans, for example, had been little distressed by the Socialists' announced intention of changing the Republic into a revolutionary socialist regime. Azaña and his allies may have calculated that the Socialists would never be strong enough to get away with it, but if that was the case, the continued participation by the left Republicans in democratic politics would probably guarantee that the CEDA would never be able to realize its own goals, either. The truth is that the existence of this double standard was at no time faced and discussed.

The new government was the "provocation" long awaited by the Socialist revolutionary committee. *El Socialista* had already declared on 25 September: "Let everyone renounce peaceful revolution; blessed be war," and added two days later: "The skies are darkly overcast en route to October. We repeat what we have been saying for months: watch for the red flare! Next month may be our October. Hard tasks and days of challenge await us. The Spanish proletariat and its leaders face enormous responsibility. We have an army waiting to be mobilized. And our international policy. And our plans for socialization."

None of these proclamations seems to have greatly disturbed the left Republicans, who were outraged only by minority rightist participation in a constitutional government. Azaña had declared in a speech of 30 August that the left Republicans would respect the results of new elections, but only if the elections were administered by the left. Should the CEDA enter the government, "we shall have to conquer [civil] guarantees with bare chests,"[69] remarkably bellicose language for someone like Azaña, renowned for physical cowardice. The left Republican *Heraldo de Madrid* concluded on the morning of 4 October: "The Republic of the fourteenth of April has been lost perhaps forever. That which begins today is of no concern to us. Our Republic we find moribund." This was a breathtaking and apocalyptic conclusion, possible only within the exaltado thought processes of the left Republicans.

When word of the new coalition leaked out on 4 October, the left Republican leaders tried in vain to reach a common formula of protest. They were to some extent hampered by the fact that formation of the new government was the result not of a partially extraparliamentary action, as in Italy in 1922, nor of a backstairs deal, as in Germany in 1933, but of normal parliamentary processes, a scrupulously constitutional coalition of the two major parties elected less than a year earlier by democratic suffrage in free elections. On the evening of 5 October Azaña's Izquierda Republicana issued its statement: "Izquierda Republicana declares that the monstrous act of handing the government of the Republic over to its enemies is an act of treason. It breaks all solidarity with the present institutions of the regime and affirms its decision to make use of all means of defending the Republic." Similar statements, which might readily be interpreted as aligning the left Republicans with the revolutionary insurrection now beginning, were delivered by Martínez Barrio's Unión Republicana, Sánchez Román's Partido Nacional Republicano, Miguel Maura's Partido Republicano Conservador (which said the new government was engendering "civil war"), the Izquierda Radical Socialista, and the Partido Federal Autónomo. The problem, of course, stemmed from the left Republicans' insistence on identifying the Republic not with democracy or constitutional law but with a specific set of policies and politicians, any change of which was held to be treasonous. On the morning of 6 October, Martínez Barrio sent his personal secretary to the office of Alcalá Zamora, insisting to the president that the only way to avoid a major armed revolt was to form a new left Republican government.[70]

The Alianza Obrera's insurrection began on the night of 4 October. Extensive planning had been under way for months, together with considerable stocking of pistols and rifles, to the extent that Moa has termed it, probably correctly, "the best armed" of all the leftist insurrections of interwar Europe.[71] Yet, though the planning was extensive, preparations were not carefully coordinated and integrated. Some parts of the plan were never carried out, and those that were remained largely disconnected. Nor was any program or set of goals announced; the program agreed upon in January 1934 was not published for twenty-four months.[72]

A general strike called on the national level began on 5 October in Madrid, Barcelona, and all other areas in which the Socialists were strong. In all but two provinces, the plans to seize centers of power with armed militiamen were scarcely even put into effect, and the few efforts made were easily quashed by the authorities. Schemes to subvert the armed police forces and the army failed altogether, the great majority of leftist sympathizers in these institutions refusing to join the rebels. The armed forces and the police supported the government almost unanimously. There was no remote comparison between the Russian army of 1917—demoralized by three years of defeat, bad leadership, and millions of casualties—and the modest but disciplined Spanish army of 1934—well rested, relatively united, and with morale fully intact. Plans to seize major centers in Madrid quickly broke down into feeble and unsuccessful skirmishes. The strike itself was at first reasonably effective, but most of the workers and their leaders simply remained at home rather than forming barricades. Two days of street-sniping by the Socialist Youth (initiated by a few vindictive shots fired at the home of Besteiro, chief Socialist foe of violence) accomplished very little. A few barricades were set up in worker districts, but in general the working masses failed to rally to the revolt. Lerroux, the new prime minister, had not believed that the Socialists would carry out their threats,[73] so martial law was not imposed until the morning of 6 October. Diego Hidalgo, the Radical minister of war, had held office since December 1933. Though he was from one of the more liberal sectors of the Radical Party and in fact had been the strongest Radical supporter of the agrarian reform, he distrusted the army chief of staff, Carlos Masquelet, as too pro-leftist and possibly sympathetic to the rebels. Hidalgo had therefore already selected a special adviser in General Francisco Franco, who seven years earlier had become the youngest general in any European army, a major hero of the Moroccan campaigns and one of the most prestigious figures in the Spanish military. In this period almost all sectors spoke well of Franco's character and ability—moderates and conservatives with admiration, leftists with a respect mixed with apprehension. Hidalgo had awarded him the first promotion to major general (*general de división*) that became available, and had invited Franco to assist the war minister during the recent army maneuvers in León and then return with him to Madrid. Soon after the revolt began Hidalgo turned over coordination of the repression to Franco, who slept in a room at the War Ministry for the next two weeks.[74]

In Barcelona the Alianza Obrera had a key ally in the Generalitat government, which had been making plans for armed resistance against Madrid, depending on the outcome of the summer autonomy crisis and the struggle for power in Madrid. It had been a major part of the plan for a leftist pronunciamiento that Azaña himself had toyed with in June and July. The earlier scheme had involved the potential formation of an alternative left Republican government in Barcelona, which would be supported by a UGT general strike, as a milder alternative to a leftist insurrection. After negotiations in Madrid and Barcelona, this had been abandoned because of the refusal of the key Socialist leaders, bent on seizing power themselves, to support another government led by the left Republicans.[75] Azaña seems then to have withdrawn from such schemes, though he moved to Barcelona on the eve of the revolt to await events there, while the Generalitat committed itself to full cooperation with the revolutionaries.

The Alianza Obrera began its general strike in the Catalan capital on 5 October with some success, in view of the fact that most organized labor was dominated by the CNT. On the following day an effort was made to extend the strike throughout Catalonia, with the assistance of the olive-shirted Escamots of the Esquerra. At the same time the Catalan police arrested key anarchist leaders for fear they might sabotage the operation. At 8:00 P.M. on the sixth Companys announced from a balcony at Generalitat headquarters: "Catalans: Monarchists and fascists have assaulted the government. . . . The democratic Republic is in great peril."[76] He declared that all authentic Republicans were in revolt and that the Generalitat was assuming full power in Catalonia. He announced formation of the "Catalan state in the Spanish Federal Republic" and invited other left Republicans (much as in Azaña's earlier plan) to establish a new provisional government of the Republic in Barcelona. The Generalitat had the backing of all the *catalanista* left Republican groups and the small worker parties of the Alianza Obrera.

Preparations for revolt had been left in the hands of the councilor of security, the extremist Dencàs. On paper he had organized some 7,000 Escamots and was able to distribute arms to some of them, but like the Socialists in Madrid, they were not prepared for very serious fighting. The popular response in the Catalan capital was not so much like the active enthusiasm of 1931 as like the passive anxiety over the threat of war among people in Berlin in September 1938, four years later: relative silence, no crowds filling the streets, people hurrying home.

The military commander of the Barcelona district was General Domingo Batet, whose Catalan ancestry had led some rebel leaders to assume or hope that he might remain no more than a passive spectator. In fact Batet was a loyal and disciplined commander who proved energetic and absolutely decisive. He declared martial law throughout Catalonia at 9:00 P.M., only an hour after Companys' announcement, and by 11:30 that night a small army detachment had moved light artillery into place for bombardment of the Generalitat. Even before that, two rounds into the headquarters of the CADCI, the ultra-Catalanist white-collar union, had killed its leader, Jaume Compte, and brought surrender, while the headquarters of the Catalanist militia surrendered equally rapidly. Bombardment of the

Barcelona city hall, the other remaining rebel center, began just before dawn, quickly producing another white flag. Companys surrendered the Generalitat at 6:00 A.M. Batet then read him a little lecture on the ills of resorting to violence and required him to announce the surrender over public radio. Dencàs had hoped for the support of Catalanist militia outside Barcelona, but many of his own police deserted instead. He fled through an escape hatch into the sewer system, an arrangement obviously prepared in advance that gave rise to much mirth. Altogether in the abortive Barcelona revolt, 78 people were killed.[77]

There was minor skirmishing in several parts of Catalonia on 6 and 7 October as local Alianza Obrera groups took over several towns, including for a very brief time part of Gerona and Lérida. They were quickly put down by the army and police,[78] though not before they had committed several killings, including the slaying of at least one priest.

Azaña, as indicated, had come to Barcelona, his intentions ambiguous. He obviously was not trying to play the role of loyal opposition to the constitutional government, which he made no attempt to warn. Indeed, his party's announcement could easily be interpreted as support for the revolt. Azaña had left Madrid on 27 September carrying only one suitcase, to attend the funeral of his former cabinet minister Jaume Carner. He spent 3 and 4 October in a series of interviews with leaders of left Catalanism. It has been conjectured that one goal was to dissuade Companys from declaring separatism when he rebelled. Azaña later wrote that on the fourth the left Catalanists offered him a place in the new provisional government they were planning, but that he refused. Late on the sixth he left his room at the Hotel Colón and moved to the home of a Catalan friend, where he was arrested three days later and subsequently placed on a prison warship.[79]

Altogether the insurrection affected more than twenty provinces. Largo Caballero's revolutionary committee had in theory named rebel commissions for every provincial capital, but Socialists in the south were still exhausted from the failed agrarian strike. There were various strikes and disorders in scattered spots of the south, where several people were killed, but no general insurrection took place there.[80] In Aragon some anarchist groups did engage in outbursts of their own, and a general strike in Zaragoza lasted from 6 to 9 October, with libertarian communism briefly declared in a few small towns.

Aside from Asturias, the only serious Socialist revolts occurred in the two industrialized Basque provinces of Vizcaya and Guipuzcoa, and in Palencia and León. The general strike was effective for several days in the industrial zone of Vizcaya, while in Guipuzcoa the Socialists temporarily took control of the cities of Mondragón and Eibar, officially proclaiming the social revolution and killing two hostages in the former. Troops were moved in from other regions, and there was some fighting before the area could be pacified.[81] In Palencia the Socialist miners' insurrection began on the fifth and controlled parts of the province for several days. The revolt broke out the following day in León (part of whose garrison had been dispatched elsewhere), and about three-fourths of the province was held for several days until military detachments regained control.

The great drama of the 1934 insurrection took place in Asturias, where a united revolutionary Alianza Obrera, based especially on the mining districts and strongly supported by the local CNT, set up the first revolutionary commune west of Germany since Paris in 1871. In a region where nearly 70 percent of all workers were unionized, the worker left was fully united. Though the strength of organized labor in Asturias had declined seriously in the face of foreign economic competition during the 1920s, the Republic had made possible a comeback. Yet because of the depression, declining productivity, and low investment, renewed labor mobilization had only heightened frustration and militancy, with younger workers particularly inflamed. The fact that the labor force remained partly rural in no way reduced radicalization,[82] so that Asturias had proportionately led all Spain in strike activity under the Republic, with the UGT and CNT increasingly making common cause.[83] This had led to their Asturian "Alianza Revolucionaria" of 31 March, also joined by smaller worker groups and eventually by the Communists, with its own goals of a "federal socialist" regime.

The revolt in Asturias began on the night of 4–5 October. The mining areas were quickly seized, with only three larger police stations holding out until the second day. The defense plan of the local authorities was purely passive, in the expectation that the police would hold out in their district posts as they had elsewhere during anarchist mini-insurrections. The force of the insurrection was much greater in Asturias, where more than 20,000 militia were quickly organized. Though some initially lacked weapons, they successively gained more arms from each police post overrun, soon seizing the Trubia artillery works and twenty-nine cannon as well. The miner militia also developed an innovation: the use of lighted sticks of dynamite as hand grenades, a device that sometimes proved initially frightening. On the sixth they moved into the provincial capital, Oviedo, a city of 80,000, garrisoned by 900 troops and 300 armed police. The local military and police commanders, somewhat weak and divided, undertook another system of passive defense organized exclusively around nine strong points in the city. Most of Oviedo, including the center of town, was then occupied by 8,000 revolutionary militiamen. In the "liberated zone," they officially declared the proletarian revolution, abolished regular money, and—given the penchant for violence of the Spanish left—also installed a revolutionary terror that took more than a score of lives, mostly of clergy. As the struggle continued, portions of the city were blasted apart by shelling, bombing, and dynamite, and there was much vandalism, looting, and deliberate destruction, as well. Lack of coordination deprived the revolutionaries of support from neighboring UGT contingents in León and Palencia, but the government was at first similarly unable to provide reinforcements for the resistance. In the initial days, the only succor for defenders came from squadrons of the air force that attempted to bomb and strafe rebel positions, killing ten people with a bomb dropped on the central plaza on the tenth.

Army reinforcements were soon being rushed toward the region, for which a new military commander had been named. Lerroux later observed that he chose from among the liberal minority in the army command in appointing the inspector general of the army, Eduardo López Ochoa, to head the main relief column. López Ochoa was a Republican liberal and a Mason and had been a leader in the pro-Republican military conspiracy of 1930. He was flown to Galicia on the afternoon of 6 October. The next day he began to make his way eastward with a modest force of some 360 troops in trucks, half of whom had to be detached along the way to hold the route open. Meanwhile a garrison of 460 soldiers and police had held out in the main Asturian coastal city of Gijón, where reinforcements first arrived by sea on the seventh, followed by larger units from the Moroccan Protectorate on the tenth,[84] so that the main relief column came due south from the direction of Gijón on the eleventh. This maneuver also involved the first historical military use of a helicopter (at least in part a Spanish invention) as reconnaissance for the column. The city was reoccupied on 12 and 13 October.

The revolutionaries' regional committee decided to abandon Oviedo on the eleventh, but the small Communist contingent protested, blaming the other worker forces for "desertion," until they finally had to admit there was no alternative. On the following day, 12 October, the Communists and a group of Young Socialists improvised their own separate regional committee in the nearby town of Sama to stop the retreat. Some militia who had abandoned positions were arrested, then allowed to go back to the fight. Asturian Communists belatedly tried to form a disciplined new "red army" Soviet-style, and even began to talk fantastically of Soviet intervention, but their initiative soon became hopeless.[85] The sharpest fighting took place between the fourteenth and seventeenth for control of the southern and eastern outlying districts that controlled access to the mining basin. By this time yet another military column had come in from the east, and López Ochoa had a total of 15,000 troops and 3,000 police in the area, equal in numbers to the revolutionary militia. After a parley on 18 October the latter surrendered, and occupation of the mining district began on the following day.

Sharp tension developed between the moderate López Ochoa and his chief subordinate, the hard-line Lieutenant Colonel Juan Yagüe, who commanded the elite Legionnaire and Moroccan Regulares units from the protectorate. Yagüe, a close colleague of Franco, complained that López Ochoa's orders had exposed his troops to unnecessary risks during the advance and that Ochoa had agreed to the regional committee's demands that the elite forces not be allowed to enter the main mining areas.[86] Critics later alleged that the commander-in-chief was too soft on the revolutionaries, who were not being required to give up all their arms. On the twentieth, a truck full of soldiers was blown up, the army reporting twenty-five fatalities. This atrocity provoked a decree from López Ochoa that anyone found with arms on his person or in his home would be tried by summary court-martial and, if found guilty, immediately executed. He also seems to have approved a number of summary executions under martial law, estimates for which range from a low of 19 to a high of approximately 50. Some sniping at troops and the police continued, and not all arms were recovered, petty guerrilla actions (or what some would label terrorism) continuing into the first part of 1935. The exact loss of life can never be precisely determined. The best estimates suggest 1,300 fatalities for the rebels, 1,100 of these in Asturias.[87] Deaths among the army and police apparently totaled approximately 450, again mostly in Asturias.[88] The revolutionaries carried out at least 40 executions in Asturias—possibly more—where the number of summary executions by the military was about as great. A total of 107 were killed in Catalonia (of whom 78 died in Barcelona), approximately 80 in Vizcaya and Guipuzcoa, 34 in Madrid, 15 in Santander, 10 in León, 7 each in Albacete and Zaragoza, and very small numbers elsewhere. The Dirección General de Seguridad announced recovery of 90,000 rifles, 30,000 pistols, and forty-one cannon, as well as a number of automatic weapons, though these figures may be somewhat inflated. About 15 million pesetas were looted from banks, of which only about a third was recovered, most of the rest going to finance leftist activities in the future; and there was much destruction of property.

After the military occupation, a thorough police sweep of the mining region took place, producing thousands of arrests. A number of prisoners were subjected to beating and some even torture, especially under the special repression conducted by Major Lisardo Doval of the Civil Guard.[89] In all Spain, more than 15,000 arrests were made, with the left claiming a total at least twice as high.[90]

There were also numerous arrests and prosecutions within the armed forces, beginning with six senior officers of the army and Civil Guard garrisons in Asturias, all of whom were sentenced to prison. One junior officer and one soldier received severe sentences for having joined the revolutionaries. In the lower ranks of the Civil Guard, nine men were condemned to prison, including one junior officer and four noncommissioned officers. Most of them, like the senior army officers, were charged with neglect of duty, but one guard was indicted for having joined the revolutionaries. Cases of desertion or mutiny among troops were rare, but with sailors it was a different story, whose attitude in 1934 would foreshadow developments in the Civil War. There were more than a few organized leftist cells among seamen, who had a closer common identity because of the physically circumscribed nature of navy life. Though none of several alleged plots of shipboard mutiny came to fruition, seventy-two sailors were arrested and prosecuted. Conversely, the only military personnel directly punished for crimes or excesses in the immediate repression were four Moroccan Regulares, summarily executed by their commander.

For the next eighteen months, Spain would be filled with atrocity stories. The right would emphasize the violence of the revolutionaries and their murders of priests and other civilians (including thirty-four clergy and seminarians, and one conservative Cortes deputy—Marcelino Oreja in Mondragón).[91] The left stressed the executions with or without court-martial, atrocities against miners' families, and the continued brutal mistreatment of some of the prisoners.[92] Needless to say, there was considerable hyperbole on both sides, though the reality was bad enough. As Gabriel Jackson would write thirty years later, "In point of fact, every form of fanaticism and cruelty which was to characterize the Civil War occurred during the October revolution and its aftermath: utopian revolution marred by sporadic red terror; systematically bloody repression by the 'forces of order'; confusion and demoralization of the moderate left; fanatical vengefulness on the part of the right."[93]

For the left the result was disaster, with extensive loss of life and many thousands of militants arrested on top of those already in jail, the detention or flight of most of their leaders, the closing of many Socialist Party and UGT local headquarters, and the general elimination of the left as a parliamentary and political force for the next sixteen months. The entire fiasco had been justified on the grounds of the sinister, fascistic intentions of the CEDA. If those intentions were as dangerous as the left insisted, the CEDA would now have an easier opportunity to strike than ever. The truth of the matter was that, as the genuinely fascist intellectual Ledesma Ramos would write some months later, much of the Spanish right was *"apparently fascist, but, in many cases, essentially antifascist"* because of its legalism and rejection of violence, whereas much of the Spanish left was *"apparently antifascist, but, in many of their characteristics and objectives, essentially fascist"* because of its use of violence and rejection of democratic legalism.[94]

Historians have been nearly unanimous in viewing the revolutionary insurrection as the beginning of the decline of the Second Republic and of constitutional government and constitutional consensus in Spain. Whereas the anarchists had never been part of the Republican mainstream, the Socialists and left Republicans had been integral to the new system and had governed the country for two years. The Socialists had now attempted violent revolution instead, and the left Republicans had provided a kind of passive support, as in fact they would continue to do in the future. Historians as diverse as Gerald Brenan, Salvador de Madariaga, Sir Raymond Carr, Gabriel Jackson, Richard Robinson, Carlos M. Rama, Carlos Seco Serrano, and Ricardo de la Cierva have described it either as "the prelude to" or as "the first battle of" the Civil War. Perhaps the most widely quoted evaluation has been that of Madariaga: "The revolt of 1934 is unpardonable. The decision of the president to call the CEDA to share in the government was not only unimpeachable, not only unavoidable, but long overdue. The argument that Señor Gil Robles intended to bring in Fascism was both hypocritical and demonstrably untrue. . . . The Asturian miners were well paid, and, in fact, the whole industry, by a collusion between employers and workers, was kept working at an artificial level by state subsidies beyond what many of the seams deserved in a sound economy. Lastly the Catalan case was no more justified."[95]

Edward Malefakis has written: "The tragedy of the Spanish left, and ultimately of Spain itself, was that in 1934 it lacked the self-confidence to ride out that crisis through which it was passing as the right had ridden out its own crisis in 1931–33." Sir Raymond Carr observes: "Socialists might have reflected that they, like the CEDA, had their own form of accidentalism. They were a party in theory committed to major social changes which must destroy bourgeois society, but they had been willing to cooperate in a bourgeois parliamentary government.

"The revolution of October is the immediate origin of the Civil War. The left, above all the Socialists, had rejected legal processes of government; the government against which they revolted was electorally justified. The left was later to make great play of the 'legality' argument to condemn the generals' revolt in July 1936 against an elected government."[96]

Richard Robinson puts it more strongly: "The Socialists and the CEDA both had ideals incompatible with liberal democracy, but whereas the evolutionary tactic was dogma for the CEDA it was not for the Socialists. The latter had accused the former of being Fascist in 1933, but whereas Largo Caballero had threatened to use violence since the autumn of 1931, Gil Robles did not make counter-threats until the autumn of 1933. It was the Socialists, not the CEDA, who turned against the democratic system."[97]

Though the Socialists would never conduct an official self-criticism —and still have not in the twenty-first century—the issue of violent revolution and insurrection would eventually lead to a split in their party. Of the top Socialist leaders—aside from Besteiro, who had always foreseen the disaster an insurrection would bring—the one who most quickly grasped the magnitude of the mistake and repented of it was Indalecio Prieto. Years later, he confessed in a speech in Mexico City on May Day 1942: "I declare myself guilty before my conscience, before the Socialist Party and before all Spain, of my participation in the revolutionary movement of 1934. I declare it as guilt, as a sin, not as a glory. . . . And I accepted tasks that others avoided, because behind them lay the danger not only of losing liberty, but the deeper danger of losing honor. Nonetheless, I accepted them."[98]

Though the leftist leaders would never publicly admit to any wrong-doing in the Socialists' turn to mass violence, they accepted the fact that they could not regain power by such means in the immediate future. Henceforth the joint goal of the left Republicans and the *prietista* wing of the Socialists would be to restore reunified political and electoral, not revolutionary, action to overcome the twin disasters of 1933–34.

CHAPTER FOUR

A Conservative Republic?

1934–1935

LERROUX'S RADIO ADDRESS TO the nation on 7 October called for calm and respect for the constitution. The prime minister expressed confidence that most Catalans would respect the established order and promised that the government would "preserve the liberties recognized by the Republic," assuring all that "the rule of law" would triumph. With occasional sniper shots still being heard in Madrid, the Cortes reopened on the ninth to applause for Lerroux, who faced the task of defeating the insurrection and presiding over the resulting repression as fairly as possible. The latter would not be easy, for just as the sanjurjada had strengthened the left Republican coalition, so the failed insurrection energized the right and even led some moderate liberals to urge extreme rigor. The rightist press was full of lurid atrocity stories and assured its readers that the revolutionaries guilty of such deeds could not be human beings. On 19 October even *El Sol* intoned: "For wild beasts capable of such monstrous deeds that even a degenerate would not be capable of imagining, we ask for severe, implacable, definitive punishment. For men, as men; for wild beasts, as wild beasts." As provided for in the Republican security legislation, military tribunals quickly set to work in *sumarísimo* court-martial proceedings to prosecute the leading figures. A tribunal in Barcelona soon delivered six death sentences, beginning with Major Perez Farrás and two other former army officers who had been commanders of the new Catalan constabulary (Mossos d'Esquadra) and militia (Somatén) involved in the insurrection.

The terms of the repression became the central political drama of the next three months. The Cortes, which had refused to restore the death penalty after the last anarchist insurrection, now wished to reintroduce the maximum sentence. All the right demanded severity, but President Alcalá Zamora, Cardinal Vidal i Barraquer, Cambó, other leaders of the Lliga Catalana, and various moderates urged leniency. The new government, though at first unanimously opposed to commutation (with the exception of the case of Captain Federico Escofet, whose involvement was limited),[1] found itself holding a series of lengthy meetings. Alcalá Zamora, in what had become a habitual extension of his prerogatives, made one of his lengthy presentations to the cabinet on 18 October, citing article 102 of the constitution, which stated: "The President of the Republic has the power to commute penalties in crimes of extreme gravity, after a report from the Supreme Court and a recommendation from the government." He made it clear that he would insist on using this authority even if the government refused to appeal cases to him.[2] The resulting tension fed a rumor repeated by Radio Toulouse that the government would be replaced by a military regime led by General Franco, but there is no indication of a military conspiracy at that point. Though his pressure and the procedure that he threatened were of questionable constitutionality, Alcalá Zamora had no intention of giving in. Two cabinet meetings were held on 31 October and two more the next day, with the president threatening to withdraw confidence and force a government reorganization or new elections. Though the report of the Supreme Court did not recommend commutation, Lerroux finally decided to capitulate in order to make peace with the president and appease moderates. After another cabinet meeting on 5 November, he announced that of the first twenty-three death sentences, twenty-one would be commuted.

The regular Cortes session also convened on 5 November, and Lerroux expressed his satisfaction to the right: "I will die satisfied for having contributed to my fatherland the service of having brought over from you, the monarchists, all those elements that now constitute the right wing of the Republic. . . . We are accused of being fascists and of having altered the spirit of the Republic. What projects have been approved contrary to spirit and letter of the Constitution? . . . There will be no modification of the fundamental laws, except by following the course prescribed in the Constitution itself." Melquiades Álvarez, the veteran Republican and leader of the Liberal Democrats, observed that he had been a leader in the popular movement of protest in 1917 but that he and his associates had scrupulously avoided common crimes and political murders. He invoked the example of the founders of the French Third Republic, who had executed Communards en masse in 1871, concluding that "with those executions they saved the Republic and its institutions and maintained order." Calvo Sotelo made a stronger speech yet, pointing out that the Spanish Socialists' "tactics differ from those of all the responsible socialist parties of Europe, since none of the latter advocate violent class struggle." In such a situation, the army was now "the spinal column" of Spain. The government easily won a vote of confidence of 233 to zero, with the extreme right abstaining. Though none of the left and left-center deputies initially returned to parliament, Martínez Barrio and Miguel Maura came back on the ninth, followed six days later by the left Catalanist deputies. After the government ended temporary censorship on parliamentary debate early in November, others began to take their seats. Meanwhile, the CEDA carried by a vote of 161 to 13 a motion that declared all deputies personally involved in the insurrection to have forfeited their seats and mandated an investigation of all trade unions, providing for dissolution of those found to have been implicated and confiscation of their assets to pay for damaged property. This measure, like so much of the repression, would never be carried out.

The first conflict of the new session was an attack on two cabinet members, Samper and Hidalgo, for their alleged irresponsibility in failing to prevent the insurrection. Without support from the CEDA, they resigned on 16 November, and the government was then reorganized. During this minicrisis, rumors of military conspiracy that had swirled for several weeks took more concrete form when two hard-line generals, Manuel Goded and Joaquín Fanjul, urged Gil Robles to adopt a firmer policy, pledging the support of the military. Gil Robles apparently told them that the CEDA would not oppose an imposition by the military, but would not itself initiate any extraparliamentary action. After two days canvassing military opinion, the two generals came back to advise that they had spoken too soon; the CEDA must continue to cooperate with the coalition government, for army leaders were unwilling to take any political responsibility and a sudden new election might return the left to power.[3]

A commission of four cabinet ministers was appointed to make recommendations on Catalan autonomy. It presented a bill on 28 November that temporarily suspended autonomy but provided that all rights be restored no more than three months after full constitutional guarantees were returned to Spain as a whole. An interim governor general would be appointed while a new committee would determine how much autonomy was to be enjoyed by Catalan administration in the interim. The CEDA added amendments that would suspend autonomy indefinitely until such time as the government and Cortes saw fit to reinstate it gradually, step by step, and the legislation was carried on 14 December. Thirteen days later the government appointed Manuel Portela Valladares as governor general. An elderly veteran of the old monarchist Liberal Party, Portela had earned a positive reputation as the last constitutionalist governor of Barcelona in 1923. He appointed José Pich y Pon, a veteran Radical politician, as mayor of Barcelona and turned the city council over to the Radicals.

Controversy over the repression continued without abatement. The right emphasized the violence of the revolutionaries and their murders of priests and other civilians, while the left stressed brutal behavior by troops in the mining district, summary executions, alleged military atrocities against miners' families, and continued harsh mistreatment of some of the prisoners. While the extreme right condemned the government's "appeasement" in commuting most death sentences, protest from the left mounted over brutal police procedures in Asturias. In Catalonia and the rest of the country the terms of repression appear to have been relatively moderate, but the Civil Guard's jurisdiction in Asturias, where the brutal Major Lisardo Doval was in charge of investigations, seems at first to have been a law unto itself. Beatings remained commonplace, and several more prisoners died. In the most publicized atrocity, a liberal investigative journalist who went by the pseudonym of "Luis Sirval" was arbitrarily arrested, then abruptly shot dead in prison by a Bulgarian Legionnaire officer named Ivanov. Continued censorship under martial law at first made independent reporting almost impossible, so a special commission of Socialists and left Republican deputies carried out an investigative mission of their own. That such a commission, composed of the participants in and indirect supporters of the insurrection, was able to function indicated how limited were the overall terms of repression. Its report dismissed the most extreme atrocity stories of both sides but presented evidence of continued beatings and torture in Asturias. Lerroux reassigned the infamous Major Doval on 7 December, but even then police practice in Asturias was not fully moderated. In January 564 prisoners signed a collective letter protesting torture in Oviedo prison. This was followed by another collective letter of protest to Alcalá Zamora, which included the signatures of moderate and conservative luminaries such as Unamuno and Ramón María de Valle Inclán. By that time the protest had become international, a depression-era equivalent of the Ferrer campaign of 1909, with the left lending it major attention throughout western Europe and the Comintern also investing considerable resources. The insurrection had captured the imagination of the European left and enjoyed extensive publicity abroad, the young Albert Camus penning a drama titled *Révolte dans les Asturies*. A commission of British Labourite deputies was allowed to visit Asturias, while in February 1935 the French Socialist Vincent Auriol talked with Lerroux as his party collected thousands of signatures on amnesty petitions in France. Though courts-martial continued, all death sentences were commuted save for two prisoners executed in February, the army sergeant and deserter Diego Vázquez, who had fought alongside the revolutionaries, and a worker known as "El Pichilatu," convicted of several killings.

Though the government had intended to be reasonable, and was in fact moderate in most cases, there was no doubt that the repression was badly handled. Justice was uneven, and in Asturias police administration was at first allowed to run wild. Though only two executions took place—both of men convicted of murderous crimes—there was much mistreatment of prisoners in Asturias. Moreover, the revolt of the Esquerra government was not adequate grounds to suspend Catalan autonomy, with no distinction between the excesses of one political group and the constitutional rights of the region.[4] After the revolt the government replaced more than one-eighth of all the mayors in Spain.[5] Continuation of the censorship was counterproductive, and eventually even the monarchist deputies initiated a Cortes debate on its unnecessary prolongation. Martial law was lifted for most of the country on 23 January 1935 but was retained for the provinces of Madrid, Barcelona, and six others in the north. Three weeks later Calvo Sotelo observed that, in the nearly four years since the beginning of the Republic, Spain as a whole had enjoyed only twenty-three days of *plenitud constitucional* (full constitutional rights). Excesses in Asturias were counterproductive, building sympathy for the left among more moderate sectors of the left-center and center. The same may be said of the government's refusal to free leftist leaders who bore little or no direct responsibility. The imprisonment of Azaña and the effort to prosecute him would also backfire, earning him new sympathy and prestige among the left and even part of the center. A further example was the policy of closing many CNT centers and arresting hundreds of anarchosyndicalists outside Asturias who had nothing to do with the revolt, a practice that encouraged mutual sympathy between anarchists and Socialists and better prospects for leftist unity than before the revolt. The insurrection had been a disaster for the Socialists, but the miscalculations of the repression had the effect of restoring much of the left's strength. Moreover, the controversy tended to weaken the government itself, dividing the center and the right.

Yet a contrary case can be made for the proposition that the repression, though initially severe in the mining basin, was generally too limited and ineffective. The center-right administrations that governed Spain from October 1934 to December 1935 followed a rightist and counterreformist socioeconomic policy and kept thousands of prisoners in jail, but made little effort to suppress the revolutionary organizations that had carried out the insurrection. Consequently the latter were soon back in business in 1935 in full force. The Republic's repression in 1934–35 was in fact the mildest by any liberal or semiliberal state challenged by major violent revolutionary subversion in nineteenth- or twentieth-century western Europe. In 1871 the Paris Commune had been drowned in a sea of blood that included thousands of arbitrary executions. The tsarist repression of the Russian revolution and mass terrorist cataclysm of 1905–1907 was proportionately more moderate than that in France but nonetheless involved at least 3,000 executions. The Freikorps and other elements that repressed the German revolutionary disorders of 1919–20 acted with greater severity than did the Spanish Republic, as did democratic Estonia, carrying out numerous executions in a very small country after the attempted Communist takeover of December 1924. The response to Socialist maximalism and Communist revolution in Italy and Hungary was an immediate upsurge of authoritarian forces in new regimes that perpetuated repression. In Spain, the Republic maintained relatively uninterrupted constitutional government, the right largely continued to abide by the constitution, support for fascism was minimal and did not increase, and many civil liberties were soon restored, followed by total restitution later in 1935, after which the revolutionaries were given a remarkably generous opportunity to take power through electoral means. Compared with other European countries, the liberality of the Spanish system was astounding. Centrist leaders refused to let themselves be pushed by the right into a harsher repression, the president of the Republic intervening directly to ensure a more benign policy. As in the case of Germany in 1932–33, a more genuine repression might have been the only way to save the Republic, for once the left returned to power, constitutional order and legality began to disappear. Thus the failure to punish the revolutionaries was of no permanent benefit to liberal democracy in Spain but may instead have hastened its demise. Atrocious as was the repression of the Paris Communards in 1871, for example, it may have assisted the early stabilization of the middle-class French Republic during the 1870s and 1880s.

The case of Finland provides an interesting comparison. Finland underwent a brief but vicious revolutionary/counterrevolutionary civil war in 1918 that was replete with atrocities. The victorious rightists at first instituted a vigorous repression that took a deadly toll. The number of leftists who died was proportionately greater than the number executed by Franco's Nationalists during the Spanish Civil War. The Finnish counterrevolutionaries were, however, essentially liberal and parliamentarian, a product of the civilized nineteenth century rather than of twentieth-century extremism. The elements initially most responsible for the bloodshed, the Communists, were outlawed, but a democratic parliamentary system remained in place. The Socialists quickly reconstituted themselves under new social democratic leadership that eliminated Bolshevik residues, and then emerged in the elections of 1920 as the largest single party in Finland, becoming a mainstay of Finnish democracy and helping to lead the subsequent war for independence against the Soviet Union.

Differences between the Finnish and Spanish cases are instructive. First, the Finnish repression was much more severe than the Spanish repression of 1934, and even at first proportionately more destructive of life than the Francoist repression of 1936, but it was more precisely targeted and soon came to an end. Second, the hard-core revolutionaries, the Communists, were permanently disenfranchised (though even they soon returned under a different name). In Spain many revolutionaries, including all the revolutionary organizations, were given full freedom by the end of 1935. Third, in Finland the bulk of the worker left responded responsibly, reconstituting itself as a fully social democratic movement. In Spain the worker left remained much more revolutionary, using elections as a means to promote extraconstitutional measures. Finally, in Finland it became possible within two years to achieve a functional liberal democracy open to the full national political spectrum. This was impossible in Spain, where the right was more extreme, while much of the left followed revolutionary tactics.

Perhaps the clearest voice of reason in the Cortes of 1935 was that of the Catalan centrist Francesc Cambó. He answered Calvo Sotelo's speech of 13 February two days later with a firm denial that democracy itself was responsible for the ills of contemporary Spanish society or incapable of producing progress and concord. The worst horrors of the present time, he stated, were occurring not in democratic western Europe but in the new dictatorships of eastern and central Europe. He pointed to another source of Spain's deteriorating condition: "We live in a period of weakening public power, such as we have never before experienced, and this weakness . . . is reflected in parliament, where I must say that I have never previously sat in a parliamentary chamber so insensitive to the wounds being inflicted on the public interest as in the present Cortes."

Legal prosecution of some of those involved in the insurrection would continue for most of 1935. Of all those indicted, the best known was Azaña, who had been placed at liberty by a decision of the Supreme Court on 28 December. Results of the judicial investigation into his role, together with facts on his indictment for earlier illegal activities in helping to provide arms for Portuguese exiles, were presented to the Cortes on 15 February 1935, the debate on the latter not beginning until 20 March. It quickly became clear that there was no evidence to connect Azaña with either the planning or the outbreak of the insurrection itself, and that the dredging up of facts on the Portuguese arms deal threatened a delicate area of foreign relations. Alcalá Zamora had told Lerroux that there was no legal reason to prosecute, even though Azaña was probably circumstantially involved on the fringes of the insurrection, and would have sought to make use of the latter had it triumphed, trying to restore the government of 1932–33.[6] This judgment of the president was probably correct. Azaña had engaged in various extralegal maneuvers between November 1933 and August 1934 to try to overturn the democratic electoral victory of the CEDA and had even indirectly threatened violence in his speeches, but he was not directly involved in the insurrection itself. He had gone further in his relations with the Socialists in 1934 than had Gil Robles in relations with the military, for Azaña had apparently made plans to use a peaceful, nonrevolutionary general strike as a political weapon, but as a pronunciamiento civil, not a violent revolution. On 6 April the Supreme Court absolved him of any charges connected with the insurrection. A vote was carried in parliament on 20 July to have him tried before the Tribunal of Constitutional Guarantees for his efforts to provide Portuguese exiles with arms to overthrow the Portuguese government, but the Radicals boycotted the session, and the vote of 189 to 68 fell short of the absolute majority (222) required to proceed to prosecution in this area.

The next round of courts-martial produced nominal death sentences for some of the main Socialist leaders in Asturias, including Ramón González Peña—arguably the most important regional figure—and the more moderate Teodomiro Menéndez, who had in fact always opposed the revolt.[7] In this case the Supreme Court recommended commutation for González Peña and several others, a recommendation that split the cabinet when it met on 29 March. Lerroux proposed commutation for González Peña and for twenty others, including Menéndez. Six other Radical ministers supported him; the three cedistas, the Agrarian, and the Liberal Democrat voted against.[8] This vote was sufficient to decide the issue but also broke up the government, with Alcalá Zamora initiating consultations for a new coalition on the following day.

Reconstitution of the coalition was not viable because both the CEDA and the Agrarians demanded increased representation and competed for key ministries. Alcalá Zamora remained determined to exclude the CEDA from any position of power proportionate to its parliamentary strength, and hit upon the makeshift solution of invoking article 81 of the constitution, which empowered him to suspend parliament for thirty days and to appoint an interim administration under Lerroux, composed mainly of Radicals but with two representatives of the president's own little Progressive Republican Party and with the independent Portela Valladares (not a parliamentary deputy) in the Ministry of the Interior in recognition of his recent labors as governor general of Catalonia. Alcalá Zamora hyperbolically termed this so-called government of experts "the best government of the Republic," but it was made up mostly of cronies of the president and prime minister. A surprising number of its members came from the García Prieto faction of the old monarchist Liberal Party, and for the first time under the Republic a general and an admiral held the portfolios of war and navy. This government finally put an end to martial law on 9 April and presided over a rather dreary anniversary of the Republic (compared with which Holy Week that year was quite festive), but its days were obviously numbered. Seeking a positive note and to identify itself with prestigious luminaries, the government awarded the new decoration of the Banda de la República to Ortega y Gasset. He refused to accept it, saying that he no longer had anything to do with politics. In doing so, he expressed the disenchantment of many moderates.

The most positive accomplishment of this interim government was to restore the functions of autonomy, except for public order, to a reconstituted Generalitat in mid-April. The new president was Pich y Pon, the top Radical politician of the region, functioning in cooperation with the Lliga. During the spring, conditions deteriorated. On the one hand, Pich y Pon handed over many top jobs to cronies; on the other, with martial law ended, the CNT became more active. Petty disorders, such as the periodic burning of streetcars, increased, as did violence against persons. On 29 June martial law was reimposed on Barcelona province.[9]

During April party leaders of the preceding coalition (Lerroux, Gil Robles, Melquiades Álvarez, and Martínez de Velasco) began to reach agreement that the only viable government would be restoration of the coalition, particularly between the Radicals and the CEDA. The Catholic party held a series of mass meetings to demand greater representation, something that Lerroux was willing to concede. Alcalá Zamora was out of alternatives, and therefore a new coalition under Lerroux was installed on 6 May. Gil Robles, now the first of five CEDA ministers, took over the key Ministry of War. Federico Salmón, one of the more progressive CEDA leaders, became minister of labor. However, the Christian democrat Manuel Giménez Fernández, who had pursued a continuing reformist policy as minister of agriculture in the autumn-winter coalition, was for that reason vetoed by the conservative majority of his own party, replaced by the ultraconservative Nicasio Velayos of the Agrarian Party. The "inevitable" Juan José Rocha (nicknamed "Miss Ministry" because he participated in so many different ministries in various governments) remained in foreign affairs. Altogether the new cabinet contained five cedistas, four Radicals (including the prime minister), two Agrarians, one Liberal Democrat, and one independent, Portela Valladares. Alcalá Zamora's main achievement in the new arrangement was continued exclusion of the leader of the largest party from the prime ministership, an office that Gil Robles had decided—doubtless erroneously—not to insist on filling, at least for the time being.

Though martial law had ended (except in Barcelona), a state of either alarm or prevention remained in effect in sixteen provinces. On 6 June the government gained approval for prorogation of this condition for another thirty days, the eighth prorogation of a state of constitutional exception under the Republic. This provided the opportunity for Calvo Sotelo to declare in the Cortes that it made manifest "that the Constitution is not viable." The Lerroux governments of early 1935 made intermittent attempts to come to grips with the dilemma of continuing censorship and introduced two new bills to regulate the press (in February and in May), but finally gave up, unable to achieve an effective balance between civil rights and the need to contain incendiary and subversive agitation.

There would be no more executions, and the new government began with a round of *indultos* (commutations), even including common criminals. The most important new prosecution was of Companys and other ministers of the rebel Generalitat. It was decided that the Tribunal of Constitutional Guarantees had jurisdiction to prosecute leaders of an autonomous regional government, and on 6 June the latter handed down its verdict that all were guilty of "military rebellion" and sentenced each to thirty years.

Military courts continued to try cases involving violence during the insurrection. During June, nine more death sentences were handed down, though it was unlikely any would be carried out, and many long prison terms were imposed. By this point, however, with martial law ended, there was much more protest from the left. Asturian miners declared their first new sympathy strike, and several judges received anonymous death threats.

May and June were a time of big new political rallies. Azaña began his comeback with a huge rally that filled Valencia's Mestalla stadium. The CEDA was at first the most active, and Gil Robles addressed an audience approximately equal to Azaña's in Mestalla stadium on 30 June. Not to be outdone, Lerroux held a Radical Party rally in the same spot a week later, announcing: "Who are the ones who have evolved? They [the right] have, and similarly in other ways. . . . I prophesy to you that the Republic has been definitively established in Spain."[10]

Monarchist leaders, keenly resentful of the CEDA's "opportunism," at that point tended to agree with Lerroux. Though considerable tension continued to exist between the Radicals and the CEDA, the prime minister was convinced that he had saved the Republic by domesticating the largest force on the right. He seems to have thought that if the left Republicans would now settle down and coalesce into one large but responsible opposition party, the function of the Radicals would be to hold the balance of power between a Republican left and a Catholic Republican right, so that he could soon look forward to an honored retirement.[11]

REPUBLICAN REFORM "RECTIFIED"

The coalition agreed on the need to "rectify" and revise the reforms of the first biennium, but there was little agreement on how far this effort was to extend. The Radicals wished to retain nearly all the reforms and only to moderate certain excesses, while in key respects the CEDA sought a counterreform, especially in religious, military, and socioeconomic policy, and a basic alteration of the constitution.

Terms of industrial relations had already begun to change under the first Lerroux governments of 1933–34, which had been a factor in further labor radicalization. The jurados had become more neutral, less pro-labor, while some of the new regulations had simply not been enforced. Nonetheless, before the October insurrection there had been no legal reversal of the basic reforms, nor had the syndicates by any means lost all the contract settlements of 1934.

The situation changed much more in the aftermath of the insurrection. Though UGT syndicates were not universally dissolved (the government being unable to prove their responsibility for the revolt), hundreds of jurados mixtos were closed down, particularly in the industrial areas, and they had already been weakened in the countryside. A government decree of 1 November 1934 established the legal category of *huelga abusiva* (roughly, illegal strike), which would henceforth apply to all strikes that were not undertaken in connection with specific labor issues or that failed to follow all legal regulations. In such a situation, employers would be free to rescind contracts and fire workers.

Federico Salmón, the new CEDA labor minister in May 1935, represented the "social Catholic" wing of his party. He sought to make the jurados more neutral and more effective by introducing civil servants as their presidents, but neither the UGT nor the CNT would participate, and Salmón virtually admitted that labor was no longer being fairly represented. In many areas the jurados ceased to operate effectively, while some concrete gains were officially rolled back. The forty-eight-hour week, for example, returned to the construction and metallurgical industries. Unemployment continued to rise. Thousands of workers had been fired by employers for having participated in political or other strikes, even though employers were officially urged not to retaliate. Growth in industrial production in 1934–35 and increased business confidence and investment under the center-right may have reduced the rate of expansion in unemployment during 1935 but certainly failed to reverse it, as employers sought to limit employment of workers who in general were still enjoying higher wages than in 1931. The unemployment statistics for 1935 (table 2) showed a significant drop in midyear because of the seasonal increase in agriculture, but overall the problem continued to worsen.

Salmón thus gave priority to reducing unemployment. He immediately introduced a new plan to spend 200 million pesetas for new construction and public works, with subsidies and insurance incentives to trigger a total volume of private investment at least four times as great. This plan was aimed at the private sector and also at the local level. It was approved in June 1935 and marked the first direct new employment scheme, designed to develop new production facilities, from a Republican government. In fact the money was spent bit by bit in small portions and never triggered the volume of new construction and employment anticipated. Subsequently Luis Lucia, one of the two most important Christian democratic leaders in the CEDA, became minister of public works in September and laid the groundwork for a new public works program that was presented to the Cortes on the eve of the coalition's collapse. These well-meaning initiatives, the second of which came too late to be approved, were too little too late and failed to reduce the rise in unemployment.

More controversial was revision of the agrarian reform. The Progres-

Table 2

Unemployment, 1934–1936

YEAR	MONTH	NUMBER OF UNEMPLOYED
1934	January	625,097
	April	703,814
	July	520,847
	October	629,730
1935	January	711,184
	April	732,034
	July	578,833
	December	780,242
1936	January	748,810
	February	843,872

Source: *Boletín Informativo de la Oficina Central de colocación obrera y defensa contra el paro,*
in J. Tusell, *La Segunda República en Madrid* (Madrid, 1970), 84, 128.

sive Republican Cirilo del Río, minister of agriculture for much of 1934, had sought to continue the basic reform while correcting certain abuses. Thus sharecroppers placed on uncultivated land in 1931–32 were evicted, the municipal boundaries law was annulled, rent revisions suspended, and procedures for evicting insolvent renters expedited, but the regular agrarian reform proceeded, more landless families being settled in 1934 than during 1932–33.

Agriculture minister in the first cedorradical government of October 1934 was the advanced social Catholic and Christian democrat Manuel Giménez Fernández. His first major act extended for one more year (until 31 July 1935) the continued occupation of formerly untilled land worked by *yunteros* (ploughmen) in Extremadura since 1932–33. Though the issue split the CEDA, Gil Robles supported it, and it passed on 20 December 1934. Giménez Fernandez' second major act was a decree of 2 January 1935 that altered somewhat the terms of administration of the agrarian reform. During the rest of the year there would be no more forcible expropriations, preference would be given to landless families with their own instruments of cultivation, and a target of 10,000 landless farmers to be settled on new land was set for the year. This was not, as the left insisted, an attempt to destroy the reform but simply an effort to make it less costly and more efficient. The total number of landless to be settled was exactly the same as had been proposed by Azaña for 1933, while the end to forced expropriations was designed at least in part to save money until a more flexible compensation system could be worked out. In fact resettlement under the agrarian reform continued at a normal rate until May 1935.

Giménez Fernández faced the most severe opposition to his proposals to benefit agrarian renters. He held to the social Catholic position that private property was a basic right but not an absolute one, its usufruct subject to regulation by objective community needs. Expanding an earlier plan by Del Río, he proposed that renters be allowed to purchase land they had worked for a minimum of twelve years at prices mutually agreed upon with owners or set by independent arbitration. Otherwise they would be guaranteed six-year leases, receive compensation for improvements made, enjoy the opportunity to have their rents set by arbitration tribunals, and be subject to eviction only for nonpayment of rent. Giménez Fernández argued that the government simply lacked funds to compensate owners for legal expropriation other than at the present slow rate, and therefore the most appropriate alternative was to make it possible for productive long-term renters to purchase their farms on the private market. This constructive proposal met a firestorm of criticism as a subversion of private property: Giménez Fernández was vehemently denounced as a *bolchevique blanco* (white Bolshevik). Its main terms had to be given up. Legislation finally approved in February–March 1935 granted renters leases for only four years and some compensation for improvements, while leaving arbitration to regular courts.[12]

When the CEDA reentered the government in May 1935, the archconservative Nicasio Velayos of the Agrarians took over the ministry. During the months that followed, many owners—possibly as many as "several thousand"[13]—took advantage of a provision in the recent legislation allowing owners to evict tenants in order to farm land directly, in many cases fraudulently, without any effort at direct cultivation. The number illegally evicted may have run into the tens of thousands, but Velayos refused to intervene to see that the rules were followed.

His proposal for a "Law for the Reform of the Agrarian Reform" was presented to the Cortes in July. It introduced the principle that there would be no expropriation of any kind without full compensation, while terms for calculating the latter were substantially altered in the landowners' favor. It annulled the inventory of properties technically subject to expropriation, making it possible for owners of eight-ninths of the lands in that category to sell off properties to third parties, grant them to children, or take a variety of other measures to gain exemption. Certain kinds of land were now totally excluded, and all collective experiments forbidden. The bill also repealed the provisions that had made possible expropriation of smaller properties (one of the most dubious aspects of the first bill) and arrangements for expropriation of rented properties. The increase in costs of administering the reform would drastically reduce the number of new farmers settled, while eligibility requirements were steeply raised. Finally, as a sop to moderates and Christian democrats, the bill did give the state the right to seize any land for reasons of "social utility," though without any strategy for doing so. In the following year, after the left returned to power, this provision would have the unintended "boomerang effect" of enabling the left to condemn sizable amounts of property for expropriation.

Velayos' new bill was vehemently denounced by the left and also by part of the center. The Falangist leader José Antonio Primo de Rivera calculated publicly that at this rate the agrarian reform would take more than 160 years to complete and warned that the amended project would last only "until the next movement of reprisal," as would indeed be the case. When the measure was passed on 25 July, the left Republicans again temporarily withdrew from parliament.

In general, 1935 was a year of severe reprisals in the central and southern countryside, with numerous expulsions and firings, lowering of wages, and arbitrary changes in working conditions. The leading conservative historian of this period judges that landowners' tactics in the south "achieved dimensions . . . of genuine cruelty," involving violence as well as the deaths of a number of Socialists and farmworkers. He concludes that "the behavior of the right in the countryside during the second half of 1935 was one of the principal causes of hatred in the Civil War and, probably, of the Civil War itself."[14]

Another basic area of reform for the cedorradical government was military policy, though there was a divergence of interest and intention between the two principal coalition partners. Altogether between September 1933 and December 1935 there were seven different ministers of war, but the two whose leadership was important were the Radical Diego Hidalgo (minister from January to November 1934) and Gil Robles (minister from May to December 1935). The goal of the Radicals had been to pacify the military—whom Lerroux considered still relatively liberal at heart—after the alleged *trituración* (pulverizing) by Azaña, in order to make them feel happier with the Republic. Of those previously prosecuted and then amnestied by the legislation of April 1934, all but the ringleaders of the sanjurjada were offered the option of retiring, going on reserve with full pay, or returning to active duty. Most took the first two options, but some figures, such as General Emilio Mola (last police chief of the monarchy), General Andrés Saliquet, and Colonel José Millán Astray, chose to return to active duty. Franco had received the first new promotion to major general, while on 19 July 1934 Hidalgo had published a decree prohibiting all political activities by the military. Lerroux took over the ministry when Hidalgo was forced out and tried to be evenhanded in constructing a personnel policy that balanced the concerns of both conservative hard-liners and pro-Republican senior commanders.

When Gil Robles entered the ministry in May 1935, leftists prophesied the worst, fearing preparation of a coup d'état. Calvo Sotelo and his ultra-rightist Bloque Nacional, having little civilian support, publicly sought military backing, with Calvo hailing the army as "the spinal column of the fatherland." Gil Robles scoffed at the idea of a coup, saying that, on the one hand, dictatorship could never solve the country's problems and, on the other, that the CEDA had adequate legal support to triumph. "The people," not the army, was the "spinal column," while the army was the *brazo armado*, the "weaponed arm" of the state for the entire citizenry and should not be involved in politics.[15] He did propose, however, to reconservatize the officer corps and army command, and to improve its combat readiness against any future subversion.

Gil Robles' command appointments were very rightist. The sometime Agrarian deputy and extreme rightist General Joaquín Fanjul became his undersecretary in the ministry, and Franco was named chief of the General Staff. Gil Robles publicly complained of "Masonic influence" in the army command, and some forty top *azañista* appointees, liberal senior commanders, were removed and in some cases placed on reserve. Old regimental names and religious services were restored, as were the combat promotions (*méritos de guerra*), which in some cases had been annulled by

Azaña. A project to lower by two years the age for passage to the reserve was blocked by the intense opposition of the president and senior pro-Republican generals, some of whom would have been eliminated by it.

There was no money to improve salaries, but in December the Cortes approved a law promoting all the *subtenientes* (sublieutenants) created by Azaña to lieutenant, thus expanding the officer corps by 3,500, so that its total size rebounded to about 14,000. The proportion of volunteers was raised to 8 percent of all new recruits, and in July a new law required all candidates for any of the police or constabulary corps to first acquire three years of active military service.

Despite the shortage of funds, a three-year rearmament plan was drawn up, projecting a new extraordinary budget to be paid for out of savings and more progressive taxation, but the latter was killed by the government. Two new brigades were created, and plans drawn up for new warplanes, tanks, artillery, and machine guns, though very little could actually be purchased.[16] The murkiest aspect of all these plans was a proposal by Cándido Casanueva, the CEDA minister of justice, to arrange for German suppliers for the military buildup, with a rake-off to go into party campaign coffers.[17] Apparently nothing came of this.

Since the end of 1933 a new army officers' semiclandestine association had been developed in Spanish garrisons. Called the Unión Militar Española (UME), it was a somewhat more rightist variant of the old Juntas Militares movement that had flourished during 1917–1919. The UME was scorned by Gil Robles, who wanted nothing to do with corporate army politics as distinct from a stronger, more conservative professional military. Its main goal was the complete reversal of all the Azaña personnel and political reforms. The UME was organized and led by monarchists, particularly the staff officers Captain Bartolomé Barba Hernández and Lieutenant Colonel Valentín Galarza, but it was a loose organization that appealed to garrison officers primarily with regard to professional concerns rather than to a political program. It may have been encouraged and protected by Fanjul and several other appointees of Gil Robles.

Educational policy also changed. The most positive accomplishments were made under Liberal Democrat Filiberto Villalobos, who served as minister of public instruction from April to December 1934, before being forced out by the CEDA.[18] Between 29 December 1934 and 30 December 1935 the ministerial portfolio became a football, changing hands seven times among six people, including the ubiquitous and persistent Rocha for a month, and ending with a brief return by Villalobos. The initial Radical governments increased educational expenditures to an all-time high of 7.08 percent of total state expenditures, before dropping them to 6.6 percent in 1935. The number of new schools constructed declined to about 1,300 in 1934, but with Catholic schools remaining open, the deficit was felt less. In July 1934 requirements and examinations for all levels of secondary education were standardized, and in August the curriculum was reorganized into successive cycles, a reform generally well received. At the same time, coeducation was ended in primary schools, and during 1935 the national school inspection apparatus developed under the left was largely eliminated. Policy became steadily more conservative in 1935. After the October insurrection student representation in the universities was abolished, while Catholic education groups became increasingly active.

Of all the changes, the ultimate for the CEDA was constitutional reform. The tactic was basically first to counter the anti-Catholic legislation, introduce aspects of the CEDA's social program to strengthen conservative institutions, and then to undertake fundamental constitutional reform. Yet though this goal was crucial, the party leadership was not in an immediate hurry, for any constitutional amendment adopted before 9 December 1935 (the fourth anniversary of the constitution) would require a two-thirds majority, whereas after that date a simple parliamentary majority would suffice. Moreover, the law required that after an amendment had been passed parliament must be dissolved, with new elections to serve as a kind of referendum on the amendment. Otherwise there was no need for the CEDA's Cortes plurality to face new elections until November 1937; thus in this critical area the leadership proceeded slowly.

Alcalá Zamora also stressed the need for constitutional reform, yet his own objectives differed in key respects, for he simply wished the Republican charter to become a more moderate and efficient, yet still essentially liberal democratic, constitution. He had made a long exposition to the first cedorradical cabinet in January 1935, proposing reform of all four of the articles pertaining to regional statutes, articles 26 and 27 on religion, and article 51 on the *cámara única* in order to create a bicameral legislature. He also proposed to change the statement on socialization of property and to make changes in twenty-seven other articles, amounting virtually to a new constitution.[19] The government appointed a parliamentary commission under the Liberal Democrat Joaquín Dualde to prepare draft proposals, but this work moved slowly, at least in part because the CEDA and some others saw no need to proceed until December.

Meanwhile there was more serious consideration of electoral reform. Party representatives first met on 16 June, and then again soon afterward. The CEDA came out for proportional representation, while the Radicals and most other Republican parties only sought elimination of the 40 percent quorum and called for cutting the largest electoral districts in half. Lerroux announced that he would take responsibility for a new electoral law that would "satisfy everyone," based on a majority system for the smaller districts and proportionality only in the four or five largest ones. His energy, however, was in serious decline, and no such proposal ever appeared. The Radicals believed that they would continue to do well with the present law, and even the small parties agreed.[20] As Alcalá Zamora later put it, this position by politicians such as Martínez de Velasco and Melquiades Álvarez would cost them first their parliamentary seats, and later their lives.

On 5 July Lerroux presented to parliament the proposals of the Dualde commission. Its preamble proudly stated: "For the first time in the history of Spain, a constitutional revision is being carried out by making use of the provisions of the existing constitution. Previous preconstitutional regimes and constitutions tended toward immutability, with the result that any change could come only through violence." The proposal contained guidelines for revising no fewer than 41 of the 125 articles in the constitution. Central would be the change of provisions for regional autonomy to safeguard public order and unity; democratization of the religious articles, with provision for negotiation of a concordat; revision of article 44, which had permitted expropriation without compensation; creation of a senate; and revision of the presidential prerogatives to give the president greater freedom to dissolve parliament but to reduce his authority over the ordinary conduct of government. The proposal gained the backing of the governing coalition but was vehemently rejected by all the left. A commission of twenty-one deputies was appointed to study it and make further detailed recommendations that could be discussed in the Cortes during the final months of the year.

These proposals were much more moderate than the goals earlier set by the CEDA and particularly by the strident JAP, their youth group. JAP publications had been calling for a much stronger executive, with limitations on the power of the legislature,[21] while at JAP meetings there were sometimes calls for a new corporative-type constitution. At various times during 1935 Gil Robles sought to disassociate himself from the authoritarian, nationalist rhetoric of the JAP—sometimes closer to Calvo Sotelo's Bloque Nacional than to the CEDA—though he took no decisive action to silence it. The CEDA leader gave some indication that he appreciated the importance of a parliament, yet he did believe that its powers and functions should be reduced.[22]

A more immediate problem was the budget. Republican governments encountered increasing difficulty in preparing a budget, not because the state was teetering on the verge of bankruptcy—almost the opposite was the case—but because of political quarreling. Agreement was handicapped by steady (though scarcely overwhelming) growth of the deficit, continued slow economic conditions (though the depression had now bottomed out), and above all by government instability.[23] In mid-1935 the problem was placed in the experienced hands of Joaquín Chapaprieta, wealthy lawyer and businessman, a former member of the Alba wing of the old Liberal Party, and last minister of labor before the dictatorship. Elected as a Republican independent in 1933, Chapaprieta had some reputation as an expert in administration and finance. His initial proposals, presented on 29 May, foresaw reduction of the past year's 750 million peseta deficit by one-third during the current year, with the full balancing to be achieved by 1937 or in the final months of 1936 through a combination of reductions in certain categories, modest tax increases and revisions, and improved collection. His reductions aimed at trimming government administration and personnel costs while retaining necessary public works and social programs. He observed: "In economic policy I don't see that the governments of the left have had a different policy from those of the center and right,"[24] and believed that with sounder management the economy might soon enjoy considerable investment from both domestic and foreign sources. Chapaprieta refloated a significant part of the public debt, but his key proposals, which included a plan to eliminate three ministries, drew strong opposition from the left, the civil service, and certain economic groups.[25]

The general lack of interest in stimulating the economy through deficit spending in a rapidly modernizing country without any crushing burden of debt was a striking feature of all the Republican governments, left or right, and at least a minor factor in their failure. This attitude stemmed in part from the excesses of deficit spending under the dictatorship, leading to the notion that it was antidemocratic and irresponsible. As a result, strong proposals for deficit spending came only from the extreme left or right, though the CEDA was also willing to go a bit further in this regard. The general reluctance, however, was but another example of the lack of clear imagination or understanding on the part of Republican leaders, though, to be fair, it should be recognized that they followed the orthodoxy of the early twentieth century in a manner similar to many other governments during the depression.

Even as it was, as soon as the Chapaprieta reform was approved by the government on 19 September, the two Agrarian ministers abruptly resigned, primarily because of opposition to restoring further areas of administration (in this case, public works) to the reconstituted Catalan Generalitat, and in part because of the potential impact of the new reform on their own ministries. There was no reason why these resignations should have precipitated a general crisis, since neither of the main coalition parties was involved and each was fully prepared to continue the coalition, but on the following day, to conform scrupulously to political precedent, the entire cabinet formally resigned, as a preliminary to reorganizing the coalition. Alcalá Zamora, however, had other ideas, and was determined to end the trend toward a conservative Republic by manipulating a new shift toward the center.

CHAPTER FIVE

Frustration of the Parliamentary System

THE GOVERNMENT REORGANIZATION OF September 1935 was another routine affair similar to the one experienced by the Azaña government in June 1933. A stable majority coalition existed, so that the vacant portfolios could be readily filled. Nothing was so simple under the Second Republic, however, for the slightest incident was seized upon by the president as an opportunity to interfere. Alcalá Zamora viewed reorganization as a new opening to weaken the cedorradical coalition and to shift the government more decisively toward the center. As usual, rather than doing the normal thing and authorizing reconstitution of the coalition of the two largest parliamentary parties—as would have happened in a fully functioning democracy—he opened another round of consultations concerning all possible alternatives, bringing the Radical Rafael Guerra del Río to despair that "we are in a lunatic asylum." The president's initial plan was to ask the distinguished speaker of the Cortes, the former Liberal Party leader and now Radical convert Santiago Alba, to form a new coalition that would include all the center-left, even the left Republicans and the most moderate wing of the Socialists, the very small Besteiro group (despite the latter's notorious opposition to government participation). Alba undertook the responsibility but found that Gil Robles would not accept coalition with any elements beyond the center and quickly gave up.[1]

Refusing to call on the leaders of either of the two largest parties,

Alcalá Zamora turned instead to the independent nonparty finance minister, Chapaprieta, and asked him to reorganize the coalition, a decision guaranteed to make the next government as weak as possible, though this did not seem to bother the president. Once more, Lerroux and Gil Robles gave in, and Chapaprieta quickly formed a new government, extending it slightly toward the center by including a member of the Lliga Catalana as minister of the navy. A tiny man, scarcely more than five feet tall, Chapaprieta was intelligent, strong-willed, and energetic. In line with his planned austerity budget, he reduced the number of ministries from thirteen to nine by combining a number of assignments. The CEDA still held three portfolios: Gil Robles in war, Lucia in public works, and Salmón in labor and justice. The heavy-handed role of the president, entitled by the constitution to designate each new prime minister (with the latter empowered to select his own cabinet ministers), was painfully obvious.

The new government was presented to the Cortes on 1 October, where it immediately faced a blast from Calvo Sotelo. The monarchist leader defined it as "a pathological crisis," the thirteenth or fourteenth in the four and a half years of the Republic, in which the government had endured seventy different ministers, individual ministries had known ten different ministers, individual ministers had held at least four different portfolios, and governments had sometimes lasted no more than thirty days, all this to the accompaniment of long-winded presidential declarations that were both "diffuse and profuse, full of gerunds and gongorine prose." Calvo charged that Alcalá Zamora not only personally determined in almost every case who would be prime minister but also interfered in the selection of individual ministers, an intervention that was technically unconstitutional. Thus "the chief of state currently directs Spanish politics. In my judgment it is not wrong for the chief of state to enjoy strong authority; quite the opposite." In Calvo's judgment, the failure lay first in the fact that the Republican system was hopelessly divided against itself and second in that "the chief of state does not support the counterrevolution," which was largely true, at a time when "the revolution" was "more alive than a year ago."

The main tasks of the new administration were financial, with Chapaprieta planning to complete his fiscal and administrative reform as soon as possible. The CEDA minister of public works, the Christian democrat Luis Lucia, was at the same time drawing up a program to benefit small rural communities with improved roads, communications, and railroad service, while maintaining the dam construction program. In addition to beginning the balancing of the budget, the new government hoped also to prepare an electoral reform that would introduce some degree of proportionality, reducing the 40 percent quorum and dividing the very largest districts. It readily won a vote of confidence, 211 to 15, obviously with very many abstentions. Chapaprieta's seventeen budget reduction decrees, which had appeared in *La Gaceta* on 30 September, eliminated five administrative sections in the Ministry of Agriculture, three in justice, and so on down the line. Government salaries and supplements over 1,000 pesetas would be automatically reduced 10 percent. Half of all vacancies in government employment would be eliminated, as would 597 doormen in the ministries and 300 official automobiles. Chapaprieta presented a fuller explanation to the Cortes on 15 October, reporting that he had already reconverted much of the debt from 5 to 4 percent and had reduced the total budget by 400 million pesetas, while taxes were being raised by an approximately equivalent amount, and improved collection during the past five months had added another 172 million pesetas in revenue. Thus, though the government planned to spend 400 million more than previously on public works and 250 million more on defense, the deficit anticipated for 1936 would decline to 148 million and would be eliminated altogether by the end of that year. It seemed an impressive feat that astonished the Cortes. Industrial production had been growing, while the 1935 harvest was excellent, creating a problem about how to withdraw excess grain from the market in order to maintain prices.

A final goal of the new government was to normalize political life, and thus all political centers in Barcelona were allowed to reopen with the exception of the extremist Estat Català. Mass meetings continued, Azaña setting a record with a huge turnout (200,000 or more) to hear him talk for over three hours—politicians of the Republic were notoriously long-winded—in a field to the south of Madrid. The CEDA announced plans for a rally of "half a million," and the Socialists were authorized to hold one of their own as well as a new national congress, though the latter never convened.

Political violence had by no means disappeared, but its pace in 1935 was the slowest of any year of the Republic. The government curiously announced that only 140 people had been killed in political violence since the start of the regime, when the true figure was more than ten times higher. All the while military tribunals continued their nominal work in repression, handing down numerous convictions for long prison terms, as well as more of the ritualistic death sentences that would never be carried out. On 6 October the only conviction for excesses in the repression took place, when one of the defendants in the Sirval murder case—Lieutenant Dmitri Ivanov, who had pulled the trigger—received the modest sentence of six months' imprisonment for homicide by negligence. The last big round of military tribunals took place in the first days of 1936, when thirty-four leaders of the Socialist militia, including the most active Socialist militants in the Civil Guard and Assault Guard, were sentenced to terms of varying lengths.

It was in this ambience of partial economic improvement, prospects for constructive reform, and delicate political balance that the principal corruption scandals of the Republic suddenly broke. The first concerned a new electronic roulette-type gambling device, known as the "Straperlo,"[2] which its owners had hoped to legalize in Spain through personal negotiations with various politicians, mainly Radicals. Apparently a number of bribes were provided, but legalization never fully took place, and the frustrated promoters finally sought compensation or revenge. David Strauss, a Dutch businessman who was the principal partner, was eventually placed in contact with the exiled Prieto and with Azaña, who urged Strauss to write to the president of the Republic, which he soon did.[3]

Rather than turn this material over to the courts, Alcalá Zamora retained the correspondence for political purposes, first bringing it to the attention of Lerroux just before the September crisis. The Radical leader brushed it aside as an unjustified triviality (which in some respects it was). For Alcalá Zamora, however, it provided further opportunity to discredit the major center party, his chief personal competitor for political space. The old Radicals had gained a reputation for corruption in Barcelona municipal politics during the early years of the century, a reputation that the expanded catchall party of the Republican years had never been entirely able to shake off. Even though it was primarily the president who had been responsible for the continuing crises since the middle of 1933, the spectacle of numerous Radical ministers—led by the indefatigable Rocha —playing musical chairs with Republican ministries had produced the cynical conviction among some that the principal motivation for frequent crises was to permit as many senior Radicals as possible to qualify for the ministerial pension. The party had expanded during 1931–1933 as a kind of moderate Republican umbrella organization without a very distinct ideology, at least compared with leftist and rightist groups, which argued politics in terms of eschatological damnation and salvation. As a normal bread-and-butter political organization, the Radicals considered patronage very important. Lerroux relied especially on his veteran cronies in the party leadership, men loyal to him personally but in some cases not especially competent, who often gave the impression of being a group of party hacks (as indeed some were).[4]

Alcalá Zamora informed the new prime minister about the Straperlo correspondence only after the first of October, and Chapaprieta was alarmed by the potential complications. He advised Alcalá Zamora not to respond to Strauss but to let him take the matter to court if he chose, surely the most sound and appropriate advice. Indeed, Alcalá Zamora might have followed the path of discretion had it not been for a petty incident a few days later. The Radicals had organized several large banquets *de desagravio* (in compensatory recognition) for Lerroux, to publicize the dubious manner in which the president had just eased him out of the prime ministership. A banquet took place in Barcelona's luxurious Hotel Ritz on 9 October, with Gil Robles in conspicuous attendance, fulsome in his praise of Lerroux. The Radical leader in response added words to the effect that one must always respect the office of the chief of state, whatever opinion one might have of any individual incumbent.[5] This observation deeply offended the president's morbid vanity, and before the next day was out he informed the prime minister that he was handing all the Straperlo correspondence over to the government rather than to the courts. The council of ministers took up the matter immediately, having received word that Azaña was about to make public reference to it in a mass meeting. It decided to announce that a complaint had been received from a foreign source alleging irregularities by certain Spanish officials and was being handed over to the prosecutor of the Supreme Court for investigation.

As soon as the announcement appeared (19 October), opposition deputies, smelling blood, insisted on a full parliamentary investigation in order to achieve maximal political effect, and the usual commission was appointed. In contrast to the parliamentary footdragging of the past two and a half years, the "Straperlo commission" moved with unaccustomed speed, reporting back to the Cortes in four days. According to the available data, David Strauss had first attempted to gain authorization for his gambling device in Barcelona at the end of 1933. Rebuffed, he returned to the Catalan capital in May 1934 and was introduced to the local Radical leader José Pich y Pon (then undersecretary of the navy) and to Aurelio Lerroux, nephew and adopted son of the party chief. They convinced Strauss to form a new corporation in which Pich y Pon and Aurelio Lerroux received 50 percent of the stock in return for gaining authorization from the government.[6] They won approval from the minister of the interior, at that time Salazar Alonso, and his undersecretary (Eduardo Benzo), though apparently no bribes were actually paid to these officials, and approval was also necessary from the prime minister, Samper. The latter's close associate, Sigfrido Blasco Ibáñez, son of the famous Radical novelist, allegedly promised to arrange matters in return for a 400,000 peseta bribe for the prime minister and a lesser amount for the minister of the interior. Authorization was obtained, and in August 1934 Strauss presented Alejandro Lerroux and Salazar Alonso with expensive gold watches valued at 4,600 pesetas each, the only money or objects of value known to have changed hands. The Strauss casino opened in San Sebastián on 12 September 1934, but within three hours it was closed by police, allegedly because of Strauss's failure to come up with bribes. An irate Strauss then demanded of Aurelio Lerroux that he return all that had been invested, but the latter allegedly convinced him that it would be possible to mount the operation successfully in Palma de Mallorca, provided that modest bribes were paid to Juan José Rocha, now minister of the navy, to Pich y Pon, Benzo, and a few others. Strauss then invested in opening a new casino in Formentera, only to see it closed within eight days, possibly as a result of pressure from local Balearic business interests. Strauss next attempted to salvage whatever he could from his investments—demanding return of 50,000 pesetas allegedly paid to Aurelio Lerroux and 25,000 to Benzo. The corporation was then dissolved, Strauss acknowledging the return of some 75,000 pesetas against 450,000 allegedly lost.[7]

The Radicals proved extraordinarily inept in their defense. After Alcalá Zamora had last pulled the rug out from under him, the seventy-one-year-old Lerroux, his energies seriously declining, seems to have fallen into a deep depression, believing his political career to be at an end. The

Radicals insisted, appropriately enough, that if anyone had committed a crime, it should be prosecuted in court, that the issues did not involve the present government, the parliament, or the Radical Party as a whole, that Radical ministers had themselves ended the Straperlo operations, and that whatever irregularities may or may not have occurred, they were no worse than those of other politicians. Strauss's letter was written in remarkably idiomatic Spanish, indicating expert assistance, and there was already some evidence of collusion by the opposition in the whole affair. Yet hardly any of these points were presented vigorously or effectively. Radical leaders seemed disconcerted and lacking in focus and energy.

The main document presented by Strauss and his lawyer was in fact unsigned and was unaccompanied by any material evidence, so its legal value was uncertain at best. The truth of all the allegations may be almost impossible to ascertain, the only valuables known to have changed hands being the two gold watches. The Strauss device was not something forbidden by Spanish legislation, and when the report was debated by the Cortes on 28 October, Gregorio Arranz, the independent head of the parliamentary commission, declared: "I would not go so far as to conclude from the materials investigated that a crime has been committed." Strauss was found to be a shady operator and something of a con artist who had had to flee Mexico eight years earlier. The commission's report nonetheless recommended that all the principals who were the target of major allegations—Salazar Alonso, then mayor of Madrid; Pich y Pon, the governor general of Catalonia; Aurelio Lerroux, government representative in the national telephone company; the Cortes deputy Blasco Ibáñez; undersecretary of the interior Benzo; and two other minor figures—resign their positions. They immediately did so.

The report caused a sensation, epitomized in the words of the Falangist leader Primo de Rivera, who declared in parliament: "Here we simply have a case of the disqualification of an entire political party: the Radical Republican Party." Some days later he shouted down from the Cortes galleries to the deputies: "Viva el Estraperlo!" This became a perfect slogan for extremists of left and right to satirize the alleged corruption of the parliamentary system. More moderate deputies also severely censured the Radicals, and their CEDA allies became increasingly zealous for prosecution. The matter was not remanded to the courts, which existed for such things, but was immediately turned into a political football to be decided initially by parliamentary vote. Salazar Alonso was spared by a mere three ballots, but all the others named in the report were indicted by parliament for regular prosecution, despite the lack of clear-cut evidence.

On the following day the two leading Radicals in the government, Lerroux and Rocha, resigned, but this move did not provoke another "presidential crisis," since by now Alcalá Zamora had worked himself into a corner and had no alternative to Chapaprieta. The prime minister reorganized his cabinet, with the Agrarian chief Martínez de Velasco replacing Lerroux as foreign minister and two minor Radicals taking the two ministries that had been held jointly by the ubiquitous Rocha.

The official judicial investigation, which began on 6 November, uncovered evidence that most of the charges were accurate. The impact on the Radicals was profound.[8] Lerroux proved increasingly listless and offered little leadership, while a kind of paralysis extended through the party. The Radicals' reputation for corruption was now overwhelmingly accepted. There was no doubt that the party did have a history of a certain amount of corruption, particularly in Barcelona and Valencia, and there was evidence of a few irregularities in government during recent years. To a lesser degree, such irregularities had occurred during the first Republican biennium, but even Alcalá Zamora recognized that most Radical politicians were no more corrupt than those of any other party. These shortcomings were a small price to have paid for the only large liberal democratic party that tried to build a Republic for all sectors of Spanish society.

Another scandal broke on 28 November, when the former inspector general of colonial administration, a onetime army officer named Antonio Nombela, made a public protest over improper payment of funds by Lerroux when prime minister, which had resulted in the firing of Nombela. This murky affair stemmed from cancellation of a colonial shipping contract some years earlier because of nonperformance of services. In April 1935 the Supreme Court had found in favor of the claimant, an elderly Catalan shipping merchant named A. Tayá, who demanded three million pesetas in settlement. The court had directed that a commission of experts determine the final sum, but Tayá, who had had dealings with Lerroux in earlier years, made arrangements for direct payment from colonial administration funds through Lerroux's undersecretary of the prime ministership, Moreno Calvo. Nombela had protested, and a subcommittee of cabinet ministers had reviewed the matter but routinely approved payment on 11 July. Now Nombela protested directly to Gil Robles, and on 17 July the council of ministers cancelled the payment, but at the same time Nombela was dismissed. He now demanded justice and the clearing of his name.

There was little doubt that some irregularity had occurred, but its significance seemed very minor. Such problems, moreover, are not normally resolved by being referred to parliamentary politics. Nombela took the matter directly to Alcalá Zamora.[9] Though Chapaprieta again saw the hand of the president trying to convert this into a political issue,[10] Alcalá Zamora was now more diffident. Pressure to take the issue to parliament this time came from the CEDA, which played a major role in the Chapaprieta government and calculated that the new scandal might break remaining Radical strength and give the CEDA full control of the parliament. The Cortes immediately voted to appoint an investigating commission, chaired, as in the Strauss case, by the independent conservative Arranz. It found that the only person at fault was the undersecretary Moreno Calvo. The report was discussed at an all-night Cortes session on 7–8 December and was approved 105 to 7, with the CEDA voting to accept and most deputies abstaining. The monarchist minority then introduced a personal motion against Lerroux for prevarication and falsification, but he was technically absolved by a vote of 119 to 60, though a similar vote against Moreno Calvo carried.

This second scandal—even though no incorrect payment had ultimately been made—completed the discrediting of Lerroux and the Radicals, with yet more complaints about Radical corruption waiting in the wings. The party was badly divided over recent policy and compromises and was losing support as some of its followers moved back to the left while the CEDA acquired a stronger position to the right. Clara Campoamor, the only woman Radical deputy and one of only three women deputies in the entire Cortes, had resigned from the party the preceding February, alleging that it had sold out to the right, and her defection was symptomatic.

The Straperlo-Nombela scandals have been compared with the Stavisky affair in France during 1933–34, when French Radical politicians were shown to have profited from corruption, resulting even in the murder of the chief witness. Ildefonso Bellón, the chief investigating magistrate in the Straperlo case, was one of the first to acknowledge publicly that, by comparison, the Spanish affair amounted to very little.

Though French politics were rocked by the Stavisky affair, the much more strongly institutionalized French Radical Party in the long run suffered only limited damage and within four years would regain the prime ministership. But in the much more fragmented, weakly institutionalized, and highly polarized Spanish system, the combined effect of the Straperlo-Nombela scandals—small potatoes though they were in themselves—was devastating.

Whereas the French case was handled through normal channels, the Straperlo affair was carefully developed by the leftist opposition, led by Prieto. Nonetheless, it might have amounted to little had it not been carefully exploited by the Spanish president, even though he was fully aware that Strauss had been trying to blackmail his own prime minister. Having leveraged Lerroux from power, Alcalá Zamora then appointed the Chapaprieta government. Though Chapaprieta had initially recognized that the case should be handled by the courts, his own political position was very weak, which was why the president had appointed him in the first place. Thus he caved in to pressure from Alcalá Zamora and others, so that the case was handled in a flagrantly political fashion, with parliament acting as both judge and jury, a procedure that violated separation of powers. Major Spanish officials were forced to resign on the unproven and unsigned word of a sordid con man who had already had to flee one Spanish-speaking country. The parliamentary commission conducted a summary investigation and refused to allow testimony from most of the accused, yet another violation of proper procedure. While the left simply sought to weaken the center and right, this maneuver was also supported by the moderate right and the extreme right. The CEDA miscalculated, believing that weakening the Radicals—as it had persistently sought to do for the past year—would strengthen the CEDA, while the extreme right simply mirrored the tactics and goals of the left, hoping to weaken parliamentary government altogether and force the CEDA to move to the right.

There were two other reasons for the extraordinary impact. One was that in Spain, unlike in many countries in eastern Europe or Latin America also trying to establish democracies, governmental officials were relatively honest and above-board in financial dealings. When cases of corruption were uncovered, the resulting outcry was consequently that much stronger.

A second reason was that many Spanish political groups argued in chiliastic terms of absolute morality and doctrinaire ideology. In so super-charged an atmosphere, the spectacle of the Radicals as a normal, democratic catchall party, given to the ordinary gamut of wheeling and dealing and involved in a certain amount of small-scale corruption, brought universal censure and the rapid decomposition of a party already being torn apart internally. The Radicals had limited internal cohesion: they were strongest on the local level, dealing with grassroots issues. They had elected more mayors, city councilmen, and provincial deputies than any other single force, yet these petty notables were in no position to provide national leadership. Most members were recent affiliates of pragmatic motivation. As the national organization foundered and the bitter, exhausted Lerroux showed that he had lost the capacity for leadership, many Radicals began to seek new political homes.[11]

THE DECEMBER CRISIS

Throughout this dreary spectacle the tiny, beleaguered prime minister struggled to carry out his budgetary and financial reform. On one public occasion he took the Cortes to task for the sectarian, partisan concerns of most deputies and their lack of interest in pressing economic issues,[12] and in this charge he was largely correct. With the Radicals in disarray, Chapaprieta's majority depended on the CEDA, most of whose deputies in fact opposed key aspects of his reforms. The Straperlo affair had required reorganization of the government, which was formed once more around the same center-right coalition. The main Radical leaders refused to participate, but two minor figures accepted ministries without authorization from the party, in a further sign of its decomposition. Still, Lerroux did not want to bring down the Chapaprieta coalition, at least for the moment. Meanwhile the government was further weakened by its handling of the great 1935 grain surplus. Outstanding weather and improving techniques had produced the best harvest in history, resulting in the collapse of grain prices. A lengthy series of partial measures was pursued to provide relief for farmers, but failed to do so, and there were many local irregularities.

The CEDA had reason to complain about the prime minister's priorities, for balancing the budget was hardly Spain's most pressing problem. The Catholic party had its own social and economic program; it wanted to spend more money on basic items such as roads, irrigation, public health, housing, and public works, and even perhaps a little more on the agrarian reform. The main concern of key internal party interests, however, was the proposed increase in taxation.

When the council of ministers met on 9 December, Gil Robles repeated to Chapaprieta that the CEDA would accept the modest increase proposed for corporate taxes but would have to vote against other features of the financial reform, especially a small rise in inheritance taxes. For the prime minister, lacking any party or majority of his own and buffeted by all manner of partisan pressures, this was the last straw. As foreseen by the CEDA, he resigned, pointing out in his note to the press that the government's failure was tantamount to "a confession by the present parliament that it lacks the capacity to complete a single regular budget."[13] For the CEDA, however, the way seemed finally to have been cleared for a Gil Robles–led CEDA coalition, since there was literally no other alternative. The Catholic leaders could congratulate themselves on their patience during the past two years, and now looked forward to their reward.

The ball was back in the court of a president who had refused to allow the leaders of either of the two largest parliamentary parties to preside normally over a government, and in Gil Robles' case resolutely denied him the prime ministership altogether. Alcalá Zamora's vision of Spain was based on the culture and the achievements of the liberal Spain of the two decades 1914–1933. During that period it may be argued that Spain made greater proportionate achievement than almost any other country in the world. It had rapidly expanded its economy, considerably improved living standards, and was restructuring its society. It had avoided World War I, won at some cost a major colonial war, and had advanced from predemocratic conditions to one of the most advanced democracies in the world. The country was undergoing a cultural flowering, and education was improving rapidly, despite the attempted destruction of Catholic schools. Thus when he had been faced at the end of September 1934 with the prospect of revolutionary insurrection and/or a coup from the right, Alcalá Zamora might well say, as he did in his memoirs, that he suddenly felt as though he had landed in an "insane asylum." As a lifelong liberal, he felt that the danger from the right was greater than that from the left, though he also recognized the latter's capacity for destructive extremism. The president nonetheless thought that it would be possible to win much of the left back to democracy, though this could not be accomplished without the presence of a strong and moderate Republican center, which he had concluded from the events of 1934–35 he himself must lead.

There seem to have been several elements in Alcalá Zamora's grand design. One was to prevent the CEDA from dominating the government, and a second was to drive Lerroux from power and cripple the Radical Party, both of which had been achieved. Like the left, the president was eager for new elections that would weaken the right, yet for this he found himself in an ambiguous constitutional position. Having already dissolved one parliament, albeit a constituent assembly, dissolving a second one might create grounds for subsequent impeachment, as provided for in the constitution. The president's more positive short-term goal was constructive reform of the constitution. He had hoped to keep the Chapaprieta government functioning under his arbitration and manipulation until at least some constitutional reforms, scheduled for discussion in the final weeks of the year, might be approved, possibly together with a fairer and more representative electoral law. Even very limited constitutional amendment, or simply a change in the rules for constitutional reform, might itself trigger automatic self-dissolution of the Cortes that voted it. Thus at one and the same time might be achieved some sort of constitutional reform and the liquidation of the—from the viewpoint of the president and the left—hated center-right parliament, without having the dissolution charged to Alcalá Zamora himself. The great unknown, however, was how the present Cortes might be kept functioning to achieve reform, in view of the mounting hostility of the CEDA and the incipient collapse of the Radicals, which the egocentric president had himself helped to precipitate, partly for selfish reasons. Like so many other politicians, Alcalá Zamora could be his own worst enemy.

As was commonly the case with the Republic's leaders, Chapaprieta had his own separate vision. He was concerned not with stimulating the economy but with balancing the budget, normally a laudable goal. Yet he imposed short-term sacrifices on an economy that was just beginning to recover from the depression, while initiating longer-term investments that would have no positive effect for at least a year, hardly the best recipe for short-term success and stability. Moreover, like so many Spanish politicians, he was not very flexible. Moderating his tax reform as the CEDA wished would not have destroyed his budget, though it would have left the budget with some imbalance, not an impossible price to pay.

Gil Robles' calculations were of course different. Though he recognized the constructive character of some of Chapaprieta's financial reforms, he did not make a maximum effort to overcome opposition to them inside his own party. With the Radicals in serious decline (also partly thanks to the CEDA), downfall of the Chapaprieta government would leave little alternative to a CEDA-led administration. Such a government would continue the conservative counterreforms of 1935, advance the CEDA's own socioeconomic program, and later begin the process of constitutional reform, provided that it could gather 51 percent of the votes, all that would be needed after 9 December. This government would produce a much more rightist reform than Alcalá Zamora desired, with a more powerful executive and an at least partially corporative structure, but the president would have scant alternative other than to dissolve the Cortes on his own initiative—another leap in the dark for Spain. That conclusion was correct, though it did not take fully into account the president's endless capacity for manipulation, and the willful recklessness with which he was prepared to pursue his ends.

Alcalá Zamora began consultations on 10 December. His first attempt was apparently to try to convince the honest, well-liked Agrarian leader Martínez de Velasco to form a new center-right coalition as a delaying action, with the Cortes suspended for thirty days. Strong opposition from the CEDA and others, however, revealed this to be impossible, while Chapaprieta remained firm in his refusal to try to reorganize the outgoing government.

On the afternoon of the eleventh, Gil Robles went back to the president once more, offering a CEDA-led government that could balance the budget despite greater funding for public works and alleviation of unemployment, complete the prosecutions stemming from the insurrection, strengthen both the economy and the armed forces simultaneously, and also begin constitutional reform. Alcalá Zamora remained unmoved, making it clear that he would never appoint the CEDA leader prime minister, presumably even if refusal meant premature dissolution of the Cortes.[14] More clearly than ever before, he was adopting a semipresidential form of government. Though this determination did not violate the letter of the constitution, it showed extremely bad judgment.

Gil Robles exploded with rage when he saw that the president would never permit the CEDA to capitalize on its partial victory in the past elections. He later claimed to have told Alcalá Zamora that by refusing to allow parliament to function normally he was inevitably pressing the country toward "violent solutions," and that if there were immediate new elections in the present state of polarization, no matter who won, the ultimate result would be "civil war."[15] Afterward he began to say privately that he would lead a campaign to drive the president from power.

Alcalá Zamora was determined to force Gil Robles from the Ministry of War as soon as possible, since he feared that the latter was using it to prepare a coup d'état. Finding the normal course of parliamentary government totally blocked, a coup d'état was precisely what Gil Robles began to investigate seriously for the first time. Alcalá Zamora's manipulations had created a self-fulfilling prophecy. Gil Robles asked his undersecretary, General Joaquín Fanjul, to take the matter up with Franco, the chief of staff, who could most effectively coordinate and unite the military, and with several other senior commanders. Gil Robles proposed not a military takeover of the government but a sort of "legalitarian pronunciamiento," by which the military leaders would force Alcalá Zamora to appoint a majoritarian parliamentary government, which would presumably have to be led by the CEDA. This formed a striking parallel on the right to the pseudolegalitarian extraparliamentary schemes of Azaña on the left during 1933–34. By the next morning, however, Franco returned a firm no, saying that the military was not united and could not possibly take responsibility for resolving a dispute between political parties and politicians so long as Spain was not facing a true national crisis. Franco characterized the present impasse as simply another, largely routine, political crisis, which in one sense was true enough,[16] and in so doing showed greater respect for the Republican constitution than had Alcalá Zamora, Azaña, or Gil Robles. This episode nonetheless marked an end to any sort of genuine majoritarian constitutional government in Spain. Franco was correct that military intervention was not technically justified, because in December 1935 there was indeed no dire national crisis, but the consequences of allowing the president to take full charge of government, while ignoring parliament, would in the long run be disastrous.

Alcalá Zamora next asked Miguel Maura to form a broad new center-right coalition, but this move quickly encountered the veto of Gil Robles, while Chapaprieta rejected repeated requests to try again. Now the only alternative to dissolution that the president was willing to consider was a ploy evidently suggested by a new counselor, Manuel Portela Valladares, another of the old monarchist Liberal Party politicians who played roles during these months. The former acting governor general of Catalonia, an independent without a seat in the Cortes who still remained in Barcelona, apparently suggested to the president the tactic of an interim government of centrist elements that would move to build a new center coalition capable of winning the balance of power in the next elections. Having painted himself into a corner, Alcalá Zamora grasped at this strategy, thinking of Maura and of Portela himself as its leaders. That Portela was not a member of parliament and had no party backing was not necessarily a weakness in the president's eyes, for it would make him more dependent on Alcalá Zamora and loyal to a new centrist coalition indirectly led by the president himself. Maura indignantly refused to participate in this most ambitious and outrageous of the president's manipulations, announcing to reporters on 13 December that Alcalá Zamora was planning a government based on "the old politics of the worst kind," which technically was true enough.[17]

A new cabinet was thus formed under Portela on 14 December, with the clear (though as yet unannounced) plan of new elections, in which it might be possible to "center the Republic" by electing 140 to 150 deputies from a new centrist bloc. Alcalá Zamora calculated that Portela, who was nearly seventy years old, would require several months to carry out the plan, and so the government was presented as a new minority centrist coalition, made up of independents and representatives of minor parties, which would begin with the closing of parliament for thirty days, under the president's prerogative. It was composed of two independents (Portela himself and Chapaprieta in finance), two Radicals (who were immediately disavowed by Lerroux), two military men (a general and an admiral in charge of the War and Navy Ministries), one Agrarian, one Liberal Democrat, one Progressive Republican, and one minister from the Lliga Catalana. The whole operation has been termed a "fantastic collage," and Alcalá Zamora's principal biographer characterizes it as a "surreal kind of situation."[18]

Gil Robles released a long note to the press on 16 December, declaring that the outcome of the crisis eliminated any possibility of accomplishing the CEDA's economic goals, such as a major new program of public works, state credit to combat unemployment and to sustain grain prices, or the strengthening of the armed forces. CEDA representatives in municipal and provincial governments throughout the country resigned, and the party's media launched a massive campaign against the new government and, by implication, against the president, whom Gil Robles was now determined to oust. The left, conversely, was jubilant, correctly reading the appointment of the new government as a prelude to new elections.

The left would immediately dub the work of the center-right in 1934–35 the *bienio negro,* a "black biennium" of destruction of Republican reforms, but this propaganda approach is too simplistic. First of all, if there was anyone to blame for the change in the political situation, it was the left, which had abandoned parliamentary action and through the use of extreme violence had skewed the spectrum yet more heavily toward the right. Second, none of the major Republican reforms had been annulled. The notion that the center-right governments had defied the left is a considerable exaggeration, for in most areas the approach was relatively conciliatory. During most of 1934–35 more was spent on education than ever before. More new schools were built, and there was an increase in teachers' salaries, with the education budget declining only in the second half of 1935. Extension of toleration to Catholic education meant that the total number of schools and of students being instructed was much greater than would have been the case under the exclusionary policies of the left. Before the leftist insurgency, Lerroux had accelerated the agrarian reform, and even during 1935 it continued at a reduced rate, with special assistance provided to renters. A reactivation of investment and business activity took place, and certain new categories of public works were introduced, while Chapaprieta initiated an important tax and fin**ⁿcial reform. There was no major decline in wages before the insurre   ⁻ᵈ ᵗⁿ ᶜ   ¹ well-being in some respects may have improved. Th   *in*ₜₕₛ hunger, which had increased from 1930 to 1933, began to decline in 1934 and 1935. Much of the labor reform had been allowed to lapse in practice, the agrarian reform was eventually reduced, and discrimination against Catholicism ended, but otherwise the reformist legislation survived, and the parliaments of 1934–35 in toto had passed 180 items of new legislation that in several respects complemented the original reforms. Nonetheless, social and economic policy had been limited in scope and sometimes inept. There should probably have been more deficit spending to reduce unemployment, but that was a common failure of the era and also of the first leftist governments of the Republic. What seemed decisive at the time, however, was the veto of further leftist reforms and the determination to limit most of what had been accomplished. Temporary outcomes of that sort are normal in representative systems, which, if honestly administered, are not designed to guarantee the monopoly of a single tendency.

To the left it all amounted to two years of reaction and sterility, and, despite the economic improvement and cultural growth, the biennium had indeed been a time of relative political sterility. Neither left nor right nor center had been able to accomplish its main goals, for which the president and both left and right were responsible. The concept of loyal opposition was totally alien to the left, the left Republicans identifying the regime exclusively with their own goals, denying effective representation or a share in power to their rivals. The anarchists and Socialists were worse yet, the former relying on violence and insurrection to achieve their own revolutionary ends, the Socialists insisting on a socialist regime that they eventually sought to impose by violence. The CEDA had, by comparison, fully observed the law as a political group, yet its own stance was sometimes provocative and threatening. The left's religious policy, of course, was so extreme that it seemed to preclude any common ground. The monarchists' activity was partially conspiratorial, primarily obstructionist.

Despite certain accomplishments, the center-right coalition governments were ultimately a political failure that fell between two stools. On the one hand, they had failed to carry out an effective repression, yet also failed to follow the logic of their own de facto moderation, doing little to conciliate the left or to encourage it to join a constitutional consensus. This contradiction was due to the basic differences between center and right. While the center might otherwise have tried to conciliate the left, the right was primarily interested in gaining greater power, resisting further compromises. As it was, what repression there was was ineptly handled politically and turned out to be counterproductive, serving to further stimulate and unify the left, and even winning sympathy for the latter among moderate elements of the center. While the repression went on, it swept a certain number of ordinary anarchists, who had not participated in the insurrection, into its dragnet. Though not able to conduct a thorough repression, the center-right governments were also unable or unwilling to undertake a true conciliation of the more moderate sectors of the left. Since the official policy ended by largely rehabilitating the revolutionaries, it would have been advisable to make a greater virtue of such an approach, possibly conducting an official investigation into the initial excesses of the repression in Asturias. Failure to do one or the other effectively, together with the rightist-oriented alteration of some of the earlier socioeconomic reforms, presented the image of a government totally hostile to the left, even though unable or unwilling to repress them consistently. The result of government policy, despite its relative leniency, was thus not to conciliate the left or to achieve any new constitutional consensus, but to continue to stimulate the hostility of the left, which in turn formally refused to repudiate the revolutionary violence of 1934. The left was ultimately responsible for its own program and actions, but the center-right governments were responsible for failing to institute a resolute policy that moved firmly in one direction or the other.

The CEDA had been patient and moderate in its political strategy, but that strategy was often not well conceived. It might have been better advised to have insisted on proper parliamentary practice and a major place in government from the very beginning, rather than constantly submitting to the president's caprice. Such delay and moderation simply led to a series of postponements, compromises, and frustrations at the hands of the president. Meanwhile the CEDA's most conservative elements sometimes dominated its economic policy, and, despite the CEDA's legalism, its youth movement experienced the vertigo of fascism and adopted a semifascist language and style, minus the key fascist ingredient of violence, which was much more typical of the left. The CEDA was also remiss in not giving electoral reform top priority. Conversely, it could not simply "declare itself Republican," as Alcalá Zamora demanded, so long as "Republicanism" meant a sectarian leftist regime that denied full civil rights to Catholics.

The major single factor in thwarting more effective government was Alcalá Zamora himself. The president maintained the laudable goal of defending a centrist and liberal democratic regime, but possessed a kind of messianic complex, a gigantic ego that led him to think that he possessed the right to manipulate every aspect of government as much as he wished. Strictly a politician of the old school, his approach was totally personalistic; he never grasped that liberal democracy would depend on rigorously liberal democratic practice, with scrupulous observation of the rules of the game. His constant interference made normal parliamentary and constitutional functioning impossible. Nothing was gained by persistent manipulation and the denial of greater access to the CEDA. Even Gil Robles' prime ministership, together with the introduction of more conservative and authoritarian features to the Republic, would have been preferable to the absolute breakdown that soon occurred following unnecessary, premature, and counterproductive elections.[19] Indeed, once Alcalá Zamora rejected the principle of majority constitutionalist government in December 1935, the Republic would never experience it again. The president's attempt to set himself above normal parliamentary procedure did not "center the Republic," but ultimately produced exactly the opposite effect.

Alcalá Zamora's decision at the end of 1935 to hold new elections within a matter of months would prove an unmitigated disaster. Since October 1934 the country had entered a state of intense polarization; premature elections would inevitably reflect that polarization. The president undoubtedly had good intentions, like most people, but they were of the kind that pave the road to hell. The notion that, under the democratic Republic, he could still manipulate the outcome through a government of cronies betrayed an appalling lack of judgment, as well as fundamental disrespect for the democratic system that he always claimed to defend. Both Azaña and Alcalá Zamora were essentially nineteenth-century personalities who did not understand the character of twentieth-century democracy. Premature elections were likely to have one of two outcomes: either the left, which now placed itself firmly on the ground of the insurrection, would win, and then proceed to implement the goals of the insurrection, bringing a new all-left regime or a civil war; or the right would win, and also move toward a different system. On the other hand, allowing the present parliament under a majority government to continue for two more years would at least provide some time for the polarization to be reduced or partially dissipated. As it was, new elections would merely be a plebiscite between a mutually exclusive left and right, followed by movement toward a less democratic regime, if not outright disaster.

Only the center parties were truly willing to reject undemocratic forces and hew to the line of constitutional democracy. A serious effort to broaden the center would thus have been helpful, whereas the president merely tried to reduce the center to his own area of manipulation, thereby nearly destroying it. All responsible leaders save the president recognized the importance of maintaining a viable coalition, prosecuting the work of government, and avoiding premature elections that might result in another pendular swing. If elections had been delayed until November 1937, there was at least some hope that polarization might decline, the center might grow slightly stronger, and the economy might continue to improve, while the increase in international tension might actually have encouraged domestic moderation. An amnesty for political prisoners in 1936 (though unlikely under the CEDA) might have taken much of the steam and bitterness out of the left, and in any case a CEDA-led coalition could not have been worse than what actually happened, and it might well have governed until 1937. Moreover, some degree of electoral reform (in the direction of greater proportionality, as strongly favored by such disparate groups as the CEDA and the Lliga, as well as the president) would have moderated extreme polarization in the next electoral results.[20]

The only large party that supported liberal democracy was the Radicals. Their very lack of doctrinairism and their willingness to compromise made them quintessentially suspect in the eyes of rigid doctrinaires of left and right, yet they were the only sizable force that always played by the constitution and the democratic book, no matter how unfairly treated. Extremist groups of left and right that decried Radical "immorality" would soon be exemplifying their own concepts of political morality by setting to work to murder each other on a massive scale, while the way they would soon be handling property and finances would make the peccadillos of the hapless Radicals look like a church picnic. Thus we see that concepts of political morality vary greatly. It is to the lasting credit of the Radicals that for better or ill they stood as the principal defenders and practitioners of a democratic Republic for all, and that fact must merit them some significant place in the history of Spain.[21]

As I have observed elsewhere, the political failure of 1935 was the more striking in contrast with Spanish success in the arts and athletics and even (very modestly) in science. The Republic had coincided with and stimulated a boom in publications, producing many new series of books and foreign translations. Theater was strong, with older playwrights like Jacinto Benavente and new ones such as Alejandro Casona, while Federico García Lorca, the brightest young star in an impressive literary firmament, saw three different plays of his premier in little more than twelve months between late 1934 and the close of 1935. Other major new poets such as Vicente Aleixandre and Jorge Guillén were making names for themselves, while Spanish painters—Picasso, Gris, Miró, and Dalí—stood atop the international art world. The cellist Pablo Casals was already internationally renowned, and new filmmakers such as Luis Buñuel were beginning to draw attention. Ramón Menéndez Pidal was at the height of his powers and already the dean of Spanish historians; he had just begun to edit the forty-volume "Historia de España" series, probably the most detailed national history in the world. In 1935 a world-famous Spanish entomologist hosted the International Congress of Entomology in Madrid, and Spain triumphed in beauty contests as Alicia Navarro, Miss Spain of 1935, won the Miss Europe title in London. The country could even boast its first twentieth-century international sports celebrity, as the Basque boxer Pablo Uzcudún had recently fought (unsuccessfully) for the heavyweight championship of the world.

CHAPTER SIX

Toward the Popular Front

IT WAS WIDELY ANTICIPATED that so irregular a government as that of Portela Valladares could only be an interim ministry serving as a prelude to dissolution of parliament and new elections. From the president's point of view, a longer rather than a shorter life was desirable, but such an administration could not be kept in power at the expense of parliament for very long. According to Portela's memoirs, his original agreement with Alcalá Zamora provided that his government would continue for at least two months, giving him time to gain firm control over the levers of administration and to construct an effective new center grouping.[1] Only in mid-February 1936 would new elections be announced, to be held at the beginning of April, yet the whole scheme was so irregular that it would not be possible to implement such a timetable.

The tall and elderly Portela, his head crowned with a mane of snow-white hair, looked to some observers like a sort of aging magician or warlock appointed to cast a spell that might somehow overcome civic fragmentation. During the second half of December he busied himself with numerous changes in personnel, involving replacements of civil governors and other local government officials in a large number of provinces, to try to build a new apparatus of political power as rapidly as possible.

The new government completely restored civil guarantees, for one of the few times in the history of the Republic. The leftist press, slowly reemerging in recent months, now appeared in full panoply. On the one hand, it featured attacks on the military and on the governments of the so-called bienio negro, and on the other, praise for the revolutionaries of 1934. There was no repudiation of the politics of violence; indeed, quite the contrary. The left treated the failed insurrection as a victory, claiming that it had showed that the forces of reaction and "fascism" would not be tolerated, that it had kept the Republic from swinging completely to the right. In this irrational propaganda, there was no recognition that in fact the effect of the insurrection had been to shift the Republic sharply to the right, the effects of which had been thwarted not by the disastrous insurrection, but by the endless manipulations of the centrist president.

At first the most active member of the new government was Chapaprieta, who assumed the initiative of trying to form a broad new center-right coalition, one that could include the CEDA, for the next elections. Since the left was known to have been hard at work in recent months to reconstitute the left Republican-Socialist alliance, it was clear to Chapaprieta that it could be defeated only by an equally broad antileft and antirevolutionary alliance of all constitutionalist, parliamentary forces of the center and moderate right. Though the CEDA had launched a furious press campaign against Alcalá Zamora and the Portela government, Chapaprieta pursued his negotiations and had an encouraging interview with Gil Robles on 19 December.[2]

A major stumbling block was the new government's announced plan to prorogue the existing budget by decree for another three months. Something of the sort was necessary, since no budget had ever been voted, but the constitution specified that only the Cortes held the power of the purse and of any budget prorogation. Alcalá Zamora and Portela took the ingenuous position that since the preceding budget had been voted by the Cortes, it was legal for the government temporarily to prorogue the same budget while the Cortes was not in session, ignoring the fact that the president was intentionally keeping the Cortes closed and once more thwarting parliamentary government. Gil Robles protested vehemently in a public letter to the speaker of the Cortes on 17 December, and there was a meeting of the leaders of the various parliamentary minorities on the twenty-third to discuss the problem. The CEDA leader became increasingly impatient. He judged correctly that Portela's goals were as much antirightist as antileftist, and on 27 December the CEDA announced that it was planning to form "a very broad counterrevolutionary front" but would not include any party that remained a part of Portela's government.[3]

Soon afterward Alcalá Zamora decided that the time had come to implement Portela's proposal to create a new center force directly from the government and abandon the feeble pretense of maintaining a functioning coalition, even if it meant holding elections sooner rather than later. When the cabinet met on 30 December, Portela Valladares launched into a violent tirade denouncing cabinet members for negotiating outside the existing government, even though he had earlier given nominal approval to Chapaprieta's efforts to deal with the CEDA. The entire cabinet resigned, as intended, so that Alcalá Zamora could immediately authorize Portela to replace all the former ministers, which he had already done, probably by prior design, by 7:00 P.M. that same day. The new government made no effort to form any functional coalition, but was composed of friends and cronies, including two dissident Radicals, one Progressive Republican, one Liberal Democrat, and various independents. This would constitute Alcalá Zamora's last and most disastrous effort to bypass parliamentary government. A note released to the press on the following day justified the new scheme as a necessary effort to create a Republican center—all the more important since the president had worked successfully to destroy the existing center—that could overcome polarization before it was too late. The budget was simply prorogued by decree, despite the dubious constitutionality of such procedure, and on 2 January *La Gaceta* carried a presidential decree suspending the Cortes for another thirty days. The object, of course, was to allow the new cabinet to gain full control of political and administrative procedures to guarantee maximum manipulation before new elections were held.

By this point the governing procedures of the Spanish Republic had begun to parallel some of the negative aspects of the Weimar Republic during its last years in Germany. In both cases presidential authority had superseded the normal functioning of parliament. Justification for this was greater in Germany, where fragmentation had become complete. In Spain a functional coalition was readily available, but was vetoed by the president. Though parliamentary government had not been so fully superseded as in Germany, Alcalá Zamora's appointment of short-term governments without parliamentary support was headed in the same direction and facilitated, rather than restrained, irresponsible behavior by the parties.

On 2 January forty-six deputies of the CEDA, in conjunction with a number of Radical and monarchist deputies, petitioned the president of the Cortes for an immediate meeting of the Diputación Permanente of the Cortes—the small standing body that could be convened when parliament was not in session—to indict the prime minister and his new cabinet for criminal responsibilities in the illegal proroguing of the budget and the "unconstitutional" suspension of parliament. Portela agreed to appear before the Diputación Permanente, whose meeting was scheduled for 7 January. One day earlier, however, he called on the president and immediately published a decree from the latter dissolving parliament, with new elections scheduled for 16 February, announcing that he would be represented at the Diputación Permanente by his minister of agriculture.

When it met, Miguel Maura denounced Portela's government: "Charges are pending against the government that meet all constitutional requirements for being pursued. And when these justified charges were pending, the President of the Republic, in agreement with the prime minister, dissolves parliament and fails to appear before the Diputación. And this is done through a government that has no identity other than presidential favoritism, and is led by an electoral manipulator certified as such many years ago, composed of six ministers who are not deputies, and four others who represent no one. That is twenty times worse than the behavior of the monarchy and has nothing to do one way or other with the Republic."[4]

Portela now set to work to concoct his new Partido del Centro Democrático (a sort of expansion of Alcalá Zamora's existing very small Partido Republicano Progresista), while the CEDA prepared to wage a massive new electoral operation of its own.

THE MARXIST LEFT

Whereas the prospect or reality of revolutionary civil war had the ultimate effect of moderating the position of most Socialists in such disparate countries as Finland and Germany, this had not necessarily been the case in Spain. One large sector of Socialists, the prietista "center" of the party, was indeed chastened by the experience of the failed insurrection, and forswore the insurrectional path for the future. The prietistas had never been given to rhetoric about the dictatorship of the proletariat. But for another large sector of the Socialist movement, those who tended to cluster around the jailed Largo Caballero, it was a different story.

Caballerista revolutionaries preached the goal of bolchevización in order to convert Spanish Socialism into the same sort of "revolutionary instrument" as Russian Bolshevism in 1917. Though their reach exceeded their grasp, their chief outlets were Luis Araquistain's theoretical monthly *Leviatán* and the new caballerista weekly *Claridad,* which an indulgent Republican government allowed to begin publication late in July 1935, demonstrating how little the continuation of partial censorship affected the revolutionary movements. Unlike the prietistas, the caballeristas rejected further collaboration with Azaña. Araquistain declared in July in *Leviatán* that "today the CEDA is nearer to Izquierda Republicana than to the monarchists of Renovación Española, and Izquierda Republicana nearer the CEDA—in terms of ultimate ideals for the Republic—than to the Socialist Party." He prophesied that the CEDA would join the moderate Republicans and go into the next elections "under a frankly Republican banner." Araquistain concluded that Azaña "and a few others like him" posited a "utopian" democracy above social classes, but assured his readers that such a project would be destroyed by inevitable historical processes. The most extreme statement of "Bolshevization" was probably the booklet *Octubre—segunda etapa* (October—second stage), written by Carlos Hernández Zancajo, president of the executive commission of the Madrid section of the Socialist Youth, and several colleagues. It urged expulsion of the moderate besteiristas from the party, calling for completion of Spain's October Revolution by a second stage that would construct a centralized Leninist organization with a secret apparatus, a revolutionary red army, and the eventual establishment of the dictatorship of the proletariat throughout the world.[5]

The Socialist organizations had to deal with alliance questions not merely with the left Republicans on their right but also with the small but now rapidly growing Communist Party on their left. The October insurrection, which the Comintern had permitted the Spanish Communists to join only at the last minute, had marked a breakthrough for the latter. For the first time they participated as a full ally with the Socialists in a revolutionary undertaking. Moreover, while the Socialist line after the insurrection sometimes waffled—Largo Caballero denying all responsibility in order to avoid a major jail term—the Communists wrapped themselves in the flag of the insurrection and fully identified themselves with it, greatly exaggerating their own role and winning much sympathy on the left.

For the Comintern, the isolationist revolutionary tactics of the so-called Third Period, introduced in 1928, were slowly giving way to a new tactic of broader leftist antifascist alliance. News of the October insurrection had been received with enthusiasm at Comintern headquarters in Moscow, though the Soviet press initially took the line that the Spanish revolt was merely a defensive struggle against fascism. Only after final defeat had *Izvestiya* declared that it had been a major step toward the complete revolutionary liberation of the Spanish proletariat. The year of the Spanish insurrection had been a time of slow realignment of the Comintern under the new direction of the Bulgarian Georgi Dimitrov. Movement toward cooperation with Socialists and bourgeois democrats was initiated first in France, setting the stage for a broader tactical re-alignment announced at the Seventh Congress of the Comintern, held in Moscow from 25 July to 21 August 1935, which introduced a new tactic of forming broader all-left "Popular Fronts." For the first time in years the Comintern leadership took the position that fascism should not be considered the same form of domination as bourgeois democracy, but was distinctly worse. The problem was made more serious by fascism's ability to generate mass support from broad sectors of the petite bourgeoisie and even from some workers.

Dimitrov announced that "a broad people's anti-fascist front" was needed, though this was held to require no change in fundamental Comintern strategy. The basis of any new alliance would still be "the proletarian united front," which must be adjusted to conditions in any given country. The reference to Popular Fronts remained ambiguous, invoking Lenin's stress on the need to consider new "forms of transition or approach to the proletarian revolution," and at one point seemed to suggest that Communists would join a Popular Front only in prerevolutionary conditions of crisis. Dimitrov stressed that it would be wrong to view a Popular Front coalition government as "a special democratic intermediate stage lying between the dictatorship of the bourgeoisie and the dictatorship of the proletariat," a stage that might delay transition to the latter. Such a coalition could be no more than temporary, a tactic for the defeat of fascism to advance "the revolutionary training of the masses."

Dimitrov explained that in a situation of crisis in various countries at the present moment a Popular Front coalition might be desirable and could even lead to a Popular Front government. The prerequisites he set for formation of such a coalition government were three: willingness to reject the policies and functionaries of the bourgeoisie, commitment of the masses to vigorous struggle against fascism and reaction, and willingness of at least a sizable part of the social democrats to support severe measures against fascism and other reactionary elements.

A Popular Front government would be a "democracy of a new type," going beyond bourgeois democracy and pointing toward a soviet democracy. This would constitute the second, more indirect, path to socialism (as first essayed in the People's Republic of Mongolia, established in 1924, though this was not an example to be usefully cited in European affairs). Such a "new type democracy" would not introduce socialism but would begin the nationalization of selected parts of the economy and distribute land to poor peasants. It was a type of government that would be formed "on the eve of and before the victory of the proletariat," and was "in no way" to restrict the activity of the Communist Party. The goal remained the insurrectionary seizure of power and the dictatorship of the proletariat. Hence the proletarian revolution remained very much on the agenda. Dimitrov emphasized: "We state frankly to the masses: Final salvation this government [of the Popular Front] cannot bring. . . . Consequently it is necessary to prepare for the socialist revolution! Soviet power and only soviet power can bring such salvation!"[6]

Much in the Popular Front tactic remained vague, but its Trojan horse aspect, or what Antonio Elorza and Marta Bizcarrondo have called its "Janus face,"[7] was made perfectly clear. As Kevin McDermott and Jeremy Agnew have put it, the Popular Front involved a change in immediate Communist tactics, but no change in overall revolutionary strategy.[8]

Defeat of the 1934 insurrection had left the Comintern leaders in Moscow not depressed but enthusiastic about the prospects for future revolutionary action in Spain. The initial Comintern line was that defeat had been due to the failure of Socialist organization, lack of support from the CNT, and failure to adopt the full Communist program. The Comintern's executive commission blew hot and cold, however, about applying the new tactic. At first it restrained the Spanish Communist leaders from going so far as the French Communists in seeking a broader antifascist alliance, warning them against "opportunist deformation" and making it clear that bourgeois parties should not participate in the antifascist front. The PCE was ordered to maintain the united front with the Socialists, but to intensify criticism of the latter's earlier democratic collaboration and to avoid any relaxation in the revolutionary struggle against capitalism, while actively developing organs of military self-defense.[9]

On 26 November 1934 the PCE leadership had first proposed formation of an organic *comité de enlace* (liaison committee) with the Socialists. During the first nine months of 1935 it sent more than ten official communications to the PSOE, proposing a variety of joint groups and activities, while complaining about the lack of Socialist response.[10] A special number of the Communist *Bandera Roja* in January 1935 was titled "The Revolutionary Unity of the Proletariat" and emphasized the need to achieve organic unity between the two parties for "the overthrow, through armed popular insurrection, of the dictatorship of the bourgeois-landlord bloc and the installation of the revolutionary power of the workers and peasants in the form of soviets." Liaison committees were formed in a few provinces where local Socialists were willing to do so. At the same time, a seemingly contradictory proposal was drawn up to make local Worker Alliances sovereign over local member parties, forming their own assemblies. This was conceived as the ultimate consummation of the united front from below and as the instrument that could prepare for revolutionary soviets, operating in conjunction with fusion with the Socialists.[11] All such continued machinations, even after suppression of the bloody insurrection, were of course possible because Spain was ruled not by a "dictatorship of the bourgeois-landlord bloc" but by a remarkably lenient liberal democracy that showed extraordinary tolerance even toward those engaged in attempting its violent destruction.

Identifying themselves more completely with the insurrection than did any other group and conducting their largest propaganda campaign in Spain to date, the Communists had taken advantage of the aftermath of the revolt to gain new followers and to bolster their reputation on the left by providing assistance to prisoners, their family members, and refugees. A key entity was the Comité Nacional de Ayuda a las Víctimas (National Committee to Aid the Victims), set up by the Comintern in Paris under the nominal leadership of Julio Álvarez del Vayo, a Socialist luminary who cooperated closely with the PCE. Initially a commission composed of three Communists and three Socialists was to supervise a fund of three million francs that had been collected in the Soviet Union, but the Socialists insisted on separate accounts. Such assistance was important to them, for the Socialists received little support from a Socialist Second International that frowned on their revolutionary activities. In addition, about one-fourth of the Spanish refugees allowed into the Soviet Union were Socialists, though when they returned over a year later many complained of poor treatment.[12] The Communists also developed a series of new fronts stemming from the insurrection, such as the Committee of Women against War and Fascism and the Association to Aid Workers' Children.

The shift in Comintern tactics first appeared in Spain in a special number of *Bandera Roja* for December 1934, announcing a new policy— formation of a Concentración Popular Antifascista (CPA) for the "struggle against the parties who have betrayed the People's Republic." Its goal would be dissolution of all nonleftist parties in Spain and initiation of a program for a People's Republic, with distribution of land to peasants and liberation of national minorities. Terminology for the new tactic in Spain would remain multiple and confusing for a full year and a half, and would never be fully unified until the spring of 1936. At first the term "Popular Front" was used in Spain only by the Spanish Section of the front organization World Committee for the Struggle against War and Fascism, which in the standard front organization tactic was seeking a broad alignment with non-Communist leftist intellectuals and left Republican parties in support of its propaganda.[13] The CPA was officially formed five months later, in May 1935, with the membership of all the Communist organizations and various fellow-traveling groups such as the Izquierda Radical Socialista, the Juventud de Izquierda Federal, and the Unión Republicana Femenina, perhaps the most important being the Juventudes de Izquierda Republicana (the youth group of Azaña's party). Despite the continuing use of inflammatory revolutionary language, the emphasis now lay on political struggle, and immediate insurrectionism was condemned. Thus when the Catalan Communist *Lluita* came out in April 1935 for the complete destruction of the bourgeois regime, it sowed confusion and had to be toned down.

By the middle of 1935 the PCE was promoting three parallel alliance tactics. The first was to promote "organic unity" and eventual fusion with the Socialists (which the Comintern felt confident would soon bring the much larger Socialist movement under Communist domination); the second was the CPA (whose name was changed in June to Bloque Popular Antifascista) as a broad alliance of the left that included sympathetic forces of the middle-class left as a sort of popular front to work for broad political goals; and the third was development and tightening of the Worker Alliances into effective joint revolutionary instruments of the worker left to prepare the ultimate transition to revolutionary soviets. Yet another new concept developed in this year of conceptual and tactical realignment was that of the *pueblo laborioso,* which might be translated as the "community of labor," a vague and ambiguous but broader term that could be used in conjunction with the CPA to bring the leftist sectors of the lower-middle classes into union with workers and peasants. All this involved the usual Communist combination of two-phase tactics, one for the short term (which required broader support) and a second one for the ultimate revolutionary phase, which was being developed at the same time.[14]

The revolutionary core of the CPA/BP was to be a properly organized Worker Alliance. In May 1935 a manifesto was launched to all "anarchist, syndicalist, socialist, and communist" workers, which lamented that, according to Communist definition, "the leadership of the Socialist Party has never seriously faced the problem of organizing and preparing the masses politically for insurrection" because it was afraid of a real worker revolution. The manifesto therefore called for complete reorganization of the Worker Alliances (naturally under Communist hegemony, though this was not spelled out) on the basis of a thirteen-point program, whose main features were:

- Confiscation without compensation of all the land of large landowners, the Church, and the government, for free distribution to farm workers either individually or collectively, "according to their own decision"
- Confiscation and nationalization of large industry, finance, transportation, and communications
- Recognition of full autonomy for Catalonia, the Basque Country, and Galicia, even as independent states
- Immediate unconditional liberation of northern Morocco and all other Spanish colonies

- Dissolution of the armed forces, the arming of workers and peasants, and a purge of "enemies of the people" (the standard Leninist-Stalinist purge term) throughout the government
- Creation of a Worker-Peasant Red Guard, with election of officers
- "Proletarian solidarity with the oppressed of the earth and fraternal alliance with the USSR"

The new-style Worker Alliance would cooperate with a broader Bloque Popular Antifascista (the alternative nomenclature for the CPA) to establish a provisional revolutionary government. These somewhat confusing and overlapping revolutionary proposals were reprised by the party secretary, the handsome José Díaz, on 2 June at a mass rally at Madrid's Cine Monumental, the largest Communist meeting since the insurrection. Only eight months after the bloodshed, he was free to boast grandiloquently and falsely that "we were responsible for the revolutionary movement of October," emphasizing that "the Communist Party of Spain claims for itself all the political responsibility derived from the victorious movement and insurrection of Asturias." He also stressed the need for a democratic program based on the Bloque or Concentración Popular Antifascista that would serve as a banner for new elections "that will have a clear antifascist and revolutionary meaning." Such elections would soon lead to a "provisional revolutionary government."[15]

In France the initial agreement for the Rassemblement Populaire between Communists, Socialists, and the Radicals was signed on 14 July 1935, some weeks before the Popular Front tactic was made official by the Comintern. The process of adjustment was, however, much slower in Spain because of the Communists' small size and lack of influence and the revolutionary posturing of the caballeristas. The year 1935 was nonetheless the time of the first significant propaganda success of the PCE, in two different dimensions. The party claimed to be putting out a total of forty-two publications in Spain—most of them legal, a few illegal—and the funding of these enterprises attested to the importance Spain now held for the Comintern. Thanks to Soviet backing and vigorous publicity, it was able to make itself much better known than before, and thanks to the practical assistance it offered and the aura of Soviet revolutionism it exuded, it was more attractive to Socialists than ever before. Support was increasing, to such an extent that 1935 can be called the first year of the rise of the party; probably most of the new members who affiliated with a Marxist party in Spain that year joined the PCE. Second, though the Communists did not convince the left that they were the main force behind the insurrection, they certainly managed to convince the right. From this time forward, the Spanish right would see the Communist Party as stronger and more influential than it actually was. Just as the left liked to call everything to the right of center "fascist," so the right more and more referred to the worker and revolutionary parties simply as "Communists." This was but one more step in an already intense polarization.

The middle of 1935 was a time of major leftist mass meetings, the aforementioned Communist rally in Madrid on 2 June being the largest Communist meeting in Spain to that point, eloquent testimony to the weakness of repression. The largest crowds, however, were generated by Azaña, particularly at his huge open-air rallies in Valencia on 26 May and at Baracaldo on 14 July. The prietistas held a few joint meetings with the left Republicans, and various rallies were held under the banner of Alianza Obrera or Frente Antifascista, reflecting the revolutionary alliances of the preceding year.

The new partial moderation of Comintern tactics raised the possibility that the PCE would now be positioned for the first time to the right of a quasi-insurrectionary Socialist Party. During the summer a debate was carried on between Luis Araquistain, chief revolutionary guru of the caballeristas, using the pages of his monthly *Leviatán*, and Vicente Uribe of the PCE's Politburo, writing in *Pueblo*, a Comintern-subsidized newspaper. Araquistain trumpeted the need to introduce the Soviet model in Spain immediately through violent revolution, whereas the Communist leader Uribe, following the new Comintern line, urged a more restrained policy.

The only new alternative on the worker left emerged in July 1935, when the very small Leninist BOC of Joaquín Maurín and the tiny Trotskyist Izquierda Comunista de España (ICE), led by Andreu Nin, merged to form a new-style independent Spanish Communist party, the Partido Obrero de Unificación Marxista (Worker Party of Marxist Unification; POUM). The new party would become famous two years later not because of its achievements but because of the manner of its suppression by Soviet power in the Republican zone during the Civil War, its revolutionary ardor emblazoned in George Orwell's famous memoir *Homage to Catalonia*.

The charismatic Maurín's analysis of the current situation appeared in his book *Hacia la segunda revolución*, published in April 1935. He contended that Spain would soon achieve conditions fully propitious for revolution, and would then find itself in a better situation than had Russia in 1917, for Spanish workers in a western European country had much more of a democratic tradition and thus could bring democracy with them into the revolution, further supported by the fact that there was much more directly revolutionary consciousness among the rural population (at least in the southern half of the country) than there had been in Russia. Thus whereas Lenin had had to renounce any possibility of maintaining a democratic type of dictatorship, the Spanish proletariat was proportionately more numerous and more mature. In Spain the proletariat would have the task of rapidly completing the final phase of the democratic revolution and of carrying it almost immediately into the socialist revolution, so that it would become a "democratic-socialist revolution." Maurín's minimum program for completing the democratic revolution—rather similar to the PCE's formula for the "new type" democratic republic of a provisional republican government—called for creation of an Iberian Union of Socialist Republics, with the right of complete secession. It included nationalization and redistribution of land, nationalization of major industry, banks, mines, transport, and foreign commerce, the six-hour day, and the arming of workers, all of which was supposed to result in a gigantic increase in production. "Organs of power" were to be "elected democratically by the workers," but, he warned ominously, the socialist state, unlike the "fascist" state, "will lack rights: it will have duties." What is striking is how near Maurín's doctrines were to those of the Comintern as the latter were being reformulated in 1935. To Communists, however, inadequate distinctions were being made between the two revolutions. They regarded Maurín's thesis as a heterodox blurring of differences, inadequately and improperly formulated in terms of a dangerous "Trotskyite" adventurism, above all lacking the tutelage of the Comintern.

Maurín also developed further his theory of fascism, defined in standard Marxist fashion as the last desperate paroxysm of capitalism in decline. He observed that fascism depended on a number of factors, such as division of the worker movement, defeat of "petit-bourgeois democracy," a climate threatening international war, and an ever more menacing state of internal conflict. Fascism faced a difficult future in Spain, he concluded, where memory of the recent dictatorship had created an aversion to overt authoritarianism. Moreover, in Spain the petite bourgeoisie was still oriented toward democracy, while fascism had no support among workers (in contrast to Italy and Germany) and did not even have the backing of the country's small industrial bourgeoisie. The small fascist movement was itself divided and lacked a significant leader. The Catholic CEDA, though large, could not really become a fascist party because its chieftain, Gil Robles, in fact "was afraid of fascism." Hence the only real basis for counterrevolutionary power would be the military, as in Portugal, eastern Europe, Latin America, and Asia. Finally, a successful fascism depended on the prior defeat of a leftist revolution, which fascism could purport to transcend. The only thing that had failed in Spain, according to Maurín, was the purely "petit-bourgeois" democratic revolution, whereas the "democratic-socialist revolution" was supposedly gaining more and more support. Despite certain inaccuracies, this was a more reasonable assessment of the prospects for a Spanish fascism than was normal among Spanish Marxists. Just as some Socialists in 1931 had seen the Spanish Republic as the start of a broader democratization in Europe that would initiate the downfall of fascism, Maurín was certain that growth of the "democratic-socialist revolution" in Spain would serve as a catalyst for the downfall of fascism in Italy, Germany, Poland, and Portugal. He fantasized that the resulting socialist states might join the Soviet Union in forming the United States of Europe. Maurín admitted that any attempt to introduce such a revolution in a western European country, with more advanced institutions and larger middle classes, would at first bring civil war, but assured his readers that such a civil war would be much briefer than the one in Russia (1918–1921), primarily because at the present time it could count on international proletarian support, and would be shielded from foreign counterrevolutionary intervention by the terms of international imperialist rivalry and the potential danger of world war. This last point was also being developed in *Claridad* by Araquistain, but they were both dead wrong, as would become clearer a little over a year later, when international factors would predominantly favor counterrevolutionary intervention.

The official founding of the POUM took place in Barcelona on 29 September. With a membership of at the very most 6,000, the new revolutionary party was officially structured on the basis of Leninist democratic centralism, but there is little doubt that it was internally more democratic than the PCE. Though the POUM contained a significant small core of intellectuals, it was essentially a worker party made up primarily of blue-collar and service workers. The native language of most members was Catalan. The formerly Trotskyist ICE had broken with Trotsky before joining the POUM, which formally rejected "Trotskyism" but would nonetheless remain friendly to Trotsky. It called the constant and ferocious Soviet attacks on Trotsky an "incitement to assassination" and occasionally published Trotsky's articles, while maintaining that the Comintern had failed as a center for world revolution and functioned merely as "an instrument at the service of the Soviet state," a view that was, of course, entirely correct.

The POUM leaders denounced the new Comintern tactic of the Popular Front, claiming that there was no inherent conflict between fascism and bourgeois democracy, because both were essentially capitalist, so that this new tactic merely reflected the opportunism of the Soviet state, alarmed by the danger from Nazi Germany. Mere defense of bourgeois democracy was held to be "Menshevist" (the Comintern had expelled Maurín four years earlier for alleged Menshevism). The Popular Front supposedly represented postponement of the class struggle, being designed primarily for the defense of the USSR. The POUM did, however, accept the need for some sort of alliance for the next Spanish elections, since these would inevitably have a "markedly revolutionary character," but any alliance should be carefully limited.[16]

FORGING THE LEFTIST ALLIANCE

All the left Republicans, together with many Socialists, recognized that the reason for their electoral disaster in 1933 had been the breakdown of the alliance. For the left Republicans, its restoration became a fundamental goal. In April 1935 a unity of action agreement was reached between Azaña's Izquierda Republicana, Martínez Barrio's more moderate Unión Republicana, and the tiny Partido Nacional Republicano. On 12 April 1935, the fourth anniversary of the defeat of the monarchy, they issued a joint declaration specifying minimum requirements for the restoration of Republican democracy as they defined it: reestablishment of constitutional guarantees (which they themselves had often denied to others), release of those imprisoned for the insurrection, abolition of police torture, an end to all discrimination against leftists in state employment, freedom for all trade unions (which they themselves would deny after they returned to power), readmission of all those fired for political reasons since October 1934, and the restoration of all municipal councils ousted by the government since that date.[17]

Since November 1934 Azaña and Indalecio Prieto had corresponded about the need to restore the alliance, Prieto making use of his freedom in exile to become the most active figure in the Socialist leadership. He quickly adopted what became the standard line among left Republicans and some moderate Socialists: that the insurrection had been fought to defend Republican democracy rather than to impose revolution, and that the full restoration of Republican democracy—meaning the left's regaining power—must be the goal. By January 1935 he had come to a meeting of minds with Azaña. The Socialists and left Republicans must reestablish their alliance in new elections, adopting a joint program within the bounds of Republican constitutionalism and arranging for a sizable number of left Republican candidacies so that the latter would have a strong parliamentary base for a new government that, given the caballerista position, must be made up exclusively of left Republicans.[18] From the outset, therefore, the plan was to create a weak minority government, beholden to the support of revolutionary Socialists—an inherently unstable formula. On 23 March 1935 Prieto wrote to the Socialist executive commission, emphasizing the importance of alliance and also mentioning the need to discipline the Socialist Youth.[19] By the end of that month, Prieto's ally Juan Simeón Vidarte, secretary of the executive commission, issued a circular that stressed the importance of Republican liberties (at least as applied to leftists), the defensive nature of the insurrection, and the moderate, responsible character of the Socialist Party.[20] Vidarte's role was anomalous because, though he had been a member of the Socialist Revolutionary Committee, he had never been arrested, a fact that caballeristas attributed to his active Masonic membership.[21] As de facto head of the Socialist apparatus, during 1935 he was in charge of articulating the massive propaganda campaign about the repression,[22] but Vidarte was a prietista who also sought to diminish revolutionary fervor. Further, on 14 April 1935, the fourth anniversary of the founding of the Republic, both Prieto and the moderate left Republican Sánchez Román published articles in Prieto's *El Liberal* on the need for unity of the left.

Largo Caballero, still in prison but with almost complete freedom of expression, protested any alliance with the bourgeois left in a letter to the executive commission on 29 April, a step that Santos Juliá has termed the beginning of caballerismo as a separate faction within the party.[23] The letter insisted on the revolutionary class nature of the party and the UGT. From this time down almost to the start of the Civil War, the Socialist press would be filled with bitter polemics among the three sectors of the party—the caballerista "left," the prietista "center," and the small and impotent self-styled "orthodox" or Kautskyist Marxists of the besteirista "right." Thus on 28 April, the day before Largo's letter, Julián Besteiro delivered his speech of admission into the Academy of Political and Moral Sciences on "Marxism and Anti-Marxism," claiming that Marx had not propounded the dictatorship of the proletariat as a necessary goal in itself and that true Marxism led to democratic socialism. He stressed further that "a socialist party out of power that accentuates the cult of violence," as the Socialists were doing in elaborating the myth of the insurrection, "can easily degenerate into a revolutionary and violent reformism with a psychology and activism very similar to those of fascism,"[24] anticipating the remarks of the fascist intellectual Ramiro Ledesma Ramos, who would observe that the Socialists were antifascist in theory but fascist in practice.

Prieto's main forum in 1935 was his newspaper, El Liberal, in which he published a series of five articles late in May, reprinted by at least eight other newspapers, on the need for a practical program of leftist unity. He pointed out that when the incendiary spokesmen of the Socialist Youth talked about those undermining socialism, their words ought first of all to be directed against the extremist actions of the Socialist Youth themselves. Collected as the booklet Posiciones socialistas del momento, they were immediately countered by Carlos de Baráibar's Las falsas "posiciones socialistas" de Indalecio Prieto, which argued among other things that a new electoral coalition would be futile because, by the time elections were next held, the cedorradical government would have totally changed the electoral law, whereas in fact the entire system should be destroyed.

During the summer of 1935 the left Republican leaders began to work on defining a common electoral program, but for some time no headway was made in negotiations with the Socialists because of caballerista opposition. Caballeristas held that the only union necessary was revival of the loose Worker Alliance, which would of course exclude the left Republicans.

Communist insistence on direct joint action between the two parties was put down (in part correctly) to the exigencies of Soviet foreign policy, while the large crowds that Azaña began to draw were at first dismissed as mere petit-bourgeois sentimentality. Araquistain pontificated that Azaña should not forget what his role really was, implying that it was essentially that of a Spanish Kerensky on behalf of the Bolsheviks/caballeristas.

There was in fact a genuine surge of *azañismo* during the second half of 1935 as he became a great national symbol for the recovery of the left, and not merely among the left-liberal middle classes. Azaña addressed the largest of all the mass meetings that year in the Campo de Comillas out-side Madrid on 20 October. At least 200,000 people (organizers claimed many more) attended what may have been the largest single political rally in Spanish history to that time, with many Socialists and Communists in the audience. Azaña's speech was moderate, invoking constitutional-ism and democratic reformism. He failed to respond to the clenched-fist salutes of many young revolutionaries.[25] It appeared that there was a significant movement of moderate opinion from the right-center back to the left-center, in revulsion against the frustrations of the cedorradical biennium and in response to the massive propaganda campaign about the repression. All the while, the azañistas had to work on both sides of their proposed alliance, convincing more moderate left Republican lead-ers such as Martínez Barrio and Sánchez Román not to cooperate with Alcalá Zamora in immediate constitutional reform or the formation of a broader centrist governing coalition, while continuing to pursue the So-cialists. Comillas seems to have impressed even the caballeristas, and on 2 November their organ *Claridad* spoke for the first time of the possibility of a temporary electoral alliance with the left Republicans, provided that the most moderate sectors of the latter were not included.

On 14 November Azaña dispatched a formal letter to the Socialist Party leadership, proposing an electoral alliance with a common program, and received a surprisingly rapid and positive response. By this point Largo Caballero was doing another of the flip-flops that had characterized his leadership during the past eleven years. He immediately convened the executive commissions of all the main Socialist groups (the party, the UGT, and the Socialist Youth), who accepted Azaña's proposal, provided that the Communist Party and its union, the CGTU, were included. That, however, was not part of the proposal made by Azaña, who initially had no intention of forming a French—or Comintern—style Popular Front, with a major Communist component.

Largo's willingness to consider an electoral alliance did not reflect any strategic moderation of his revolutionary goals, for close association with the Communists was for him equally or more important. The latter were following their split-level unity program, calling for a broader leftist union on the one hand while seeking to expand the Worker Alliance as a revolutionary instrument on the other. This task had proved more difficult than anticipated. Whereas the party had claimed to be participating in sixteen provincial Worker Alliances in April, many proved phantasmal, and two months later the number was down to eight. A further Communist gimmick was to form "workplace" Worker Alliances in factories, but only a few of these were organized in Vizcaya and in Seville.[26]

At a large Communist meeting in Madrid on 2 November, Díaz reported on the recent Seventh Comintern Congress, but his speech revealed little Popular Front moderation. He called for a broad new Bloque Popular of antifascist democracy to "to conquer fascism definitively," after which he stressed the importance of moving to a worker-peasant government en route to the dictatorship of the proletariat. Díaz emphasized that "we fight directly for the dictatorship of the proletariat, for the soviets. We declare this clearly, because, as the party of the proletariat, we do not renounce our objectives. But at the present moment we understand that the struggle is being waged not on the terrain of the dictatorship of the proletariat, but on that of the struggle of democracy against fascism as the immediate objective."[27] At this point the Communist term in Spain for the alternative tactic was the Bloque Popular, and by December the party claimed to have organized BPA committees in fifteen cities, though only five of these were provincial capitals.[28] For the first time the Communists made progress in Barcelona, where their Partit Comunista de Catalunya was outflanking the new POUM in its relations with the other small Catalan Marxist parties. On 12 January 1936 the PCC entered into an agreement to form a special liaison committee with the Unió Socialista de Catalunya and the Partit Català Proletari while seeking to extend this to the Catalan federation of the Socialist Party and to Estat Català.[29]

Even in France the longtime Socialist leader Léon Blum was showing interest in the Comintern line about "organic unity" between the Socialist and Communist parties, though Blum apparently fantasized that if this were achieved the French Communists could then be convinced to break with Moscow. With this the case by the end of 1935 among part of the moderate leadership of French Socialism, the Comintern was hoping for much more from the partially "Bolshevist" Spanish Socialists. Largo Caballero, who had steadfastly refused in court to admit any connection with the insurrection that he had planned for nine months, was briefly released from prison by the "ferocious repression" in November to visit his sick wife. He used this liberty among other things to meet with Vittorio Codovilla, the chief Comintern representative in Spain, who quickly telegrammed Moscow that "Largo agrees about the essentials of the decisions of the Congress and their application in Spain." Largo accepted the Communist proposal for fusion of the two syndical movements by which the small Communist CGTU would simply enter the UGT (a process begun soon afterward), but he did insist that the redevelopment of the Worker Alliance should be formed exclusively from above, by the parties themselves, and not by fusing membership from the base.[30]

At that point the Spanish Communists were more immediately concerned with unity with the Socialists and a broad Worker Alliance than with a French-style Popular Front with middle-class parties, even though the latter was readily accepted—and even sought—as a temporary electoral tactic. In December the Spanish-speaking Jacques Duclos, a top Comintern operative and French party leader, was sent to Madrid to hold extensive conversations with Largo Caballero in his prison cell over a period of three days—further eloquent testimony to the extreme liberalism and broad extension of civil liberties by what the Communists called the "fascist dictatorship" in power. By that time the French parties had converted their Rassemblement Populaire into what the Communists called the Popular Front, a firm electoral alliance for the balloting that would take place in France the following year. The Comintern then began to give priority to forming a similar pact in Spain. This effort was henceforth supported by Largo, who insisted that the PCE must be included in any broader electoral alliance, and must also participate in approving the alliance's program, but otherwise adopted a position to the left of the Comintern's. In an article that appeared in *Claridad* on 23 November, the still-imprisoned Socialist leader called once more for the Bolshevization of Spanish Socialism and establishment of the dictatorship of the proletariat without the distinctions and nuances that the Popular Front tactic had introduced into Communist discourse. Such was the feebleness of the legal prosecution of the insurrection that seven days later the "Spanish Lenin" was officially discharged by the court system for alleged "lack of evidence."

The deep differences within the Socialist Party were faced at a meeting of its national committee on 16 December. Largo continued to insist on participation of the Communists in preparing the program of a new electoral alliance, even though that had been rejected by the left Republican leaders. At this point—obviously to provoke and weaken Largo Caballero—Prieto craftily reintroduced an old issue that had divided the party leadership on the eve of the insurrection: he moved that the Socialist parliamentary minority be bound in its actions by decisions of the executive commission and national committee. Largo was vehemently opposed to this step, fearing the power of the prietistas in the party apparatus, and earlier had temporarily resigned his presidency of the national committee over it. He viewed the proposal as an attempt by moderates to gain political leverage and took the position that in a revolutionary organization all major decisions should be taken unanimously. When the national committee carried Prieto's motion by a vote of nine to five, with two abstentions, Largo resigned definitively, and was quickly joined in resignation by his three closest supporters on the party's executive commission. The increased antipathy, now amounting to outright hatred, between Prieto and Largo Caballero had broken into the open and was beginning to split the party. Henceforth the executive commission and national committee of the party would be dominated by the prietistas, while the UGT would be dominated by the caballerista left (even though two of the latter's most important regional groupings in Asturias and the Basque provinces were largely pro-prietista). Though the caballeristas claimed to have the support of most of the Socialist rank and file, the party apparatus was in the hands of their rivals. In this situation, the UGT in effect increasingly split from the party and began to function almost as its own separate Socialist movement.[31]

Negotiations between Socialists and left Republicans quickly accelerated after Portela announced elections, though the official pact of what (to Azaña's distaste) soon became known as the Popular Front was not announced till 15 January 1936. The appellation "Popular Front" was never its official name, but the term soon came into common use because of its zealous propagation by Communist propaganda. Largo and the UGT did not participate directly in the negotiations but managed to establish certain conditions. First, the alliance would be strictly for electoral purposes (as distinct from Prieto's plan to maintain close collaboration with a post-electoral left Republican government); second, though the new program would be a Republican, not a revolutionary, program, the Socialists and other worker parties would make clear the differences between this temporary electoral program and their own goals; and third, all other worker groups and parties who wished to participate should be allowed to join. Thus, though the Popular Front program was negotiated by leaders of the left Republicans and the Socialist Party, the resulting alliance was joined by the Communist Party, the tiny Partido Sindicalista of Angel Pestaña, and the new POUM.[32]

If Prieto had faced considerable difficulty in gaining the agreement of the Socialist left, Azaña had continuing difficulty with the two most moderate left Republican parties. Initially, Martínez Barrio had sought a union of the left Republican groups alone but was convinced by Azaña that the support of the Socialists was indispensable. Having agreed to that, the pliable Martínez Barrio did not balk at eventual inclusion of the Communists and other elements of the revolutionary left, though some in his party did. Conversely, Felipe Sánchez Román, who headed arguably the most prestigious law firm in Spain and was leader of the tiny Partido Nacional Republicano (made up largely of progressivist professional men and a few of the more progressive small industrialists), had always recognized the indispensability of the Socialists and played a major role in negotiating final terms of the alliance's program, much of which he is said to have written himself. On the night of 14 January, however, just before the program was issued, Sánchez Román withdrew his little party from the Popular Front. He was the most intelligent and one of the most moderate and responsible of the left Republican leaders, and probably the one whom Azaña respected most. His withdrawal has usually been attributed to his opposition to inclusion of the Communists in the Popular Front.[33] As El Sol reported on 26 January, he rejected the goals of all the revolutionary movements and had concluded that it was a flagrant contradiction for erstwhile proponents of the Constitution of 1931 to join forces with those who would destroy it.[34] Sánchez Román had insisted that the program include "the express prohibition, even in propaganda, of revolutionary tactics and the need to suppress the militarized youth groups,"[35] but when Azaña himself refused to champion this position, Sánchez Román withdrew.

Initially the caballeristas and Communists had prepared an electoral program that called for confiscation of all large landholdings without indemnity (contradicting the legislation of 1933), a purge of the army and the administration, expulsion of all religious orders, and new legislation that would outlaw all conservative and rightist parties, thus achieving the "new type" all-leftist republic called for at the Seventh Congress of the Comintern.[36]

The official manifesto of the Spanish Popular Front, however, was quite different. It called for "the rule of the Constitution" (something for which the Popular Front parties themselves had shown no respect) but contradictorily demanded immunity for the insurrection of 1934. It insisted on a "broad amnesty" for all political crimes, including murder, committed after November 1933 and rehiring of all state employees who had been suspended, transferred, or fired "without legal procedure or for motives of political persecution," as well as the rehiring of all employees fired for political reasons. The manifesto went on to declare: "Instances of violence by agents of the security forces that took place under the reactionary governments require the investigation of concrete responsibilities to clarify individual guilt and punishment." In other words, though there would be full amnesty for violent revolutionary crimes, including premeditated murder, there would not necessarily be similar immunity for those charged with repressing such crimes. This stance ran exactly parallel to the policy of the military rebels six months later, who would prosecute for "armed rebellion" those who had refused to engage in armed rebellion. All this was naturally read by opponents of the Popular Front as an indirect endorsement of revolutionary violence.

The manifesto called for reform of the Tribunal of Constitutional Guarantees "in order to prevent having the defense of the Constitution entrusted to consciences informed by convictions or interests contrary to the health of the regime." Other goals included reform of the Cortes to expedite the work of parliamentary commissions, reform of judicial procedure and purging of conservative judges, purging of police personnel and packing the police with leftists ("of recognized loyalty to the regime"), and revision of the Law of Public Order (written by the left themselves), "so that, without losing any of its defensive force, it provides the citizen with a greater guarantee against arbitrary use of power."

In economic affairs, "the Republicans do not accept the principle of the nationalization of land and its free distribution, as requested by the delegates of the Socialist Party." The manifesto proposed instead economic assistance to agriculture, a new and more progressive tenancy law, and stimulation of collective forms of production. "The Republic of which the Republican parties conceive is not a Republic dominated by social or economic class interests, but a regime of democratic freedom." Therefore "the Republican parties do not accept the worker control requested by the representatives of the Socialist Party," nor would they agree to nationalization of the banking system or an obligatory unemployment subsidy, but promised full restoration of the social legislation of 1931–1933 and above all support for wages of farmworkers. The manifesto pledged to stimulate and protect industry and to assist small business, stressing the need to follow "a strict criterion of subordination to the interest of the economy as a whole." Major expansion of public works received high priority. The manifesto also called for more progressive tax relief but failed to provide details, while urging more efficient collection and administration.[37]

The manifesto could not resolve the differences between the left Republicans and the revolutionaries, but merely listed some of them. It could not propose a strong and unified majority coalition government, even if the Popular Front won, because the Socialists would not join such a government. Thus it could at best promise only a weak minority government subject to all manner of pressures, not a return to the relatively stable government of 1931–1933. But Azaña was desperate to regain power above all else, and he emphasized from the beginning that this was not merely an electoral alliance but a strategy for creating a new left Republican government, even though technically only a minority government, that would hold power with, he hoped, the support of the revolutionaries.

Azaña wrote of the program to Prieto that "a Trajan would be needed to carry it out; or if not, a parliament that could work steadily, day and night, for six years, without opposition, without an opposition press, without anarchosyndicalism, without any commercial interference, without any depreciation of the currency, without opposition conspiracies, without strikes."[38] To that extent he confessed that the alliance program was a utopian project, revealing how little his political scheme had to do with reality.

The relative moderation of this program has often been stressed by historians, yet its proposals for "Republicanization" would require a large-scale political purge and totally partisan staffing of public institutions, which, as events would reveal, would soon lead to all manner of abuses. Moreover, a large part of the Popular Front did not really support the Popular Front program, but intended to bypass it immediately. For the caballeristas, this was no more than an electoral alliance, not the basis for the long-term government of Azaña's utopian dreams. The Popular Front program was thus not really the program of much of the Popular Front, but rather of the left Republicans and to some extent of one sector of the Socialists. How even this program could be sustained against the pressure of the revolutionaries, since the government would be dependent on their votes, was never addressed or explained.

The character of the Spanish Popular Front can be better understood by comparison with its only European counterpart, the Popular Front in France. The latter also represented a heterogeneous coalition linking Socialists, Communists, middle-class liberals (mainly the French Radicals), and several small leftist parties. The goals of the French Popular Front were to enhance the power of the left and to defend the existing French democracy against the menace of fascism. It also proposed social reforms, but included only one revolutionary party of any consequence, the Communists. Though the French Communists had the same Comintern-imposed goals as the PCE, the much more stable French political environment made it impossible for them to be presented in the same aggressive terms as in Spain. Nor could a parallel be drawn between the two Socialist parties, since only a very small left wing of the French party was interested in "Bolshevism." The goal of the French Socialists in their relations with the Communists was not self-Bolshevization, but converting the Communists to social democracy. The French Popular Front did not demand amnesty for violent revolutionaries. It did not propose major institutional changes to ensure the future political predominance of the left, but made democracy a value in its own right. Finally, the Spanish left Republicans were scarcely the equivalent of the French Radicals, a large, established middle-class party that scrupulously respected constitutionalism and generally supported conservative economic principles. The French Radicals even managed to impose the technical title "Rassemblement Populaire," since "Popular Front" was identified too closely with the Comintern, though it was the term most commonly used. The French Radicals were liberal democrats devoted to constitutional and parliamentary government, even if they were not in power, a stance that did not apply to the more sectarian Spanish left Republicans. At the slightest whiff of real "Hispanization" of the French Popular Front, the Radicals would have pulled out, as they eventually did anyway. The only Spanish left Republican leader who sustained equivalent principles was Sánchez Román. Together with the social democratic, nonrevolutionary French Socialists, the Radicals provided a more stable basis for government, for Socialists and Radicals could collaborate in forming a democratic, parliamentary, and law-abiding coalition. Thus the French Popular Front represented more of a democratic consensus and lacked the radical overtones of its Spanish counterpart.[39] All Popular Fronts contained inherently contradictory forces, however, so that the French coalition began to break down within only a year of taking power; and the same thing might have happened in Spain had not the Civil War intervened, despite Azaña's complacency with the extreme left. The Spanish Popular Front thus stood to the left of its French counterpart, and this circumstance, when combined with the hard-rightist and counter-revolutionary position of its main adversaries, contributed to a decisive national polarization that never took place in France.

For the left Republicans, alliance with the worker and revolutionary left was the only way to regain power for themselves, but it must be questioned why such exclusive power had come to dominate all other values for them. For example, the idea of a broad center Republican coalition with more moderate elements was rejected out of hand by most of their leaders. Yet if they were serious about their professed principles, they could not explain why violent revolutionaries were more desirable allies than Republican constitutionalists. Hatred of the liberal president was one major consideration, even though it was he—and not the disastrous insurrection—that had denied full power to the CEDA.

The only worker revolutionary party represented in the Popular Front central committee was the Socialist Party. The Communists were denied a seat by the left Republicans, who in turn offered to admit a UGT representative, but this proposal was spurned. There seems to have been a good deal of conflict over apportioning candidacies among the parties on the various electoral lists, with the Socialists at first demanding the lion's share. Nonetheless, the original Azaña-Prieto plan was carried out to the extent that the left Republican parties gained the largest portion of electoral candidacies, even though it was more than doubtful that they would provide the lion's share of the vote, in order that a future all-left Republican government would have a slightly less narrow base. Altogether 193 left Republican candidates held places on the Popular Front ticket, compared with 125 Socialists. The other small worker parties were given only 25 candidacies, 19 of which went to the Communists, potentially the only party other than the left Republicans to be overrepresented, thanks to the caballeristas.[40] The FAI-CNT once more rejected electoral participation, with the declared intent of campaigning against it. In fact, anarchosyndicalist propaganda in this regard was vacillating, so that most observers concluded that many, perhaps most, members of the CNT would vote for the Popular Front, even though such a position was adopted only by the CNT leadership in Asturias, and even there unofficially.[41]

All spokesmen for the worker left emphasized the tactical nature of the alliance. Ironically, the Socialist electoral campaign was led by Largo Caballero, now out of jail. Prieto remained in exile, having never been cleared of involvement in the insurrection, and participated through newspaper articles. On 12 January, just before formation of the Popular Front, Largo emphasized that an electoral understanding did not constitute a return to social democratic reformism, stressing that the Republic must be transformed into a "socialist republic." "Let it be quite clear that we are not mortgaging our ideology or our freedom of action in the future."[42] In his first major campaign speech, Largo emphasized that the function of the Popular Front was simply to free the thousands of leftist prisoners and restore predominance to the left generally. On one occasion he declared that fortunately the Spanish working class was "ideologically different from those in other lands," not being characterized by the attitude of "permanent submission" found in most European countries, and that "this spirit of indiscipline exhibited by the working masses will be their salvation!"[43] *Claridad* affirmed a "two-class" theory rather similar to that of the POUM, declaring that though the left Republican petite bourgeoisie might survive for the time being with electoral support from the workers, ultimately it would have to merge with the latter in a worker revolution or return to the bourgeoisie proper. Thus when on 9 February Martínez Barrio—the archrepresentative of the petite bourgeoisie within the Popular Front—repeated his standard maxim that the task at hand was "a conservative enterprise," this hardly corresponded to the position of the worker left. Even the posture of the prietista leadership of the Socialist Party was not as moderate as it has usually been presented, or at least was not able to control all the leading party organs, for *El Socialista* trumpeted on the same day as Martínez Barrio's statement: "We are determined to do in Spain what has been done in Russia. The plans of Spanish socialism and of Russian communism are the same. Certain details of the plan may change, but not the fundamental decrees."

The party that gained the most proportionately from the Popular Front was the Communists; for the first time in their history they were part of a major alliance. Since their true leadership was in Moscow, not Madrid, the PCE leaders went to the Soviet Union in mid-January for final instructions. Dimitri Manuilsky, their Comintern supervisor, explained once more that the Seventh Congress had mandated a merely temporary acceptance of the Bloque Popular (i.e., Popular Front) for short-term electoral purposes, whereas the basic goal remained the same: "That is, the dictatorship of the proletariat, the destruction of the bourgeoisie through violence, the rupture of class collaboration," and the establishment of the Soviet model. It was important, he said, that Largo Caballero be made to understand the importance of the role of revolutionary soviets, or their direct functional analogue, in Spain's revolutionary process. Therefore even during the electoral campaign the PCE must go beyond the Bloque Popular itself, and announce vigorously its program of completing the full bourgeois democratic revolution as soon as possible, since the goal was the "democratic dictatorship of the proletariat" (Lenin's slogan in November 1917). Expansion of Worker Alliance groups was indispensable, for they could subsequently play the revolutionary role of soviets as the alternative to, and subversion of, even the "new type" republic.[44] The conclusion was that in the short term the party must advance a "program of democratic-bourgeois revolution" that recognized the maintenance of democratic liberties (up to a point), but that would go beyond the official Popular Front program by demanding confiscation of large landholdings and a purge of the army.[45] Meanwhile, in a large joint Socialist-Communist rally on 22 January in Madrid, Largo Caballero spoke and the young Communist leader Jesús Hernández announced that the two groups were working toward a united revolutionary Marxist party to achieve "armed insurrection for the conquest of power and the establishment of the dictatorship of the proletariat."[46]

The Spanish Communist leaders faithfully implemented Comintern guidelines during the four-week election campaign, which enjoyed a large infusion of Comintern funds that helped to cement the new term "Popular Front."[47] In the official Communist daily *Mundo Obrero*, Díaz called on 3 February for "complete freedom for the Catalan, Basque, and Galician peoples" and insisted that "monarchist and fascist organizations must be dissolved," proposing to outlaw all the right. At a large meeting on 11 February, five days before the balloting, Díaz emphasized that the function of the Popular Front was simply to complete the bourgeois-democratic revolution, while preparing to move on to the dictatorship of the proletariat. "The decisive blow" would come through "insurrection," as in the Russian October, the ultimate model.[48] On the same day he published an article in *Mundo Obrero* to stress that the forthcoming elections were not merely "elections of a normal type," as in standard bourgeois democracies such as the United States, Great Britain, or Switzerland. The Spanish elections would instead be plebiscitary, to determine a new regime that would first carry out the Popular Front program and then go on to socialism. On the fourteenth, two days before the balloting, *Mundo Obrero* called attention once more to the ultimate goal of a "worker-peasant government," whose revolutionary program was then presented, and soon republished, in an official pamphlet. In this outline, the soviets were called Worker Alliance groups, and a three-step strategy was detailed: first, a victorious Popular Front and completion of its program, which would then be replaced by a worker-peasant government, which in turn would prepare establishment of the dictatorship of the proletariat.[49]

Altogether, the Popular Front represented a gigantic step toward the unity of the left, especially of the worker left. The common jail experiences of militants from diverse organizations during the repression of 1934–35 made the notion of unity much more tangible. Anarchists were now more disposed to vote for Marxists, while relations between the Communists and the Socialist Youth, in particular, drew ever closer. To the latter, the Communists represented a genuine revolution, a categorical and victorious Marxism-Leninism, which preached the unity of the left without giving up revolutionary goals.

The propaganda of the worker parties was virulent, laden with atrocity stories of the repression, full of abstract but vehement and emotional calls for destruction of the political enemy. Much was made of the supposed

30,000 leftist prisoners in jail, when the true figure was scarcely more than half that.[50] Whatever the precise number, the repression and the lack of amnesty for the thousands of prisoners were the strongest weapons in the Popular Front's campaign arsenal, rallying the support of moderates and of anarchists who otherwise might not have voted. Yet, in view of the strong campaign being waged by the right, there was no overconfidence, and there was no mere assumption of a decisive victory. During a well-publicized interview on the eve of the elections, Largo Caballero gave voice to pessimism and virtually prophesied defeat.

CHAPTER SEVEN

The Elections of February 1936

PORTELA VALLADARES WAS PROUD of the fact that the electoral campaign period restored full civil liberties for one of few occasions in the history of the Republic, but he found it more difficult to make headway with his new Partido del Centro Democrático than he had supposed. A large part of society was already politically mobilized, so that old-style administrative and electoral manipulation could in most cases no longer be carried out effectively. The Spanish political system had become too democratic to be readily responsive to government machinations. In so tense a situation, with nearly all political space already occupied, creation of a significant new political force *ex nihilo* was almost impossible. Portela had hoped to have at least one more month before announcing elections, but the opposition of the right had made such a delay impossible. About the first of February he tried to gain time by proposing to Alcalá Zamora that the date of elections be postponed until around the tenth of March (according to the forty-day delay that the constitution permitted the president to impose), but Alcalá Zamora demurred, replying that doing so would create too many complications.[1]

Portela has claimed that the president's bottom-line request was to do all he (Portela) could to see to it that the left gained increased representation, even as many as 180 seats, while Portela was hoping that centrist forces might win at least 100 seats, to mediate between a weaker right and a stronger left. He calculated that the Lliga would win the majority in Catalonia, gaining at least 20 seats, and that the centrists would win 40 more between the south and the Valencia region, with 20 to be added in Portela's native Galicia (its low mobilization making it more amenable to manipulation) and at least 20 more from all the rest of Spain.[2] Little of this, however, proved to be within his grasp.

The manifesto of the Partido del Centro Democrático on 28 January rejected both "civil war" and "red revolution," stressing constitutional process, national unity, and progress. Yet the manifesto itself was vague and full of liberal platitudes, so that, however more desirable the latter might have been than the extremisms of left and right, the new formation failed to present a completely clear image. In general, Portela looked more toward alliance with the left than with the right, but, though the Popular Front seemed somewhat more friendly at first, a regular left-center alliance was achieved only in Lugo province, where the prime minister dominated the political machinery.[3] A major goal was to complete the breakup of the Radicals so as to win over as many as possible of the latter's members and followers, but such a maneuver only weakened the center further. Portela enjoyed significant strength in only a few provinces of Galicia and the southeast, and on 7 February he announced that his party would be willing to ally with the right in districts where an understanding was not possible with the left. The consequence was that center-right alliances were eventually formed in various provinces of the south where the right was willing to ally because of relative weakness.[4] In Alicante province Portela first tried to reach understanding with the right; when that proved impossible, he dealt with the left, placing the provincial government and most municipal councils in the hands of left Republicans and Socialists. To this the right responded by offering more favorable terms, whereupon the new leftist government figures were replaced by decree with rightists.[5] The final result was that Portela was able to present candidacies in only about half of Spain's electoral districts, and when alliances were formed, they usually had to be made with the weaker side.

The most vigorous campaign waged by moderate parties occurred in Catalonia and the Basque Country. Both the Basque Nationalists and the Catalan Lliga mobilized major efforts. The remnants of the Radicals struggled as best they could and made their strongest campaign in Catalonia. As a result of numerous defections, they were able to field only seventy-eight candidates, and of these only twenty-three gained places on broader center-right coalition tickets.[6]

The right was much stronger than the center but never so united as the Popular Front. After it became clear before the end of January that Portela was engaging in all manner of manipulation and administrative irregularities designed to reduce the rightist vote, Gil Robles and even the centrist Chapaprieta seriously considered withdrawing from the elections, but Santiago Alba is said to have talked them out of it.[7] The monarchist groups demanded a broad national alliance of the right on a maximalist program, a sort of more extreme version of the Popular Front in reverse, but this the CEDA wisely rejected. Instead, on 20 January Gil Robles came to an agreement with the Radicals, the Agrarians, and small sectors of rightist Republicans on a program of defense of the Republic and parliamentary government, though the CEDA would campaign for fundamental constitutional revision.[8] The rightist coalitions were sometimes referred to during the electoral campaign as the "Bloque Nacional," but no such bloc existed, the term properly referring more strictly to the ultrarightist monarchist coalition that Calvo Sotelo had earlier sought to organize. All CEDA alliances were made for individual districts only. Where the left was strong, as in the south and in Asturias, the CEDA formed center-right alliances. In more conservative Salamanca, it allied with the Carlists and Agrarians, and in Carlist Navarre with the Carlists only. In Catalonia a broad Front Català de l'Ordre was formed by the CEDA, the Lliga, Radicals, and Carlists. In the long run, the CEDA electoral strategy was excessively ambiguous and opportunistic, for a more broadly categorical alliance with the center would have probably benefitted both the center and the moderate right, as Chapaprieta had always argued.

The CEDA campaign was in technical terms the most elaborate in Spain prior to 1977. No medium of expression was overlooked. The electoral message was carried by neon lights, telephones, radio broadcasts, specially prepared short movies, and big mural signs, with fifty million leaflets and 10,000 posters printed. Gil Robles and other party leaders were in constant motion, sometimes traveling by airplane. A half-million leaflets were said to have been mailed to voters in Madrid alone, and the huge sign in the Puerta del Sol, the center of the city, was three stories high.

The basic theme of the CEDA's campaign was proclaimed in its slogan "Contra la revolución y sus cómplices!" (Against the revolution and its accomplices!). Just as the Popular Front dwelt endlessly on an exaggerated version of the repression, CEDA propaganda harped on the insurrection, the atrocities of the revolutionaries, and the marked increase in crime under the Republic, not eschewing various extravagances about the collectivization of the family that had allegedly occurred in the Soviet Union. At times, however, the CEDA seemed to be campaigning against Alcalá Zamora as much as against the left; the president was repeatedly denounced for having blocked government access and for being in complicity with the left, the first charge being valid and the second largely invalid. The CEDA also publicly denounced quite a few of the manipulative abuses being committed by Portela Valladares in his effort to create a new government-led center.

As usual, JAP spokesmen were more extreme than the main CEDA leaders. JAP crowds acclaimed Gil Robles fascist-style as "Jefe, jefe, jefe!" (echoing "Duce, duce, duce!"). JAP leaders proposed to depose the president and to give full power to a new rightist executive, dissolving the Socialist Party and writing a new constitution, presenting their own version of a "new-type republic" diametrically opposed to that of the Comintern. Gil Robles and the main leadership tried to maintain the party's basic ambiguity, cautiously refusing to commit themselves to a precise blueprint for all the changes to be wrought if the CEDA won the absolute majority for which it aimed. Though it was claimed that by this point the CEDA had suffered twenty-six "martyrs" slain by the left,[9] he specifically rejected concepts of "destruction" or "annihilation" of the enemy, as used by the revolutionaries, and even spoke of the CEDA's "Christian understanding" of its adversaries, implying that the left could still play some role in a Spain governed by the CEDA. There were no threats to overturn law and order, though pressure from the JAP forced Gil Robles to announce during the final week of the campaign that the main goal of the CEDA in the next Cortes would be revision of the constitution. The CEDA was supported by a pastoral letter issued by the primate of the Church in Spain, Cardinal Gomá, at the close of January, titled "Por Dios y por España" (For God and Spain). It urged Catholics to vote for the parties that defended Catholic interests, but emphasized the importance of "avoiding all violence" and also spoke of charity toward the left and the need to "respect the freedom of those who do not think like yourselves."[10]

The main *tremendismos* (inflammatory statements) on the right came from Calvo Sotelo and the monarchists, who held a clear and unambiguous position. Calvo Sotelo insisted that in 1934 the left Republicans and Socialists had killed their own constitution and that a democratic Republic was already dead, because by the winter of 1936 the majority of politically active Spaniards no longer recognized it as legally or morally binding or planned to respect it in the future, but insisted on either a leftist or rightist regime. He reiterated that Spain needed an authoritarian, corporative, unitary, Catholic, and nationalist state. Calvo Sotelo continued to hail the military as the country's "spinal column" and voluntarily accepted the labels "militarist" and "praetorian" (as he did that of "fascist"), since only the military could save Spain from the revolutionary outburst and civil war that were looming. He was categorical that these elections would be "the last for a long time,"[11] as proved to be the case.

At the same time, there were many voices of reason and moderation. In the provincial *La Publicidad* of Granada, a moderate pro-Republican newspaper, one writer lamented that "listening to the speeches of party leaders or reading their writings and manifestos, one reaches the conclusion that at the present time none of them has a clear and sure vision or has made a conscientious study of the social, economic, and psychological situation of our country in the light of its history and the evolution of ideas and systems in the world. We live amid wildly gesticulating political epilepsy. This seems to be a land of the possessed or of simians."[12] A significant minority of Spaniards sought a rational middle ground but found most political space already occupied by left and right.

Though both polarities constantly emphasized the plebiscitary and decisive, even eschatological, character of the contest, there were comparatively few incidents during the campaign and only a few people killed, as in 1933. The principal complaints had to do with constraints employed by conservative forces in the countryside of Granada, a province in which 4,000 gun licenses had been issued in a comparatively short time. The stock market actually rose during the campaign, largely in the expectation of some sort of rightist victory, even if not an absolute majority.

THE ELECTORAL RESULTS
Conditions for the balloting on 16 February were good, and the elections were generally free and fair. The only areas where there was noteworthy evidence of corruption or coercion were parts of Galicia (subject to ma-

nipulation by the government and in La Coruña by left Republicans) and in Granada, where balloting in some rural districts was forcibly dominated by the right.[13] Early returns from urban districts indicated a stronger showing by the left than many had anticipated, partly because of electoral support from anarchists, and by the late evening it was clear that the Popular Front was winning, though the dimensions of the victory were not yet clear. The official recording (*escrutinio*) of electoral results would not take place until four days later, on 20 February.

It was evident by 17 February that the Popular Front had not merely won but would hold a parliamentary majority. That fact was not contested at the time, but subsequently there were much controversy and confusion about the overall totals in the popular vote, made the more confusing by the functioning of the alliance system. The government never published exact overall figures, and the Catholic *El Debate* was the only national-level newspaper to publish relatively full and precise reports for all provinces and major districts. The results later sparked polemics, and historians would subsequently advance guesstimates strongly influenced by political preferences.[14] These estimates might suggest such broad disparities in the popular vote as nearly five million for the left and less than four million for the right, a figure apparently arrived at by adding for the Popular Front the results of the second round of balloting in several provinces on 1 March, while subtracting from the right and center all the votes subsequently annulled by the highly partisan new Cortes, as well as those from which the right withdrew in the second round. Ultimately the only way to reconstruct the outcome accurately was to compile the original vote totals for each district as reported in the press, a task carried out thirty-five years later by the historian Javier Tusell and a group of colleagues. The resulting data are presented in table 3.[15]

It is clear from the cumulative totals that the Popular Front won the popular vote, but its margin may be judged either large or small depending on the categorization of the remaining votes gained by center-right alliances, which, together with the strictly rightist vote, exceeded the total for the left. Of nearly ten million voters, 47.2 percent voted for the Popular Front and its allies, while 45.7 percent voted for the right and its allies. If all the latter vote is categorized as rightist, then the right is calculated to have trailed by only 1.5 percent among total eligible voters, while the votes cast exclusively for the center alone amount only to 4.1 percent for

Table 3

Results of the Elections of 16 February 1936

CATEGORY	TOTAL NUMBER OF VOTES	PERCENTAGE OF ELECTORATE
Eligible voters	13,553,710	—
Votes cast	9,864,783	72.0
Popular Front	4,555,401	—
Popular Front with center (Lugo)	98,715	34.3
Center	400,901	5.4
Basque Nationalists	125,714	—
Right	1,866,981	—
Right with center	2,636,524	32.2

Source: J. Tusell Gómez et al., *Las elecciones del Frente Popular* (Madrid, 1971), 2:13.

Portela's Centro Democrático, or to 5.4 percent, if the Basque Nationalist vote is added. The totals may vary further depending on how independent tickets are categorized. In the computation of Ramón Salas Larrazábal, the combined vote for rightist alliances (including center-right) and independent rightist tickets amounted to 4,511,031, compared with 4,430,322 for the left, or 46.43 percent for the former compared with 45.6 percent for the latter.[16] This method of computation may or may not be more misleading, however, and what would ultimately be determinate would be the concentrations in individual districts, not the popular vote, given the nonproportional allocation of winning seats.

If, however, the vote is broken down by tickets for each district and by individual parties, a different pattern emerges. A precise breakdown is admittedly very difficult, perhaps in some cases impossible, because of the complexity of the alliance system and the existence of several minor or incomplete tickets. The best approximation has been achieved by Juan Linz and Jesús de Miguel, who have tried to separate out individual party totals, particularly with regard to the center-right coalition tickets. (See table 4.) Their results are less definitive than the broad totals given above but suggest that the Popular Front directly received about 43 percent of

Table 4

Deputies Elected in the *Primera Vuelta* of 16 February 1936

POPULAR FRONT	NO.	RIGHT	NO.	CENTER	NO.
Socialist	88	CEDA	101	Centrist Party	21
Izquierda Republicana	79	Traditionalists	15	Lliga Catalana	12
Unión Republicana	34	Renovación Española	13	Radicals	9
Esquerra Catalana	22	Agrarians	11	Progressives	6
Communists	14	Rightist independents	10	Basque Nationalists	5
Acció Catalana	5	Conservatives	2	Liberal democrats	1
Leftist independents	4	Independent monarchists	2		
Unió Socialista de Catalunya	3	Spanish nationalist	1		
Galicianists	3	Catholic	1		
Federal Republicans	2				
Unió de Rabassaires	2				
POUM	1				
Partit Català Proletari	1				
Revolutionary Catalan nationalist	1				
Partido Sindicalista	1				
Independent syndicalist	1				
Esquerra Valenciana	1				
Total	**263**		**156**		**54**

Source: J. Tusell Gómez et al., *Las elecciones del Frente Popular* (Madrid, 1971), 2:82–83.

the votes cast, that the right directly received only 30.4 percent, and the various center and right-center groups a collective total of 21 percent, with 5.6 percent of the votes going to unclassifiable candidates.[17]

The abstention rate of 28 percent—compared with 32.6 percent in 1933—indicates that, despite the frenzy in some quarters, Spanish society as a whole was not as hyperpoliticized as it may have seemed. It is doubtful that more than 1 to 2 percent of the abstention can be directly attributed to rightist coercion in the provinces, though a small part of it was undoubtedly due to those anarchists who still refused to participate in elections. The rate of abstention was highest in Cádiz, Málaga, and

Seville, where illiteracy and poverty coincided with considerable support for anarchosyndicalism.

The leftist vote was strongest in the south and southwest—the agrarian regions of poverty and of UGT and CNT strength—and also in the east, where the left was well organized and there was a historical tradition of opposition, as well as in much of the northern littoral and in Madrid. It was stronger particularly in most of the main cities, where masses were more readily mobilized. Anarchist participation was a real help in some areas, while in certain districts the Popular Front drew moderate or middle-class votes that had gone to the center-right in 1933 but had been alienated by the frustrations and repression of 1935.

The right, by contrast, did best in its typical strongholds of Catholics and smallholders in the north and north-center, though it had significant elements of strength in various parts of the country. The CEDA remained the largest single party, drawing at least 23.2 percent of all votes cast, whereas the Socialists drew 16.4 percent and the two main left Republican national parties a combined total of 19.6 (though admittedly it is different to sort out accurately the Socialist and left Republican vote, the difference being due in part to the greater number of left Republican candidacies). The CEDA's allies, however, added fewer votes, so that the CEDA gained only 19 percent of the seats with 23.2 percent of the vote, whereas the two main left Republican parties gained 27.2 percent of the seats with 19.6 percent of the vote.[18]

The elections were a disaster for the center, not so much because of a decline in the absolute number of votes as because of Alcalá Zamora's manipulations and the weak position of the center parties in those alliances they were able to form. Altogether, the various center and right-center candidates drew about 21 percent of the vote, down from 26.3 percent in 1931 and 22.3 percent in 1933, but in the first elections the center had often been allied with a victorious left and in the second with a victorious right. In 1936 the center parties had either to run independently or in some cases ally with a weaker right in provinces where the latter had less strength. The machinations of Alcalá Zamora had helped to destroy the only sizable center party, while the bizarre effort to substitute a novel ad hoc formation conjured by a strictly caretaker government failed completely. In half the provinces Portela was not even able to present candidates, while the Radicals were deserted en masse by their former voters. The tiny center

liberal parties of Miguel Maura and Sánchez Román were scarcely better off. Only eight of the seventy-eight Radical candidates were elected,
six as allies of the right, two as independents. Of these, three were later
denied seats by the Popular Front parliament, and one of the remaining
five became an independent, leaving only four Radicals under the leadership of Santiago Alba in the final Republican Cortes. Of all the changes of
behavior reflected by the 1936 elections, one of the biggest was probably
made by a sizable number of moderates who had previously voted for the
Radicals and now made up the most conservative wing of those voting for
the Popular Front. Radical voters were often more liberal than the party
leaders, and in the second round of balloting two weeks later, apparently
even more former Radical votes went to the left.[19] The center won a few
seats in alliance with the Popular Front in La Coruña and Lugo provinces
in Galicia, probably two of the most corrupt and manipulated contests.
Though the Basque Nationalists, who refused to band with either left or
right, maintained most of their ground, their vote declined from 1933.
In a generally polarized contest, none of the autonomist movements did
particularly well in and of themselves.

The absolute majority of seats won by the Popular Front represented a
breathtaking pendular swing from the 1933 results, yet this was the effect
of bloc voting for alliances and a heavily disproportionate electoral law,
the Spanish voting pattern in fact being considerably more stable than
the outcome in parliamentary seats made it appear. The great majority of
the votes were cast in much the same way as in 1933, the main differences
being the shift by former Radical voters and the partial participation of
CNT members. The main change was thus not so much toward extremes
of right and left as a shift from the center or right-center to left-center, together with the achievement of leftist electoral unity and somewhat greater
participation by the extreme left. Though impossible to measure, there
was also the phenomenon of the *voto útil*, the "useful vote" cast by an un-
determined number of moderates who figured that either the left or right
would win and did not want to waste their vote, casting it for the side they
opposed less. And the effects of the electoral law and alliance system exaggerated the results in many districts. In Madrid, despite a relatively close
popular vote, the Popular Front won fourteen seats, the right only four.
In Andalusia, where Cortes seats went very heavily to the left, the right
and center-right combined won about 45 percent of the popular vote.

Moreover, despite the massive representation of left and right and the partial disappearance of the center in parliament, the tendency of the vote was not so extreme as it appeared. The left Republicans led the Popular Front list, drawing the highest number of leftist votes in thirty-six provinces, compared with only eight for the Socialists. In Madrid, Azaña and the moderate Julián Besteiro, not the caballeristas, drew the largest number of votes, and altogether the left Republicans held 151 of the 263 Popular Front seats. Communist candidates invariably came in last on the list and in fact were overrepresented as a result of their success in gaining a surprising number of candidacies on victorious Popular Front tickets. The fascistic Falange drew only 46,466 votes, or scarcely more than one-half of one percent of the total, possibly the lowest voting percentage for a principal national fascist party in all Europe. Even so, it drew 7,500 votes in an Andalusian province such as Jaén, where, had its total been combined with the right, the Popular Front would have been defeated.[20]

Caballerista Socialists nonetheless argued, with the support of considerable evidence, that in fact the left Republicans had been deliberately overrepresented in the composition of the electoral lists to give them the parliamentary strength to form their own government. The consequence was somewhat to underrepresent the Socialists, at least by comparison with left Republicans,[21] while the CNT, by its own choice, was not directly represented at all.

Even so, the relative authenticity of the electoral map produced by the elections was confirmed five months later, when the Civil War began. The division of Spain into two armed camps roughly conformed to the electoral results.[22]

One of the most remarkable results was that ultimately seventeen of the twenty-two Communist candidates gained seats, though this was a consequence of the support of the caballeristas, who saw to it that the PCE, like the left Republicans, was overrepresented on the candidate lists. It was not necessary for voters in a given district to vote for all the names on a given alliance list; in fact, even when they won, Communist candidates drew fewer votes than did their left Republican and Socialist allies. The left, of course, was jubilant over the results, for they had converted a crushed insurrection into a decisive electoral victory. The Popular Front had scored its first major triumph in Europe—though in fact most members of the victorious left had little sense of the Popular

Front as a particular Communist strategy, as it was increasingly regarded abroad. Much more important was the fact that the victorious left spoke and acted as though they were totally oblivious of the fact that they had won fewer popular votes than the center and the right combined. They believed that they had won not a democratically qualified success, but an absolute mandate to work their will on Spain.

THE PRECIPITOUS RESIGNATION OF PORTELA VALLADARES

The electoral result at first stupefied the right, which had been fairly confident of victory, though none of the rightist spokesmen in the first days impugned the validity of a Popular Front triumph. The electoral mechanism of the Second Republic, though far from perfect, was generally fair and representative. The electoral process had been reasonably orderly, with exceptions: six people were killed in various parts of the country, and approximately thirty were injured. By the evening of 16 February crowds were demonstrating on behalf of the Popular Front in a number of cities. Several churches and other religious buildings were torched, with more serious disorders spreading on the day following. By midnight on the sixteenth the CEDA had received reports that civil governors were reluctant to control the crowds and that the latter were interfering with the recording of electoral results. Since no careful research has ever been done on this issue, it is impossible to say just how serious and widespread these disorders were.

The first reaction of the CEDA was very similar to that of the left Republicans in November 1933, the difference being that the reaction of the former was particularly triggered by the reports of rioting and interference, which had not taken place in 1933. In the early hours of 17 February both Gil Robles in person in Madrid[23] and Francesc Cambó by telephone from Barcelona[24] spoke with the prime minister, warning that major disorders were beginning that might affect part of the results, as well as constitutional order, urging him to suspend constitutional guarantees and declare martial law. The difference between Azaña's proposal in 1933 and that of Gil Robles in 1936 was that the latter did not propose holding any new elections—at least for the time being. Portela's account is that he replied that he, too, was profoundly disappointed and apprehensive, fearing that such intensely polarized elections might be the prelude to civil war, but that he could not function as dictator. He had presided over the electoral process and was reluctant to do anything that might invalidate it, however disappointing the results. Moreover, he was too old and had no ambition to rule by force. Third and perhaps most important, he had no political party or organized force of any consequence on which to rely, or any appropriate ideology for such a crisis, having been a lifelong liberal. Finally, though he feared the situation might deteriorate rapidly, the full effects would not be felt for some weeks or months, while in the immediate aftermath of the elections there would be little support for a dictatorship.[25] He therefore planned to resign as soon as possible after the registering of the electoral results on 20 February. When it was objected that this step was too precipitous and that Martínez Barrio had remained in office for a month after administering the elections of 1933, Portela insisted that the circumstances were entirely different, since Martínez Barrio had been a leader of one of the major winners in those elections and thus had the support of the second largest party in the new Cortes. Meanwhile, the steady expansion of disorder with each passing hour only strengthened his resolve to resign as soon as possible.

Army Chief of Staff General Franco also became increasingly alarmed. Late on the night of 16 February he telephoned the inspector of the Civil Guard, General Sebastián Pozas, urging the need to quell all disturbances, but, according to Franco's later testimony, Pozas refused to adopt any special measures. Later still, General Joaquín Fanjul came to the War Ministry to report that disorders were becoming extreme in some districts. After being contacted by Gil Robles, Franco awakened the minister, General Nicolás Molero, who allegedly agreed that he would urge the prime minister to declare martial law.[26] According to Gil Robles, however, the ultimate decision was made by Alcalá Zamora, who refused to declare martial law.

Alcalá Zamora presided over a special meeting of the council of ministers about noon on the seventeenth, immediately after a violent disturbance had been ended in Madrid. That day a number of mass jailbreaks took place in several parts of the country, followed by more the next day. Immediately after the meeting, Portela announced the imposition of a constitutional state of alarm, which included prior censorship, for eight days, and added in his press release that the president had already given him signed authorization to impose martial law whenever he might deem it necessary.[27] During the day civil governors resigned in three of the provinces in which disorders were most extensive, and military units were ordered into the streets of several cities to maintain order. According to the prime minister, Franco visited him around 7:00 P.M. to urge him "courteously and respectfully" not to resign but to remain in office indefinitely, making use of the martial law decree if need be. He promised the support of the army, but again Portela demurred.²⁸ Franco testified that he visited the prime minister about 2:00 P.M. on the eighteenth to insist that the situation was getting out of hand and that martial law must be imposed but that the prime minister simply replied that he must "sleep on it" (*consultar con mi almohada*). Franco added that later that afternoon several other senior commanders came to tell him that the army must act on its own, if necessary, but that he replied they must first consult their regimental commanders to determine the degree of support. Since many of the replies were negative, Franco refused to take any further initiative.²⁹

Portela has stated that at Gil Robles' insistence, he met the latter once more at a secluded spot on the highway at the northern edge of Madrid, again resisting his urging to remain in power and ignore the election results.³⁰ The latest news from around the country was even more discouraging, and on the eighteenth *El Socialista* insisted that he resign immediately. Portela became convinced that it would be very difficult to resist further the left's vehement, sometimes violent, insistence that all prisoners be released immediately and that the local government officials removed from office in 1934 be quickly reinstated. The leftist disorders and acts of violence had begun the night of 16–17 February and would continue with only brief abatement until the Civil War. Had Portela Valladares had the courage and resolution to impose martial law, the president would probably have supported him, since the caretaker ministry supervising elections was supposed to remain in office for several weeks thereafter to certify fully and terminate the electoral process, including the segunda vuelta, where necessary. Portela, however, was an old man who felt as though he had been left suspended in midair over a volcano; he arranged to meet Martínez Barrio that evening (18 February) in order to inform Azaña that Portela planned to resign within less than forty-eight hours. The news caused visible displeasure to the Republican Union leader, for he and his colleagues were not eager to assume immediate governmental responsibility for quieting the leftist masses.³¹

By the morning of the nineteenth the press had picked up rumors of military conspiracy and a possible coup that had first begun to circulate during the electoral campaign. When the cabinet met in mid-morning, new reports of demonstrations, church burnings, and prisoner takeovers or liberation in various jails were even more numerous than the day before, and the ministers agreed unanimously to resign at once. Portela was of the opinion that the left Republicans were encouraging the rioting, and that they should take responsibility for government as soon as possible. At the Ministry of the Interior en route to the presidential palace, he found Franco waiting to see him. Franco again insisted that Portela not resign but impose martial law. When the latter objected that parts of the army might not cooperate, Franco allegedly replied that units of the Legion and Moroccan Regulares could be moved in from Africa to stiffen discipline. Yet, though Portela agreed with much of what Franco told him,[32] his mind was made up.

Portela then went directly to Alcalá Zamora to present the resignation of the entire cabinet. The president resisted the impropriety of such a maneuver, insisting that the present government continue until the new parliament opened, if necessary imposing the state of martial law for which a decree had already been signed. In the face of Portela's refusal, Alcalá Zamora insisted on calling the entire cabinet to the presidential palace, but found that the only incumbent ministers willing to face the situation were the two armed forces commanders in charge of the Ministries of War and Navy, both of whom were excluded by the constitution from holding the position of prime minister. The government thus resigned on the nineteenth, not even waiting for the official recording of the electoral results that would take place on the morrow, bringing with it the mass exodus of many provincial governors and other local officials, who resigned in a panic without waiting for adequate replacements.[33]

The flight of Portela and his colleagues made a difficult situation much worse. Leftist street pressure had resulted in an immediate and unconstitutional leftist takeover before the electoral results had been properly registered, a fact that could only help the left further, though it may not have led to any immediate falsification of results. It would mean, however, that the electoral commission of the new Cortes would meet in March under the eye of a leftist government and act arbitrarily to take even more seats away from the center and right.[34]

CHAPTER EIGHT

The Left Returns to Power

THE NEW LEFT REPUBLICAN government under Azaña was quickly assembled and took over before the close of 19 February. Azaña was displeased with the unseemly haste of Portela's resignation, for it required the new administration to assume office well before the responsibilities of its predecessor had ended. He wrote in his diary: "The normal thing would have been for the government to wait until the Cortes meets before resigning. Today we do not even know the precise electoral results or how much of a majority we have. . . . We take over unexpectedly, a month before the Cortes convenes, and our situation will be the more delicate and difficult without the support of parliament. . . . I always feared that we would return to power in difficult conditions. They could not be worse. Once more we must harvest grain while it is still green."[1]

Since the new government had from the start been designed as an inevitably weak minority government composed exclusively of left Republicans, Azaña hoped to assemble as broad a representation of the latter as possible, reaching as far to the left-center as Martínez Barrio's Unión Republicana (which he partly distrusted as being composed mainly of former Radicals) and even to Felipe Sánchez Román, whom he continued to respect greatly even though the latter had withdrawn from the Popular Front. Sánchez Román rejected Azaña's offer, fearing correctly that the present concept of government was a design for chaos, and that under

185

existing circumstances the new ministry would be subject to intolerable pressure from the worker left. Yet again Sánchez Román proved correct, demonstrating that there was nothing in the least unforeseeable about the course of the new Azaña government, except that most of the left Republicans preferred not to see.

Of the thirteen members (including the prime minister), no less than ten were from Izquierda Republicana and its affiliates, two were from Unión Republicana, and one was a left-liberal Republican independent. Nearly all were professional men (mainly lawyers and professors), and several were from wealthy backgrounds. Azaña followed Portela's precedent in naming a general to the War Ministry in the person of the elderly Carlos Masquelet, a liberal and pro-Republican general who had been one of his advisers during 1931–1933. Masquelet also replaced Franco as chief of the General Staff.

Azaña addressed the nation by radio on the following afternoon (20 February). His message was perhaps the most conciliatory since he had first become prime minister in 1931, declaring that "the government speaks with words of peace. Its hope is that all the nation may share its goals of pacification and reestablishment of justice and peace. . . . So long as all limit themselves to the constitutional rights guaranteed each of us no one need fear the pressure of the government. Only he who is not at peace with the rule of law and public authority need fear the rigor of the government, which in no case will depart from its duties and the law. . . . The people can rely on our careful fulfillment of what we have promised. . . . Let us all unite under our national flag, where there is room for both Republicans and non-Republicans, and for all who are inspired by love for the fatherland, for discipline, and for respect for constituted authority."[2]

Public order was a problem from the first moment. Arson, vandalism, and demonstrations tinged with violence were reported in at least eleven provinces, and probably a good many more, with numerous attacks on local offices of rightist groups and even in some instances on those of the Radical Party. Violent jailbreaks to free leftist prisoners also sometimes freed common criminals, adding to crime and disorder. Azaña further noted on the twentieth that "people are going to take out their anger against churches and convents, and the result is that as in 1931, the government is born with scorching [con chamusquinas]. The result is deplorable. They are behaving just as though they had been paid by our enemies."[3]

As in 1931, however, he was little concerned to protect the churches and convents being torched. His choice for minister of the interior fell on the amiable and honest Amós Salvador of Izquierda Republicana, a well-liked architect and landowner of some wealth who lacked the energy and ability for so difficult a task.[4] For the key post of director general of security, the new government appointed José Alonso Mallol, a middle-aged former Radical Socialist who had served as civil governor of two different provinces during the first biennium. Mallol would subsequently acquiesce in the policy of restoring to their commissions various revolutionary Civil Guard and Assault Guard officers convicted of armed rebellion in 1934.

The most pressing task was to fulfill the campaign pledge of a general amnesty for imprisoned revolutionaries as soon as possible, for hundreds had already taken the law into their own hands in provincial jails.[5] The Diputación Permanente of the Cortes was hastily convened on 21 February and, with the cooperation of the right, quickly agreed to general amnesty for all those convicted or imprisoned for political and social crimes since the elections of 1933, conditions that also included the freeing of a number of Falangists amid the approximately 15,000 officially released on the following day.

The government then dissolved about half the municipal councils in Spain, in most instances reappointing members of the left who had been sacked in 1934, on the grounds that since the latter had in most cases been legally elected they should serve out the remainder of their term of office, regardless of whether they had been involved in armed rebellion. Similarly, new *comisiones gestoras* were appointed for all those (largely rightist) provincial governments where the first leftist administration had installed them during 1931–1933.[6] Civil governorships went primarily to left Republicans, but the Socialists (partly thanks to alliance with the Communists) gained more positions in municipal government than did any other party, particularly in the south. Though some of the civil governors tried to restrain the political purges of state employees on the provincial and local levels, in some parts of the country they failed completely. In Granada province, for example, some local municipal governments were simply forcibly seized by the Socialists,[7] a little like the actions of the Fascists in northern Italy in 1921–22.

Upon his release from prison, Lluis Companys, former president of the Catalan Generalitat, made a radio speech to his Catalan constituency that praised the insurrection of October, and refused to return to Barcelona until autonomy had been fully restored. After two long sessions, on 26 February the Diputación Permanente finally agreed to language that authorized the Catalan parliament to resume its functions and to elect a new president, which it did by once more selecting Companys on the same day. The full system of Catalan autonomy was quickly restored. While still in Madrid, Companys attended a large Socialist-Communist rally in the Plaza de Toros on 26 February, where he gave the clenched-fist revolutionary salute amid red flags and portraits of Lenin and Stalin.

He returned to Barcelona on 2 March to a euphoric mass greeting. Once more he hailed the alleged achievements of October and then restored nearly all the cabinet members who had gone down to defeat in the insurrection. Notable exceptions were the protofascist Catalan paramilitary leaders of that affair, the interior councillor Dencàs and the police chief Badía, who did not return. (The latter, together with his brother, would shortly be shot down by anarchist gunmen in one of the innumerable adjustments of accounts during that late winter and spring.) Henceforth Companys would look toward conciliation with a leftist Madrid and with the worker left inside Catalonia.[8] On 3 March the Tribunal of Constitutional Guarantees declared unconstitutional the legislation of 2 January 1935 that had annulled Catalan autonomy.

The Popular Front victory march in Madrid on 1 March was estimated to involve about 250,000 people. The Socialist and Communist components stood out with their thousands of uniformed youth, revolutionary emblems, and party anthems. More important, however, was the government's decree that day requiring all employers to rehire all workers fired for political reasons or for political strikes since the beginning of 1934, and to reimburse them for wages lost to the extent of not less than thirty-nine days' wages nor more than six months', depending on individual cases. Nothing was said with regard to the violent crimes that any workers might have committed against their employers, for which total immunity was provided. On the following day civil governors and district labor boards began to put the new law into effect. The Madrid Chamber of Commerce and Industry and other employer organizations protested that whatever had been done by employers had been fully legal under previous legislation, that they had violated no previously existing law, and that the new edict would generate chaos and crushing costs. Rightists would later claim that in at least one instance a widow left in charge of a business was forced to reemploy a worker responsible for her husband's death in a political altercation.

Second-round elections were held on 2 March. These were required wherever the leading ticket received less than 40 percent of the vote, but thanks to the alliance system this occurred in fewer provinces than in 1933, being required only in Castellón, Soria, and the Basque provinces. The right largely withdrew, so that the left did better than ever, though three of the five provinces were moderate districts. The right threw their support in the Basque country to the nationalists, who then won in Vizcaya and Guipuzcoa, while the two seats in Alava were divided. Altogether the Popular Front, which in the first round had led for only five seats in these five provinces, gained eight seats, the right (which had led for eleven) added only three, while the center (mainly Basque nationalists) gained nine, including a seat in Soria for Miguel Maura.

The initial response of the CEDA was conciliatory. Party leadership was temporarily left in the hands of the Christian democrat Giménez Fernández,[9] who told *El Adelanto* of Segovia on 22 February that the CEDA was simply "the right wing of the Republic" and would always act "within legality and under the Republic," as it had heretofore. During the first two weeks after the elections, *El Debate* outlined the terms of civil concord: obedience of the law, dissolution of all paramilitary militias as had been decreed in France two years earlier, a reasonable program of economic expansion that all could support, along with equal respect for Catholic education. When the CEDA national council met on 4 March, it declared that the vote totals had shown the party to be stronger than ever (which was technically correct), though with fewer deputies because of the way the alliance system had functioned. It promised to continue the "legal struggle" and would support the government "in whatever affected public order and the national interest," but would oppose "whatever was revolutionary."[10] At the first meeting of the new CEDA parliamentary delegation on 19 March, Giménez Fernández dramatically raised the question whether the party would support "democracy or fascism," and the CEDA delegation opted for democracy, though with the proviso that if democracy became impossible the party would be dissolved so that the members could go their own way (as eventually happened during the Civil War).[11] Giménez Fernández still hoped that it could become a fully Christian democratic conservative party, though he had already observed that at the time "anyone who does not allow himself to be run over is called a fascist." This circumstance inevitably stimulated people to say, "Well, if you have to run the risk of being called a fascist to avoid being forcibly dominated by those who are neither better nor more numerous, let them call us fascists."[12] In fact, already the youth group of one of the most democratic sectors of the party, the Derecha Regional Valenciana, was indeed going its own way, having begun secret talks with army officers about the possibility of armed rebellion. Though the official position of the party was clear, its more volatile youth were beginning to cross other boundaries.

After the new government took office, the level of disorder declined temporarily, and by the end of February there seemed to be a more positive mood, reflected by a slight rise in the stock market. This trend did not survive the first week of March, in which violence and disorder increased precipitously, remaining at a high level until the end of the month, when there was a slight improvement.

The biggest disturbance took place in Granada, where, allegedly in response to a violent incident by the right, a series of disorders and acts of property destruction was climaxed by a general strike and mass riot on 10 March, including the burning of the press and offices of the conservative newspaper *El Ideal*, as well as of rightist political centers, a number of churches, and at least two private homes. The violence spread to many of the smaller towns in the province, while in the city of Granada at least two people were killed. As Macarro Vera describes it, "The provincial governor had become so irresponsible as to give papers to the Socialist and anarchist militia as deputies of his authority, and in the days following they carried out searches of the homes of rightists,"[13] as though the conservatives were to blame for destroying their own property. The policy of the civil governor of Granada provided the first major instance of two initiatives that later became more common: authorization of revolutionaries to serve as auxiliary police, which guaranteed that the law would be even more severely abused; and the increasingly common tendency, after violence and disorders by the left, to arrest primarily only rightists, as though they were to blame for the disorders by the left. On this occasion, however, the government did react to the abuse of justice, sending a new governor who belonged to Unión Republicana. He disciplined all sides and had at least 300 people arrested, ranging from the criminals setting fires and destroying property to conservatives trying to protect themselves.[14]

Most of those killed in political assaults were rightists or nonleftists slain by leftists, though some leftists were also killed by rightists and Falangists. Most of the casualties suffered by the left were inflicted by the police trying to put down demonstrations and riots.[15] Salvador feebly tried to reassure public opinion that the situation was not as grave as it appeared, the worst incidents being perpetrated by "bands of youths" who were not members of political parties, which in some cases was technically true, though their political allegiance was clear enough. The main leftist leaders occasionally issued statements discouraging violence by their supporters, but the extremist youth groups were largely left free to act on their own.

The standard excuse of leftist leaders was that violence stemmed from provocations by the Falangists and the right, and that any actions by the left were simply responses to such provocations. For the most part, this was untrue, and with regard to the first weeks after the elections, totally false. The truth of the matter was more nearly the other way around. When violence came from Falangists (and occasionally from the right), it was at least initially in response to persistent violence from the left. Immediately after the elections, José Antonio Primo de Rivera declared a truce in propaganda attacks by his party against the new government and in other hostile acts against the left. In a manner typical of his poor political judgment, José Antonio was, like much of the left, captive to the myth of Azaña, whom he thought a potentially great leader who might begin to carry out the "national revolution."

The government and the revolutionaries responded with a determination to shut down fascism in Spain, a basic goal of the Popular Front. On 27 February local Falangist centers throughout the country were closed by police for illicit possession of arms by their members. No effort was made to check leftist centers. The government later acknowledged that "some fascists" had been killed in Almoradiel. On 6 March two members of the Falangist trade union, the Confederation of National Syndicalist Workers, who failed to support a leftist strike and were employed in the demolition of the old Plaza de Toros in Madrid were shot to death and two others gravely wounded, while four Falangist workers were killed that day in Galicia. On the following day, a member of the Falangist student syndicate, SEU, earlier shot in an attack on an SEU meeting in Palencia, died of wounds. On 11 March two young law students, one Falangist and the other Carlist, were shot to death in Madrid, allegedly by members of the Socialist Youth. Since the elections, fourteen Falangists had been killed in various parts of Spain, and others gravely wounded. In Madrid alone between 6 and 11 March, there had been four fatalities.[16] The major Falangist response was not, however, merely more of the same, but, as is frequent in such confrontations, a counterescalation. On the morning of 13 March several gunmen fired on the well-known Socialist leader and law professor Luis Jiménez de Asúa, one of the authors of the Republican Constitution. He managed to flee unharmed, but his police escort soon died of wounds. Since this was no longer a case of the right's being attacked by the left, but vice versa, the police made a serious effort to carry out arrests, jailing several Falangist students, though the real gunmen escaped by air to France.[17] Burial of the slain police escort then became the occasion for another demonstration and riot. A rightist newspaper office was set ablaze and never resumed publication, and two major churches in downtown Madrid were torched, one being completely gutted. However, the subsequent official statement by the Dirección General de Seguridad placed the matter in clearer perspective than have subsequent writers, relating the *atentado* on Asúa to the preceding deaths of "some fascists" in Almoradiel, the killing of the workers on the sixth, and of the students on the eleventh.[18] There was one fatality in the disorders attending the funeral of the police escort, and two Communists were said later to have been killed in a second Falangist attack.[19]

The attempt on Asúa represented something of an escalation, for amid all the violence of the Republican years the major party leaders, frequently accompanied by armed escort (at least since 1934), had scarcely ever been targets of direct assassination attempts. Azaña held a long meeting of the council of ministers, followed by an official statement urging calm and order. What was clear was that the *atentado* had come from Falangists, the only categorical fascist movement in the country, though small and isolated. Although the great bulk of the violence under the Republic had always come from the left, the Azaña government depended exclusively on leftist votes and reasoned that the abolition of the Falange would only improve public order and reduce the provocation and excuses of the revolutionaries. On 14 March the entire national leadership of the party, including José Antonio Primo de Rivera, were arrested, and a sweep was made of many leaders in the provinces as well. The official arrest report on José Antonio simply read "Arrested as a fascist," though no legislation existed which made it illegal to be a "fascist" any more than to be a Communist or anarchist. Three days later a Madrid court ruled the entire party an illicit organization for illegal possession of arms and violent activities. In this manner "fascism" would simply be abolished in Spain by decree. The whole affair was an example of the extreme politicization of justice under the leftist regime, for there was a long list of leftist organizations that had engaged in much more illicit possession of arms and violent activities than had the Falange, though none of them was outlawed. When the initial charges against José Antonio Primo de Rivera were nullified after appeal to a higher court, the government continuously filed new accusations against him, some of them of doubtful authenticity, in order to keep the Falangist leader under permanent detention, before finally executing him along with thousands of other Falangists after the Civil War began.

The Falange could no longer operate as a regular political movement, but the Republic was not yet a police state. Though the party was driven underground, new recruits far exceeded those arrested. These came especially from the JAP, now disillusioned with the moderate, legalist tactics of the CEDA. The outlawing of the party may have helped to effect a momentary decline in violence during the latter part of March, but Falangists were determined to retaliate, and the activities of the revolutionary left continued to expand. The rate of violence picked up again during April and thereafter continued at a high level.[20]

At the same time, the government was bewildered by the constant excesses of the revolutionary left. Azaña had somehow thought that his alliance with revolutionaries would not encourage revolutionary activity, that the worker parties would be content with radical parliamentary reformism once the left had gained full control of government. He wrote to his brother-in-law and best friend on 17 March: "We are headed downhill because of the persistent anarchy in many provinces, by the sly disloyalty of Socialist policy in many areas, by the brutality from various sources, by the ineptness of authorities, by the crazy actions of the 'Popular Front' in nearly every town, and by the nonsense that some of the Republican deputies of the majority are starting to speak." Azaña further lamented,

"I think there have been more than two hundred killed and wounded just since the government took power."[21]

On 27 March *Política*, the organ of Azaña's Izquierda Republicana, declared that "it becomes almost anodyne to repeat that fascism is not fearsome because of its numbers but because it can grow through demagogy and sterile agitation. Therefore any tactic founded on a theory of 'permanent revolution' has been discredited by its catastrophic results in Germany and other countries affected by fascism. . . . It is incomprehensible how forces that never stood for worker extremism [the Socialists] can repeat methods defeated elsewhere and fall victim to the illusion of a revolution that is bereft of the process described by Marx." Though leftists might (sometimes with good reason) grumble about conservative judges who were too lenient with imprisoned Falangists, the police were in fact much more rigorous with the latter than with the thousands of leftist lawbreakers, while more often than not overlooking leftists who attacked Falangists.[22]

Luis Romero has penned perhaps the best analytic summary of the dialectic of violence that unfolded during the late winter and spring of 1936:

> The government proved incapable of maintaining order, and bloody incidents—including deaths and severe wounds— stained all of Spain. Churches, monasteries, rightist centers, all manner of religious art of greater or lesser value were burned or sacked in widely scattered areas. In mid-March a furious iconoclastic assault in Yecla set fire to churches and particularly destroyed a large number of images. On the twenty-second the Liberal Democrat Alfredo Martínez, briefly a minister of labor in the first Portela government, was killed in Oviedo. On the morning of the thirty-first a nineteen-year-old medical student, Antonio Luna, described as being of "fascist" ideology, was shot at by three or four gunmen on leaving his home in the center of Madrid. That same day four individuals in Seville shot down Manuel Giráldez Mora, described as *afiliado al fascio* and who had worked as a dock foreman. . . .
>
> What happened was that the Republicans were required to pay for the victory which the Popular Front had given them. Only a very few times did the disorders stem from members of

Izquierda Republica or Unión Republicana; the authors of the assaults as of the arson and other acts of destruction were usually Socialists or Communists, and on occasion anarchists. And although it has been customary to blame the extremism on the followers of Largo Caballero, in moments of direct action those of Prieto did not remain behind.

Rightists also showed themselves capable of direct action, though in this period they usually acted . . . on the defensive. Primarily in the smaller towns supporters of the CEDA frequently took up weapons; depending on whoever drew up the report they might be given the label "fascist" pure and simple (whether as killer or victim), and there was no more to it. Rightist publicity drew attention to arson, destruction of property, or other horrors without explaining how they began; in some cases it could be verified that they were the consequence of the "death of a Socialist," or even two. . . . Falangists were also active, and from this time forward, even more so; in their cases they boasted of it then and afterward, which permitted other elements, who exercised greater discretion, to place all the blame on the Falange.

There has been so much exaggeration in books published during the Civil War and afterward that to accuse Falangists became a meaningless cliché. Some deliberately employed exaggeration as a political weapon, but others did so because they really believed. Later they simply copied each other.[23]

Romero observes further that rightists, especially outraged by anticlerical violence and destruction, used the religious issue to attract moderates and people of modest means: "The tolerance of the government, which reacted to the disorders only slowly and feebly, attracted to the right many Spaniards who, because of their weak economic position, precarious incomes, or meager social circumstances, had no reasons other than religious ones to join those who were their natural 'class enemies.' The bourgeois left which governed—rabidly anticlerical and with a high percentage of Masons among its leaders—thought it had found an escape valve for the left in attacks on the Church."[24]

Some sectors of the Republican left reacted with greater alarm than did the government. In mid-March governors of five different provinces resigned because of their inability to deal with these problems, and in some cases because they felt that the government itself was not making a serious effort to maintain order. Ultimately this situation raised the question of the future of the Popular Front. Technically no more than an electoral coalition, it had formally ceased to exist as soon as the elections were over. The parties that had made up the Popular Front were divided between the outright revolutionaries on the one hand and the left Republicans on the other, with the semimoderate, sometimes radical prietista Socialists in between.

The need for a new coalition for the municipal elections, scheduled to take place in March, revived the issue of continuation of the Popular Front. The left had always been stronger on the municipal level than on the national level, so that now the Marxist parties felt that their position was reversed from that of the candidacies for the Cortes elections, when the left Republicans had got the lion's share. Socialists and Communists demanded the majority of the candidacies for mayors and municipal council seats for themselves, and declared they were in no mood to give in. Azaña lamented to his brother-in-law on 29 March, "They have become so irresponsible as to say that they are doing so in order to dominate the Republic from local governments and proclaim dictatorship and the soviets," with the result that "neutral people are now scared to death. Panic about a Communist takeover is equivalent to panic about a military coup."[25] Yet, though severely irritated, Azaña was not yet profoundly disturbed, dismissing the revolutionaries' stance as "stupidity." It may indeed have been "stupidity," but the Marxist parties were dead set on it. The prime minister still blithely assumed that the Kerenskyist role that the latter assigned to the left Republicans was no more than theatrical posturing, when in fact it was their determined policy, and one for which, as events proved, he would have no answer.

Edward Malefakis has suggested cogently that the failure to take energetic measures to restore order at this stage was crucial, because it would have been easier to do in March than later on, when things got even more out of control.[26] The pattern of complacency and partisan administration of justice thus became a determined policy, which involved a crucial complicity in the escalation of partisanship and breakdown. Not all the wiser or more moderate members of Azaña's own party agreed with this approach. The distinguished medievalist and Izquierda Republicana leader Claudio Sánchez Albornoz, for example, posed the question whether the contradictions between the Popular Front parties were not so fundamental as to make the present government unviable. Before the end of March he spoke with Azaña about the need to work toward building a different, more moderate and stable, parliamentary majority, even if that meant doing without the support of the Socialists.[27] Indeed, such an alternative was probably the only democratic solution, but remained anathema to Azaña. He saw no hope of ever realizing his nineteenth-century petit-bourgeois utopia of anticlerical radicalism in the twentieth century without mass support from the Socialists. He was seemingly incapable of understanding that instead of restraining the revolutionary process, he had become its enabler.

THE MILITARY

Spain's perennial "problem of the military" had supposedly been solved by the Azaña reforms of 1931–1933, but the left soon found that this was not the case. At great expense, Azaña had resolved much of the problem of a perpetually swollen officer corps, but he and the left, generally, had made the "political problem" of the military worse with each passing year. The political intervention of the military had stemmed not from irrepressibly unnatural desires on the part of the military themselves, but from the persistent division, disorder, and lack of access in civilian politics and government. In 1930, when out of power, the Republicans had shown no reluctance to attempt a military revolt of their own, and the revolutionary process that they encouraged further polarized and radicalized political opinion. In 1931 the military had accepted what was presented to them as an orderly, united democratic polity. Growing disorder and disunion, however, together with the hostility of the left toward the military, stimulated an increasingly negative reaction.

Rather than transcending the errors of the past, the left was determined to repeat them. The old issue of military "responsibilities" that had played a major role during 1921–1923 and 1931 was thus resurrected by the Popular Front, in an even more partisan and politicized manner. Its demand for amnesty for all those involved in the October insurrection, regardless of the nature of their crimes, did not include military and police personnel charged with "excesses" during the repression. According to the twisted logic of the left, the former were justifiable acts of political expression, the latter crimes meriting punishment. Those who had rebelled against the legal order were blameless; those who had defended the constitutional regime might have committed crimes. While the latter proposition was entirely possible, there was no objective reason why it should have been judged by a different standard than the former. The left thus clearly prefigured the logic of the military rebels a few months later as they prosecuted for "military rebellion" precisely those army officers who had refused to participate in military rebellion.

Most outspoken on this issue was the vitriolic Dolores Ibárruri ("Pasionaria"), who had already gained fame as the leading propagandist of the burgeoning Communist Party. She declared in a speech of 1 March: "We live in a revolutionary situation that cannot be held back by legal obstacles, of which we have had too many since the fourteenth of April [1931]. The people impose their own legality, and on the sixteenth of February they asked for the execution of their assassins. The Republic ought to satisfy the needs of the people. If it does not, the people will cast it down and impose their will."[28] The Azaña government found that it could not resist these demands, echoed by almost every sector of the worker left, and on 10 March arrested General López Ochoa, the former inspector general of the army who had been commander of the Asturian campaign (in which, paradoxically, he had been criticized by military hard-liners as too lenient toward the rebels). A Civil Guard captain and several other officers were also arrested.

Discussions about the need for a military coup were not exactly a secret to government leaders, who reassigned all the top commands, placing nearly all of them in the hands of pro-Republican or at worst politically neutral senior commanders. Franco was removed as chief of staff and named military commander of the Canary Islands, where he would find it very difficult to conspire directly with other generals. Fanjul, former undersecretary, was left without assignment. General Goded, the director general of aeronautics, was similarly moved to the Balearic Islands, General Mola from command in Morocco to the twelfth brigade in Pamplona, and so on down the line. After reassignments had been completed in mid-March, one estimate calculated that of the twenty-two top commands in the army, fourteen were held by loyal Republicans, four by conservatives, and only three by potentially active conspirators. Much the same policy was followed with regard to Civil Guard officers. A decree of 21 March opened the category of *disponible forzoso* (without assignment) for officers under suspicion, and during the five months down to 18 July the government shifted 206 of the corps's 318 captains, 99 of the 124 majors, 68 of the 74 lieutenant colonels, and all 26 colonels.[29] The leftists earlier expelled from the army and police units for involvement in the events of 1934 were restored by decrees of 22 February and 2 March.

Hatred of the military was so intense among the left that there were frequent cases of public insult to army officers and even a few instances of physical assault. Azaña noted in his diary that a young aide to the new minister of war, a junior officer of irreproachable conduct, had been shoved around by a leftist crowd, and on 13 March the minister of war issued a note expressing "indignation about unjust aggression" against officers, urging the latter not to allow themselves to be provoked. The ministry also denied publicly that there was any danger from the "military conspiracies" being rumored and declared that the military deserved the respect and support of all, being "the strongest support of the Republican state."[30] This position may seem rather fanciful in view of later developments, but at that point it made sense to the government, which would need the support of the military in its delicate balancing act between leftist revolutionism and a renewed Republican radicalism that must somehow remain constitutional.

The government had indeed ensured the loyalty of most top commanders. The eventual rebellion of 18 July would be supported at the active command level only by the director general of Carabineros (Gonzalo Queipo de Llano), two of the major generals (Miguel Cabanellas and Franco), and two of the brigadiers (Goded and Mola). Yet the shift in assignments alone was hardly enough to prevent conspiracy, which had begun among the hard-core right in the military on the evening of 16 February and never ceased thereafter.

A semisecret organization did exist, the Unión Militar Española (UME), and by the spring of 1936 it claimed 3,436 members, or about one-fourth of the officer corps, together with the support of 1,843 retired officers and 2,131 noncommissioned officers.[31] The political coloration of the UME was antileftist, but beyond that its program was vague. It had certain qualities of a military trade union, but it lacked tight structure and leadership and thus was not an effective instrument of conspiracy.

A more directly political leftist counterpart, the Unión Militar Republicana Antifascista (UMRA) had been created in 1935 by fusing the Unión
Militar Republicana (created in Morocco the preceding year) and the very
small, clandestine Communist-led Unión Militar Antifascista. The UMRA
had no more than a few hundred members, but among them were two
generals, including the new director general of aeronautics, Miguel Núñez
de Prado. Masonic membership was also important in the UMRA, whose
two main branches were in Madrid and Barcelona.[32]

On 8 March some of the leading antileftist commanders held a meeting in Madrid at the home of a CEDA leader who was a reserve officer.[33]
Five hours of talk failed to produce full accord or a detailed plan of action,
though the participants agreed to be ready to rebel if the revolutionary
sector of the Socialists took power or there was a grave emergency threatening complete breakdown. The retired General Rodríguez del Barrio was
left to serve as a kind of liaison and organizer in Madrid, but his efforts
during the next month only led to the imprisonment of two commanders
and produced no results. A vague deadline of 20 April came and went
without consequence. General Sanjurjo was conceded a certain seniority
among rebels, but he lived in Portugal and made little effort to organize
anything himself.[34]

Thus by the early spring multiple strands existed but no effective
plot. Until he fell ill, Rodríguez del Barrio tried to coordinate schemes in
Madrid with several other generals, Sanjurjo vegetated in semi-isolation in
Lisbon, Franco took a command out in the Atlantic Ocean, and the various
UME groups remained uncertain and without central organization. The
Carlists semisecretly trained their own militia but were noteworthy only
in Navarre. The Falange had been legally dissolved, its members driven
underground. Even so, they rapidly increased in numbers. Some of the JAP
were now turning toward the Falange and in a few areas making their own
paramilitary plans, but after 19 February the CEDA had quickly returned
to legality. Calvo Sotelo and the more extreme monarchists preached a
corporative dictatorship sponsored by the military but lacked significant
support, either civil or military.

The prime minister and minister of war hesitated to purge the military directly, for several reasons. On the one hand, Azaña and his colleagues held army officers in low esteem and doubted their ability to
organize an effective revolt. On the other, government leaders dared not

abandon altogether efforts at coexistence with the right. The additional paradox was that the army was ultimately the only protection of the Azaña government from its subversive allies of the revolutionary left, should the leftist relationship break down completely, an entirely possible eventuality. Thus the government hesitated to go beyond tepid gestures such as a decree of 18 April that allowed it to suspend the pension of any retired officer found to belong to an illicit organization, such as the Falange. The government was playing with fire, or more precisely, was playing with two different fires, but that was a policy deliberately chosen by the left Republicans. They feared to try to extinguish either fire altogether for fear that the other would get out of control. This policy, such as it was, continued for five months until it ended in disaster.

THE DEEPENING SOCIALIST SPLIT

The electoral victory only deepened the tensions within Socialist ranks. The prietistas continued to maneuver for a semimoderate course in alliance with left Republicans, while caballeristas steadfastly vetoed any participation in government, and even, in some cases, mere cooperation with it. They insisted on a radical policy that would seek alliance with the Communists, and even with the CNT.

The main internal issue facing Socialists was first of all their own national leadership, since Largo had resigned his position in December and the present executive commission was more than three years old, having been chosen after the Thirteenth Party Congress of October 1932. On 8 March new elections for the leadership of the Madrid section of the party were won by the caballeristas—who usually referred to themselves as *de izquierdas* (leftists) or "Marxist revolutionaries"—by a margin of three to one. The left Socialists thus held control of the Madrid section of the party and most of the UGT, their main base of support. The prietistas—otherwise called *centristas*, or "moderates"—held control of the national party apparatus, direction of the party daily *El Socialista*, the strong Basque section of the UGT,[35] and much of the Asturian section of the UGT. Yet after the resignation of Largo and three supporters from the executive commission, the withdrawal of two other members meant that the executive commission consisted of Prieto and four supporters, altogether less than half the nominal membership. A new party congress would be crucial. The caballeristas insisted that it be held in their Madrid stronghold, while the prietistas opted for delay and a possible autumn congress in Asturias, where they were stronger. The result was stalemate, with neither leftists nor semimoderates able to impose their policy on the other.

The strategy of the left Socialists was to force the Azaña government, after swiftly completing its putatively Kerenskyist task, to give way to a Socialist government, presumably (though never clearly) by legal means. Since the party held only a fifth of the votes in parliament, a Socialist-led revolutionary government would have to be a coalition supported by the Communists but also by others; in its initial stages it would require the voting support of the left Republicans, as well. In other words, the existing relationship of the Socialists and left Republicans would have to be reversed. There was no plan or preparation for a direct revolutionary takeover, despite much rhetoric about the "dictatorship of the proletariat." The only other alternative considered was the necessary response to a military or rightist coup attempt, which would take the form of a revolutionary general strike, followed by transfer of power to a Socialist-led regime.

THE ROLE OF THE COMMUNISTS

In this situation the Communist Party was able to play a significant role for the first time. Seventeen Communist deputies made the party a minor parliamentary force, and Communist influence was also bolstered by close relations with the Socialist Youth, the assistance provided to victims of the repression by Socorro Rojo Internacional (International Red Relief), and a multitude of front and auxiliary organizations, from women's, cultural, and sport groups to the now rapidly growing and prestigious Amigos de la URSS.

After the elections a PCE delegation hurried to Moscow, where the Comintern leadership prepared a new document to guide the Spanish party in what was termed the "Revolution being developed in Spain." Even though the Azaña government was not a true Popular Front government but simply a "bourgeois government of the left," it should be both supported and pressured in the right direction. The Comintern directive stated that "it is necessary to present a platform of demands with the goal of isolating Acción Popular [CEDA] and the other reactionary parties from their base and undermining their economic support," leading to large-scale confiscations. Equally or more important was "to develop a mass movement outside parliament," making Worker Alliance groups "genuine collective mass organs of a worker-peasant democracy" and gaining recognition for them as "legally recognized government organs."[36] Or, as Antonio Elorza and Marta Bizcarrondo put it, "under the cover of supporting the Popular Front, what Manuilsky proposed was a new version of the preparations for the Soviet revolution."[37] Dmitri Manuilsky, head of the Comintern executive commission, also prepared a letter to José Díaz, secretary of the PCE, who had remained in Madrid, to stress that "the next few weeks are the ones that will have major, perhaps decisive significance" for "the very fate . . . of the democratic revolution in Spain," requiring mass mobilization, aggressive action, and party unification with the Socialists.[38]

Mundo Obrero declared two days after the elections that "we must follow the path of completing the democratic-bourgeois revolution until it leads us to a situation in which the proletariat and the peasantry assume responsibility for making the Spanish people as free and happy as the Soviet people through victorious realization of socialism by means of the dictatorship of the proletariat." (These words, written less than three years after the mass famine and destruction wrought by Soviet collectivization, and on the eve of the Great Terror, read today almost as a macabre exercise in black humor.) The party newspaper then came out with new demands on 25 February:

- Confiscation of all lands not yet in the hands of the peasants, which the latter may work either individually or collectively
- Cancellation of all peasant debt, increase in wages, and reduction of the workday
- Nationalization of industrial enterprises, banks, and railroads
- Liberation of oppressed peoples: Catalonia, Vizcaya [sic], Galicia, and Morocco
- Suppression of the Civil Guard and Assault Guard
- Arming of the people
- Suppression of the regular army and liquidation of officers; democratic election of commanders by soldiers
- Fraternal alliance with the Soviet Union

The Communist line was thus perfectly frank. There was no "Trojan horse" pretense of merely supporting bourgeois democracy. Instead, the minority left Republican government should be pressed to complete rapidly the program of the Popular Front, after which the left should quickly move to the more radical program advanced by the PCE, carrying out large-scale confiscation of land, nationalization of basic industry, destruction of the existing police and armed forces, and—if not already accomplished—the political elimination of the conservative parties and the mass arrest of their most active elements. Vittorio Codovilla, Comintern adviser in Spain, opined that the weakness of the minority left Republican government would prove to be a great advantage, enabling it to be guided along rapidly and then replaced.[39] This judgment, at least, proved to be fully correct. After the broadening of the left and the elimination of the right, the left Republican government must give way, as explained in a *Mundo Obrero* editorial of 24 February, to a "worker-peasant government." This sequence obeyed the classic Marxist-Leninist scheme in which a worker-peasant government, once the final phase of the democratic revolution had been completed, would initiate the direct transition to socialism, though it would not itself constitute the dictatorship of the proletariat and the full construction of socialism. In a joint PCE-PSOE meeting just before the elections, Díaz had emphasized the difference between the latter and the initial worker-peasant government.[40] Though the PCE wanted to move rapidly toward a worker-peasant government, it nonetheless continually reproached the caballeristas for premature references to the dictatorship of the proletariat.

Contrary to the notion often advanced that the Communists occupied a moderate position in the Popular Front, PCE spokesmen were normally the most vigorous, and usually the most coherent, of all sectors in demanding completion of the Popular Front program immediately so as to move rapidly beyond it. The most extreme statements were often made by Ibárruri, as in her public speeches demanding immediate "revolutionary justice" against the CEDA and those in power in 1934. She and other Communist spokesmen insisted on not merely the arrest of everyone in positions of authority when the democratic constitution had been enforced in 1934 but also the official outlawing of conservative and rightist parties,[41] a major step toward consolidation of the "new type" people's republic as defined by the Comintern's Seventh Congress. Other revolutionary groups made similar demands, though not in such consistently orchestrated style. Outlawing of the Falange in mid-March was seen as the first step in outlawing all rightist organizations.

The PCE was still not a mass party, but its significance had grown disproportionate to its numbers. Comintern discipline made it a totally united party, in complete contrast to the fragmented Socialists. Soviet assistance provided ample financial support for mass propaganda and broader mobilization, as well as a subtle (and cynical) capacity for maneuver that was beyond any of the other Marxist parties. Moreover, as a Comintern movement it could invoke the Soviet experience of Communist struggle and triumphant revolution that gave it a dynamic, rapidly growing appeal, to that extent unequaled by any other revolutionary organization.

Outside parliament, however, it was sometimes the POUM and left Socialist spokesmen who made the most sweepingly extreme statements, declaring that Spain would soon be ready for the dictatorship of the proletariat, without making the distinctions and qualifications of the PCE concerning all the more limited preliminary steps. One of the most categorical spokesmen was, as usual, Luis Araquistain (who in only one more year would find himself in violent opposition to the Communists). During the electoral campaign Araquistain had delivered a lecture in Madrid on "The Historical Parallel between the Russian and Spanish Revolutions," a position that he continued to elaborate during the months that followed. He flatly denied the contention frequently made by Besteiro that only the historically unparalleled prior disintegration of civic institutions had made possible the Bolshevik takeover in Russia. Araquistain similarly derided Besteiro's analysis (which repeated the earlier Menshevik analysis regarding Russia itself) that Spain had not yet completed the prior development of capitalism outlined by Marx. According to Araquistain, "history, like biology, is full of leaps." The current underdevelopment of Spain was supposedly equivalent to that of Russia in 1917, making Spain ripe for revolution. The events of 1931–1934, particularly the last year, constituted "Spain's revolution of 1905." Its middle classes and conservatives were weak, while the Republic itself had done no more than create "a weak state" that could no longer resist revolution. "These undeniable objective facts lead me to think that Spain might very well become the second country where the proletarian revolution triumphs and is consolidated, while I do not worry especially about counterrevolutionary dangers from abroad. The great powers around us are too preoccupied with their own problems. . . . In the final analysis, the Soviet Union would not permit other European states to intervene in a socialist Spain." Hence "the historical dilemma is fascism or socialism, and only violence will decide the issue," but given the weakness of "fascism" in Spain, socialism would win.[42]

Araquistain returned to the theme in the March number of his monthly *Leviatán:* "In Spain historical conditions are extremely similar to those of Russia at the end of the nineteenth and the beginning of the twentieth centuries: a capitalism already in its financial phase, without a haute bourgeoisie capable of effective leadership and with a petite bourgeoisie lacking political parties, that will have to end up coming to the Socialists; a weak state and a proletariat eager for power, conscious of its historical mission, and with a capacity for revolution like no other in the world outside Russia, and cured, also like no other, of all illusions about democracy under a capitalist regime."

RELATIONS BETWEEN THE REVOLUTIONARY PARTIES

Following Comintern instructions, leaders of the PCE gave special priority to the "triple unification" with the Socialists, meaning unification of the parties, the trade unions, and the youth organizations. In mid-November 1935 the executive commission of the UGT had officially accepted the entry of the small Communist CGTU into the Socialist trade union organization, but months were required to carry out the process, which still had not been completed by March 1936. More promising for the Communists was the keen interest of the JS (Socialist Youth) leaders in promoting rapid unification for their group. Comintern bosses were in fact concerned about the irresponsible extremism and possible Trotskyism of JS activists; they underlined the requirement that a united youth organization accept direction from the Comintern and recognize the leadership of both Stalin and the USSR as homeland of true socialism; but as early as 21 February Codovilla was able to telegram that the JS leaders accepted all these requirements. A small delegation headed by the JS leader Santiago Carrillo then immediately went to Moscow, where his combination of prudence, firmness, and revolutionary zeal evidently made a good impression;[43] in turn Carrillo and the other Young Socialists were even more impressed by the center of Soviet power, and by Manuilsky's advice about the way to adjust the revolutionary process to the situation in Spain.[44]

On 4 March the PCE's central committee sent a long letter to the executive commission of the PSOE, proposing formation of Worker Alliance groups, led by Socialists and Communists, but "freely and democratically constituted," at every level. To that date the AOs had generally languished, but they remained high on the Comintern agenda, and could become the instrument for the joint action of the two principal Marxist parties, the goal being "rapid execution of the pact of the Bloque Popular and the struggle for our own program of a worker-peasant government." The latter would involve the frequently mentioned large-scale land confiscations; nationalization of large industry, banks, railroads, and transportation; major social reforms; "national liberation" of Catalonia, the Basque Country, and Galicia; immediate unrestricted liberation of the Moroccan Protectorate; dissolution of the army, Civil Guard, and Assault Guard; and "proletarian solidarity with the oppressed of the entire world and fraternal alliance with the Soviet Union." This twelve-point program was almost identical with the party's earlier thirteen-point program, save for elimination of the point calling for financial aid to smallholders. The worker-peasant government was thus to establish an economic structure similar to that of the Soviet Union under the New Economic Policy of 1921–1928.

Moreover, the central committee proposed formation of liaison committees at all levels to begin the merger of the two organizations into "the Marxist-Leninist single party of the proletariat," on the programmatic basis of "complete independence from the bourgeoisie and complete rupture of the social-democratic bloc with the bourgeoisie, with prior achievement of unity of action; recognition of the need for the revolutionary overthrow of the domination of the bourgeoisie and installation of the dictatorship of the proletariat in the form of soviets; renunciation of any support for the bourgeoisie in case of an imperialist war; construction of the party on the basis of democratic centralism, assuring unity of will and of action, tempered by the experience of the Russian Bolsheviks."[45]

During the electoral campaign the sixty-six-year-old Largo Caballero had stressed that the left Socialists were not separated from the PCE by "any great difference. What am I saying! By no difference!" He added, "The fundamental point: the conquest of power cannot be done through bourgeois democracy." Largo had lamented that "there were even Socialists" who failed to perceive the beauty of a Socialist-Communist dictatorship and still "speak against all dictatorship."[46]

On 5 March, the day after the Communist letter, the caballerista executive committee of the UGT proposed to the Socialist Party apparatus and the JS that a new joint committee be formed of two representatives from each of the worker parties in the Popular Front, to join forces to carry out the Popular Front program. On the sixteenth the Madrid section of the party, now also dominated by the caballeristas, adopted a statement declaring that "there is no alternative to establishment of revolutionary socialism" through the "dictatorship of the proletariat. . . . The organ of that transitory dictatorship will be the Socialist Party." It would secure the unity of all the proletariat and present a program roughly similar to that announced by the PCE for a worker-peasant government, the Madrid section hoping to gain complete support for this agenda at the next party congress. A few days later it announced that it would urge the party congress to give priority to creation of a united party with the Communists.

The extremely small besteirista sector of the Socialist Party was in despair. That same month the besteirista Gabriel Mario de Coca completed the manuscript of a short book denouncing "the Bolshevization of the Socialist Party." He concluded:

> I close my work with the impression of Bolshevist victory in every sector of the party. The Socialist parliamentary minority will be impregnated with a strong Leninist tone. Prieto will have few deputies on his side while Besteiro will be completely isolated as a Marxist dissenter. . . .
>
> The outlook that all this leaves for the future of the working class and of the nation could not be more pessimistic. The Bolshevik centipede dominates the proletariat's horizon, and Marxist analysis indicates that it is on its way to another of its resounding victories. So that if in October 1934 it only achieved a short-lived Gil Robles government accompanied by suspension of the constitution and the most horrible, sterile shedding of working-class blood, it can now be expected to complete its definitive work in the future.[47]

This prophecy, accurate as a long-term prognosis, nonetheless exaggerated the problem as of March 1936. Prietista domination of the Socialist Party apparatus meant that Communist proposals would be stonewalled for the time being. No process of unification of parties in fact ever began, while the internal chasm between caballeristas and prietistas continued to broaden. On 19 March *Claridad* published the goals of the caballeristas—a worker regime, collectivization of property, "confederation" of the "Iberian nationalities," and dissolution of the regular army—but these were not accepted as working goals by the prietista leadership.

Communist fusion tactics were successful only with the Socialist Youth. On 5 April the Juventudes Socialistas Unificadas (United Socialist Youth; JSU) was officially created, merging the 40,000 or more members of the Socialist Youth with their 3,000 Communist counterparts on terms that amounted to a Communist takeover.[48] Until that date Communist leaders continued to make ardent revolutionary proposals; on 1 April *Mundo Obrero* insisted: "All power must go to the worker and peasant alliances, which with national scope will be the organs responsible for exercising the dictatorship of the proletarian class, rapidly surpassing the bourgeois democratic stage, transforming it into a socialist revolution."

The Communists proposed to deal with the CNT primarily through expansion of the AO. The caballeristas were more directly interested in joint action with the anarchosyndicalist confederation, but the CNT was wary and tended to rebuff UGT overtures, especially when these suggested a possible fusion of the two large worker movements. CNT spokesmen lamented that "no one ever knows how it would be structured, and frequently it is oriented toward the absorption"[49] of the anarchosyndicalists. By contrast with the persistent Marxist-Leninist prophecies of caballeristas, Communists, and POUMists, CNT spokesmen always insisted that "the Spanish revolution must be of a libertarian type."[50] Nonetheless, by the spring of 1936 there was more fraternal feeling between CNT and UGT members than there had been for many years. The common experience of repression had brought them closer together, as did the common expectation of decisive new victories. There would be many joint UGT-CNT strikes that spring, even though strong rivalry would remain, as well.

THE COMISIÓN DE ACTAS

The Cortes opened on 15 March with a pro forma session presided over by the *presidente de edad* (oldest member), a well-known rightist from Cádiz. His refusal to close the session with "Viva la República!" led to tumult, and Communist deputies sang the "Internationale" in the Spanish parliament for the first time. Thirty-three political parties were represented. There had been a large turnover of deputies, as in 1931 and 1933, with a host of new faces. Even among the Socialists, who with the CEDA enjoyed the greatest continuity in size of delegation, nearly half the party's deputies

were new to parliament. The Cortes approved continuation of the existing state of alarm for another thirty days (it would in fact remain in place
until the beginning of the Civil War), and on the following day Martínez
Barrio was elected president (speaker). More incidents followed, and on
20 March several leftist deputies had to be physically restrained from assaulting a conservative member.[51]

Under the Republican system, the first major task of a new parliament was to elect a *comisión de actas* (electoral commission) to review the
electoral results and determine if they should be cancelled or reversed
in any district on account of fraud or other improprieties. This meant in
effect that the victors in each election had the power to sit in judgment on
the losers and determine if their parliamentary representation should be
reduced still further. This power had been exercised with moderation by
the center-right in 1933, but the Popular Front, consistent with its intention to eliminate all political opposition it could, intended to conduct a
sweeping review of all the districts won by the center and right in 1936.
The extreme left demanded cancellation of nearly all rightist victories,[52]
judging, as *El Socialista* put it on 20 March, that "not a single deputy of the
right can say that he won his seat fairly." Membership of the commission
was voted on 17 March with a heavy leftist majority.

As Carlos Seco Serrano has explained it, "The leftist majority in parliament was not so absolute as to provide the complete quorum required for
the automatic approval of legislation. The Comisión de Actas would soon
act to correct this, reassigning a number sufficient to beat all the records
of the old monarchist regime in manipulation."[53]

In the words of Madariaga, "With a majority won, it was easy to make
it overwhelming. . . . All results were annulled in certain provinces where
the opposition had won, while friendly candidates who had lost were
declared elected. Thus various deputies from the minority were evicted
from parliament. This was not merely the result of blind and sectarian
passion but the execution of a deliberate plan of broad scope. Two results
were sought: to make of parliament a convention, smash the opposition,
and guarantee the strength of the most moderate sectors of the Popular
Front."[54]

The commission began on 24 March by annulling the election of
two conservative candidates in Burgos and Salamanca, both conservative
districts. When rightist deputies asked for investigation of the close leftist

victory in Valencia and the Popular Front triumph in Cáceres, their request was ignored. Giménez Fernández demanded that all results be judged by the same standard, and on 31 March the rightist deputies temporarily withdrew from parliament.

The nearest thing to a clear example of fraud and coercion may have been the election in Granada. As Macarro Vera says, "In view of the results of all the previous elections in this province, fraud had every likelihood of having been carried out."[55] Since the change in government, 10,298 firearms had been confiscated in the province, mainly from the right. At the time of the elections, rightists had apparently employed all the notaries in Granada, so that the left had to rely on "temporary certification of state employees" to verify the voting. Seventy affidavits were obtained from citizens of Granada attesting to threats of force, economic pressures, and vote fraud. In a number of poor pueblos no votes were recorded for the left, while in one mountain town (Huéscar), all 2,000 votes were recorded for the right.[56] Altogether, the left alleged 55,000 false votes. The right contended there were no more than 3,000, saying that the left was trying to throw out all the votes in certain districts, whereas evidence presented by the latter, even if accurate, presented grounds for challenging only 16,000, which would still not be enough to give them victory. Though a full and careful examination of all evidence was not completed, the results were annulled and new elections mandated.[57] A similar verdict was rendered for Cuenca province, where it was judged that if all fraudulent votes were thrown out, the victorious right would hold less than the required 40 percent, though in this case the evidence was more dubious and the Basque Nationalists refused to vote with the majority as they had done previously.

The region of Galicia had the worst record for electoral manipulation, but the Radicals, who had won the minority in Pontevedra, were unsuccessful in obtaining any reexamination of the Popular Front majority vote there. The leftist triumph in La Coruña was procedurally somewhat dubious, but Azaña refused to consider annulment, because it might leave his crony Santiago Casares Quiroga without a seat. There was much more interest in annulling the rightist vote in Orense, for that would deprive Calvo Sotelo of his place. Ibárruri's incendiary and scurrilous speech encouraging the commission to throw out this vote proved too overheated, however, and was counterproductive. Calvo Sotelo was himself allowed to speak and made a telling address. He pointed out the unlikelihood of there having been as many as 106,000 fraudulent votes, as alleged by the Communists, and dwelled on the contradictions in the review process. If Spain were to have a Marxist or totalitarian dictatorship, elections would be of no consequence, he said, but if a democratic Republic were to continue, it could do so only on the basis of respecting electoral results. He concluded by comparing the current purge with Hitler's elimination of Communist deputies after he became chancellor, and this analogy seemed to give the left Republicans some pause. The majority reconsidered, much to the anger of the extreme left, and Calvo Sotelo was permitted to keep his seat.

The final result was complete annulment of the elections in Cuenca and Granada, both of which the right had won, and partial annulments affecting one or more seats in Albacete, Burgos, Ciudad Real, Jaén, Orense, Oviedo, Salamanca, and Tenerife. New elections would be held in the first two provinces; elsewhere seats were simply arbitrarily reassigned to the Popular Front majority, though the center also gained a few seats, and in Jaén a seat taken from the Radicals was awarded to the CEDA so as not to appear totally partisan. No evidence was produced of clear, overt fraud except in Granada and perhaps in parts of Galicia.[58] Irregularities in Galicia were mostly ignored, since there they had benefitted the Popular Front more than the right. In no case was a seat taken from the left. The right charged that the elections had been stolen by the left in four or five provinces where the disorders of 17–20 February had made it possible to falsify the results, and Alcalá Zamora was of the same opinion. This accusation was categorically denied by the Popular Front deputies on the commission, and the charges were never investigated. Altogether 32 seats changed hands. Martínez Barrio's relatively small Unión Republicana benefitted more than any other single party. After all these reassignments, the final composition of the Cortes was 277 seats for the left, 60 for the center, and 131 for the right. Electoral fraud had been frequent in the history of parliamentary government in Spain, but this explicit and highly formalized reassignment of voting results was without precedent.

During these proceedings the chairman of the commission, Indalecio Prieto, resigned, not because he objected to disqualifying rightist votes in principle, but because he felt that the Popular Front majority was simply going too far. He also would have preferred to see a more nonpartisan investigation of the electoral process in Galicia, though there Alcalá Zamora

THE LEFT RETURNS TO POWER 213

seemed at first as concerned to protect the machinations of the Portela administration as the Popular Front was those of the left.[59]

The final judgment by the most thorough study of the 1936 elections concludes:

> If irregularities did not alter the proportionate total votes
> gained by each side, the number of seats . . . was gravely
> affected by the work of the Comisión de Actas, which can accu-
> rately be called distressing. If it is more appropriate to accuse
> the right at that time of having a mentality more reactionary
> than conservative and of having exploited the most politically
> ignorant sector of the electorate, it is also appropriate to charge
> the left with looking more toward momentary benefits than
> to the long term and of acting in a totally partisan manner in
> determining the validity or invalidity of the voting. The left
> should have understood that, in the long run, they would have
> benefitted more from the consolidation of the democratic sys-
> tem than from creating a momentarily large majority, encour-
> aging the right to adopt the path of subversion. Moreover, this
> was especially the responsibility of the left Republicans, since
> the Communists and a large number of the Socialists had al-
> ready placed themselves outside the democratic system. It was
> the left Republicans, who theoretically constituted the firmest
> support of the Republic, who benefitted most from the redistri-
> bution of seats and who, even so, were subsequently incapable
> of facing up to extremism in the new Cortes directly. Finally, it
> was the left Republicans who, after the personal intervention of
> Azaña to prevent the exclusion of Calvo Sotelo, made reference,
> in the words of one of their deputies, to the "need to sacrifice."
> That phrase is sufficiently expressive of their abandonment of
> democratic practice.[60]

This time Alcalá Zamora agreed with the right:

> Though the Popular Front's parliamentary delegation was
> near an absolute majority, certainly with more than 200 seats,
> it still failed to achieve a majority in the voting. It achieved
> an absolute majority, and an overwhelming one, in the

postelectoral administration, full of violence and manifest illegality. . . .

The flight of civil governors and their tumultuous replacement with anonymous and even irresponsible appointees permitted the registration of votes to be made by amateurs, mailmen, wandering workers, or simply by crooks with whom anything was possible. . . . And in the second-round elections on 1 March, even though few seats were involved, fraud was employed, and the government got what it wanted. How many results were falsified? . . . Cáceres could not be denied . . . and with regard to . . . all Galicia, as was also the case unfortunately with Almería, all the results should have been nullified even though they appeared to be properly registered. The most general calculation of the number of postelectoral changes would be eighty seats, though of that approximate number . . . not all were done for the benefit of the Popular Front, since the price of complicity was to give some to the opposition. . . .

The worst and most audacious frauds were carried out by the Comisión de Actas. . . . In the parliamentary history of Spain, never very scrupulous, there is no memory of anything comparable to what the Comisión de Actas did in 1936.[61]

CHAPTER NINE

The Left Consolidates Power

MARCH—MAY 1936

THE POPULAR FRONT PROGRAM pledged a policy of "Republicani-zation" of state personnel and administration, but exactly how far this would go was not clear. Whereas some historians have described Azaña's program in 1936 as restoration of the policies of 1931–1933, he himself had said that it would be "in no way" (*de ninguna manera*) like that of the first biennium.[1] Whereas in 1930 he had said that liberalism must be "radical" and "sectarian" in order to succeed, by 1936 the Republican left was adopting a position yet more radical and sectarian than three years earlier, though the Popular Front program specified that left Republicans did not accept economic socialism. Exactly how a minority left Republican government could function, depending on the support of revolutionaries, was at no point seriously discussed, for the revolutionaries had made it clear that they did not accept the Popular Front program itself as a long-term basis for government, but only as a stage in the enhancement of their own power. While the left Republicans spoke of Republicanization, and their revolutionary allies of preparing for revolutionary dictatorship, any discourse of democracy or equal rights disappeared.

It was clear that the new Azaña administration would be both more interventionist and more radical than the earlier government. If the most important factor here was the pressure of the worker parties, this also suited the leftward turn taken with the official formation of Izquierda

Republicana in 1934, distinctly more statist and interventionist than its predecessor, Acción Republicana. One obvious target might be unemployment, which, according to official statistics, continued to worsen. Though the economy generally was recovering during 1935–36, the recovery had not yet affected the number out of work, which stood at 843,872 by the end of February 1936.[2] That figure amounted to nearly 9 percent of the active population. It probably did not reflect all the hidden unemployment in the countryside, but did include the partially employed, so that it may have exaggerated absolute unemployment in the cities. Moreover, in parts of the south names of workers were sometimes not removed from the unemployment file after they had found employment, in order to retain maximal state support. The first major step in this area taken by the government was its law of mandatory reinstatement of workers who had been fired for political reasons. This went beyond the original Popular Front program, which had only specified rehiring state employees.

Tensions were keenest in the countryside. The winter of the Popular Front victory was extremely rainy, the second wettest of the century to that point, resulting in heavy farm losses and increased rural unemployment. Whereas urban unemployment was not remarkable and in the past year had increased by little more than 5 percent, in some rural areas unemployment had increased by more than 20 percent. Living standards had not fallen overall, for the incipient recovery had produced a slight increase in consumption under the center-right government, but the continued increase in unemployment, coinciding with the electoral triumph of the left, stimulated rapid expansion of rural syndicates, as they regained their 1933 level of membership and increased further.[3] Radicalization of the farmworkers' mood, at least among the activist sector, reached a new high. On 3 March villagers in Cenicientos, a small hill town in Madrid province, occupied grazing land that they claimed had once been part of village common lands and was now largely abandoned. This was the first in a lengthy series of illegal direct occupations of land involving scores of villages and tens of thousands of farmworkers and smallholders, first in Madrid, Toledo, Salamanca, and Murcia, and then in other provinces of the center and south.

The new director of the Institute of Agrarian Reform (IRA) declared before the end of February: "The concept of private property, with all its privileges and prerogatives, with regard to land, is as antiquated in fact as it is in theory."[4] Mariano Ruiz Funes, the new minister of agriculture, published a decree on 3 March encouraging yunteros (paid ploughmen) who had been evicted from land in Extremadura during the preceding year to petition for restoration. These terms were rapidly expanded; by 20 March Ruiz Funes had "eliminated all other exemptions and authorized the Institute of Agrarian Reform to occupy immediately any farm anywhere in Spain if it seemed socially necessary."[5] Such sweeping and arbitrary action could be carried out legally because, ironically enough, the infinitely maligned Radicals had succeeded in introducing such a provision under a rightist minister of agriculture in the preceding year's legislation: confiscation without compensation was permitted when deemed necessary "for reasons of social utility." The right had expected to be in a position to prevent any such actions from being carried out, but the new government employed this measure to head off direct action by revolutionary syndicates of the landless, or nearly landless, though it failed in the attempt.

Despite Ruiz Funes' efforts to expedite transfer of land, settlement of yunteros proceeded at a measured rhythm for two weeks, with some 3,000 gaining authorization to occupy land. The Socialist FNTT decided that this transfer was too slow, and at dawn on 25 March it launched a mass occupation of land in Badajoz province, with about 60,000 farmworkers and renters participating. Though troops were ordered in by Azaña and some activists were arrested, the government soon gave in, withdrawing the troops and releasing the prisoners on the thirtieth. The mass occupation was soon resumed, then legalized ex post facto by the government.

Takeover of local government in much of the south by the Socialists had established what Macarro Vera describes as "dictatorship in the small towns,"[6] with arbitrary seizure of property, forced assignment of workers to employers, and a purge of local government employees. Orders from the Ministry of the Interior directing them to cease arbitrary action and to respect private property were ignored.

For the spring grain harvest, the government reestablished the turno rigoroso (hiring strictly according to the list of local workers), replaced the presidents of the jurados mixtos, and began to impose fines on landowners who violated the new labor contracts. These measures, though more extensive than those taken during 1931–1933, failed to prevent a massive outburst of farm strikes. The Ministry of Agriculture recorded

192 between 1 May and 18 July, approximately equaling the total for all
1932 and nearly half the number during the preceding highest twelve-
month period (1933). Socialists and anarchists now sometimes cooperated,
producing broad district stoppages. During some weeks in late spring, at
least 100,000 farmworkers were on strike at a time.

Rural labor costs increased enormously, at a much higher rate than
during 1931–1933. In many provinces harvest wages were set at eleven
to thirteen pesetas a day, approximately twice the rates for 1935, and at
least 20 percent more than in 1933. Moreover, rural unions often imposed
agreements on limiting machinery and other structural reforms. Turno
rigoroso meant taking on many inexperienced local registered workers,
while the policy of labor *alojamiento* (direct assignment or "lodging" of
workers on a specific piece of land) was frequently imposed in the south,
in some cases with workers directly taking over land to work or requiring more workers to be hired than there was work for. Though by June
even the government was publicly insisting that wages should be based
on achievement of a specified production norm, the syndicates seem to
have agreed on a slowdown. The most thorough study has concluded that,
compared even with the highest preceding levels (1933), by June and July
rural labor costs had in toto risen by 50 to 60 percent.[7] At this point the
goal of the FNTT and CNT was not so much revolutionary seizure as a
drastic alteration in the terms of labor and syndical domination of the
present agrarian economy.

The government sought to expedite agrarian reform through legislation that Ruiz Funes presented to the Cortes on 19 April. This reduced
considerably the maximum exempt property limits (from 16.6 to 62.5
percent, depending on category), restored the original compensation levels
of 1933, and gave the government complete power to seize any piece of
land "for reasons of social utility." Another bill two weeks later proposed
to initiate expropriation through taxation, levying a surtax of more than
100 percent on landowners with agrarian incomes of more than 20,000
pesetas a year. Moreover, on 2 June the Cortes voted to restore all land
taken away from new tenants during the center-right biennium, and a
more drastic version of the original 1932 agrarian reform Law was passed
on 11 June. As indicated in table 5, much more land was redistributed in
the five months from March through July 1936 than in the five preceding
years of the Republic.

Table 5

Land Distribution under the Popular Front, March–July 1936

MONTH	NUMBER OF FARMERS SETTLED	AREA OCCUPIED (HECTARES)
March	72,428	249,616
April	21,789	150,490
May	5,940	41,921
June	3,855	55,282
July	6,909	74,746
Total	**110,921**	**572,055**

Source: *Boletín del Instituto de la Reforma Agraria* (March–July 1936), in E. E. Malefakis, *Agrarian Reform and Peasant Revolution in Spain* (New Haven, 1970), 377.

It is the consensus of specialists that these figures are incomplete, since the IRA was slow in recording transfers. During June and July the press reported land transfers that did not appear in IRA statistics, while Ruiz Funes himself declared publicly that as of 19 June 193,183 campesinos and their families had been settled on 755,888 hectares,[8] probably a more nearly accurate statistic. The IRA seems to have gained some control over the process during the spring. Though the terms were accelerated to hit wealthy landowners harder and to subject more land to potential expropriation, the ruedo clause of 1932, which affected modest owners, was not revived. While land was being confiscated from the wealthiest, medium-scale owners who had lost land were being paid something approaching market value, and potential new tenants could take advantage of arrangements that would enable them to fully purchase a certain amount of land. Even so, these dramatic changes did not suffice to restore peace to the southern countryside.

Rapid and sweeping prosecution of the land reform was the only clear economic policy of the new government. Despite the left's carefully contrived total domination of parliament, the Azaña administration was slow to take concrete new steps to combat unemployment or other lingering effects of the depression, so that the most incisive comments in the Cortes about economic problems came from centrist and rightist spokesmen, as well as from the Socialist dissident Besteiro. The Azaña government never completed a full budget, though it did increase spending in most categories. The Chapaprieta reforms were categorically rejected, and the state payroll expanded, with considerable new hiring, always of bona fide leftists.[9]

An obvious goal in labor policy was full restoration of the jurados mixtos as they had been in 1932–33, but this was approached piecemeal; action was not taken on a national scale until 28 May.[10] As indicated earlier, on 3 March the government had decreed blanket reinstatement and compensation for workers fired for political reasons, though it resisted demands from Communists and Socialists that employers who had previously violated labor regulations be jailed. The government obviously faced an avalanche of labor demands, particularly after the beginning of the massive strike wave in April, whose goals were not simply better wages and working conditions, but categorical changes in labor relations, such as the thirty-six-hour week and retirement with pension at age sixty. The reduced forty-four-hour week was soon instituted in metallurgy and construction, but employers lacked resources to meet many of the new demands. Labor costs rose precipitously, and during the spring the rate of bankruptcies increased. Trade unions sometimes opposed the closing of businesses and demanded to be allowed to take them over. Eventually, in May, the government announced plans for major spending increases to combat unemployment and for more progressive tax legislation, but these measures were not implemented before the start of the Civil War.

The other major area of government activism was education, where Marcelino Domingo returned as minister. He immediately announced plans to close schools still taught by religious personnel no later than the middle of 1936. A decree of 29 February announced creation of 5,300 new state teaching positions. Domingo claimed that in 1931 Spain had needed 27,151 new "schools" (classrooms) and that 16,409 had been constructed, 12,988 of these during 1931–1933. Of the remaining shortage of 10,472, half (5,300) were to be built in the remaining ten months of 1936, and the remainder completed no later than 1 May 1938.[11]

Domingo issued another decree on 6 May authorizing district education inspectors to make temporary arrangements in areas where new classrooms were badly needed but for various reasons could not be constructed. This in effect authorized what became a series of takeovers or confiscations of private schools and other facilities, which even Izquierda Republicana's official organ *Política* acknowledged on 29 May were sometimes of "doubtful legality." Five days later spokesmen of the Lliga Catalana in parliament protested that there had been many arbitrary seizures of private schools. In some cases schools were closed simply on the grounds of having given confessional instruction. On 4 June a CEDA deputy claimed that in the twenty-five days before 15 May a total of seventy-nine private schools with 5,095 students had been closed, taken over, or set afire.

The Azaña government, as might be expected, was absorbed in domestic affairs and paid little attention to the dramatic events currently breaking in Europe and Africa. Despite the intense antifascism of the Popular Front, Azaña had no interest in participating further in economic sanctions against Italy for its invasion of Ethiopia—an attitude in sharp contrast to that of the last parliamentary government, headed by Chapaprieta. Azaña feared diplomatic, economic, and military complications that Spain was in no condition to face. According to Madariaga, the Republic's spokesman in Geneva, "The first thing that Azaña said to me was 'You have to free me from article 16 [on sanctions]. I want nothing to do with that.' That was his official language. His unofficial language was: 'What does the Negus [the deposed Haile Selassie] mean to me?'"[12] The left Republican leaders did not see themselves as involved in any great international struggle between democracy and fascism, and categorically refused to help another country assaulted by fascism. After the Civil War began, this attitude would change. Having themselves failed to support Ethiopian independence, they would bitterly complain about the lack of support or intervention by the western democracies on behalf of the Spanish revolution.

THE EXPANSION OF VIOLENCE AND DISORDER

During April disorders increased further, assuming four different forms: attacks on and arson of religious buildings, strikes and demonstrations in the towns that often took a violent turn (and sometimes involved more arson), the direct occupation of farmland in certain central and southern provinces either as a permanent takeover or to impose new worker-control labor conditions, and direct clashes between members of political groups, usually carried out by small hit squads or death squads of the left (mostly Socialist and Communist, occasionally anarchist) and of the Falangists (and very occasionally of other rightist organizations).

In the words of Madariaga,

The country had entered a plainly revolutionary phase. Neither life nor property was safe anywhere. It is sheer prejudice to explain matters with partial variations of the word "feudal." It was not only the owner of thousands of acres granted his ancestors by King So-and-so whose house was invaded and whose cattle were left bleeding with broken legs on the smoking fields of his lands. It was the modest Madrid doctor or lawyer who possessed a villa of four rooms and bath and a garden as big as three handkerchiefs, who saw his house occupied by landworkers, by no means homeless and by no means hungry, who came to harvest his crop: ten men to do the work of one, and to stay in his house till they finished. It was the secretary of the local gardeners' union who came to threaten the young girl watering her roses that all watering had to be done by union men; it was a movement to prohibit driver-owners from driving their own cars and to force them to accept a union driver.[13]

In the countryside farmworkers sometimes ran into either armed police or armed landowners. During 1934–35 the previous governments had granted 270,000 private licenses for firearms, mostly to rightists, and in many provinces conservatives were far from defenseless,[14] though some of these licenses were rescinded and weapons confiscated under the new administration. In the provinces of Málaga and Seville six farmworkers were killed on the first of April, allegedly in the "invasion of estates." Later that month four workers were shot and killed by the Civil Guard in Huelva, apparently after a demonstration got out of control. The police or Civil Guard also suffered one or more deaths each week, sometimes in direct clashes, sometimes in sniping attacks. The most notorious political murder during the first half of April was the killing by Falangists on 13 April of Manuel Pedregal, a Madrid judge who had sentenced the accomplices in the Asúa atentado. In Barcelona April was the most violent month of the spring, with numerous cases of arson and bomb explosions, some of them in connection with a major CNT metallurgical strike. The CNT also committed at least four political murders that month, killing the Badía brothers of Estat Català as well as two nonleftist workers, but then disorders subsided somewhat.

The most notorious incidents occurred in Madrid, the principal center of violence. During the Republic Day parade on 14 April, a Falangist threw a smoke bomb at the presidential reviewing stand, and when the Civil Guard paraded, insults were shouted by part of the crowd. Several Guard officers, off duty and in civilian clothes, reproved those jeering near the presidential stand. At that point a number of leftists opened fire, killing a fifty-five-year-old Guard officer in the crowd and wounding two other off-duty Guardsmen as well as a woman and child. The burial of the Civil Guard, Lieutenant Anastasio de los Reyes, two days later was turned into a major rightist demonstration and a pitched battle in the streets of Madrid. Though the funeral procession had been prohibited from marching directly through the city, its leaders insisted on doing so, and it was fired at by leftists on numerous occasions. Altogether six people were killed—apparently all members of the funeral procession—and many were wounded.[15] That same day there was also a major leftist riot in Jerez, something of a repeat of the events in Granada on 9–10 March, with the burning of two newspaper offices and the temporary arrest of "class enemies." It produced numerous injuries but no reported fatalities.

Azaña was increasingly embarrassed and even frightened by the persistent disorder,[16] but he clung to the usual line on 17 April, declaring that the Madrid events had stemmed from a fascist provocation. On that day the government introduced new legislation stipulating that retired officers who joined illegal political groups would automatically lose their pensions, while one retired monarchist general engaged in conspiracy was exiled to the Canaries and numerous Civil Guard officers were reassigned. The courts were also beginning prosecution of those charged with crimes during the 1934 repression, bringing conviction of a Civil Guard sergeant for killing a Socialist mayor. His sentence of twelve years' imprisonment and a 15,000-peseta fine was said to have been the first of this sort in the history of the Civil Guard.[17]

Conditions varied greatly from province to province. Some were relatively unaffected, and in some the authorities made more of an effort to maintain order than in others. Near the bottom was Fernando Bosque, civil governor of Oviedo, quoted by *Mundo Obrero* on 20 April as saying: "I have appointed Popular Front delegados [political militants used as auxiliary police] throughout Asturias, who have been carrying out antifascist sweeps [*batidas*] with good results: they have jailed priests, doctors, municipal secretaries, and whomever else it may be. They fulfill their tasks admirably. Some of the delegates are Communists, and even like Fermín López Irún, sentenced to death for his participation in the events of October. . . . The one in Taverga has jailed the local telegrapher and the court secretary; the former is let out during the day to do his work and locked up at night. Among those in prison are two canons from Covadonga." These remarks, boldly published by the aggressive Communist press, raised a scandal in Madrid, however, and eventually Bosque, who had been moved from civil governor of Huesca to Oviedo on 11 March, was forced to resign, as the interior minister finally announced on 18 June.[18] Nevertheless, Bosque's frank statement made clear why there would not be public order under the left Republican administration, as the policy of naming leftist militants as special police delegados became more common. This sinister process, which has never been studied, bore some similarity to the policy of the new Hitler government three years earlier of naming Nazi militants as special *Hilfspolizei*, or auxiliary police. The steady politicization of police functions would culminate in the killing of Calvo Sotelo on 13 July, the ultimate catalyst for civil war.

The threat of violence was present even in the Cortes. In the words of a Socialist historian, "The parliament, as soon as it began to function, asphyxiated the government. It acted as a sounding board for civil war, reflecting and exacerbating the nation's own turbulence. The deputies insulted and attacked each other by design; each session was in continuous tumult; and since all the representatives—true representatives of the nation—went armed, a catastrophe could have been expected any afternoon. In view of the frequency with which firearms were exhibited or referred to, it was necessary to resort to the humiliating precaution of frisking the legislators as they entered."[19]

THE IMPEACHMENT OF ALCALÁ ZAMORA

Both the left and right had campaigned against the president during the elections. The CEDA, in particular, convinced that he had robbed the party of its earlier mandate, made little secret of the fact that if it won it would ask the new Cortes to review the last dissolution of parliament, with the aim of deposing Alcalá Zamora according to the Constitution. Azaña and the Popular Front gave clear indication of heading in the same direction.

Yet the president's aim had never been to hand all power to the left, and after the complete failure of his strategy in the elections, Alcalá Zamora directed his animus against the left and the new government, whose extremism and irresponsibility he now found even more intolerable than he did the CEDA. There is little doubt that Alcalá Zamora had sought the ultimate good of the Republic as he understood it, but his vain, pompous, and personalistic style, with its constant manipulations—however austere in financial matters—had placed him at odds with nearly all the leading politicians of the left and right, and even of the center. During the first weeks of the new Azaña government, Alcalá Zamora met several times with the council of ministers and tried vainly to encourage greater moderation and discipline. In his view, the new administration was using the state of alarm and partial suspension of constitutional guarantees not to maintain law and order but to give a free hand to the forces of disorder.[20] Relations grew ever more tense, and Azaña claimed that he forced the president to back off on more than one occasion by speaking to him in harsh and aggressive language.[21]

In one of the numerous incidents of arbitrary and totally illegal arrests that occurred under the Azaña government, relatives of Alcalá Zamora himself were seized in Alcaudete, in Córdoba province. Their release was secured by dispatch of a truckload of Assault Guards, but the latter did nothing to punish or restrain those responsible or to halt their seizure of farmland. As Alcalá Zamora complained to the government, the Republican police were not trying to restore order but rather "practically placed it in the hands of the lawless; they ordered local authorities to follow the dictates of the latter."[22]

He urged Azaña to announce a detailed legislative program as soon as possible and to proceed through legal channels with positive remedies, but on most issues the government dawdled. Conversely, Alcalá Zamora protested one of its first decrees, the terms for blanket reinstatement and compensation of workers fired in 1934, since in some cases, according to the president, "the owners of small family businesses were now required to rehire the murderers of a father or a brother. . . . According to a former governor of the Banco de España, the latter was required to take back an employee who had fired seven gunshots at an administrator."[23] Alcalá Zamora recalled that he did manage to firmly veto one proposal "that was absolutely illegal . . . and in violation of the Constitution itself. It would have created special ad hoc municipal committees to fix arbitrarily the production expenses of each landowner and would also have had the power to confiscate totally without indemnity any agrarian goods to re-assign to whatever individual or collective they saw fit. Moreover, all legal appeal was denied and any administrative appeal was also denied if, as might be expected, the local tyrants ruled unanimously."[24] He added:

> There was a moment when I had some hope that this tolera-tion of anarchy would be ended. That was after we had received word from leading diplomats like [Plácido Álvarez] Buylla, [Au-gusto] Barcia, and Madariaga of the alarm this created abroad, reflected even in the sarcastic jokes of Soviet diplomats. Then the government brought for me to sign the termination of sev-eral provincial governors, but on such honorific terms that it was like voluntary resignation. I signed this formula of unmer-ited benevolence with regard to the governor of Jaén, respon-sible for outrageous acts against my family and myself, which required the utmost delicacy on my part, but I sent back the de-crees for those of Cádiz, Granada, Murcia, and Logroño, advis-ing the government that at the very least it could officially fire them if it was unwilling to prosecute them for dereliction of duty. The ministers admitted that I was right but still asked me to sign lenient terms in order not to provoke the Popular Front. And these were extreme cases that had even created humiliat-ing international complications: arson against the homes and factories of political enemies; guards murdered with their own weapons; and a bloody clash with a barracks in which several people were killed.
>
> . . . The government often tried to hide from me what was going on . . . but in one meeting of the council I was informed of the burning of two churches in Alcoy carried out by the local city council as a whole. I invited the ministers to rectify the situation but the minister of justice said it was under the juris-diction of the minister of the interior, who silently exhibited his usual disdainful indifference, encouraged and directly pro-tected by Azaña.[25]

By the end of March the major new issue, aside from the partisan deliberations of the Comisión de Actas, was the municipal elections, which the government had scheduled for all Spain save Catalonia in early April. There had been no municipal elections since the start of the Republic except for those held in a minority of districts in 1933. Though the constitution stated that half the seats were to be placed up for election every three years, the government now planned total plebiscitary municipal elections. Moreover, the revolutionary parties were demanding the great majority of candidacies and promising that wherever they won, victory would mark the local beginning of the "dictatorship of the proletariat." The CEDA protested that this plan for total renewal all at once was unconstitutional, and that moreover under the present climate of violence, intimidation, and partial censorship, fair campaigning and honest elections would be impossible. Alcalá Zamora agreed and warned moreover that a leftist victory would generate a revolutionary demand for a new leftist system—variant proposals for a kind of people's republic, already present in leftist propaganda—analogous to that stemming from the Republican triumph of 12 April 1931.[26]

The president still possessed the constitutional power to dismiss the government, all the more since it remained technically a minority government, as he had done many times in the past. There was speculation that he might dismiss Azaña and ask Manuel Rico Avello to form a more responsible left Republican government on a broader basis. On 30 March he told the centrist Lliga leader Juan Ventosa that at the next cabinet meeting he would declare his total opposition to the irresponsible policy of the Azaña government.[27] On the following day Chapaprieta urged him to go further and dismiss the reckless Azaña cabinet, adding that he believed the president could count on the support of the army should this produce a crisis.[28] Alcalá Zamora was reluctant to go that far because it would bring the country close to civil war. Instead, at the next cabinet meeting—the last Alcalá Zamora would have the opportunity to attend—he vigorously attacked the government's prorevolutionary security policy, its toleration of widespread leftist disorder, the personal irresponsibility of individual cabinet ministers and of Azaña himself, the irregular awarding of a large number of parliamentary seats both during the turmoil of 16–19 February and in the manipulations of the Comisión de Actas, the need to cancel what would be abusive and arbitrary local elections in the present climate of terror, and the absolute need to return to constitutional government immediately.[29] In so doing, the president signed his political death warrant.

The only concession made by the Azaña administration was to postpone
the upcoming municipal elections, but here the prime minister's principal
motivation was to avoid the looming split between moderate and revolutionary sectors of the Popular Front and the danger that the elections
might even be won by the right.[30]

On 3 April Azaña addressed the first regular session of the new Cortes.
Exhausted, having slept very little the past two nights, he warned that the
country's problems had become severe. He referred to the "eclipse of the
sense of justice and of the sense of pity that threatens the Republic" and
declared that Spaniards were facing "the last chance not merely for the
peaceful and normal development of Republican politics, but even for the
parliamentary system itself." Though he announced a radical economic
policy of imprecise contours, he also made an appeal for order and harmony that was generally well received by both sides. The stock market in
fact rose on the following day, and the government seemed momentarily
to have gained a breathing space.

As Alcalá Galve has put it quite accurately, "A full examination of the
political trajectory of Azaña reveals that his leftism was not originally pro-
grammed, but grew progressively." Azaña moved as far left as he judged
necessary first to regain and then to hold power. Other considerations
were largely secondary. "To present Azaña as a scrupulous follower of
Republican ethics and legality and of respect for democracy, as has been
done by many historians and by his biographers, offends the evidence."
Rather, he adjusted his policy to double games with antigovernment insurrections, manipulations to cancel legal elections and conduct arbitrary
ones, immunity for mass crimes, and, progressively from 1934 on, the
adoption of a radical new economic program—totally unknown to his first
government of 1931–1933—so that Azaña "changed his ideology from the
bourgeois leftism of his first biennium toward a direction compatible with
the extremist forces that supported him."[31] Or, as José Ma. García Escudero
put it, "when a Cánovas was needed, he preferred to be Robespierre."[32]
Azaña undoubtedly sought to gain control of the revolutionary process
rather than surrender to it, but in this he failed as well, for no matter how
far left he moved, the revolutionaries would always outflank him.

He promised to govern within the law and the constitution, but
insisted:

There is another kind of obstacle: the reactions and aggres-
sions of the economic interests affected by government policy.
Yes, it is correct that we are going to infringe [*lastimar*] interests
whose historical legitimacy I am not going to question, but
which now constitute the main part of the disequilibrium from
which Spanish society suffers. Now those who accuse us of
destroying the Spanish economy wish that our earlier program
[of 1933] had not been interrupted, because now the sacrifice
will have to be much greater! We come to break the abusive
concentration of wealth wherever it may be, to harmonize social burdens and to recognize only two types of citizens: those
who participate in production and those who live off the labor
and effort of others. The privileged elements of Spain will
have the option of accepting the sacrifice or facing desperation.

As usual with Azaña, this rested not so much on economic analysis as
on the esthetic level of rhetoric. There were no details and no discussion
of technical economic problems other than a reference to "the growing
interventionist activity of the state in regulating the problems of production and labor."[33] His Socialist ally Prieto told him that the speech had
been "hollow," for lack of specificity, but it was an effective piece of rhetoric
whose terms were so vague that the speech was generally well received
by much of the right, even though it reflected Azaña's standard tactic of
blaming all difficulties on the other side.

The CEDA returned for the opening of the Cortes, and at a meeting of
its parliamentary group the great majority voted to continue to cooperate
with the government. *El Debate* had earlier suggested that an understanding might be possible on the basis of disarming all political militias and
undertaking a broad national program to overcome unemployment and
the depression. The government had made it clear, however, that it proposed to disarm only the Falange, not its own supporters, and to impose
its own program of prerevolutionary economic redistribution of property,
vague and slow though it was in developing this.

Even before Azaña's opening address, a petition had been presented
to the speaker of the Cortes asking that article 81 of the constitution be invoked, which granted a new parliament produced by a second dissolution

during one presidential term the right to review such action and, if it found this action unjustified, to proceed to a vote on the deposition of the president. The petition had been organized by Prieto—providing further evidence that he was not merely the "moderate" social democrat defined by some—and was signed by 17 deputies from the worker parties, mainly Socialists. The initial argument held that the dissolution of 1933 should count as a regular dissolution, not the pro forma ending of a short-term Constituent Cortes, since the first parliament had continued for nearly two years after the constitution had been completed. The counterargument was that the additional labor of the Constituent Cortes during 1932–33 had involved primarily the passage of complementary legislation required to put the constitution into effect, and there was considerable evidence that many political leaders had viewed the Constituent Cortes in exactly that light. The CEDA was now moderating its position on Alcalá Zamora, realizing that his removal would simply permit the left to consolidate total power. Spokesmen for the center and right held that the matter was so complicated that it should go before the Tribunal of Constitutional Guarantees. There was also the question of article 82, dealing with impeachment pure and simple, which stipulated that a motion to depose a president must first be backed by 100 deputies, with three days' notice given of debate, and that the motion must be carried by three-fifths of the chamber. Prieto preferred to avoid article 82, for fear of not having enough votes. The initial proposal carried 181 to 88, with many abstaining. It stipulated that Alcalá Zamora had carried out two regular dissolutions of the Cortes, exhausting his presidential powers, and mandated the crucial debate on 7 April as to whether the dissolution of 1936 had been unnecessary and hence illegal. If that were the decision, it would produce automatic removal of the president.[34]

Azaña remained uncertain for three days. In December 1931 he had taken the position that dissolution of the Constituent Cortes should not count against the president, and the publication of his diaries and memoirs many years later would reveal that he took that position on five different occasions. Moreover, more than a few left Republicans hesitated both to manifest the hypocrisy of deposing the president for doing what they had incessantly beseeched him to do for more than two years and to make the presidency a mere football of partisan passion. Finally, there was the consideration that if the Popular Front judged illegal the elections that had placed it in power, its results logically should be cancelled and new elections held, placing the Popular Front majority at risk. The great danger, of course, was that in 1936 Alcalá Zamora would use the presidency against the left, just as he had used it effectively against the right during 1934–35. As was customary with Azaña, sectarianism won out. In typically hyperbolic language, he wrote: "I said to myself that I could not shoulder the responsibility of leaving the Republic's worst enemy in the presidency."[35] His decision to commit the government to impeachment largely determined the outcome. For Azaña, the impeachment crisis had the additional advantage that it could be used as an excuse to postpone the municipal elections, which threatened either the rupture or the outright defeat of the Popular Front. By concentrating on the attack on the president, the leftist alliance sustained itself, and for the time being sidestepped the thorny issue of municipal elections.

During the three-day interim that followed, Chapaprieta twice visited the president, who insisted that he would not resign, that it was indispensable for the stability and survival of the Republic that its first president complete his initial term, and that if he resisted an unconstitutional "parliamentary coup d'état," he would be supported by the armed forces. Chapaprieta replied that if Alcalá Zamora was so convinced, he must dally no longer but act decisively, immediately withdrawing confidence from the Azaña government and appointing a new, more moderate government that would respect the constitution, restore law and order, and gain the support of a large political spectrum and, crucially, of the armed forces.[36] This, in fact, was the logical continuation of the way Alcalá Zamora had acted during the preceding year, in which his actions had been distinctly more arbitrary. At that moment, this would have been the best alternative and was much more justifiable than his actions between September 1935 and January 1936. By now, however, Alcalá Zamora had lost his nerve, possibly as a result of insistent advice from his closest counselor, his son Niceto, a law professor at the University of Valencia.[37]

The argument employed on 7 April was byzantine, to say the least. It justified deposition on the grounds that the recent dissolution was "not necessary" because (1) it should have been done much earlier, and (2) when it was done, it was done improperly, with an attempt to manipulate the outcome. There was of course some truth in the latter charge. Prieto read aloud excerpts from Gil Robles' campaign speeches declaring that the

January dissolution was unjustified. Alcalá Zamora had alienated almost all the major political personalities. No one spoke in his favor, though some leaders of the center and right urged a more careful and deliberate procedure, either by invoking the more complex means provided by article 82 or by referring the matter to the Tribunal of Constitutional Guarantees. Miguel Maura warned, "Why must you stain the honor of parliament by making people think you are motivated solely by political passion? Listen well! What is being decided this afternoon is more than a mere personal or political case: it is the essence of the Republic itself." The Popular Front deputies understood that well enough and intended to conform the "essence of the Republic" completely to their own domination by removing the last obstacle to full power. The leftist leaders seem to have been aware that Alcalá Zamora was at least toying with the idea of trying to dismiss the Azaña cabinet, an action consistent with what he had done many times in the past. His removal and replacement by a leftist president would remove that danger. The vote to depose was 238, with only 5 of Portela's deputies voting no, the right and the rest of the center abstaining.

Again, to quote Madariaga: "Now this parliament, which owed its existence to the presidential decree, a decree which turned a majority of the right into a majority of the left and which therefore proved, at any rate to the satisfaction of the left, that the nation had changed its opinion radically . . . did not hesitate to show the world that the Spanish Republic was incapable of keeping its first president in office for more than half his term, and . . . it committed itself to the most glaring denial of logic the history of a free nation can show."[38]

This destructive action has been almost universally condemned by historians, ranging from the dean of late twentieth-century Marxist historiography in Spain, Manuel Tuñón de Lara,[39] to Javier Tusell, the leading specialist on Spanish political history of the twentieth century.[40]

The constitution provided that the speaker of the Cortes would succeed to a vacant presidency until a special election could choose new delegates (compromisarios) to select the next president, so Martínez Barrio was sworn in as acting president that night. Then the Cortes, apparently feeling that it had no serious matters to discuss amid the national crisis, took eight days off.

Outraged, Alcalá Zamora made no gesture of rebellion. He knew that he might have been able to rally military support to keep himself in power (and indeed one general staff colonel, Valentín Galarza, urged him to do so), but he wished to take no personal responsibility for unleashing the grave crisis that he saw ahead.[41] As he later wrote: "It is possible that if I had resisted, what became a three-year civil war might have lasted only three months, weeks, or days, but even if that—which was then so uncertain—had been so, it would then have been *my* war, *mine* with its deaths, horrors, iniquities, and crimes against conscience. As it was, it became their war of one side and the other, as they boasted of false and execrable glories, of popular and national epics and triumphal years: such deceitful glories, with their terrible responsibilities, are for them instead."[42]

THE PARLIAMENTARY DUEL OF 15–16 APRIL

The new Cortes began its regular work on 15 April, when Azaña first presented his legislative program. This included reparations for political persecution by the center and right (though no compensation for the large-scale destruction wrought by the left), full restoration of Catalan autonomy, reform of the rules of the Cortes to expedite the legislative process, and reform of the rules for electing members of the Tribunal of Constitutional Guarantees and for selecting the president of the Supreme Court, to assure leftist dominance. All this had been part of the Popular Front program, and to a large extent the first two items had been carried out by decree. In toto, this program—whose limitations would soon infuriate the revolutionary left—could hardly be considered an adequate response to the protorevolutionary ferment gripping much of the country. Azaña also, somewhat more vaguely, planned significant socioeconomic changes to placate the revolutionaries, but no genuine plan ever emerged.

He emphasized that "the phenomenon we are witnessing in Spain is the access to political power of new social classes, a phenomenon that we can locate in the first third of this century." "For the moment," the government was especially concerned with unemployment and with labor problems in the countryside, though persistent deficits, weak finance, and a negative balance of payments severely limited state resources. Azaña admitted that the economy was in serious condition, declaring that it was important to stabilize foreign debt so as not to risk vital imports. He declared that it would be necessary to reduce expenses in certain unspecified areas while redistributing income through progressive taxation, expanding public works, and accelerating agrarian reform. Wages must be maintained and yet sufficiently controlled to prevent inflation. Azaña concluded that major reforms must be undertaken on a virtually self-sustaining financial basis, a task so difficult that he was unable to provide specifics. As was typical of his approach, he made no effort to come to grips with the widespread violence and disorder, but approached it as a kind of philosophical spectator, presenting standard *leyendanegrista* (Black Legend) clichés so dear to the hearts of the left: "Knowing as I do how deeply rooted violence is in the Spanish character, this cannot be proscribed by decree, yet we still hope that the time has come when Spaniards will stop shooting each other," adding that owing to "pity and mercy" certain excesses, presumably by the left, had not been repressed by the government. But then, if the present situation was merely a result of the "Spanish character," his government could presumably wash its hands of the matter, as to some extent it did. The whole performance reflected the contradictions of the Popular Front alliance, and the absence of any government policy for coming to grips with the present situation.

Calvo Sotelo and Gil Robles replied for the right. The former, speaking for the radical right, demanded a drastic alternative through regime change, while the CEDA leader accepted the present government and sought to influence it to alter its policy, such as it was. In a marathon speech whose text and appendices filled eleven pages of the *Diario de las Sesiones,* Calvo Sotelo presented the first of what would become a series of statistical reports on alleged acts of violence, declaring that between 16 February and 1 April a total of 74 people had been killed and 345 wounded in political incidents, and 106 churches burned, including 56 completely destroyed. The government offered no statistics with which to challenge this report, which more than a few historians have taken to be substantially correct, as indeed it seems to have been. Calvo Sotelo then cited speeches by revolutionary leaders indicating that this was just the beginning of revolutionary destruction. He warned that, as opposed to the dictatorship of the proletariat, "I want to say in the name of the Bloque Nacional that Spain will be able to save itself through the formula of the authoritarian corporative state."

Gil Robles then spoke amid shouts and tumult, saying that necessary social reforms would have the CEDA's votes, but that rightists were being assaulted all over Spain and that legal social reform no longer seemed to be the goal of the left, while the government made only feeble efforts to channel these actions within legality. He warned against the idea of trying to govern for only half of Spain: "A considerable mass of Spanish opinion which is at least half the nation will not resign itself to die." Turning to Azaña, Gil Robles added: "I think that you will suffer a sadder fate, which is to preside over the liquidation of the democratic Republic. . . . When civil war breaks out in Spain, let it be known that the weapons have been loaded by the irresponsibility of a government that failed to fulfill its duty toward groups that have kept within the strictest legality." This prophecy, both of the result of the government's irresponsibility and of Azaña's own political fate, proved completely accurate.

In a speech later in the same session José Díaz, secretary general of the Communist Party, declared that Gil Robles "will die with his shoes on." This was no more than standard revolutionary language, but, as speaker of the Cortes, Martínez Barrio called Díaz to order and had the remark stricken from the record. Benito Pabón, of the tiny Partido Sindicalista, the most moderate of the worker parties, then urged those parties to support the government more loyally because "Azaña has not used violence against the excesses of the workers."

Parliament met the following day in a supercharged atmosphere created by the De los Reyes funeral procession, which at one point threatened to march on the Cortes. Azaña began with his customary bluff and braggadocio, claiming once more that the disorder was simply inspired by the right and its "prophecies": "I don't intend to serve as anyone's guardian angel. The honorable gentlemen should show less fear and not ask me to extend them my hand. Did you not want violence, were you not disturbed by the social institutions of the Republic? Then take to violence. Be prepared for the consequences." Of all Azaña's many foolish and irresponsible speeches, this one probably broke all records. To say that the CEDA's five years of activity within Republican legality simply showed that it "wanted violence" was the most delirious incendiarism. The spectacle of a parliamentary prime minister inviting the opposition to civil war would have been incomprehensible anywhere but within the context of the Spanish Popular Front. Azaña himself would be the first to be dismayed when the right finally took him up on his invitation, demonstrating once more the hollowness of his position.

Azaña underlined the importance of maintaining the unity of the left: "We must not permit a single break in our coalition. I will not be the one to open it." This revealed the essence of his policy—solidarity with the revolutionaries through thick and thin. To avoid conflict with them he had already cancelled the municipal elections, and for the same reason would accept a policy of coercion for the new Cortes elections in Cuenca and Granada. This posture made impossible a reconciliation even with the center, and made inevitable the breakdown of what was left of Republican democracy. Only the rejection of revolutionism and violence accompanied by formation of a broader government of conciliation would make possible continuation of the democratic system. Any such change Azaña was determined not to make, because it would also require renouncing total domination by the left. On such a basis, democracy could not long survive, and no decision was more important than the one taken by Azaña himself.

Probably realizing that his call to civil war was mistaken excess, he then tried to step back from the precipice he had just approached. Turning to Gil Robles, he demanded: "With what authority do the honorable gentlemen challenge those who once through either vengeance or confusion launched a revolution? Vengeance is an instinct that ought not to enter personal life and even less public affairs. At no time does anyone have a right to take justice into his own hands. . . . No one can describe with sufficient vividness and vigor not merely the opposition but the repugnance felt by the government for certain events that are sporadically occurring. No one can doubt the exertions of the government to prevent or repress them. I am convinced that flames are an endemic malady in Spain; once heretics were burned, and now saints are consumed, at least as images." This rhetorical effort, which ended by once more blaming the present crimes on an allegedly essentialist "Spanish character," simply exposed Azaña's own defects of character and his inability to cope with reality, typical of the radical intellectual in politics. He then went on to criticize reporting in the foreign press, which he blamed for discouraging the spring tourist trade. For Azaña, everything was always the fault of someone else. He would never accept any blame or criticism until 1938, and then it was much too late.

Juan Ventosa of the Lliga later concluded his own remarks with a much more telling observation: "Simply listening to this debate, simply hearing the declarations made yesterday and today—repeated insults, incitement to political assassination, invocation of that barbarous and primitive form of justice called the law of revenge [*Talión*], the strange and almost absurd demand that only the right be disarmed, but not everybody— simply attending and observing the zeal for persecution and oppression revealed by some sectors of the chamber, you can clearly see the genesis of all the violence occurring in the country."

SPECIAL ELECTIONS IN CUENCA AND GRANADA

On 9 April the government announced that, pursuant to the verdict of the Comisión de Actas, the rightist electoral triumphs in the provinces of Cuenca and Granada had been annulled, and new elections were scheduled for 5 May. Both sides geared up for a maximum effort. The CEDA prepared a *candidatura de batalla* (combat candidacy) for Granada, made up of five young and determined CEDA candidates, four Falangists, and one "independent" (in fact Carlist), Colonel José Enrique Varela (himself already active in military conspiracy). The union with the technically illegal Falange created something of a sensation and was a measure of the extent to which things had changed in only two months. Similarly, the Popular Front candidacy was composed entirely of representatives of the worker left, who refused further concessions to the left Republicans, a further portent of the new state of affairs.

The simplest description of the new electoral campaign in Granada is to say that the terms of the original campaign were reversed and even exceeded. In February there had been rightist coercion against the left, while in April and May the opposite held true. Gil later claimed that at one point the right was offered a deal that would have allowed it the three minority seats. He denounced this pressure in a letter to the minister of the interior, which he had read into the Cortes record.[43] Failing that, the obstruction to which the right was subjected became so great that it withdrew from the Granada elections altogether. According to Macarro Vera, the most serious researcher on Andalusia in the spring of 1936, the campaign in Granada "was carried out in a climate of authentic terror by the left without precedent in any previous election. The Socialist and Communist militia imposed their own law in the streets, frisking and physically assaulting their class enemies, even arresting and imprisoning them without the authorities doing much to interfere. The results were scandalous."[44]

For Cuenca the original rightist ticket was reorganized on 23 April

238 THE LEFT CONSOLIDATES POWER

to include the names of the monarchist leader Antonio Goicoechea, to-gether with José Antonio Primo de Rivera and General Franco. It was Primo de Rivera who privately insisted from prison that Franco's name be withdrawn, for it gave the rightist ticket too military a look and would only increase government pressure. Franco reluctantly agreed,[45] but on 27 April the provincial electoral commission ruled in favor of a petition from Prieto that no new candidates be allowed to stand who had not received at least 8 percent of the disputed vote in the original election. In 1933 there had been a complete rightist victory in Cuenca, and in the original vot-ing of 16 February 1936 the left had failed to gain a single seat. The left was determined to reverse that situation; to give proper tone to the new campaign, a considerable number of the Socialist militia group known as "La Motorizada" were given official deputy police status for the campaign as *delegados gubernativos*,[46] just as had been done in several other locales. This was part of the process by which the left Republican government (and local Socialist authorities) mixed activists of the worker parties into the regular police structures.

Meanwhile on May Day there was a large joint Socialist-Communist parade down the Castellana in Madrid, said to involve as many as 300,000 people, with the chant of "Hijos sí, maridos no!" (Children yes, husbands no) by some of the young women activists, particularly scandalizing middle-class Catholic citizens. This mass demonstration was peaceful, but some in other parts of the country led to the usual skirmishes, with several killed and many injured.

Two days later occurred the notorious *bulo de caramelos* (candy scare) incident in the capital when a rumor swept through one worker district that nuns in one of the few remaining Catholic schools were distributing poisoned caramels to their pupils—an indication of the state of hysteria induced by leftist propaganda. One church was soon torched and reli-gious personnel attacked, and on the following day six Catholic churches and schools were set ablaze, some forty religious personnel and Catholic laymen attacked, and at least one killed.[47] On the night of the fourth the government felt the need to announce that no poisonings had in fact taken place, the whole matter being put down by leftist leaders to more "provoca-tions" by the right, who supposedly incited leftists to burn churches and attack their fellow rightists.

In the city of Cuenca, the local CEDA center and several other rightist offices, together with at least one church, were burned on 1–2 May. The new delegados gubernativos arrived on the evening of the first and for the next three days ruled with an iron hand, making campaigning by the right almost impossible. Prieto also drove in late on the first to deliver the principal leftist campaign address. He later wrote: "When I arrived at the theater, there smoldered nearby the ashes of a fire which had consumed the furnishings of a rightist center that had just been attacked by the masses. A number of important monarchist personages were holed up in a hotel in the center of town since the night before. The atmosphere was frenzied."[48] The Socialist leader went on to give one of his most important and complicated speeches of the year, in which he endeavored to stimulate the left to victory while trying to discourage the sort of disorder and violence still going on at that moment outside the theater. Prieto indicated his satisfaction with Franco's withdrawal. While praising the general's professional skills, he observed that these made Franco precisely the sort of figure who might most effectively lead a potential military revolt, diplomatically adding that "I would not dare attribute any such intentions to General Franco himself."

Prieto dedicated a major part of the speech to the problem of public order. While carefully stressing the standard line that the real cause of most of the current excesses stemmed from the reaction to the allegedly unjustified severity of the repression following the October insurrection, he insisted that the time had come to call a halt and to show greater discipline.

> It's time to stop! Enough, enough! Do you know why? Because in these disorders . . . I can find no trace of revolutionary strength. If I could, I might praise them. No, a country can stand the convulsion of a true revolution. . . . What it cannot stand is the constant strain of public disorder with no immediate revolutionary goal; what a nation cannot stand is the drain of public authority and its own economic strength, with constant unrest, tumult, and alarm. Simple souls may say that this unrest is produced solely by the dominant classes. That, in my judgment, is erroneous. The pernicious effects of that unrest will soon be suffered by the working class itself as a result of the upset and possible collapse of the national economy. . . . Abroad people consider Spain an insolvent country.

> If disorder and tumult become a permanent system . . . the
> result will not be the consolidation of revolution or the building
> of socialism or communism. The result will be desperate anar-
> chy of a kind that is not found within the creed of libertarian
> anarchism itself; the result will be economic disorder that can
> destroy the country.

His final warning, once more completely accurate, was that continuation
of the disorder and destruction would only increase the possibility of a
"fascist" reaction.[49]

The next four days, which concluded the campaign in Cuenca, gave
no evidence that Prieto's words had had the slightest effect. Several com-
panies of Assault Guards had been assigned to patrol the province, and
the civil governor ordered preventive arrest of scores of rightists, so numerous that special emergency jails had to be established to hold them
until the balloting was over. A sweeping victory for the Popular Front
was recorded amid armed coercion and flagrant fraud, with the prietista
delegados playing a leading role, casting some doubt on the sincerity
of the speech that their leader had just given and making a mockery of
his call for moderation. It was typical of Prieto that on the one hand he
wanted greater responsibility and restraint but on the other was equally
determined that the left totally dominate the electoral process. Prieto's
somewhat schizophrenic attitude was similar to that of Azaña. In toto, the
electoral process in Cuenca and Granada may have been less free than the
elections that Hitler conducted in Germany in March 1933.

Romero has penned the best epitaph:

> The May elections in Cuenca were an episode that can be prop-
> erly described as shameful, in which Prieto played a leading
> role, taking much of the responsibility. Every kind of outrage
> and abuse was committed, with extreme coercion and bold-
> faced illegalities. The civil governor, the electoral board, and,
> as a fitting climax, the young men of the 'Motorizada,' pistols
> in hand, won those elections without glory. Primo de Rivera
> was deprived of a seat that he had won in popular votes, after
> the governor announced that his votes simply would not be
> counted, as occurred in various districts, and that announce-

ment by the leading authority in the province intimidated others.[50]

On the following day Calvo Sotelo arose in the Cortes to read his latest data on violence, claiming that forty-seven people had been killed in political affrays between 1 April and 5 May. One of Azaña's closest associates, Santiago Casares Quiroga, now minister of the interior, replied that the government "is the first to condemn and execrate the lamentable events that have occurred," but that nonetheless the only real problem came from the right, not from the leftists who were killing and burning. "Only the right worries me, while the social revolution does not worry me at all," he stated, falsely claiming that "in the proletarian masses I have found loyalty and aid in getting out of this situation." A major goal of government policy, he said, was to disarm the right, from whom 13,000 weapons had been confiscated in Granada province and 7,000 in Jaén province. He did not explain why, if the right was being disarmed, violence was not diminishing, and said nothing about disarming the left. Calvo Sotelo replied that it was irrational to suppose that the violence stemmed merely from rumors that the right launched in order to injure itself, adding that the right did not want a civil war, but that in order to avoid civil war violence must cease on both sides. Fascism "here and abroad is not a primary initiative but a secondary response. It is not an action, but a reaction."

Two days earlier, José Antonio Primo de Rivera had decided on a fundamental change in Falangist strategy. He had previously been uncertain about potential military conspirators, but had given up hope of normal political relations or due process of law under the left Republican regime. Consequently he drafted a *Carta a los militares de España*, later distributed as a clandestine leaflet, urging the military to prepare rapidly for decisive political intervention.[51] Since the end of April the multiple strands of military conspiracy had begun to come together in clearer form for the first time, though this development was known only to a small minority within the military.

AZAÑA BECOMES PRESIDENT

No other candidate was in a position to contest the presidency with Azaña. He himself would evidently have preferred to see the office of chief of state in the hands of Felipe Sánchez Román, whose stature in Azaña's eyes was inversely proportionate to the minute size of his party and its parliamentary strength. Since Sánchez Román was not a member of the Popular Front, this was impossible. Largo Caballero preferred the candidacy of the meteoric Alvaro de Albornoz, who stood clearly to the left of Azaña, but Albornoz tended toward the completely irresponsible and had little support. Thus the Unión Republicana quickly nominated Azaña and, after overcoming the initial resistance of Azaña's own Izquierda Republicana—which was reluctant to lose his leadership to the more distant office of chief of state—Prieto helped swing Socialist votes in line, and the matter was quickly settled.

Voting for electors (compromisarios) for a new presidential election took place on 26 April. With much of the right abstaining, these elections were swept by the left, the Popular Front winning 358 compromisarios to 68 for the opposition. Azaña was overwhelmingly chosen by a special assembly of electors in the Crystal Palace of Madrid's Retiro Park on 10 May. The formal ceremony took place on the following day, when Gil Robles claims to have been impressed by the extreme pallor and seeming numbness of the new president.[52]

The motives of the main leftist leaders in elevating Azaña to the presidency were subsequently a matter of controversy. The left Socialist Araquistain would later insist that the whole affair was a Machiavellian plot to deprive the government of its top leader, sweeping Azaña aside into the presidency in order to leave the administration in the hands of a weaker figure who would be unable to restrain the revolutionaries; but, like much from Araquistain, this seems an exaggeration,[53] and is not supported by other evidence.[54]

With regard to Azaña, it has been speculated that he hoped to be more effective in stabilizing the regime from the presidency—that he took the new office for positive reasons—as opposed to the interpretation that he accepted the presidency largely from the negative consideration that he was tired, discouraged, and could not control events and that it was better to make his escape into a more withdrawn and ceremonial office. There is inadequate evidence to resolve this question, and an either/or conclusion is perhaps unrealistic. There is little doubt that at some level Azaña wished to escape, a desire he had earlier expressed on various occasions, but, as several of his friends have testified, he also expressed the

the last regular government of the Republic included seven ministers from Izquierda Republicana, three from Unión Republicana, one from the Esquerra, and one Republican independent, Juan Moles, in the crucial Ministry of the Interior.

This feeble effort was Azaña's last direct political initiative before the Civil War began. Henceforth he would withdraw into the presidency, preoccupied, it would seem, with esthetics, arguably his main interest. He initiated a major redecoration of the Palacio de Oriente, temporarily residing in the Casita at the Pardo palace (near the building that would be Franco's personal residence for thirty-six years). He expanded the presidential budget, drastically expanding the fleet of limousines,[66] and lent his attention to preparing new legislation that would establish severe penalties for attacks on the president and his family. Thus he fiddled while Spain burned, seemingly more intent on his personal comfort and security than on the well-being of his country.

Azaña had accomplished his basic goal of establishing leftist domination of political power and of some other institutions, the chief partial exception being the military—a crucial exception. On only one further occasion, the night of 18–19 July, would he make a belated effort to establish a broader and more effective coalition government. By then, however, the Civil War had already begun, and it would be too late.

CHAPTER TEN

Breaking Down

THOUGH NEARLY ALL SERIOUS observers agreed that the country was in dire need of a return to legality, order, and reconciliation, Casares Quiroga's inaugural speech to the Cortes, presenting his new minority cabinet on 19 May, offered the exact opposite, pledging an all-out assault against the right. Casares complained that "after five years the Republic still needs to defend itself against its enemies," once more conflating the Republic itself with the policies of the left. The government's policy, he declared, would be "an all-out attack" against these "enemies," which sounded dangerously like an effort to promote civil war. Any "declared enemy" would be "crushed." Casares went on to complain that the courts were too lenient with nonleftists, and that special legislation would be brought forward to promote the politicization of justice. Most widely quoted was his conclusion: "When it has to do with fascism, I will be unable to remain impartial. I declare to you that this government is belligerent against fascism."

Casares' appointment had pleased *Claridad,* which on 13 May had hailed it as one of the best possible because of the new prime minister's outspoken partisanship. Nonetheless, not merely moderates but also some left Republicans were critical of his "belligerency" speech, for its partisanship and ambiguity,[1] since leftist propaganda routinely called all rightists "fascist." Casares did add in his remarks that the left must also

248

obey the law and must renounce "political strikes outside the law, illegal takeovers, and acts of violence," a tacit admission of the many abuses that were occurring. Conversely, the speech had almost nothing to say about the grave economic problems that were developing, except to emphasize pursuit of the agrarian reform and an intention to double the amount spent on public works.

The parliamentary session that day was one of the most tumultuous, with much shouting, interruption, and verbal abuse. Gil Robles warned once more of the danger of civil war unless the law were firmly applied to all, while Calvo Sotelo became engaged in an exchange of insults with a Socialist deputy. Ventosa found Calvo Sotelo's remarks too partisan but pointed out: "I think that the 'enemies of the Republic' are the people who daily provoke public disorders and create the state of anarchy that is consuming the Republic. In every country where fascism has been installed it was preceded by disorders and persecution like those occurring in Spain today. . . . I call your attention to the evident similarity that exists between the political situation of Italy in 1920–21 and of Germany in later years."

It was abundantly clear that the Casares Quiroga administration would not provide the answer to Spain's problems, and conversations continued among moderate leaders about forming a stronger and more practical new coalition. The same personalities who had been active in April and early May were still involved, and the proposed leader continued to be, for want of any alternative, Indalecio Prieto. The well-known journalist Manuel Aznar wrote in *El Heraldo de Aragón* on 29 May that "every day there is more talk of a Prieto government, as well as the names of its ministers." Yet the fulcrum continued to rest on Prieto's willingness (or not) to split the Socialist Party, now experiencing further internal turmoil. One scenario had the executive commission of the party approving government participation (even though this would still be rejected by the UGT), with Ricardo Zabalza of the FNTT, a UGT dissident, taking over the Ministry of Agriculture, Miguel Maura the Foreign Ministry, and Lucia of the CEDA the Ministry of Communications (apparently for purposes of national unity). Maura was perhaps the most assiduous promoter of a broad constitutional coalition stretching from the left-center to the right-center, but its success would depend on the large parties, where agreement was lacking.

Giménez Fernández, who was actively involved in these discussions, penned the following analysis years later, shortly before his death:

From April onward, Besteiro, Maura, Sánchez Albornoz, and I talked about a possible government of the center that would extend from the Socialist right of Besteiro and Prieto to the demo-Christian left of Lucia, in order to combat the demagogy of the fascists and the Popular Front. Unfortunately, this proposal, at first opposed by neither Gil Robles nor Prieto, could not be carried out because of the following obstacles:

(A) The political blindness of Martínez Barrio, who, in order to gain seven representatives for his party in the looting of parliamentary seats from the right, could not understand that his group had moved from being the balance of power in parliament to merely being swallowed up by the left and, as events would prove, totally ineffective.

(B) The fear of Azaña that he was losing control of the left and therefore accepted the move to the presidency, unable to grasp that with the removal of Alcalá Zamora he had in fact lost the strongest support for the more moderate policies he himself suddenly began to favor.

(C) The obstinacy of Prieto, who, in order not to be deemed a traitor, refused to split the Socialist parliamentary delegation so long as he had the support of only a minority of it . . . lacking eight deputies who would not make a decision in enough time to provoke the crisis that, according to Sánchez Albornoz, Azaña would have been willing to solve by appointing a government led by Prieto (since Sánchez Román refused the premiership).

(D) The increasing pressure for rebellion and civil war from the right, especially the Juventudes de Acción Popular, who, enraged by the abuses of the extreme left and the leniency with which the latter were accepted by public authorities, passed in waves to the Falangists or Carlists, while financiers assisted those preparing a revolt, and finally, by the end of May, Gil Robles told Lucia and me that a centrist solution was becoming impossible.[2]

Though there was some evidence that support for his position was beginning to grow within the Socialist Party, Prieto continued to hold back,
—————————————————————————————— ----tallize. while on the right Gil Robles
ε. Under certain conditions
l coalition with CEDA votes,
approve CEDA participation
with the version of Giménez
ɔed any further participation
ɪns on 2 June, and some time
:d altogether.[3] Some days later,
the results of the fraudulent
ménez Fernández gave up on
:s to his home in Seville until
ɪother. The situation was now

ɔga government pressed ahead
:pression on the one hand, and
minister of public instruction,
than his predecessor Marcelino
: it:

ɪruary ordered inspectors to
egations. Apparently these
ɔls on their own initiatives.
ɪowever, it would seem that
ɪregations and the illegal
:ame, in effect, official policy.
schools be closed unless
ɪ state schools. The minister
suffer for their sins of omis-
ntly the state system since
ɔorarily withdrew from the
ɪsulting language as much as
ɪse to the Catholic conscience

Catholic schools being closed, but in
ɪs persistent harassment of religious

activities, as well. As Malefakis writes, "Priests were harassed unmercifully; churchgoers were made to feel that it was unsafe to attend Mass."[5]

The government was "belligerent" not merely against "fascism" and Catholic schools, but also against the independent judiciary. On 3 June new legislation was introduced to create a special tribunal, as provided for in article 99 of the constitution, to bring charges against judges and prosecutors accused of failing in their duties. This was to be composed of five magistrates from the Supreme Court as judges of law (*jueces de derecho*) and twelve special jurors (jurados) to render verdicts. Over the protest of the right, the measure was approved on 10 June, and another law was approved to provide greater political control over choosing new presidents of the Supreme Court. A total amnesty for all crimes by the left was finally approved on 3 July, and six days later the Cortes passed another measure for the forced retirement of judges and prosecutors, which the right charged was simply another weapon to use against conservatives.

After public order, the most serious problem facing the new government was economics. Prices were increasing rapidly, the peseta was in serious decline, and stock prices had naturally fallen. The Azaña government had taken the position that all economic problems had, as usual, been caused by the right, and had pursued a contradictory policy of expanding major budget categories and pursuing a more interventionist tack while hoping to stabilize the peseta and reduce both the trade imbalance and the national debt. The progressive tax reform proposed by Gabriel Franco, Azaña's finance minister, had never even been discussed in the Cortes, where the deputies were too busy denouncing each other. Franco had eventually resigned because it was not possible to fund significant new public works while controlling the debt, and the government refused to set priorities.

Casares Quiroga's inaugural speech of 19 May referred only to maintaining the acceleration of the agrarian reform, completing restoration of all the labor legislation of 1931–1933, and adding another 100 million pesetas to the 90 million already allocated to public works to combat unemployment. The left Republican government was committed to changing relations between capital and labor to give the latter much more power, but did not intend to eliminate market functions altogether and could not think its way through ensuing problems. It feared to introduce clearcut policies in several key areas. No reply was possible, for example, to criticism from the center and the right that the Spanish administration was the only new leftist government in Europe without a serious fiscal strategy, neither clearly deflationary nor clearly reflationary (though in practice somewhat nearer the latter). The government was going beyond the original Popular Front platform in economics, but instituted piecemeal measures and never managed to prepare a budget. Finally, on 30 June, it asked the Cortes to prorogue the preceding budget for the third quarter of the year. In parliament the only lucid remarks about the economy came from the center and the right.

The worst economic dislocation took place in parts of the central and southern countryside, while urban industry was affected somewhat less. Nonetheless the major increases in production costs, due to boosts in wages and fringe benefits, coupled with the loss of new investment, resulted in both lower production and lower productivity. Deficits in both the budget and the balance of payments increased, though the former did not raise an immediate problem. The activity of Catalan industry apparently declined, in the face of lowered demand at home and abroad and flight of capital.[6] From late May to the beginning of the Civil War center and rightist deputies in parliament bore unceasingly on the government's lack of policy to deal with the expanding crisis. By mid-June rightist spokesmen were even praising Léon Blum, leader of the more moderate and non-revolutionary Popular Front government in France, for having developed a coherent plan of national reconstruction that brought capital and labor together, with national wage rates and clear agreements, to which, as usual, the Casares Quiroga government had no response. Later Fernando Valera of Unión Republicana admitted that the government could never deal with unemployment when it could not even draw up a budget, was suffering both a fiscal and balance of payments deficit, and was dealing with an industrial structure that was not strong enough to absorb all the labor reinstatements mandated by the February decree.[7]

THE STRIKE WAVE AND LABOR DISTURBANCES OF MAY AND JUNE

Major strike activity had not been a primary feature of the first weeks after the Popular Front victory. The first negative measures taken by some business interests—abandonment of a number of enterprises, various lockouts, and above all the flight of capital—had been responses to the election results but not at first the result of major new trade union pressure. The Azaña administration, as mentioned earlier, had moved quickly to begin to restore the structure and authority of the jurados mixtos, even though this strategy was not made fully official until 30 May and new legislation that completely reestablished their original character was not approved by the Cortes until 20–21 June.

Massive strikes reappeared only with warmer weather in midspring, with a great increase in May that continued at an even more intense rate in June. During those two months alone, strike activity was approximately as great as in all of 1932 or 1934 (minus October), and for the first six and a half months of 1936 was greater than for 1933 (the previous high), if the total number of strikers is considered as well. The absolute volume, which may have involved as many as one million workers at the same time by late June, was proportionately no greater than that of the strike wave that developed in France following the Popular Front electoral victory there in May. The French strike wave of late May and June is thought to have involved possibly as many as two million workers at its height, roughly the same proportion of the labor force as in Spain. The main difference was that in France the government quickly channeled the strikes into practical economic settlements, while the massive work stoppages in Spain took on a prerevolutionary tone.

This was not because the CNT and UGT were demanding immediate collectivization of industry or the land (at least in most instances), but because the terms often demanded were so extravagant that they were beyond the ability of employers to pay or, if fully granted, would have amounted to de facto worker control. They were also frequently successful in imposing the closed shop, resulting in the firing of a considerable number of Catholic trade union members and precipitating a rapid decline of the smaller Catholic syndicates. In June the headquarters of the national Catholic labor organization was closed by the government, part of its policy of closing down rightist organizations, properties, and initiatives, as the revolutionary parties publicly urged.[8] All this occurred while the official unemployment rate remained at about 800,000 (approximately the same total as in France, indicating that registered unemployment was proportionately nearly twice as much in Spain—though again Spanish statistics included the partially unemployed). This figure underscores the essentially political character of the strikes, a feature stressed by many

Table 6

Strike Activity during the Republic

YEAR	NUMBER OF STRIKES
1931	734
1932	681
1933	1,127
1934	594
1935	181
1936	1,108

1936 BY MONTH	NUMBER OF STRIKES
January	26
February	19
March	47
April	105
May	242
June	444
July	225

Source: Boletín del Ministerio de Trabajo, 1936.

commentators. As the parliamentary spokesman of Unión Republicana admitted, the strikes were not "purely economic" in origin but "of a moral and social character."[9]

The large seamen's strike in May had international repercussions, tying up Spanish shipping in some foreign ports as well. By early June the dockworkers and crewmen had won total victory with a large wage increase, reduction in hours, and major fringe benefits. The terms of settlement would nominally require such an increase in manpower that there were neither enough crewmen nor enough space in the crewmen's quarters of Spanish merchant ships to hold them, leaving some vessels to idle in port and Spanish commerce facing catastrophic loss. Prieto warned on 25 May that the terms impending would provoke "an infinitely greater crisis" than the preceding exploitation of dockworkers and crewmen.[10]

In Barcelona the demands of hotel employees would have wrecked the hotel industry. When owners offered to cede part of their property to workers as shares in return for a more cooperative settlement, the CNT refused. In similar actions, the Valencia streetcar company and an Andalusian rail line were forced into dissolution, their services taken over by local government. In April the director of Echevarrieta shipbuilders had been arrested because his company had not been able to pay the large amount in back salaries imposed by the government. After a general strike in May, the provincial government finally agreed to pay the 200,000 pesetas involved. The Sociedad Metalúrgica de Peñarroya had made a deal with labor in April to establish a "labor rotation" so as to avoid terminal dismissals as its production declined by 50 percent. This arrangement doubled proportionate labor costs, which could not be paid. Even so, the workers presented new demands in June that, if accepted, would mean total bankruptcy.[11] Less spectacularly, hundreds of smaller businessmen were being ruined. In some cases the workday was being reduced to six hours. The minister of industry announced that he had an "educational" responsibility to change the terms of industrial relations, so that it was not surprising when on 14 May the Bloque Patronal demanded to know whether the government was taking the position that capitalist employment was to be abolished.[12] Similarly, small businessmen were asking whether the government "had decided to put an end to their historical role."[13] After the contractors' association gave in to exorbitant demands by striking CNT construction workers in Seville, the secretary of the CNT national committee, Horacio Prieto, urged his comrades to moderate demands before desperate employers, now willing to concede anything reasonable, were pushed into the arms of a protofascist reaction.

Under these conditions, in some categories unemployment inevitably increased, general production declined, tax receipts dropped, and more and more capital fled the country. It became increasingly difficult to fund the debt and to float government bonds. Business leaders pleaded with the government to take decisive measures to stabilize the economy and reach some sort of overall agreement with the trade unions. On June 7 *La Veu de Catalunya* published a "manifesto" signed by 126 local and regional employers' associations. It expressed willingness to accept most of the Popular Front's economic program but urged the government to take immediate measures to control economic anarchy, suggesting a temporary end to wage increases, reform of labor tribunals to achieve fair arbitration, and a national "labor conference" to try to straighten things out. Resolutions of the extraordinary assembly of the national chambers of commerce and industry in Madrid, as reported in *El Sol* on 26 June and 5 July, expressed the same concern. These urgent pleas were virtually ignored.

Perhaps the most conspicuous and conflictive single strike was initiated by the CNT in Madrid construction on 1 June. The CNT's Sindicato Único de la Construcción (SUC) in Madrid had expanded greatly, particularly by championing unskilled workers. On 19 April it had voted to demand a thirty-six-hour work week, a pay increase of 15 to 17 percent for skilled and semiskilled workers, and a 50 percent increase for the unskilled (peones). These demands were assumed in toto by the UGT the following month to avoid being outflanked. Employers, facing ruinous cost increases, took a hard line, and soon after the strike began it involved 110,000 workers, construction workers having been joined by allied trades. As usual, the CNT refused to cooperate with the jurado mixto, though the UGT was willing to do so, and therefore the Ministry of Labor unilaterally presented its own settlement on 3 July on the basis of a forty-hour week and salary increases ranging from 5 to 12 percent—very generous under the circumstances, but not ruinous for employers. UGT strikers voted three to one to accept these terms, which were rejected by the SUC. Even ugetistas were slow to return to work, and the strike was still in effect when the Civil War began.[14]

Major strikes often involved large-scale demonstrations and sometimes violence, the CNT particularly not being reluctant to use violence to keep strikes going. In late spring, some 60,000 shop clerks were on strike in Barcelona, and it was claimed that approximately half the workers in Madrid were off the job by July, though conditions, as usual, varied greatly from province to province.

Even leaders of the Socialist left became somewhat concerned. On 22 May the executive commission of the UGT ruled that there should be no further UGT strikes without direct authorization from the pertinent national federation, but this mandate was sometimes ignored. From about the second half of May the pro-Republican press registered increasing alarm, and *Política,* the main organ of Izquierda Republicana, called with mounting frequency for law and order. On 23 June the editors of *Solidaridad Obrera* also admitted that the strike wave had got out of hand and recommended that the CNT as a whole might want to push for lower prices rather than ever-more-unrealistic wage settlements. Alternately, CNT leaders suggested that the syndicates might wish to save their strength for the great revolutionary general strike at some unspecified point in the future. The leadership of the Communist Party also began to work to moderate the strike wave, though it had very limited influence among organized labor.

The greatest labor disorder was to be found not in the cities but in the countryside of the south-center and south. On 11 June the Cortes finally voted to restore the original agrarian reform law of 15 September 1932, but the right protested that the radical decrees of recent months, taking advantage of the clause that had been inserted in 1935 to permit confiscation without compensation "for reasons of social utility," had gone far beyond the original legislation. More serious than any confiscation of larger properties were the labor problems and great cost increases resulting from new wage settlements and alojamientos. The initiative in the southern countryside was taken more by the Socialists than by the CNT, and in Andalusia and Extremadura power lay less with national or provincial government authorities than with the municipal governments, often dominated by Socialists, and with the local Casas del Pueblo. The goal of Socialist policy in the south was ultimate collectivization but in the short run aimed less at changing the property structure immediately than at inverting the power relationships so that labor could dominate property owners. In one sense, this was consistent with general Socialist policy since 1931, which had always been to use the Republic to introduce radical changes that could open the way to socialism without establishing it immediately or through a direct violent revolution per se (in that sense, the insurrection of 1934 had been a partial aberration, not in its revolutionary goals but in its insurrectionary tactics of mass violence). The goal seems to have been to make landowners use up whatever reserves of capital they possessed to benefit workers, with no need to expropriate them formally until they had already handed over most of what they previously possessed.

By April large-scale alojamientos had been decreed, particularly in the provinces of Cordoba, Granada, and Huelva. In Cordoba this was decreed at the level of the provincial government, though more commonly just at the local level. Wage rates in Cordoba were reduced considerably, however,

for those benefiting from alojamientos, in order to avoid immediate bankruptcy of landowners. This move was accompanied by arbitrary arrests of
landowners and others charged with resisting the new measures, and also
by widespread theft of the olive crop and illegal cutting of trees. Coercion
of workers not in leftist syndicates mounted, to the point where farm
laborers in Seville province who were members of Unión Republicana protested to Madrid that the FNTT was refusing them work as nonmembers.
Alojamientos and informal "invasions of estates" increased during May,
becoming more frequent in Seville and Jaén provinces, even though in the
latter two provinces the provincial governors made futile efforts to control
such actions. The labor offensive benefitted greatly from the policy of the
Azaña government in imposing many Socialist mayors, sometimes even
in areas where the Socialists were in a clear minority. Totally one-sided
terms were imposed on the provincial levels, so that in Seville province
the workday was reduced to a mere six hours, which also included the
time spent in walking or riding to work, as well as all rest periods. Among
the arbitrary measures imposed by some municipal governments in the
south were surcharges on the normal wages, 100 percent increases on
taxes of landowners, and requirements to undertake specific repairs on
homes or properties, whether needed or not, that would employ more
workers.[15] Harvest wages in the south were generally set at eleven to thirteen pesetas per day, though the syndicates sometimes demanded more.
"This meant more than a doubling of 1935 wages and an increase of some
20 percent over the pay scales of 1933, a year in which the profit squeeze
on producers was so great that it contributed" to the downfall of the first
Azaña government.[16] In Jaén wages rose 46 percent over the level even
of 1932, so that by May some landowners in the south began to abandon
their properties and move to the cities to live off capital.[17]

Landowners in Seville province had already held an assembly in mid-
April to complain of a reign of terror in the countryside, even before conditions reached their most extreme. In mid-May petitions were made to
the government by both the Federación Patronal Agrícola in Seville and
the national Confederación Española Patronal Agrícola; both asked for the
enforcement of law and order, declaring that they were willing to accept
the new regulations so long as they went no further and were enforced
honestly, without additional excess.[18] This was a totally unprecedented
position for landowners to take, and a dramatic expression of their sense

of desperation. On May 27 the governor of Badajoz province reported that some farmworkers would not accept even wages of twelve pesetas a day, more than double what they had received the preceding year.[19] Sometimes even smallholders and renters had to make payoffs to avoid ruinous alojamientos.[20] Landowners could not understand why the left Republican governments permitted such extremism and anarchy, since they considered the left Republicans, as Azaña considered himself, to be "bourgeois" and in favor of private property. The Popular Front program had never specified such drastic changes, but by May that program had been exceeded in every respect. The more liberal landowners seem in fact to have been the most bewildered, not grasping that the left Republicans had long since abandoned liberalism and had embraced an unofficial devil's bargain with the revolutionaries. There does seem to have been some concern on the part of the Casares Quiroga government to protect small and medium landowners as well as laborers who were members of Republican parties, but this could not be done without forcefully applying the law, something that the government normally would not do for fear of the reaction from the Socialists. There were, however, occasions when the provincial governors did intervene to control excesses on the local level.

Even acceleration of the official agrarian reform under Ruiz Funes and the IRA became increasingly disorderly. Ruiz Funes annulled all the transfers that had been carried out in 1935, so that most of the small number of families who had received land the preceding year were forced to relinquish it. He did, however, seek to maintain the principle that land confiscated from smaller owners would be compensated at a rate near market value, though larger owners would be paid proportionately much less. Moreover, the average size of new legal allotments was only 5.5 hectares (about 12 acres), and Ruiz Funes admitted in the Cortes on 27 May that in fact it could not be expected that the economic success rate for such smallholdings without capital would be more than 40 percent, so that in effect the government was admitting that for the most part its accelerated agrarian reform was not likely to work. Thus the government's Servicio Agronómico recommended seizing all properties beyond a small size, since otherwise there would not possibly be enough land. Occasionally the new beneficiaries might leave the land they were given, saying they preferred "a daily wage to the benefits of direct cultivation."[21] Employers began to demand that all wage settlements include production standards, specifying how much effective work was being purchased by the enormously increased wages. Production standards were rejected by Socialists and Communists, of course, but the inept labor minister Lluhí admitted on 1 July that production standards were probably desirable. In Cortes interpellation, the opposition charged that, on the basis of the Ministry of Labor's own official statistics, the cost of the total harvest would exceed its market value, an assertion to which Lluhí and Ruiz Funes had difficulty replying.

The greatest proportionate labor action of the late spring was a sort of provincial agricultural general strike begun by the CNT in Málaga province. During the first two weeks of June this was supported by the provincial FNTT and Communist syndicates and spread to the towns, becoming a sort of rural-urban general strike in which at one point possibly as many as 100,000 workers had walked out.[22] Similar conditions prevailed in southern mining. A huge strike in Huelva was won by the UGT, but conditions imposed on the large Rio Tinto mining company proved counterproductive. A requirement to rehire 3,000 workers and pay back wages soon began to bankrupt the company; new layoffs began in June.[23]

The FNTT resolutely rejected minimal work or productivity standards and also rejected as inadequate the government's proposal to give land to 100,000 new settlers per year. The CNT, which was adding members rapidly in the southern countryside, set even more radical terms. Forced alojamientos and *siegas por asalto* (arbitrary entry to harvest on the workers' terms) drove smaller landowners to the brink of ruin, yet did not meet all workers' demands either. Increased labor costs were apparently encouraging some large landowners to move more rapidly toward mechanization, though new labor contracts in the southern countryside placed specific restrictions on the use of machinery.[24] Continued bad weather, late planting and harvesting, and lack of credit for small farmers all compounded the problems, leading the Ministry of Agriculture to forecast a 27 percent decline in the wheat harvest, compared with the bountiful year preceding.[25] Some farmland was simply abandoned, and smaller owners sought to hire only the most minimal labor. The most extreme conditions probably prevailed in Badajoz province, where over one-third of all adult rural males had already received some land, and the proportion may have been nearly as great in Cáceres. This property transfer only whetted the appetite for further economic relief, producing arbitrary actions on a large scale as "thousands of workers wandered around . . . in a futile search for jobs" in Badajoz province, "which seems to have been in complete chaos on the eve of the Civil War."[26] By the end of June the UGT had begun a national campaign for the immediate uncompensated expropriation of all land not being cultivated, and illegal takeovers of one form or another were apparently still continuing in certain provinces.

A precise census of all the land that changed hands in these months will probably never be possible. A leading social historian concludes: "Our hypothesis, though it is not certain and needs to be tested further, is that the de facto occupation of land, whether by *yunteros* (Extremaduran ploughmen), by legal beneficiaries of the agrarian reform, new settlers on confiscated land already in process of reclassification, or simply de facto occupation—sometimes in the form of alojamientos—registered by rural police commissions with the Junta Provincial Agraria, may have amounted to about one million hectares by the time the Civil War began."[27] This calculation, the best that can be made without much more research, would amount to about 2.5 percent of the 40 million hectares of agrarian property in Spain, but 5 percent of the approximately 20 million hectares of cropland. This was not yet a revolution, but it could be seen as the beginning of one. The shift in landownership had already provoked massive consequences in some of the southern provinces, where the share of cropland that had changed hands was much higher than 5 percent.[28]

By mid-June the harvest had not yet begun in some southern districts because the syndicates were demanding even higher wages. On 10 July the Patronal Agraria of Seville province sent a study to the civil governor showing that the cost of the harvest would exceed its value, while in Cordoba province a number of smallholders affiliated with left Republican parties sent their own petition to the government. It stated that under current conditions their own economic activity had become futile and suggested that the IRA should simply take over their lands, ending with the salutation *salud y República* (good health and the Republic—a standard leftist salutation).[29] A decree in the *Gaceta de la República* on 11 July forbade illegal takeover of lands belonging to small and medium proprietors, but enforcement remained unlikely under the current government.

There was a generalized flight of larger landowners from the countryside into the cities. The governor of Córdoba province announced that he was checking to see if he had the authority to stop this, in order, as a critic of his put it in the Cortes, to "require them to remain in their respective towns, asserting a novel legal theory that inverted standard exiles and deportations, turning them inside out." On 22 May, in order to keep people from fleeing abroad, the minister of the interior had told civil governors to be very restrictive in the criteria for issuing passports.[30] By late June and early July newspapers were reporting an increasing number of statements by landowners that they would have to abandon cultivation, while statements by government officials seemed to indicate that they realized that wage increases had become excessive.

There are no data on the absolute number of arrests, but arbitrary detention was frequent. In Antequera, for example, all members of the local section of the monarchist Renovación Española were arrested as "fascists," a move that apparently astounded them, since they had no dealings with the Falange. The latter was indeed growing in Andalusia because of the prerevolutionary situation that had developed. At the time of the elections, it had had scarcely more than 2,000 members in Andalusia and in terms of social composition was something of an elitist club of the upper classes. By 18 July it had expanded to 9,000 members, with laborers and employees who had been pressured by the left joining in significant numbers. According to one study, 47 percent of the Falangist membership now came from workers and employees,[31] while in the city of Almería 80 percent of the leaders were drawn from these strata.[32]

Yet the great majority of the farmworkers in the UGT and CNT seem to have had little notion of a thoroughgoing economic revolution. Most evidently wanted much higher wages or land of their own to work on easy terms. As Julián Besteiro warned in the Cortes and as an agrarian expert pointed out in *El Sol* (15 and 17 July), the real effect of all the strikes and rural harassment, especially in the southwest, was not to effect a positive revolution in ownership and production but to divert as much as possible of the short-term income to farmworkers and to some smallholders. Mechanization was thwarted, and medium- and sometimes even smallholders were being ruined without any real attempt to build the basis for a more modern efficient rural economy. The economic consequences of the agrarian prerevolution in the south were primarily destructive.

The Socialist—or at least the UGT—position was that the time had come for the socialization of land and industry, though no plan was presented. On 9 June the government introduced legislation aimed at the mining industry in Asturias and Leon, providing that mine shafts and deposits no longer being actively mined be taken over as worker cooperatives, though their low productivity might produce no more than the reorganization of poverty. By the end of the month Socialist and Communist deputies claimed that the extent of abandonment by landowners was so great that in some areas the harvest process should either be taken over by local government authorities or handed to the farmworker syndicates.

The charges of "provocation" made against landowners was particularly dubious, as Malefakis says, not only because the latter would be losing an enormous amount of money if they failed to harvest their crops but also because landowners were, in general, poorly organized as an interest group.[33] Moreover, the situation could be expected only to deteriorate later in the year, because once the harvest was over even more owners would abandon cultivation.

Since the cost of the harvest in the south would often exceed its value, even the nationalization demanded by Socialists would accomplish nothing unless real wages could be considerably lowered. The government could respond to the left only by conducting massive expropriations, but that move would not itself solve the problem, the full depth of which would be revealed by the revolutionary collectivization after the Civil War began, when the syndical organizations could not provide work or land in eastern Andalusia even to all those left over after military mobilization had begun. Because of bad weather and highly disturbed conditions, the wheat harvest of 1936 would be the worst in years. By the beginning of summer even a few left Republican deputies in parliament began to question how the government could face the multiple and mounting economic problems, which had no immediate solution. As Macarro Vera has written, "What is indisputable is that none of the economic recipes contained in the Popular Front program had any value as relevance and that those charged with their implementation were in utter disagreement. . . . In July 1936 it would seem that none of the Popular Front parties was even concerned to face up to the conundrum."[34]

GROWTH OF VIOLENCE

Many strikes were accompanied by violence, which had begun to increase in mid-April. The incidence mounted with warmer weather, hitting a high point around 25 May and remaining very near that level for the next seven weeks. Falangists and rightists were killed by the left, leftists in turn were slain mainly by Falangists, striking (usually demonstrating) workers were shot at and killed by police, and sometimes policemen were killed in return. After Falangists killed a Socialist newspaper editor in Santander on 3 June, four Falangists or suspected Falangists were slain in that city during the next forty-eight hours.

One of the more bizarre sets of incidents, which caused no fatalities, started in Alcalá de Henares on 15 May, when several officers of the local army garrison were assaulted by leftists, who then set fire to the home of one of the officers. The Socialists of Alcalá next petitioned the government to transfer the two regiments of the local garrison, alleging fascist and conspiratorial proclivities among its officers. Casares Quiroga agreed, and the units were ordered to be ready to move within forty-eight hours. When the officers protested, a number were arrested, court-martialed, and sentenced to varying prison terms, heightening the sense of outrage among the military. Similarly, after an affray between workers and the Civil Guard in Oviedo on 23 May, protests against the use of force by the latter led to the arrest and prosecution of five Civil Guard officers.

The heaviest mortality from any of the explosions of violence took place near the small town of Yeste, in Albacete province, southeast of Madrid, on 29 May. The inhabitants of a neighboring hill pueblo called La Graya had lost much of their livelihood following inauguration during the previous year of a new dam in the valley below, one of the accomplishments of the Republic's public works program. Approximately 1,000 families had drawn their living from logging and other activities in the area now under water, while the remaining forest in the hills above could not be exploited economically for the opposite reason—too great a distance between the felled logs and the water needed to transport them. The Azaña administration had imposed a new all-left comisión gestora as the government of Albacete, despite the fact that the right had just won the Cortes elections there. It had opened some small public lands for private timbering by local workers, as well as expanding public works and arranging alojamientos; but all these measures failed to end unemployment. With the coming of warm weather, many began to take the law into their own hands, illegally cutting timber on private property, though it could not be marketed in large quantities, and cultivating private land. After complaints from landowners, the local workers were ordered to cease such activity, and nineteen Civil Guards were dispatched to La Graya. On the evening of 28 May, six young hotheads attempted to assault the guards, who managed to arrest them. This move brought out a large concentration of workers and their families from surrounding villages, who blocked the road on the twenty-ninth when the Civil Guards attempted to take their prisoners to Yeste. The local Socialist mayor tried to defuse the situation by arranging to have the prisoners temporarily released, but one local militant seized a guard's gun and killed him with it (though according to another version the latter had been struck in the head with a logging hook). The Civil Guards alleged that they were then physically assaulted by the large crowd, which they estimated at up to 2,000, all the guards being said to have suffered some sort of injuries, ranging from minor bruises to serious wounds. According to their version, three at first managed to hold onto their weapons, drawing off from the crowd just enough to pour volley after volley into them at point-blank range. The gunfire immediately sent the crowd into a panicked flight, and as other guards were able to bring weapons into play, they joined in the shooting. By the time the crowd had got out of range, seventeen lay dead and more than thirty had been wounded.[35]

This bloody incident reflected the sense of desperation and rage among poor workers, as well as their extreme hostility and aggressiveness, and also the oft-demonstrated inadequacy of the Civil Guard—in terms of both training and equipment—to handle crowd control humanely. It drew a storm of protest from the extreme left, which alleged another police atrocity equivalent to that at Arnedo in 1932 or Casas Viejas in 1933, though the circumstances were quite different. The matter was aired in the Cortes on 5 June, where it was agreed to leave it in the hands of an investigative judge.

The government's only response to these incidents was to arrest more Falangists and to close the local centers of sections of the CNT that prosecuted strikes by illegal or violent means, ignoring the jurados mixtos. Neither of these policies had much effect, for both the fascist and anarchosyndicalist organizations were growing rapidly. It is no exaggeration to say that for every Falangist arrested—and there were eventually several thousand in jail—five or more new members joined in order to participate in direct action against the left. Calvo Sotelo charged in parliament on 6

May that 8,000 to 10,000 rightists were then in jail, probably an exaggeration. Falangists claimed that seventy of their members had died violent deaths between November 1933 and 1 June 1936, while cedistas claimed to have lost twenty-six members to violence before February 1936. These latter claims would seem to be approximately correct.

What was undeniable was the sudden growth in support for the now illegal organization, and the extent of the reaction among the right in general. The left Christian democrat Ossorio y Gallardo lamented on 10 June in *Ahora* that the behavior of the left had become irrational and destructive, with no positive outcome in view: "The Popular Front was created to combat fascism, but the way things are going in Spain, the only fascism is going to be that of the Popular Front."

Agustín Calvet ("Gaziel"), the respected conservative editor of Barcelona's *La Vanguardia*, wrote in the latter two days later:

> How many votes did the fascists have in Spain in the last
> election? None: a ridiculously small amount. . . . Today, on
> the other hand, travelers returning from different parts of the
> country are saying: 'There everybody is becoming a fascist.'
> What kind of change is this? What has happened? What has
> happened is simply that it is no longer possible to live, that
> there is no government. . . . In such a situation, people instinc-
> tively look for a way out. . . . What is the new political form
> that radically represses all these insufferable excesses? A dicta-
> torship, fascism. And thus almost without wanting to, almost
> without realizing it, people begin *to feel themselves* fascist. They
> know nothing about all the inconveniences of a dictatorship,
> which is natural. They will learn about these later on, when
> they have to suffer them.
>
> . . . Fascism is, in the cases of France and Spain, the sinister
> shadow projected across the land by democracy itself, when its
> internal decomposition turns it into anarchy. The more the rot
> spreads, the more fascism expands. And therefore the deluded
> concern that the triumphant Popular Front shows about a de-
> feated fascism is nothing more than the fear of its own shadow.

Nor did the partial censorship, which continued, have any effect in dampening passions. As one American scholar put it: "Government censorship tried to suppress the news of strikes and assassinations because the ministers feared the contagion of violence. Copy for daily newspapers had to be rushed to the official press bureau for examination; the deleted sections appeared as blank space or with broken type. The Paris *Temps,* arriving a few days late in Madrid, was often more informative than the newspapers of the Spanish capital. Only when one gathered a bunch of provincial papers and turned to the pages entitled Social Conflicts could one fully realize the scope of labor discontent for which there were no official statistics."[36]

The national council of Izquierda Republicana issued a public statement on 30 May that lamented, "Spain has been viewed abroad as a country in permanent civil war, incapable of democratic coexistence. The Republic is considered an unstable, interim regime, whose consolidation is made difficult by the Republicans themselves."[37] It urged all the local sections of the party to do everything possible to calm passions and maintain legality. The party newspaper *Política* continued its calls for moderation. On 11 June the parliamentary delegations of Izquierda Republicana and Unión Republicana approved a joint resolution asking the government to undertake stronger measures to restore order. In the days that followed *Política* praised the French CGT for having just signed a sweeping new national labor agreement dampening the strike wave in France, while it continued to denounce the CNT for flaunting the arbitration of jurados and seeking to ruin the UGT. It championed the position of the petite bourgeoisie, but underscored the importance of the alliance between petit-bourgeois left Republicanism and organized labor—not grasping that this indeed may have been a major part of the problem—while assigning major responsibility for social and economic turmoil to the larger employers. The only real polemic between *Política* and *Claridad* took place during the second half of June, when the former blamed the Socialist left for the conflict within the Socialist Party, which, it claimed, subverted the latter and the unity of the Popular Front.

On 11 June the government, as usual, asked the Cortes to extend the state of alarm for thirty days more, and on the morrow issued new orders for the disarming of those who possessed weapons illegally (though scarcely any Socialists were ever arrested), together with new sanctions against employers who flouted labor regulations and new measures to end strikes conducted by illicit means. This move was accompanied by further reassignments in military and Civil Guard posts. The government was now more aware that it was conducting—with the utmost confusion, uncertainty, and incoherence—a battle on two fronts, so that by mid-June Casares Quiroga was making positive remarks about the Civil Guard. Before the end of the month, for several of the southern provinces he also appointed new civil governors who he hoped would apply the law more energetically.

ALARM IN THE EMBASSIES

The pronounced increase in disorder during March naturally caused alarm in the foreign embassies, the greatest concern being shown by those of Britain, France, Portugal, and Germany. In France conservative newspapers began to speculate more and more about the likelihood of either revolution or civil war in Spain. The most alarmed government was the Salazar regime in Portugal, for it had been the target of armed conspiracy abetted by the Spanish government during the first Azaña administration, and feared another attempt by Spanish authorities to destabilize it, as indeed part of the left was demanding. Reassurances from Madrid did little good, and the mood in Lisbon was markedly hostile, as Claudio Sánchez Albornoz found when he arrived as the new ambassador in May. The Portuguese left was heavily represented in Madrid, where, according to the Portuguese police, some 200 gathered between April and June to join in the organization of the Portuguese Communist Party and to initiate negotiations to attempt to create a Portuguese Popular Front and prepare other actions against the Lisbon regime. Some of the Portuguese residents in Madrid were terrified and besieged their embassy with demands for measures to protect themselves and their property. Portuguese authorities meanwhile permitted Spanish rightists to conspire against the Madrid government and to broadcast a series of hostile radio programs from Portuguese soil.[38]

In Madrid the embassies of Germany, Italy, and Portugal were the targets of numerous threats as well as hostile demonstrations. On 2 April the ambassadors of Argentina, Britain, Germany, the Netherlands, and Switzerland met to discuss the issue of granting asylum should violent revolution break out, a concern that would soon prove prescient. By mid-April the German ambassador had transferred his residence to Paris, leaving the embassy in the hands of the chargé.[39]

In this regard, the attitude of British diplomats and government leaders was of considerable importance, and it revealed growing alarm, fueled by the perception that Spain was going the way of Russia. This was only increased by the murder of the British director of a textile factory in Barcelona, prompting official notes of protest to the governments in both Madrid and Barcelona. Largo Caballero's frank remarks to the British press soon afterward merely confirmed this alarm, when he stated flatly that the future of the Casares Quiroga government depended in large measure on the Socialists. Though he supported the government, he said, he doubted that it could long survive, after which the Socialists would take over and introduce their own program. This was exactly what British officials feared.[40]

A "CATALAN OASIS"?

Catalanists love to emphasize what they term the *fet diferencial de Catalunya*, and to that end the Lliga newspaper *La Veu de Catalunya* introduced on 4 March the metaphor of *l'oasi català*, not so much as a factual description but as the goal of a calm, well-ordered Catalonia, to which Catalans should aspire in contrast to the disorder then engulfing most of Spain. It was indeed the case that Lluis Companys, once more president of the Generalitat, did make more of an effort at conciliation in Catalonia than did the national authorities in Madrid. Though the regional government arbitrarily closed a number of the right-center Lliga's local centers, the Lliga made a serious effort to be a responsible and loyal opposition, so that by early July Companys had reversed course and begun negotiations to reach a new understanding between the moderate left and moderate right in Barcelona.[41]

Yet the "oasis" metaphor is considerably exaggerated. The Generalitat, like the government in Madrid, attempted to restrict the news and avoid public information concerning the number of conflicts and disorders, and certain earlier studies noted only three political killings in Barcelona between the elections and the start of the Civil War. More recently, however, the investigation of the Catalan press by Jordi Getman-Eraso has yielded a total of fifteen politically related killings for the period,[42] less than half as many as in Madrid but the same as the average for Seville, Málaga, and Granada (though lower in proportion to population). The majority of the killings in Barcelona were related to CNT labor conflicts. Strike activity was intensive and often accompanied by violence, though not normally by fatalities. Twenty-one bombs were exploded in Barcelona during the month of April alone, and armed robbery neared a record, registering a total of eighty robberies in the city during the first six months of 1936, each involving theft of 500 pesetas or more. Barcelona may have been somewhat less frenzied than Madrid, but in general it also reflected the violent and conflictive character of these months.

THE DRIVE FOR REGIONAL AUTONOMIES

The tidal wave of change unleashed by the Popular Front victory quickened all the autonomist and regionalist movements. Restoration of Catalan autonomy was followed by a new initiative from Basque nationalists. The demonstration effect thus provided, together with the obvious examples of new worker initiatives on every hand and the support by the left Republican administration, energized autonomist forces in all the major regions. Indalecio Prieto, the most influential non-nationalist leader in Bilbao, understood that further delay in moving toward Basque autonomy would only strengthen the more extreme nationalists, while the Basque Nationalist Party now grasped that autonomy would come only from democracy and not from or in conjunction with the right. A special Cortes committee was established, composed of José Antonio de Aguirre (leader of the Partido Nacionalista Vasco), a Basque Socialist, and a Basque left Republican who were to work out proposed terms of Basque autonomy, and on 24 May Prieto declared in Bilbao that he was determined to achieve Basque autonomy as soon as possible, even if it were his last political accomplishment. A new statute proposal was given to this committee in April, and approval was nearly ready by mid-July.

At the beginning of May representatives of the three Aragonese provinces met in Caspe to begin work on a statute for Aragon, closely modeled on that of Catalonia.[43] Delegates of the Agrarians and the CEDA commenced work on a statute for Castile and Leon on 20 May, though dissidents wanted to include only Old Castile and Leon, while on 9 June the city council of Burgos voted in favor of a statute for Old Castile alone. A campaign was launched in Gijón on 29 May to rally support for an Asturian statute, while broader efforts were already under way in the Valencian region. On 6 July a body of delegates met in Seville to begin drafting a statute for Andalusia, and on the fifteenth a similar body met in Santa Cruz de Tenerife to prepare a document for the Canary Islands.[44]

The process was farthest advanced in Galicia, where the autonomist campaign was actively promoted by the Popular Front. A plebiscite to vote on a newly prepared statute was held on 28 June, with official electoral participation of 74.52 percent, of whom 74 percent were recorded as voting in favor. These results surprised all objective observers, since Galicia traditionally had the highest abstention rate in Spain, and the turnout registered for the general elections of February had been considerably lower. In fact before the plebiscite Galicianists had struggled to gain an exception to the constitutional requirement that an absolute majority vote in favor of any proposed autonomy statute. It was generally concluded that there had been massive manipulation, particularly after it was found that in some rural, typically abstentionist, districts 100 percent of the electorate had been recorded as voting in favor. The new statute was officially submitted to the Cortes on 15 July for final ratification.[45]

With autonomist campaigns developing all over Spain, there were demands on both the radical right and the revolutionary left for complete standardization of the process. Calvo Sotelo declared in *ABC* on 20 May that there should be autonomy statutes for all regions or none, while the Marxist-Leninist POUM touted creation of an "Unión de Repúblicas Socialistas de Iberia," a sort of Iberian Soviet Union.

CHAPTER ELEVEN

Competing Utopias

THE REVOLUTIONARY MOVEMENTS IN THE SPRING OF 1936

BY 1936 SPAIN HAD become home to the broadest and most intense panoply of revolutionary movements of any country in the world, in itself a remarkable situation, and one that surely requires some explanation. The notion that this circumstance was due simply to "backwardness" or "social injustice"—the standard explanations—is superficial. Spain was not one of the most backward countries in the world, nor was it one of the most unjust, though it was far from being fully developed and had some major social problems. Any coherent theory of revolution in the modern world has first to recognize that potentially revolutionary situations do not develop among the poorest and most downtrodden societies—for the simple reason that they are indeed extremely poor and downtrodden and lack all empowerment. Revolutionary movements, like other modern political phenomena, require rather the opposite—at least a certain level of education and development. Revolutionary situations do not develop from conditions of massive oppression, but rather in countries that have recently undergone a certain amount of growth, improvement, or development that stimulates a psychological disposition to seek or desire even greater change. Revolutionary aspirations then come to the fore after the period of improvement is temporarily frustrated, creating new problems, disappointments, and frustrations, for which a revolutionary solution is then sought. This state of affairs in turn must be accompanied politically by conditions of relative liberalization and/or incipient frustration and breakdown. Such a sequence of change before the development of a revolutionary situation may be accurately applied, *mutatis mutandis,* to France in the late eighteenth century, to Russia in the early twentieth century, and to Spain in the 1930s. This is not a matter of backwardness or level of development alone. France in the 1790s was one of the most modern countries. Russia in the early twentieth century was making very rapid progress but in some respects remained quite backward and had never experienced democracy. Spain in the 1930s occupied an intermediate position.

Between 1917 and 1933 Spain had experienced one of the most vertiginous rhythms of change of any country in the world, beginning with the economic growth that started in World War I and then accelerated during the 1920s. Very rapid economic, social, and cultural change was followed by the dramatic democratization of 1931. This was the Spanish equivalent of the sudden democratization that had occurred in many other lands after the war, delayed in the Spanish case by the country's neutrality, which enabled its old regime to cling to power for a few more years. The delayed Spanish democratization, however, was all the more dramatic and explosive when it did occur, and had a greater impact on Spanish society than had been the case in a number of other European countries in 1919–20. The result, as argued in chapter 1, was to bring about the most fundamental of revolutions—the revolution of rising expectations. This can be one of the most profound of revolutions, for it takes place in the minds and emotions of millions of people.

Indeed, the democratization of 1931–32 may simply have been too abrupt, extensive, and radical for the country's good, lacking sound institutionalization or the moderating power of constitutional monarchy. A gradual and progressive democratization of the institutions of the parliamentary monarchy would have been more advantageous, for it would have taken place within an institutional and political framework more nearly capable of channeling, moderating, and balancing the democratization within constructive boundaries.

As it was, the great democratization enormously heightened expectations on the left, which were then in large measure frustrated. Many circumstantial factors intervened—the effects of the Great Depression, the rise of the radical new ideologies of left and right, the influence of the

Soviet model, the fear of fascism on the left, the continued existence of a major social problem such as that of the immiserated landless laborers of the south, the apparent weakness of Spanish conservatism (at least until 1933), and the remarkable weakness of Spanish nationalism prior to this time. Nationalism had become the greatest source of strength for rightists and counterrevolutionaries in most European countries, but seemed to have little effect in Spain save in the centrifugal form of the peripheral nationalist movements, which appeared only to reemphasize the weakness of all-Spanish nationalism, at least before the Civil War. This combination of circumstances enormously encouraged and radicalized the left, who were convinced that their historical moment had finally arrived, and that in Spain counterrevolutionary opposition was bound to be weaker—despite the votes of the CEDA—than in most other European countries. A powerful Spanish counterrevolutionary nationalism would emerge when the Civil War began, but it seemed to have little presence before mid-1936.

One major problem of the Spanish revolutionaries, however, was their diversity. Their ranks included the world's only mass anarchosyndicalist movement, a large and radical Socialist movement—by far the most radical in Europe since the demise of Italian Socialism—and two different Communist parties, the regular Muscovite PCE, now growing rapidly, and the smaller but hyperrevolutionary POUM. To their right stood the radical but nonrevolutionary left Republicans, with whom all but the anarchists were allied in the Popular Front, and whom all but the more moderate sector of the Socialists sought to use as their Kerenskyist stalking horse. The left Republicans shared none of these utopias, however, and hoped to use and moderate the revolutionaries as much as the latter hoped to use and radicalize them, creating a high-stakes political game whose future was very much in doubt. The revolutionaries soon won this competition, but the outcome might have been more uncertain had the Civil War not broken out when it did.

All the leftist movements agreed on the principle of unity to defeat and exclude the right, but otherwise their own agendas diverged sharply and were in some cases mutually exclusive. This circumstance was occasionally commented on by some leftist leaders who wondered how there could possibly be a successful collectivist revolution in Spain when the collectivists would inevitably quarrel so sharply among themselves.

THE CNT

The anarchosyndicalist Confederación Nacional del Trabajo had been until 1930 the only worker mass movement in Spain, and also the most revolutionary except for the Communists. Its strategy under the Republic had proven disastrous, however, for the three revolutionary mini-insurrections of 1932–33 had exhausted the movement and had also produced a split in its ranks. Such enervation and division, the effects of the repressions that had followed each insurrection, and the disillusionment of ordinary militants had cost the movement approximately half its membership of nearly a million workers.

To reunify the movement, the second extraordinary congress in the history of the CNT met in Zaragoza during the first ten days of May. The delegates officially represented syndicates numbering 550,595 members. This marked a decline of 40–50 percent from the organizational high point in 1931–32, though the decline was now being rapidly made good by an active campaign of expansion in which the new strike offensive and competition with the UGT played major roles. The CNT secretariat's report ridiculed the revolutionary pretensions of the caballerista Socialists, declaring that the rhetoric of the "Spanish Lenin" reminded it of the fable about the frog that wanted to become an ox. It further stressed that the internal division and "indecision" of the anarchosyndicalist movement in the past two years had permitted the Communists and other Marxist parties to grow at their expense and had allowed the bourgeois left to take over the government once more with a policy "exactly as at the time of Casas Viejas."[1]

The committee charged with investigating the CNT's role in the October insurrection attributed both the initiative and the fiasco in that enterprise to the "rage of the Socialists for having been thrown out of power." An equal share of blame was attributed to Azaña, "the head of socializing radicalism, the most cynical and coldly cruel politician ever known in Spain." The feeble effort by Catalanists and by Socialists beyond Asturias was ridiculed, and the nonparticipation by the CNT elsewhere was justified by the fact that "it did not want to be the sacrificial vanguard for factions that would have finished off in cold blood our survivors from the struggle against the government." Union with the UGT was declared possible only on the basis of the latter's absolute renunciation of any collaboration with a Republican government, agreement on "completely destroying the political and social regime," and the support of 75 percent of the membership in a referendum.[2]

The congress endorsed once more "the insurrectional method for the conquest of social wealth." A report on the installation of libertarian communism declared that the goal was to abolish private property and reorganize society on the basis of syndicates and autonomous communes to form a "Confederación Ibérica de Comunas Autónomas Libertarias." The army and police would be abolished, all weapons handed over to the communes, and the theory of the nonexistence of God taught in schools.[3]

Though relations with the UGT remained difficult, there was more cooperation on the local level than ever before, as a growing number of the multitudinous new strikes became joint CNT-UGT initiatives. On 24 May Largo Caballero publicly embraced a CNT leader at a meeting in Cádiz, yet most of the differences persisted. In a number of major strikes the CNT seized the initiative in opposition to the UGT, whose leaders sometimes tried to follow a more prudent course than the one indicated by revolutionary rhetoric.

"Competitive radicalization" between the two movements reached its climax in Málaga, where a strike by CNT fish salters was opposed by the local UGT fishermen's syndicate. In retaliation, on 10 June CNT gunmen killed a Communist city councilman who had taken the initiative against them, and then amid his funeral procession shot down the Socialist president of the Málaga provincial assembly. Gunmen from the Marxist parties soon killed one cenetista as well as the eleven-year-old daughter of another, caught in the crossfire. The government closed all CNT centers in the province, but violence continued as the CNT declared a general strike. Police reinforcements were rushed in from Madrid, and many cenetistas were arrested, while Socialists and Communists distributed leaflets accusing the CNT of serving "el fascio."

Anarchists continued to emphasize that they would never accept any Marxist "dictatorship of the proletariat," and that the Spanish collectivist revolution must be libertarian. *Solidaridad Obrera* declared on 2 June that although the Casares Quiroga government might call itself "belligerent against fascism," in practice "the government is belligerent against the CNT." It insisted that the Popular Front was the very opposite of a revolutionary alliance of workers and in fact persecuted anarchosyndicalism.

Despite the relative success of reunification, a divergence had begun to emerge between the main rural sectors of the CNT in the south and the chief industrial core in Catalonia. The Andalusian syndicates threw themselves into the furor of southern rural activism, which they were willing to press as far as possible, even into the beginning of a revolutionary change. The attitude of the burgeoning CNT affiliate in Madrid was similar. In Catalonia there was a great deal of strike activity and some violence, but the CNT leaders in Barcelona made an effort to discourage extremes of activism. Leaders in Catalonia sought to emphasize reorganization, institutional expansion, and the building of solid unified cadres, postponing at least for the moment thoughts of revolutionary change. They set their face against the insurrectionism of 1932–33, which they labeled a mistake, insisting that at this point the emphasis must be on developing strength for the future. None of this obviated the violence of CNT activists in Barcelona that spring, but indicated that it did not form part of any immediate revolutionary strategy, even though at one point the Catalan president Companys lamented that he feared this might be the case.[4] Indeed, the CNT leadership in Barcelona sometimes sounded like the UGT prior to 1934, emphasizing the importance of overcoming unemployment more than preparing for revolution.

In Barcelona there was also a new political attitude. CNT leaders now for the first time saw the Republic, completely under leftist control as a result of the Popular Front elections, as a regime worth defending. There was some sense of "antifascist unity," which had not existed before. A search for military weaponry, which became active by the late spring, was aimed not at promoting a new insurrection, but at arming activists to resist a feared insurrection by the right. Catalan CNT leaders were not pleased by the reaffirmation of "libertarian communist" revolution and insurrectionism at the Zaragoza conference, engineered especially by Andalusians, which they saw—at least for the time being—as a misplaced emphasis. Similarly, *Solidaridad Obrera* deplored the intraleftist violence that occurred in Malaga. This did not mean that cenetistas had the slightest intention of seconding the plans of the Marxist parties, but in Barcelona, at least, there was a new emphasis on organization and a more careful, measured approach. The ultimate goal of a libertarian revolution remained a chimera; as far as the Catalan leadership was concerned, it could not presently be attempted by loosely organized insurrections, the anarchist equivalent of military pronunciamientos. Nonetheless, communication between the revolutionary movements was not good, and thus Comintern bosses in Moscow would continue to fear that a major threat to the stability of the leftist Republic might come from anarchist insurrectionism, which they urged PCE leaders to discourage. In fact there was no single unified CNT policy in the spring of 1936. While the Catalan leadership had for the time being become more moderate, many activists in Barcelona, as well as CNT groups in other parts of the country, showed little interest in following their lead. Another immediate attempt at major insurrection was not, however, in the offing.

THE SOCIALIST SCHISM DEEPENS

Growing national polarization did not narrow the split between the Socialist "left" and "center," which before July only deepened. This development made impossible any coherent response by the Socialist Party and the UGT to the crisis of the Republic. The left was determined to prevent any new coalition to strengthen the left Republican government and constantly labeled all who supported one as "traitors" who merited expulsion, while the prietista center—lacking any real majority in the party but controlling the executive commission—saw its efforts stymied.

The left was not itself a completely united group but, as Santos Juliá has pointed out, consisted of four distinct nuclei:

- The majority of the UGT, led by Largo, constituted the main force. Despite their radical stance, UGT leaders eventually became somewhat frightened by the massive new strike wave. Despite their vilification of Prieto and Besteiro, they wanted to avoid an official split in the party and the UGT, and despite all their pro-Communist talk, they shied away from further mergers with the Communists after the Communist takeover of the leadership of the new United Socialist Youth (JSU).
- A second sector was composed of the rhetoricians of revolution grouped around Araquistain and the editorial staff of *Claridad*. Though they were the principal providers of revolutionary rhetoric, they were more interested than Largo in supporting the Casares Quiroga government, which Araquistain saw as essential to the long-term strategy of the Socialists.
- A third sector was the JSU, whose leadership was taken over by the

Communists in March–April. Earlier receptive to the POUM argument of moving directly to revolution, the youth movement now fully
adhered to the Communist line of loyalty to the broader Popular
Front formula.
- There was also a small number of crypto-Communists in the Socialist
Party, such as Araquistain's brother-in-law Julio Álvarez del Vayo,
who had some limited influence but did not constitute an organized
subgroup. Only the crypto-Communists were really interested
in splitting the party and joining the Socialist left with the
Communists.[5]

Much of the Socialist left was ambivalent toward the Popular Front.
There was mounting tension in the south between Socialists and left Republicans. The Socialists promoted radical activity on the local level and
from the seat of municipal governments, which they often controlled,
while the left Republican civil governors sometimes made serious efforts
to restrain them from seizing property, firing nonleftist municipal employees, or engaging in all manner of acts of religious persecution. On
24 April caballerista municipal officials in Almería officially declared the
rupture of the Popular Front in that city, apparently the only occasion when
this was formally done.[6] But any such initiative was vehemently rejected
by the national leadership of the party, as was the caballerista notion that
the Popular Front should be replaced either by a broader Worker Alliance
or a new "liaison commission" of the PSOE, UGT, JSU, and PCE.

Despite Araquistain's boast to an American reporter that "we Spanish
Socialists are now more advanced, more communistic, than the Communist Party,"[7] the left was based on the trade unionism of the UGT, and
showed little sense of the Leninist concept of a "vanguard party." The
only strategy for winning power was to await the collapse of the Casares Quiroga government or hope to ride the reaction to a failed military
coup. With the continuation of radical reform that weakened capitalism
and the right, at some point, in some fashion, the Socialists were to take
over and establish the "dictatorship of the proletariat." Araquistain tried
to compensate for the absence of a concrete strategy for this by prattling
on about the role of a revolutionary *caudillo* for the masses, provoking *El
Socialista* to complain on 13 May that *Claridad* "is forging the universal
authority of a future dictator." Two days later *El Socialista* complained that

all the talk of immediate revolution made no sense because the Spanish left was so divided and presented such diverse models: each of the various Marxist parties would attempt differing definitions of the dictatorship of the proletariat, the CNT insisted on a completely separate revolution of libertarian communism, and the prodemocratic sector of the Socialists still supported the democratic Republic (however much in the breach). The result of insistence on violent revolution would simply be "civil war among the workers," as would indeed occur twice during the revolutionary conflict that followed.

On 25 May the prietista executive commission convened a meeting of the party's national committee, which decided that the next party congress would meet in Asturias in October. Special elections were announced to fill the vacant positions on the executive commission, and the center nominated a moderate slate headed by Ramón González Peña, while warning through the national committee that local party sections which failed to follow party regulations and instructions would be dissolved. The caballeristas who controlled the Madrid section of the party countered with their own slate, led by Largo, and made plans to convene their own party congress in Madrid at the end of July, though the center warned that this would be a schismatic meeting which would only make the party split official.

Intraparty conflict reached a high point at a Socialist meeting on 31 May in the southern town of Ecija, where Prieto and González Peña tried to address an increasingly hostile Socialist audience that included many caballeristas. Shouted insults and hurling of rocks and bottles were climaxed by gunshots, with the centrist leaders beating a hasty retreat to their waiting cars. They fled town at breakneck speed, pursued by local leftists in other vehicles. There were several injuries, and Prieto's personal secretary was temporarily captured on the highway by pursuers and carried back to town before being freed by the Civil Guard.

The war of words became even more bitter as Prieto charged Largo with having betrayed the party in October 1934. Prieto began to sound increasingly pessimistic, *La Petite Gironde* of Bordeaux quoting him on 15 June as saying: "It is unjust to consider all rightists as fascists. The fascist danger doesn't exist unless it is generated by the left. The next congress of the Socialist Party will produce a split." Two days later he declared in his own newspaper, *El Liberal,* "In view of the dangerous turn being taken by events we should consider whether our critics [of the right] may not be partially correct." And after the Socialist leader Jiménez de Asúa introduced a bill in parliament for construction of a special prison for political detainees—an ominous sign for what was still supposed to be a democratic Republic—Prieto remarked, "Let them prepare the jail for us as comfortably as possible, if we are not lucky enough to get across the frontier next time. If the future once more holds for us imprisonment or exile, we shall deserve it. For senselessness."

When results of the special election to the executive commission were announced by the prietista secretariat at the end of June, the González Peña slate was declared the winner, 10,933 to 10,624 for Largo Caballero, with 2,876 invalid votes. This seemed a very low vote in view of the 59,846 names on the party membership rolls,[8] but the party administration had systematically invalidated votes from local caballerista groups who had not maintained their dues or were guilty of other infractions, while ignoring ballots from JSU members, who had no proper claim to party membership.[9] And as Juan Linz has noted, "in the plebiscite on calling an Extraordinary Congress, sought by the left but opposed by the center, *El Socialista* quoted the figure of 59,846 dues-paying voters (with a quorum of half plus one amounting to 29,924) and 13,427 valid votes, while 10,573 were annulled for various reasons, so that the ballot was 16,497 votes short."[10] Accordingly the party leadership announced that the motion for a special immediate congress had been defeated.

The caballeristas cried foul, probably with some justification. On 2 July *Claridad* asserted that in fact nearly 22,000 votes had been cast for Largo and claimed further that at a recent congress in Jaén the revolutionary platform, including the building of a broad Worker-Peasant Alliance and a unified Socialist-Communist party, had carried by 1,438 votes to 523. It suggested that a special investigating committee, selected half by the executive commission and half by the Madrid section of the party, be chosen to scrutinize the electoral results, but the executive commission quickly decided to have none of that.

During the second week of July, Largo was in London to represent the UGT at an international trade union congress. There, once more, he struck down the line assiduously cultivated by moderates, which tried to present the 1934 insurrection as an effort to "save Republican democracy," stressing instead that the insurrection had been strictly a "class movement."[11] On 10 July another Andalusian provincial Socialist congress, this time in Cádiz, supported the left position by a vote of eighty-eight to two.[12]

COMMUNIST POLICY

Communist policy during the electoral campaign and its aftermath had followed a two-tier program that made no effort to hide its long-term objectives: strong support for the Popular Front and the left Republican government, while constantly pressuring it for ever-stronger measures against the economic and political interests of the right, which would make possible the beginning of the "Republic of a new type," in which before long a Socialist-Communist "worker-peasant government," supported by a broad Worker Alliance, would take over, the last phase before imposition of the "dictatorship of the proletariat."

The Comintern began to consider the need for greater tactical caution during March and April, following Hitler's successful bid for the remilitarization of the Rhineland. Dimitrov telegrammed new instructions to PCE leaders, emphasizing the importance of organizing mass mobilization of Spanish workers in opposition to Hitler's policy.[13] The worsening strategic situation made Spain more important to Moscow, but also implied the need for greater caution, and at first the line in Spain changed very little. Codovilla had sent a long report to Moscow on 4 March declaring that the Azaña government was moving rapidly toward completion of the Popular Front program and was even going beyond it, which technically was correct. He went on to say that "the revolutionary situation is developing rapidly. A revolutionary solution to the land problem cannot be long delayed, and with expansion of the struggle, the problem of power itself. Hence the question of alliances plays a decisive role. To organize them and popularize the program of a worker-peasant government, the party is taking measures to reinforce its work in the agricultural regions. The influence and organization of the party grow continuously."[14]

During March and early April the PCE continued to emphasize development of Worker Alliance groups. A plenum of the central committee meeting in Madrid from 28 to 30 March concluded that "the present government, because of its bourgeois character, cannot fully complete the democratic revolution." Hence the party must prepare to go beyond it to install a "worker-peasant government." Díaz continued to call for expansion of Worker Alliance groups as "future organs of power,"[15] and Codovilla seemed convinced that pressure from the left would soon lead to breakdown of the present structure of the Spanish state, reporting to Moscow on 4 April: "The current situation of tension cannot go on much longer, and great struggles are in the offing."[16]

At this point the Comintern leadership became concerned that the situation in Spain was moving too fast and might get out of hand. With the international situation deteriorating and the French Popular Front, much more moderate in tone than its Spanish counterpart, proceeding nicely and about to face general elections, a blowup in Spain could be counterproductive. Dimitrov and Manuilsky replied on 9 April that any danger of a breakup in the Spanish Popular Front or the left Republican government should be avoided, and the same was true with regard to any danger of a new anarchist insurrection. Excessive strike demands by either the CNT or UGT should be vigorously resisted: "Do not allow yourselves to be provoked, and do not precipitate events, for at this time that would be harmful for the revolution and would only lead to the triumph of the counterrevolution." Thus "in all the activity of the party it must be kept in mind that, in the present situation, the creation of soviet power is not the order of the day, but that, for the time being, it is only a matter of creating the kind of democratic regime that can bar the way to fascism and counterrevolution and generally fortify the positions of the proletariat and its allies."[17] The Comintern line and previous statements by the PCE had made it clear that this "kind of democratic regime" would have little in common with liberal democracy. Though it would use the façade of democratic legitimacy to strengthen its position, it would employ democratic institutions to begin the process of building a people's republic that would exclude all nonleftist elements and constitute the first major phase of the revolution.

In practice, the Comintern's shift toward a more moderate tactical line proved confusing for the PCE leadership, which continued to promote the formation of Worker Alliances throughout Spain, Diaz referring to them in a speech as late as 11 April as "future organs of power."[18] In the major debate that took place in parliament on 15 April he did not disguise the fact that the ultimate goal of the party remained the "dictatorship of the proletariat." Only after that point did the shift in the Comintern line begin to be more fully implemented. Public calls for expansion of a new and more revolutionary Bloque Popular were dropped in favor of almost exclusive support of the existing Popular Front. The party even began to discourage strikes for such goals as the thirty-six-hour week, declaring that the present forty hours was acceptable. It insisted on major changes in the status of labor only through formal Republican legislation and finally withdrew its opposition to compensation for the confiscation of land. Whereas before it had opposed the existing system of Republican autonomy statutes in favor of breaking up Spain into a series of nominally independent states, it now supported the country's existing territorial structure and its formula of autonomy statutes. The Communist goal now was a strong, united, exclusively leftist Republican state that could eliminate the right by harassing or legislating it out of existence. Similarly, the Communist position emphasized strong Spanish support for the Soviet Union—with which the Republic still had not established diplomatic relations—and the League of Nations, Dimitrov repeating that the top priority of the Comintern was defense of the Soviet Union.[19]

Even so, adoption of a more moderate tactical line did not involve any fundamental disguise. Santiago Carrillo, chief leader of the new JSU and by this time a de facto Communist, declared forthrightly in *Mundo Obrero* on 10 May that the Worker Alliances now being formed would become the Spanish version of revolutionary soviets, revolutionary organs for the "dictatorship of one class." They would be the basic "insurrectional organ without being conceived as the organ of power." Their deployment would of course involve civil war, which the Alliances would prosecute. He added, "But once the proletariat is in power, has the civil war ended? For if it has not ended, as seems probable, the Alliances will continue fighting against the enemies of the proletariat; the army that has been built up through insurrection will also continue the struggle once in power." On 27 May *Mundo Obrero* again endorsed the ultimate formula of a "worker-peasant government," which it called in standard terminology the "democratic dictatorship of the workers and peasants."

Amid this prerevolutionary euphoria Codovilla and Jesús Hernandez reported to the Comintern in Moscow on 22 May, presenting a glowing account of the situation in Spain that clearly impressed their superiors. According to Elorza and Bizcarrondo, when they reported that Communist municipal councilmen were already exercising considerable power in a number of towns and even determining which opponents should be thrown into jail, Dimitrov enthused, "That is a true democracy indeed!"[20] When, however, Codovilla and Hernández raised the question whether such favorable conditions should rapidly lead to the development of the "democratic dictatorship of the workers and peasants," Dimitrov quickly quashed such speculations, emphasizing that the current priorities were simply the strengthening of the Popular Front and decisive victory over fascism.[21]

The subsequent resolution of the Romanskii Lender Sekretariat (Latin Section) on Spain remained cautious, reaffirming established goals: continued agitation and completion of the triple alliance (labor, youth, and party) with the Socialists, while being sure to gain the support of moderate Socialists as well. Farmland should continue to be confiscated, but in an orderly way according to the legislation of the agrarian reform. Strikes should be used "rationally," and there should be no general strikes. Communist syndicates should strive for worker control in industry, but for the time being the party should promote nationalization only of the Bank of Spain and of the railroads, measures supported by some bourgeois progressives. Agitation should particularly target youth and the armed forces and should give priority to expansion of the Milicias Antifascistas Obreras y Campesinas (MAOC). All "monarchist" organizations—meaning apparently all conservative groups—should be officially outlawed, their property confiscated, and their leaders arrested, the Catholic Gil Robles and the liberal democrat Lerroux being specified by name. The "democratic revolution" should first be carried to full completion, creating a new form of leftist people's republic with all nonleftist forces eliminated.[22]

In the first draft of this resolution, some elements of the earlier, more directly revolutionary program surfaced, with instructions to try to expand Worker Alliance groups as "organs of the struggle for power" by the revolutionary masses; but these were soon dropped. The final draft emphasized supporting the Popular Front, with Alliance groups functioning as democratically elected committees to deal with concrete issues under the aegis of the Popular Front. Yet the more moderate tactical line being imposed by Dimitrov and his chief assistant for southwest Europe, Palmiro Togliatti, does not seem to have penetrated fully to Codovilla and the Spanish leaders, so long incited to revolutionary maximalism. It was hard for them to avoid falling back into more standard terminology, particularly given the ambiguous meaning of many Communist terms.[23]

May Day 1936 in Madrid produced the biggest Communist demonstration in Spain to that point, with thousands of party members marching in unison and the uniformed JSU, now generally (though not entirely) under Communist control, parading in the paramilitary style of the era. Party membership was increasing rapidly, having risen from 9,200 in May 1934 to 11,275 on the eve of the insurrection before dropping in 1935 under the weight of the repression. As the latter eased, membership reached at least 14,000 by February 1936, with the party officially declaring twice as many. During the spring and early summer membership doubled and tripled. By July the party claimed to have 100,000 members, though the real affiliation may have been no more than half that figure.[24]

This was impressive growth but still not a full-fledged mass movement. Nonetheless, many Spanish conservatives seemed convinced amid the prerevolutionary turmoil of the spring and early summer that Communism was growing by leaps and bounds. The military rebels and their allies who initiated the Civil War on 18 July would soon fabricate documents in an effort to prove that a Communist takeover of the Republic was scheduled for August, which was a complete falsehood. Yet it remains a fact that conservatives were genuinely convinced that Communist and hence Soviet power in Spain had become very great. Certainly, the PCE did everything it could to foster such an impression, presenting an image of rapidly expanding power, inevitability, and triumphalism. Communists in fact made up but a small minority of the immense leftist march on May Day, but, like their Bolshevik predecessors in 1917, they focused on the capital and did everything possible to magnify their presence in Madrid. Certain aspects of the revolutionary style, such as the gigantic hammers and sickles, the massed clenched-fist salutes, and the provocative chants of young Socialist and Communist women, particularly impressed middle-class onlookers. Even more important was the embracing of Bolshevization by so many Socialists, since the latter were a large movement that had already led one major revolutionary insurrection.

THE POUM

By the spring of 1936 the most consistently revolutionary position was held by the POUM, whose executive committee had declared in the preceding December that it was "the true Communist party of Catalonia and of Spain."[25] In the sense of being a native Spanish Communist party not controlled from abroad, this claim was undoubtedly correct. Andreu Nin, its number-two leader, held that the electoral victory of the Popular Front had been made possible only by the preceding insurrection, which he declared the only secure road to power. When the Cortes opened on 15 April, Maurín was the only Popular Front deputy who vehemently criticized the Azaña government directly, denouncing first of all the prime minister's opening speech in which the latter attempted, albeit feebly, to calm the country. Even more than the caballeristas, the POUM had become the party of civil war, though in its arrogance it assumed that the right was so weak that a civil war could not last long. The official POUM position was that the Azaña government should immediately give way to a more radical Popular Front transition administration, which would prepare for a "worker government,"[26] in much more accelerated fashion than the Comintern was willing to countenance at that time.

In its revolutionary maximalism, the POUM inveighed against pacifism and the League of Nations as mere bourgeois formulas. Both the POUM and the anarchist FAI denounced the current Popular Front tactic in general and also criticized Socialist support for League sanctions against Italy after the latter's invasion of Ethiopia, saying that such support assumed that it was possible to work with capitalist powers and that there was a difference between capitalism and fascism. The POUM still sought to build "a great revolutionary party." It agreed with the PCE's priority of expanding rapidly the Worker Alliance groups and in May proposed formation of a liaison committee with the PCE and PSOE. POUM leaders termed rejection of this proposal further proof that their party was "the sole defender of the socialist revolution within the bosom of our proletariat."[27] Largo Caballero proposed that the POUM merge with the Socialists, an invitation that was indignantly rejected, though some of the local Socialist Youth sections declared that they would not go through with the current JSU merger unless the POUM youth were also included.

COMMUNIST POLICY TOWARD THE OTHER MARXIST PARTIES
To the dismay of the POUM, the other small Marxist parties in Catalonia were drawing closer together. The consequences of the October insurrection had radicalized the once somewhat moderate Unió Socialista de Catalunya, which in June 1935 had asked to be admitted to the Comintern as a "sympathizing section." A liaison committee was formed at that time

between the USC and the Partit Català Proletari, and was joined in December by the Catalan Communists (PCC) and a few months later by the Catalan Socialists. By 23 June 1936 the committee had reached agreement on seven points: joint identity as a class party of workers and peasants, democratic centralism, support for the Comintern, defense of the USSR against imperialist war, national liberation, the revolutionary conquest of power by armed insurrection, and the imposition of the dictatorship of the proletariat. It looked as though the Comintern goal of a united revolutionary Marxist party in Catalonia was about to be realized, but it would be very small, with only about 2,000 members, compared with 5,000 for the POUM in all Catalonia, though the allied parties were slightly more numerous than the POUM in Barcelona. Based on the Catalan section of the UGT, they also had a combined syndical membership of 80,000, larger than that of the POUM.[28]

The POUM also accepted the responsibility to "defend the USSR," but its leaders asserted that the best way to do this was through outright revolution in Spain, while control of a new Catalan Marxist party by the Comintern, POUMists alleged, would mean that its components could not be "objectively revolutionary" and would even place themselves "to the right of social democracy."[29] Similarly, when the merged JSU began to set up a Youth Front with left Republican youth, the POUM denounced this as a move to the right.

Comintern unification tactics vis-à-vis the Socialist Party itself were less successful. Their main achievement was formation of the JSU, which went ahead rapidly in the spring. The conversion of Carrillo meant that Communists dominated the national JSU leadership from the start, though in the slow unification of the two syndical systems the Communist unions were easily overshadowed. The caballeristas had some interest in unification of the two parties so long as they believed that the Socialists could absorb the Communists, but after the results of the youth merger this seemed much less likely. Neither major section of the Socialists had a clear position concerning new expansion of the Worker Alliance. The caballeristas of the UGT had more interest in some sort of revolutionary alliance with the CNT, and some progress had been made in mutual relations, but more common was a kind of "competitive radicalization" between the major syndical movements.

The most intense intergroup conflict among the revolutionary left was the Comintern's campaign against "Trotskyism" in Spain—meaning the POUM—which was intensified in the latter part of April. The PCE advanced the line that Maurín was "paid by fascist gold," and in June *Mundo Obrero* insisted that he was "a renegade at the service of reaction." Whereas Carrillo and young JS radicals had once been the sector of Spanish Marxism most sympathetic to the former BOC, with Bolshevization Carrillo and JSU spokesmen now spearheaded the attack against the POUM, seconded not merely by the entire apparatus of the PCE but also by ultra pro-Communist elements of the Socialists, such as Margarita Nelken and Álvarez del Vayo. By late spring POUM spokesmen were complaining of assaults and attempted sabotage of some of their meetings, and even some local JSU figures in Catalonia protested the attacks, while PCE leaders sought to persuade Largo Caballero that the POUM should be eliminated from the Worker Alliance and any other alliance mechanism.[30]

The earlier tiny Izquierda Comunista de España, led by Nin, had been categorically Trotskyist until 1934, and the BOC generally sympathetic to Trotsky, though never formally Trotskyist. Formation of the POUM in 1935 had in fact marked a final break with Trotskyism, even on the part of Nin, since it was based on categorical rejection of Trotsky's preferred tactic of "entryism" into existing Socialist parties. For his part, Trotsky had not reciprocated Maurín's admiration, denouncing the latter's concept of "democratic-socialist revolution" as pure nonsense, since in Russia in 1917 the proponents of democratic revolution and of socialist revolution had been on opposite sides of the barricades. From Trotsky's point of view, the democratic revolution had been completed in Spain, and the Popular Front as led by petit-bourgeois left Republicans was merely recapitulating it. While denouncing what he called "the treachery of the POUM," he insisted that in Spain a revolutionary struggle had to be waged against the Popular Front.[31] Maurín himself declared in *La Batalla* on the symbolic first of May that "I am not a Trotskyist . . . but . . . ," making clear that none of the POUM leaders considered themselves insulted by the term, for Trotsky had "one of the best-organized minds of the socialist movement" and was "the greatest Bolshevik leader after Lenin."[32]

The POUM sharply protested Socialist and Communist support for the Casares Quiroga government as the two larger Marxist parties withdrew earlier demands for dissolution of the Civil Guard and a total purge of the army. As early as November 1935 Maurín had called for reorganization of the armed Worker Alliance militia of 1934 and repeated this more and more insistently during the spring of 1936. PCE spokesmen denounced such a position as "a Trotskyist provocation," while the POUM claimed that the MAOC, of which the PCE proudly boasted, "did not exist." The latter charge was incorrect, for the MAOC, though numbering only a few thousand (mainly in Madrid), did receive paramilitary training by politically affiliated army and police officers and by several Communist militia leaders who themselves had been trained in Moscow. The POUM made at least some effort to give its own youth group (Juventud Comunista Ibérica) a little paramilitary training, and increasingly turned to direct action in strikes and agitation.[33]

Reorganization and expansion of Worker Alliance groups largely failed to take place. Only the PCE had given this as much attention as had the POUM, but as Comintern tactics became increasingly moderate the party talked of the AO less and less, while the caballeristas, as usual, were interested in the AO simply as an expansion of Socialist power. Therefore with the opening of the Cortes in April the POUM adopted the new tactic of calling for formation of an all–Popular Front government to pursue a more radical policy, but once again generated little support. When, by mid-June, approximately 110,000 workers were on strike in Madrid, party spokesmen hailed the situation as the beginning of the worker revolution;[34] but strike activity in some parts of the country subsequently declined. On the worker left only some of the Communists and prietistas had anything approaching a realistic sense of the potential strength of the right. Thus three days after the assassination of Calvo Sotelo in July—which would be the final catalyst for civil war—Maurín said to a friend in Madrid that nothing was likely to happen for the time being and left for a meeting of the POUM regional committee in Galicia.

THE POPULAR FRONT IN FRANCE

May was a time of euphoria for the Comintern in southwestern Europe, with everything looking more and more positive in Spain and a clear-cut electoral triumph of the other Popular Front being consummated in France only two months after the French Senate had finally ratified the Franco-Soviet defense pact. Victory in France seemed to provide further evidence of the utility of the Popular Front tactic. Altogether the three main French Popular Front parties increased their combined vote totals by only 1.5 percent over the preceding elections but as a bloc scored a decisive victory. The Radicals, as the right wing of the alliance, in fact declined, their share of the total vote dropping from 20.07 to 16.57 percent. The Socialist vote remained about the same, drawing votes away from the left wing of the Radicals but losing slightly more to the Communists, in toto holding fewer seats than in the preceding parliament. The big winners were the French Communists, who jumped from twelve seats and only 8.4 percent of the vote in 1932 to seventy-two seats and 15.3 percent in 1936. The PCF was now by far the largest Communist party in western Europe and entered the second of its three major phases of growth, shooting upward from 87,000 members in 1935 to 326,500 by 1937, at which point it had a larger membership than the French Socialist Party. Trade union support grew equally rapidly. Moreover, the victory of the French Popular Front touched off an enormous strike wave—largest in French history to that point—much more quickly than had the elections in Spain, though that may have been partly due to spring as opposed to winter weather.

France was not Spain, however, and the French Popular Front was not the Spanish Popular Front. Their programs were in some respects superficially similar, but the French program was more moderate, aimed at the defeat of fascism but not at the elimination of democracy and of all conservative forces from French politics and institutions. In France as in Spain, the Communists did not enter the government, but in France the large Socialist Party was relatively united, contained only a small revolutionary wing in no way equivalent to the *bolchevizantes* in Spain, and now assumed government responsibility for the first time. The Socialist leader Léon Blum, who stood to the right of all the Spanish Socialist leaders save Besteiro, presided over a governing coalition made up primarily of Socialists and Radicals. The new French government was thus more broadly based than its Spanish counterpart and was both stronger and more moderate, and hence not subject to Kerenskyist leveraging from the extreme left, which in any case was weaker in France. Blum negotiated a relatively quick end to a strike wave that had briefly included the occupation of a number of factories, with major gains for labor. The government then enacted a much more coherent and moderate legislative program than its counterpart in Madrid, though the social and political balance had been changed. A new climate of labor indiscipline took hold, greatly alarming the right, but there was no takeover of property, except through very limited government nationalization. Though political polarization also increased in France, there was very little violence.[35]

Moreover, the lower-middle-class liberal democratic Radical Party was by this point considerably different from the left Republicans in Spain, more stable and more democratic. It absolutely refused to play a Kerensky-ist role vis-à-vis the worker left and exercised a considerable moderating influence on the government. Instead of moving ever further left like the Spanish left Republicans, who had adopted a semi-Socialist economic program and whose youth group had formed an alliance with Communists, it was frightened by the postelectoral strike wave and soon began to move toward the right.

A REVOLUTIONARY FUTURE?

By the late spring of 1936 Spain had moved much farther left than France, and had become much more destabilized in peacetime than any large European country since 1848. Yet the left remained profoundly divided regarding ultimate goals, and there was no hegemonic revolutionary project. All the revolutionary movements sought to replace the existing Republic with their own utopian system, but only the Communists had anything approaching a coherent project, and the Communists were still a comparatively small force. None of the revolutionary movements was in a position to impose its goals, and all depended on the minority left Republican government to provide a cover of legitimacy for the continuing deterioration of social order and economic activity.

CHAPTER TWELVE

The Final Phase

MAY–JULY 1936

SOME MODERATE REPUBLICANS LOST hope for the Casares Quiroga government within a matter of days, and soon a few proposed more dramatic alternatives. Ever since the inauguration of Azaña as president, a number of the left Republican leaders had held to the idea that only a government with plenary powers, if necessary including the imposition of martial law, could redeem the situation. This was sometimes referred to as a legalitarian "Republican dictatorship." Claudio Sánchez Albornoz was one of its proponents, and years later he would write that after arriving in Lisbon on 14 May to assume the duties of ambassador, "for many nights I slept restlessly, with the telephone beside my bed, waiting for official notice from Madrid of the temporary proclamation of the Republican dictatorship that would save Spain. But the word I awaited never arrived, and Spain continued its sadly anarchic course."[1]

Felipe Sánchez Román had refused Azaña's suggestion that he lead the new left Republican government, because he did not believe the present formula of minority government to be viable, but he actively participated for some six weeks in discussions about the formation of a larger and stronger majority coalition. He decided that a new formula was needed, and a meeting of the leaders of his tiny Partido Nacional Republicano (PNR) therefore approved the following declaration on 25 May:

At the present time the PNR, its authority increased by having foreseen the difficulties that the Popular Front would face and enjoying the freedom of movement provided by its absence from the government, has the responsibility of uniting other Republicans in an understanding of the seriousness of the situation, recognizing the failure of the so-called Popular Front in its present form and the need to take measures to save the country and the Republic.

Political agreement should be based on the following measures:

- Immediate execution of the program of the defense of the Republican state, vigorously reestablishing the principle of authority together with a program of social reform and economic development agreed upon by the Republican Left, Republican Union, and National Republican Parties.
- Fulfillment of the reforms benefiting the working class that were included in the Popular Front electoral program.
- The taking of necessary measures to prevent those social and political forces that are actually most interested in the execution of the program from being the greatest obstacle to its accomplishment.

The following steps should be taken:

a. Severe repression of incitement to revolutionary violence.
b. General disarmament.
c. Dissolution of all political, professional, economic, or religious organizations whose activity gravely threatens the independence, constitutional unity, democratic-republican form, or security of the Spanish Republic.
d. Prohibition of uniformed or paramilitary societies.
e. A law establishing the legal responsibility of leaders of political organizations for the crimes provoked by the latter's propaganda.
f. Prosecution of local government authorities for the infractions of law that they may commit in exercising

their functions. Where circumstances require, mayors may be relieved of supervision of public order and this function transferred to other authorities.

g. The rules of parliament will be reformed to improve the structure and functioning of parliamentary committees, so that with the assistance of technical agencies new legislation can be completed more quickly.

Señor Sánchez Román will present our request to the leaders of the Republican Union and Republican Left Parties. Once an agreement has been reached, the Socialist Party will be publicly invited to participate in a new government to carry out this program.

Should the Socialists refuse to collaborate, the Republicans will urge the President to form a government of representatives of all the Republican forces [presumably referring to the center parties] willing to support the program approved by the left Republican parties. A team of Republican ministers recognized for their authority, competence, and prestige will be appointed. They will govern above the level of party politics, rejecting any kind of demagogic appeal.

If the government does not receive parliamentary support, Cortes sessions will be suspended in conformity with constitutional statutes.

Alternately, parliament might be presented with a bill authorizing the government to legislate by decree, under the powers granted by article 81 of the constitution, regarding concrete matters that demand urgent attention.[2]

This seems to have been the only concrete plan for dealing with the crisis presented by any of the Republican parties. It was coherent, responsible, and practical, and, had the other Republican parties agreed to it, the democratic system might yet have been saved. Not for nothing was Sánchez Román the political figure whom Azaña perhaps most respected for measure, wisdom, and judgment,[3] but the president showed no inclination to take this sage, if drastic, advice from his friend. It would have required him to drop his exclusively left-sectarian strategy and would officially have broken the Popular Front.

Nonetheless, the PNR's proposal, in some ways a logical alternative to the earlier project of a Prieto majority coalition, found support among some of the most moderate and sensible left Republicans, as well as among some sectors of the center, and perhaps with Prieto himself. It was apparently discussed at a meeting of Izquierda Republicana and Unión Republicana parliamentary groups, who may have passed the proposal on to the Casares Quiroga government, which rejected it.[4] Casares declared that there was no need for a special coalition or a government with extraordinary powers, asserting in the next Cortes session on 16 June that such an alternative would "open the way to dictatorship."

During the final two months of the Republic the Cortes served as the only political sounding board not subject to censorship, and during this last phase the principal spokesmen for the two sides were the prime minister on the one hand and Calvo Sotelo on the other. Though Gil Robles and representatives of the center still held the podium from time to time, Calvo Sotelo, more categorical and uncompromising, increasingly became the voice of the right. Both Casares Quiroga and Calvo Sotelo were Galicians, yet totally different in physique, style, and political loyalties, and cordially detested each other. Casares was slender, intense, emotional, physically ill with a consumption that was controlled but never quite cured. Calvo Sotelo was broad-shouldered, a burly and corpulent bull of a man, vigorous, analytical, and with greater emotional control, yet also categorically outspoken.

The session of 16 June was possibly the most dramatic and oft-quoted in the history of the Republic. Gil Robles read another of his periodic statistical summaries of disorder, alleging that from 15 February to 15 June 269 people had been killed and 1,287 injured in political violence, 160 churches totally destroyed, and 251 churches and other religious buildings damaged. The total volume of assaults on churches and other Catholic buildings, and on the clergy, had reached a massive level.[5] During the month since Casares Quiroga's appointment, there had been 69 deaths, and 36 churches had been destroyed. Gil Robles concluded with a final list of disorders, which he said had been committed during the past twenty-four hours, reporting that the British Auto Club had informed its members that it was unsafe to drive in Spain because of random violence and extortion of money from motorists on the highways.

Calvo Sotelo then rose, declaring that this was the fourth time in three months that he had addressed in parliament the problem of public order. By this point the session had grown stormy, with frequent interruptions and name-calling, a tactic that Calvo could not resist using against the prime minister himself when the latter interrupted his speech with a remark. Calvo insisted that the situation could be rectified only by an "integral state" of authority, and that if such a state had to be called "a fascist state," then "I declare myself a fascist." Casares next took the floor to denounce the preceding speaker, declaring that "after what the honorable gentleman has said in parliament, I shall hold him responsible before the country for whatever may or may not occur." Given the state of affairs in the country, this offered the unprecedented spectacle of a constitutional prime minister rhetorically signing what would be seen later as the death warrant of a member of parliament. Casares also denied that International Red Aid or other radical groups were practicing extortion on the highways—a flagrant untruth on his part, since Alcalá Zamora had been one of the victims,[6] and in fact the government had vainly issued an order on 11 May to civil governors to put an end to it.

As usual, Juan Ventosa of the Lliga provided the most objective analysis:

> What most alarms me about today's session is the optimism
> of the president of the council of ministers, who finds the situation acceptable enough and even agreeable. I leave for him
> the responsibility for that statement before Spain and the world
> abroad, since the events occurring here are well known everywhere. And the gravest aspect is his argument that what is happening today is justified because of what happened two years
> ago. But can the excesses and injustices of some justify the outrages, injustices, and violence of others? Are we perpetually
> condemned in Spain to live in a regime of successive conflicts,
> in which the access to power or triumph in elections initiates
> the hunting down, persecution, or liquidation of adversaries?
> If that were so, we would have to renounce being Spaniards,
> because civilized life would be incompatible with our country.

Even worse, he said, was the fact that the prime minister had officially declared "that the government was belligerent," engaged in a kind of civil war, rather than in administering fairness and impartiality. Thus "the words of the honorable gentleman cannot lead but to further violence." Ventosa further denounced the new legislation to "republicanize the judiciary," terming it a project to "destroy the independence of the judicial power," and concluded: "Maintain the Popular Front or break it; do whatever you please, but if the government is not prepared to cease to be a belligerent on one side and to impose on all equally the respect for law, it is better that it resign, for above the parties is the supreme interest of Spain, now threatened with catastrophe."

Joaquín Maurín then rose to make exactly the opposite point, that "the government has not even carried out the hundredth part of the Popular Front program"—a completely silly charge. He called for an all–Popular Front government led by the revolutionary parties, the nationalization of a large part of the economy, and the elimination of fascism. He had now changed his analysis of the fascist threat in Spain, terming it "today a real danger."

After Gil Robles spoke a second time, Calvo Sotelo rose to utter the most famous paragraph of his life, often quoted subsequently as a kind of epitaph:

> Señor Casares Quiroga, my shoulders are broad. The honorable gentleman is quick and facile in threatening gestures and words of menace. I have heard three or four of his speeches as prime minister, and in all of them were words of threats. Very well, Señor Casares Quiroga, I am fully notified of your threats. . . . I accept with pleasure and shirk none of the responsibilities that may be derived from acts that I perform, and I also accept those of others if they are for the good of my country and the glory of Spain. . . . Let the honorable gentleman measure his own responsibilities, review the history of the past twenty-five years, and observe the sad and bloody tones that envelop two figures who played premier roles in the tragedy of two peoples: Russia and Hungary. They were Kerensky and Karolyi. Kerensky represented ignorance, Karolyi the betrayal of a whole millenary civilization. The honorable gentleman will not be Kerensky, because he is not witless; he is fully aware of what he says, what he keeps silent and what he thinks. May God grant that the honorable gentleman may never be able to compare himself with Karolyi.

Julián Zugazagoitia, the editor of *El Socialista,* later wrote that this session

was one of the days when I saw Prieto most worried. His concern was deepened by great irritation: "This chamber has no
sense of responsibility. I don't know if we are really deaf or
merely pretend to be. The speech that Gil Robles delivered this
afternoon was extremely grave. When I heard behind me outbursts of laughter and stupid interruptions, I couldn't help feeling shamed. Gil Robles, who was fully conscious of what he
was saying, must feel for us a mixture of pity and scorn. I remember that the chief of the CEDA told us that his party, after
a careful examination, had developed its activity within the or-
bit of the Republic but that he personally was not sure if he had
made a mistake by so advising his colleagues, and that in any
event his authority and influence to keep them from breaking
with the Republic was less every day. 'This decline of my authority,' he said, 'stems from the conduct of the Republic and
the decline of my own faith that it can become a legal channel
of the national will.' And he even added: 'I condemn violence,
which promises no good result, and deplore that many and
dear friends accept that hope as the only solution.' The meaning of those words could not be clearer. The CEDA itself is being absorbed by the movement that the military are preparing
together with the monarchists. With a gesture of fatalistic despair, Prieto added: 'Only one thing is clear: that we are going
to deserve a catastrophe because of our stupidity.'"[7]

With all hope for a broader left-center/center majority coalition apparently at an end, the increasingly desperate situation was analyzed by
Miguel Maura, one of the founders of the Republic, in a series of six widely
read articles in *El Sol* from 18 to 27 June. He concluded that

in rural and provincial affairs the anonymous, radicalized
masses rule through the governors controlled by the Jacobin
committees of the Popular Front, whose disorders and excesses
are legalized by the mayors and specially appointed presidents
of provincial boards, a veritable Bolshevist plague that is devas-

tating the country. Peaceful citizens live with the sensation that laws are a dead letter and that arson, assaults, destruction of property, insults, murders, and aggression against the armed forces no longer count in the penal code for those who wear a red and blue shirt [of the JSU] or the insignia of the hammer and sickle. The clenched fist is safe-conduct and talisman for the greatest excesses.

There could not fail to be a reaction. This has taken shape in the alarming form of what is called "fascism." People have joined that movement en masse. . . . though of authentic Italian Fascism it has only the name and a few of the doctrinal postulates, of which the majority of its affiliates are ignorant.

Today the Republic is no more—though I would like to believe unconsciously—than the tool of the violent revolutionary sector of the working classes, which, shielded by the liberal democratic system and the blindness of certain leaders of the Republican parties, is preparing in minute detail an assault on the government and the extermination of capitalist and middle-class society. . . . They tell us this themselves in their newspapers and public meetings.

. . . If the Republic is to be this, it is inexorably condemned to swift extinction at the hands of those who claim to be its defenders or, which is more probable, at the hands of a reaction from the opposite direction.

Maura called for a multiparty "national Republican dictatorship" to save the country, but he added, "I do not harbor the slightest hope that my reasoning can convince those who currently bear responsibility for government." This dismal conclusion was correct, for Maura's telling analysis, accurate in both perspective and detail, merely drew upon the standard denunciations from the left Republican, caballerista, Communist, and anarchist press. *Política* blustered on 28 June that the proposal was "as reactionary as anything that could have been thought up by a leader of the extreme right." Four days earlier this forum of the nominally moderate left had assured its readers that if the CEDA ever got back into government "it would establish a fascism as fierce and inhuman as that of the Nazis."

The only Popular Front group that seemed to show any concern was

Unión Republicana, which held a national congress from 27 to 29 June in Madrid. Martínez Barrio warned his followers that "what the Spanish people cannot endure is to live in a state of constant insurrection" and proposed as a possible solution "governmental collaboration with the Socialists, even giving them the leadership." Though his closing address declared that the Casares Quiroga government would not soon come to an end, Martínez Barrio repeated that in the long run they must look toward Socialist collaboration, and possible leadership. References to a possible Prieto government could still be found from time to time in the left Republican press,[8] and Prieto was quoted by a French newspaper on 2 July as saying that what the Republic needed was a government that was not "dictatorial, but authoritarian. Authority must reside, more than in persons, in institutions."[9]

As Ángel Ossorio y Gallardo had written a few days earlier: "No one is happy with the present situation. I talk with representatives of all sectors of the Popular Front, and in private conversations all reveal themselves to be as worried, preoccupied, and anguished as the conservative forces. This is the truth, the pure truth, though it is always covered up in the service of party politics." He added: "And if this is so, who is really in favor of the present frenzy? Whom does it benefit? What we are seeing would make sense only if the revolutionaries could be sure of winning the revolution. But they are blind if they believe that. In Spain the triumph will be won not by the first revolution, but by the second: that of reconstruction."[10] Here Ossorio approached the ultimate truth of the matter: most of the revolutionaries were indeed overconfident that they could win a revolutionary civil war, even though the odds were not as much in their favor as they liked to think.

The final major Cortes debate began at 7:00 P.M. on 1 July and lasted twelve hours, marred by frequent shouts and incidents. Deputies were involved in pushing and punching each other on at least two occasions, one CEDA deputy was expelled from the chamber, and Martínez Barrio, president of the Cortes, even threatened to walk out in protest. This was also the session in which the Socialist Ángel Galarza replied to Calvo Sotelo with the remark that against the latter "anything was justified, even personal assassination," words that Martínez Barrio ordered stricken from the record but that were picked up by several journalists.[11] The words of Galarza were also predictive of his own future role, for only a few months later as minister of the interior in the wartime revolutionary Republic he would preside over mass executions in Madrid.[12] Galarza constituted a good example of the way in which the threats and violence of leftists under the Republic carried over into the mass murders of the Civil War.

One of the main items in the final session was the right's interpellation of Ruiz Funes, the agriculture minister, which the Socialists, with their usual respect for the procedures of parliamentary government, attempted to guillotine but failed for lack of votes. José Ma. Cid spoke for the Agrarian Party, reciting a long catalog of abuses in the countryside, concluding with the query: "Does the government wish to convert the capitalist system into a Marxist one? Let it say so with all clarity!" Ruiz Funes replied that the government had to wrestle with grave problems, including no less than 8,000 claims for damages still facing the Agriculture Ministry over lost jobs and illegal wage reductions in the preceding two years. He insisted, not entirely convincingly, "In all the labor problems with which I deal I respect the limits of economic profitability. I will not tolerate anyone insinuating that the government is going along with a movement toward socialization."

In this final stage, the only leftist group—aside from the POUM—with a clearly defined policy was the Communist Party. The Comintern line remained unchanged in the final weeks before the Civil War: unity of the Popular Front and the left Republican government must be sustained, but the legal mechanisms of the Republic should be employed to their maximum to convert the Spanish Republic into the "new type of democratic republic," totally dominated by the left. (This was particularly ironic in view of the fact that in the only existing "new type of democratic republic," the People's Republic of Mongolia, Communist collectivization had just had the effect of destroying up to one-third of the population. Needless to say, this was never discussed in Spain.) Such a policy would require full use of all legal resources—and some illegal ones, but always in the name of "the Republic"—to repress and outlaw the right. As *Mundo Obrero* put it on 10 June, "The attitude of the enemy requires an all-out attack." "We have reached the limits of what is tolerable. . . . The government has been too tolerant." A true Popular Front policy would demand "destroying every area of support for fascism in the judicial system, in the army, and in the armed police. Punishing the reactionary acts of the employers. . . . Imposing a solution on the conflicts they have provoked." There should be a drastic purge of all the army and the police, while the Communists prepared the MAOC as what the central committeeman Antonio Mije called their "armed militia" to be "the men of the future Worker-Peasant Red Army of Spain,"[13] an accurate prophecy of what would indeed take place a few months later. Only after this phase had been completed would the time come for violent insurrection against the remnants of the bourgeois Republic to establish a Soviet regime, a worker-peasant government.[14] At the same time, the Communists tried to hold back the most incendiary Socialist and anarchists, and during June the leadership of the PCE in Seville urged that the high-handed seizure of church buildings should temporarily be ended, as it made the left appear too extreme and lawless.

Two of the Communist priorities for the current Popular Front phase—confiscation of sizable amounts of land and beginning of direct elimination of the rightist groups—had already been initiated piecemeal by the government, even though the latter did not define these in the same terms. On 1 July the Communist delegation in the Cortes submitted to other Popular Front delegations a legislative proposal to order the arrest of everyone in any position of responsibility at the time of the Asturian insurrection from Lerroux on down to local officials, subjecting them to plenary prosecution and confiscation of property.[15] This was a logical extension of the "People's Republic" tactic of using nominal Republican legality to subvert constitutional order. Confiscation of property directly violated the constitution, however, and was not accepted by the left Republicans. On 9 July, however, the Communists succeeded in carrying their agenda to the point that all the other Popular Front groups agreed to delay the summer parliamentary recess until the question of "responsibilities" for the repression had been settled. Conversely, the numerous violent crimes of the left would continue to enjoy immunity.[16] The "new type Republic" seemed to be well under way.

While caballeristas publicly called from time to time for creation of a "revolutionary militia," they did little in practice. Though many fewer in number, Communists were much better organized. A Comintern adviser on paramilitary and other violent subversive activities, Vittorio Vidali (who went by the pseudonym "Carlos Conteras"), arrived in May and was assisted by Enrique Líster and several other young leaders who had undergone training at the Red Army's Frunze Academy in Moscow. In mid-June the party announced that its MAOC forces in Madrid numbered 2,000, with the goal of becoming "a mass organization of semimilitary character," thus constituting "the organizational basis for the future Worker-Peasant Red Army."[17] Terrorist sections were split off from the MAOC proper so as not to compromise the latter. They carried on urban guerrilla warfare against Falangists in Madrid but tried to avoid killing policemen, so as not to arouse greater alarm among the middle classes. Communists were also influential in the formation of the Unión Militar Republicana Anti-fascista (UMRA), a small organization of leftist officers who sought to counter rightist organization within the armed forces. They would later claim that the UMRA was an outgrowth of the tiny Unión Militar Anti-fascista that the party had set up in 1934.[18] In addition, Líster directed a secret "antimilitarist section" that collected information and sought to sow revolutionary subversion among Spanish soldiers.

The last eight regular sessions of the Cortes in early July were devoted primarily to discussing the restoration of traditional common lands to municipalities and a possible drastic surtax on the wealthiest landowners. As the summer heat increased, interest waned and attendance declined. Parliament also took up the issue of extending further amnesty legislation, with center and rightist deputies maintaining that any such move would be unjust unless it included amnesty for those who had defended the legal order in 1934.

There were a few signs of moderation. *El Sol* opined on 2 and 8 July that the outcome of the elections to the Socialist Party executive commission offered hope that Socialist policy would now assume a more moderate direction, though in fact this was not precisely Prieto's own conclusion. *El Sol*'s speculation was belied by the fact that on the second of July it, together with other papers, published a new "Manifesto of the Executive Commission" of the Socialist Party, which denounced "any effort to take a step backward in Republican policy" and insisted that "the attitude of the Socialist Party is, in its fundamentals, exactly the same as in the autumn of 1934." This reaffirmation of the insurrection was hardly a call to moderation. Nonetheless, after a special caucus of the Popular Front deputies and visits by the Socialist executive commission to the prime minister on 9 and 10 July, there was renewed speculation about a possible change in government. Rumors conjectured that the left might have lost control of the Socialist parliamentary delegation, which might now be willing to support a more broadly based coalition, though there has never been any evidence to support such a speculation. In an interview with an Argentine reporter on 11 July, Calvo Sotelo opined that despite the increase in strikes he believed there was less danger of another leftist insurrection than there had been in February, and he turned out to be correct that none of the revolutionary parties was planning any such action in the immediate future.

Yet violence continued with little abatement, as did church burnings and the confiscation of religious property. A group of CEDA members from the east petitioned the Ministry of Justice that in a district in Valencia province comprising forty-one towns, with a combined population of 100,000, all churches had been closed and eighty-eight priests expelled. A new sequence of political killings had begun in Madrid on 2 July, and a major incident occurred in Valencia on the evening of Saturday, 11 July, when four armed Falangists briefly seized the microphone of Radio Valencia to announce the imminent outbreak of the Falangist "national syndicalist revolution." This provoked a leftist riot in Spain's fourth-largest city that put rightist centers to the torch and was quelled only after a regiment of cavalry was ordered into the streets.

Four days earlier *El Socialista* had lamented that "the system of violence as party politics is expanding in menacing proportions, though every civilized value is outraged by the shameful murder of citizens. A psychological regression has reduced us to political 'gangsterism.'" In contrast to his earlier position, Prieto now believed that there was no longer any hope of redeeming the immediate situation; he apparently accepted some sort of breakdown, blowup, or armed revolt of the right as almost inevitable and not long to be delayed. He did not totally abandon calls for moderation, though these had often been ignored by his own followers, but emphasized more than ever before the importance of the unity of the left. This had become something of a problem in Andalusia, where the Socialists had earlier momentarily broken with the other Popular Front parties in Almería; and in Seville and Huelva, where Unión Republicana leaders were distancing themselves from the incendiary practices of the local Socialists and Communists.[19] Prieto now sought to minimize the differences between the revolutionaries and the moderates to achieve unity in the face of the militant reaction he believed was very near. He urged the government to be more vigilant, writing in *El Liberal* on 9 July that "a man well prepared is worth two, and a government already prepared is worth forty."

By the beginning of the second week of July the lines were therefore hardening more than ever before. Calvo Sotelo and key leaders of the CEDA had already been informed that a military revolt was imminent and had pledged their support.

CHAPTER THIRTEEN

The Military Conspiracy

THE SPANISH MILITARY CONSPIRACY and revolt of 1936 may be the most widely written about, if not the most thoroughly investigated, in world history. Numerous details have been lovingly recounted, often with embellishment and frequently with the masking of the whole truth, in the official and unofficial historiography of the long Franco regime to which it gave rise.[1]

Ultra-right-wing monarchists had begun to conspire against the new regime almost as soon as the monarchy had collapsed, while the religious persecution that quickly developed gave sharp stimulus to the revival of Carlism in 1931.[2] Very few monarchists, however, were willing to become involved in serious conspiracy during the first two years of the Republic, so that the abortive rebellion of General José Sanjurjo in August 1932 gained success only in one garrison (Seville) and quickly collapsed. The sanjurjada was the weakest of all the early revolts against the Republic and enjoyed less support than any of the three anarchist revolutionary insurrections of 1932–33. The founding of the journal *Acción Española* did begin to provide the theoretical basis for what was termed the *instauración*, not restoration, of a new kind of neotraditional, clerically Catholic, and corporative-authoritarian monarchy;[3] but the alfonsino political party, Renovación Española, was never able to generate popular support. The two monarchist groups, the Carlist Comunión Tradicionalista and Renovación Española, were between themselves incapable of gaining more than 10 percent of the vote, and sometimes not even that.[4] Not altogether surprisingly, after the partial victory of the legalist right in the elections of 1933, the extreme right despaired of generating a successful overthrow of the regime through its own strength and turned to Mussolini's Italy, signing an agreement with the Italian government on 31 March 1934, which would provide Italian financial support, military training facilities, and a limited amount of weapons to assist an eventual revolt in Spain to restore the monarchy.[5] The very need to look abroad was evidence of the weak base of this conspiracy, which predictably produced nothing and by the following year had become a dead letter.

The revolutionary insurrection of October 1934 polarized Spanish society to a much greater degree and stimulated new interest in a change of regime, but at the same time the defeat of the insurrection and the apparent strength of the new conservative Republican government during most of 1935 took the edge off that interest. The only popular support for the extreme right lay among the agrarian Carlists in Navarre, far too small a base for the kind of insurrection that would be required in the politically mobilized Spain of the 1930s. With most conservative opinion represented by the semimoderate, legalistic CEDA, the only force that possessed the strength for a change of regime from the right was the military.

The military, however, were almost as divided politically as Spanish society as a whole. During the greater part of the nineteenth century, the political sentiments of the Spanish military had been rather liberal, and indeed most of the military revolts during the so-called era of pronunciamientos (1814–1874) had been on behalf of one liberal cause or another. The only military dictator in Spain had been Primo de Rivera, who was never head of state.[6] With the emergence of modern radical politics, the military generally moved toward a more conservative position, but only to a certain extent. Some officers still supported liberal policies,[7] and the experience of the politically bankrupt Primo de Rivera regime soured nearly all the senior military on overt political responsibility. The proof of this lack of interest was the almost complete absence of opposition to the coming of the Republic in 1931.

The Azaña government of 1931–1933 proceeded as ineptly with the military as with Spanish society as a whole, often treating them as enemies of the new regime even though this was not the case, making special efforts to insult the military as a professional group, and emphasizing that they enjoyed no respect in the leftist scheme of things. Though Azaña succeeded in arousing the hostility of many of them, the military still showed little interest in playing a political role. Their sympathies ranged from moderate liberal to conservative, with a small leftist minority and a rightist monarchist minority that was not much larger. Hence all efforts to promote military intervention between the spring of 1934 and the spring of 1936 failed completely. As Franco had put it during the winter of 1936, the military were first of all too divided internally, and did not support any one political position. Any effort to intervene overtly or to promote a coup by military initiative alone was bound to end in failure.

The only attempt to develop an active new plan for insurrection during 1935 had been made by the leaders of Falange Española. This quickly became a null issue, because of the complete weakness of the Falange, which had scarcely as many as 10,000 members in a country of nearly 25 million, and which completely failed to generate support among the military.[8] Such plans had been abandoned well before the elections of February 1936, and in the immediate aftermath were not at first resumed, as José Antonio Primo de Rivera sought vainly to call a sort of political truce. Like many others, he was captive to the myth of Azaña and wanted to give the new administration an opportunity to provide effective leadership. The initiative in violence was taken primarily by Azaña's allies on the worker left, who began lethal new assaults on Falangists, the latter quickly responding in kind. This response had in turn provoked the government's action of mid-March, by which it obtained a court ruling that declared the Falange an illicit organization. Rather than the end, however, that was only the beginning of violence, and subsequently the Falangists resumed their planning for a violent insurrection.[9]

The electoral victory of the Popular Front prompted a wide variety of responses on the right in favor of some form of armed reaction. As seen earlier, several senior commanders had begun to conspire at the first news of the electoral results, and General Franco, the circumspect chief of staff, had been sufficiently alarmed to urge the political leadership to carry out a sort of constitutional coup. Franco nonetheless did not ultimately swerve from his original conclusion that the military were simply too divided and too weak to act on their own, an assessment that was undoubtedly correct. The new Azaña government then moved rapidly to place nearly all the top commands in the hands of politically reliable generals, so that the proliferation of meetings and murmurings by the military that followed at first had no effect. A small group of retired generals met several times in Madrid but were powerless to act, and when some of them met with Franco and a few other commanders early in March before Franco's departure to take up his new command in the Canaries, all they could agree to do was to keep in touch and be prepared to take action if any of the revolutionary groups took over the government.

As tension grew during March and April conspiracy on the right expanded by leaps and bounds, but without any overarching structure. A semisecret army officers' association, the Unión Militar Española (UME), had been organized at the close of 1933 and had several thousand nominal members but was originally conceived as a kind of professional organization for corporate military interests, without specific political identity. UME groups generally tended toward the right, however, as more and more military opinion swung in that direction during the spring of 1936. Local UME cells began to conspire in various garrisons, but at first only as individual groups without much interconnection. The self-styled "junta of generals" (none of whom held commands) continued to meet sporadically in Madrid but lacked any means to control active units. Calvo Sotelo and other monarchist leaders sought to encourage military conspirators, but their influence was very limited; the most restive military in fact looked on the rightist civilian politicians as failures worthy of little respect. The Carlists resumed training of their own militia in Navarre and in a few other localities, and even formed their own Supreme Carlist Military Junta across the French border in St. Jean de Luz, but for the time being remained isolated. What most reflected the changed climate, however, was the fact that even some of the most moderate sectors of the CEDA had begun to change their stance. For example, the Valencian branch (DRV), which had been the large sector nearest Christian democracy, lost control of its youth group, which had begun to plot armed action against the new government within days of the Popular Front victory, though once more on its own and without any broader network other than contact with a few officers in nearby garrisons.

More than a little of this was known to the Azaña and Casares Quiroga governments, but not surprisingly the latter were skeptical that such a kaleidoscope of potential insurgency could ever come together successfully.

The right had remained divided throughout the Republican years, and only once had an effort at armed action taken place, immediately ending in abject failure. The government's memory was correct, but its calculations were shortsighted, for as the revolutionary process advanced, militant opposition to it would also grow and would grope its way toward greater unity. Moreover, a new symptom had appeared in April: the distribution of false leaflets, apparently concocted by rightist agents provocateurs, containing detailed plans for leftist revolution, with blacklists of rightists to be eliminated.[10] The senior officer who eventually emerged as organizer of a centrally planned revolt was Brigadier General Emilio Mola, a veteran of the Moroccan campaigns and the last director general of security for the monarchy, who in the latter position had shown great leniency toward the left. Mola was first recognized as leader by the heads of various UME sections in north-central Spain at the end of April. A national network of conspiracy began to take shape only during the following month, for the response of the military was slow but cumulative as incidents multiplied and tensions spread. Issues of authority and legitimacy were difficult to resolve.

The senior military rebel under the Republic was Sanjurjo, but since being amnestied he had lived in Portugal, and he lacked either opportunity or ability to organize a successful conspiracy from abroad. Thus by the end of May he transferred his active authority to Mola, who planned to establish Sanjurjo as acting head of a military junta after the revolt materialized.[11]

Mola first engaged in rudimentary political planning near the end of April in a document titled "Private Instruction No. 1." This envisioned the result of a successful rebellion to be not a restored monarchy but a "military dictatorship," to be assisted by provincial committees made up of diverse allied entities, which he described variously as "political groups," "individual societies and individuals," and "militias" that were "dedicated to the cause" and "counterrevolutionary." With regard to the leftist foe, "action must be violent in the extreme in order to subdue the enemy, who is strong and well organized, as soon as possible. Certainly all leaders of political parties, societies, or trade unions opposed to the movement must be arrested, applying to them exemplary punishment to strangle any strikes or attempts to rebel."[12] Such terms, though quite rigorous and perhaps a euphemism for summary execution, nonetheless did not forecast the absolutely massive repression, affecting thousands of ordinary leftist militants, that would commence after the revolt began.

This rudimentary sketch became somewhat more detailed in a memorandum drawn up on 5 June, about a week after Mola had been recognized as the overall coordinator of conspiracy for the entire country. Titled "The Directory and Its Initial Tasks," it stipulated that the form of a new regime was to be not a restored monarchy but a "republican dictatorship." The initial government would consist of an all-military "Directory," a term taken from the Primo de Rivera regime. It would provide a "Portuguese" or "Pilsudski" type of solution rather than building a revolutionary fascist or "Italian" type of system. The memorandum concluded with the statement: "The Directory will guarantee no change in the republican regime during its administration, maintaining no change in any worker claims that have been legally obtained" and "will create a strong and disciplined state." The Constitution of 1931 would be suspended, to be replaced by a new "constituent parliament" chosen by voters who must be in possession of a new "electoral card," a requirement that would exclude illiterates and criminals. There would be some vestiges of liberalism, such as "separation of church and state, freedom of worship, and respect for all religions." Regional commissions would be established to solve the agrarian problem "on the basis of developing small property," but permitting "collective cultivation where the former is not possible."[13]

The chief problem for Mola was the army itself. The officer corps was also a bureaucratic class, and most officers were not eager to involve themselves in a desperate undertaking that might easily lead to their ruin. They had to be concerned about their families and their pensions. The Republican government still existed, and the constitution was still the law of the land, even though its guarantees were less and less enforced. The revolutionaries had not yet tried to take over the government directly, and much of the military seemed willing to go along with Azaña's gamble: after a few more months, the revolutionaries might moderate their demands and the crisis would ease. Military activism had been a disaster in Spanish politics between 1917 and 1931; most officers were aware of this fact and all the less eager to throw themselves into the fray. Furthermore, the ferocious propaganda of the left made it clear that in any radical confrontation, defeated military dissidents would not be treated as leniently as had sometimes been the case in the past. Thus many would-be rebels committed themselves fully to the revolt only after reaching the negative conclusion that it would be more dangerous for them if they did not, a situation that matured fully only in mid-July.

Liaison between the military and civilian groups was poor. Mola eventually received financial support from the CEDA after the beginning of July, but in fact never spent most of the money.[14] Neither the monarchists nor the CEDA had organized paramilitary strength to offer,[15] and Mola viewed them with distaste as untrustworthy failures.

The principal, indeed almost the only, antileftist force engaged in direct action was the Falange. Yet despite his open letter at the beginning of May urging the military to rebel, José Antonio Primo de Rivera had the same opinion of the military that Mola had of civilian politicians. He did not fully agree to Falangist participation in a military revolt until 29 June and then limited it to a time frame of eleven days. Mola tried to set a target date of 10 July but then had to cancel it because of inadequate support and also because of the arrest of one of the chief Falangists involved. Carlist leaders were even stickier to deal with, and on 9 July Mola momentarily gave up hope of gaining their cooperation.

Elsewhere the situation remained confused and problematic. Franco, arguably the most important single figure, was very reluctant. He believed in armed insurrection only as a last resort, arguing that the government should be given more time to change its policies and begin to restore order. As late as 23 June he wrote to Casares Quiroga, insisting that the army was basically loyal but urging the prime minister to adopt a policy of greater respect for the military and for law and order. As late as 12 July Franco is said to have sent an urgent message to Mola saying that the time had not yet come to rebel.[16]

General Manuel Goded, military commander of the Balearics, was equally uncertain. A moderate liberal, he had originally been strongly pro-Republican and had played a prominent role in the first year of the new regime before turning against it. According to one version, he became alarmed by news that the rebels were trying to purchase arms in Germany and might seek assistance from Fascist Italy.[17] He apparently tried to establish contact with Azaña to urge a change of course, while also seeking contact with Winston Churchill and the veteran Radical leader Albert Sarraut in France.[18] Nothing came of these maneuvers.

Many officers would act only on direct orders from above, which were not likely to be forthcoming. The conspiracy continued to be weakened by the fact that it was based primarily on preemptive considerations. A successful counterrevolution could be mobilized, it seemed, only in the face of a matured revolutionary threat, yet the revolutionary left, by design, would still only go partway. Economic disorder was great, there was considerable violence in certain areas, and the government made it clearer than ever that it was a partisan of the left and would not provide impartial administration and enforcement of the law. But the left was altogether disunited, and there was as yet no revolutionary action aimed at the immediate overthrow of the Republican state.

Hence the decisive importance of the murder of Calvo Sotelo (treated in the next chapter). To many it symbolized a radicalism and government complicity completely out of control, an end to the constitutional system. The immediate reaction of the government, which refused to do anything to reassure the right but as usual blamed the victim, proceeding to ever-more-arbitrary arrests of rightists, seemed only to confirm this opinion. For the next thirty years apologists for the military revolt would refer to fake documents alleging that the killing of Calvo Sotelo was but the prelude to a Communist plot to seize power a few weeks later. In fact no concrete leftist plan to take over the government existed, for all the revolutionary groups, in one way or another, intended to squeeze every ounce of advantage out of the leftist Republic first, and that agenda was far from complete. As far as the Communists were concerned, their explicit plan was to hew to a nominal legality that would be used to achieve absolute leftist predominance, outlawing the conservative parties. At the same time, all the revolutionary groups stated that they considered the remaining days of a parliamentary government to be numbered and expected a revolutionary regime to follow in the near future. This position was clearly outlined in manifold public pronouncements during the spring and summer of 1936. But most followed variants of the "people's republic" tack by which legal and pseudolegal means would be used to create a "safe" revolutionary situation.

Subsequently there was much speculation as to why the left Republican government did not take more stringent action to avert a major revolt. The conspiracy was not exactly a secret; though key details were not known to the government, rumors had flown for months, certain civilian contacts had been arrested, and some of the most active plotters were known to be hostile. The government had in fact taken more than a few measures to keep the army under control. Nearly all the top command assignments had been changed, and most of the generals with active commands were, as events proved, loyal to the regime. Thousands of civilian activists, Falangist and rightist, had been arrested, and some of the top conspirators had been placed under at least partial surveillance.[19]

There were deep-seated reasons why Azaña and Casares Quiroga did not go further. The "Azaña gamble" to exploit the revolutionary left on behalf of a leftist parliamentary Republic was a dubiously calculated risk that inevitably placed the government between two fires. Azaña's policy was staked on maintaining the Popular Front, yet the government was always in danger of becoming its prisoner or hostage rather than its ally. The possibility of some sort of break with the revolutionary left was not to be discounted, though Azaña and Casares Quiroga were themselves determined not to be responsible for precipitating it. Should that break occur, however, revolutionaries in the streets could be fully neutralized only by a comparatively strong army in the barracks. Azaña wished to be the ally of the revolutionary left, but not its prisoner. After gaining the presidency of the Republic, he became increasingly anguished, frightened, and withdrawn. In a conversation with Gil Robles immediately after his elevation, he seemed already to have lost his customary arrogance, declaring: "I don't know where we are going to end up. Your friends should at least give some margin of confidence. They should not create complications, because I already have enough problems with the other side."[20] One of the keenest students of the president declares that worries about the military conspiracy "in the agonized concern of Manuel Azaña did not play as much of a role as did the attitude and actions of the extreme left."[21] Added to this was the left Republicans' scorn for the military, whom they considered inept and politically insignificant, scarcely able to mount more of a threat on their own than had Sanjurjo in 1932.

Thus to Azaña and Casares Quiroga, their military policy seemed sensible and coherent. Some measures had been taken, while the danger from the right—considered by the left a spent force, already on the historical trash-heap—might be overestimated. The sanjurjada had been a feeble affair, and the military themselves were obviously divided. The easiest time for them to have acted would have been between October 1934 and February 1936; yet they had done nothing. In their view, a more aggressive policy to neutralize the military might simply crystallize a determination that would otherwise largely remain latent, while also leaving the government increasingly defenseless before the revolutionary left. Casares Quiroga had begun to speak highly of the Civil Guard, whose discipline he now needed, and he pooh-poohed any excessive worry about the military, which he put down to personal hysteria, or fear, or outmoded sectarian attitudes.[22] Spokesmen of the revolutionary left had so frequently referred to Casares' role as that of Kerensky that, according to the Socialist Vidarte, he placed a photo of the Russian leader in his office to remind him that he must avoid such a fate.[23] Juan Moles, the independent Republican interior minister, thought it important not to provoke the military into a reactive sense of solidarity.[24] As a consequence, leftist officers in the Assault Guards and UMRA had become strident critics of the prime minister.

The government sought to monitor the conspiracy without being unnecessarily provocative. Thus the Ministry of the Interior sent out circulars to heighten vigilance of rightist groups and on 2 June specified: "The Ministry has been informed of emissaries sent to various garrisons with the goal of organizing a military movement. It is necessary to exercise extreme vigilance in the most discreet manner over important leaders and suspicious military activities, taking appropriate measures and informing the Ministry of any information acquired."[25] Yet the month of June passed without military subversion, and there were numerous complaints about public insults to the military, which were frequently inflicted by the revolutionary left. The Republican minister of war himself complained of this and of excessive surveillance; accordingly, the Ministry of the Interior sent out another circular on 27 June urging that due vigilance be combined with an effort to maintain "coexistence" and to avoid unnecessary "conflict."[26]

There is testimony that Casares Quiroga first informed the council of ministers in a meeting on 10 July that a military conspiracy indeed existed, and might in fact break out within the next forty-eight hours. He provided more than a little information, though the government had not been able to identify "El Director" (Mola), the head of the conspiracy, who signed the main documents. The government had the option of aborting the movement by a series of immediate arrests, yet it lacked conclusive proof regarding the ringleaders and thus would not be able to prosecute them effectively. Such niceties were not observed in the cases of Falangists or monarchists, but, for the reasons listed above, the government felt it necessary to treat the military with a constitutional correctness that it rarely showed to rightists. The alternative was to wait for the movement to mature—always assuming that it would be little more than a repeat of the sanjurjada—and smash it completely once it began, which was the decision already taken by Azaña and himself.[27] In retrospect this decision seems delusional, yet as of 10 July the government's reading was not altogether inaccurate. There was manifest reluctance among many officers to join any revolt. Had it not been for the traumatic events of the night of 12–13 July, things might have worked out more or less as the government calculated.

CHAPTER FOURTEEN

The Assassination of Calvo Sotelo

THE EXTREME POLITICAL TENSION of the summer of 1936 obscured the fact that the vast majority of Spaniards were leading normal lives and even spending an unusually large amount on entertainment. Movie theaters—with greater proportionate seating capacity than in any other European country—were full, and there were numerous summer festivals and special athletic events, the most unusual of which was the international "People's Olympics," scheduled to open in Barcelona on 19 July, in antithesis to the regular Olympics being held in Berlin that summer.[1] The People's Olympics had strong political overtones, but elsewhere millions were simply trying to enjoy themselves and to forget political and social strife.

The final and conclusive round of violence began in Madrid on 2 July, when JSU gunmen fired on a bar frequented by Falangists, killing two Falangist students plus a third customer. On the following night, Falangist gunmen sprayed with gunfire a group of workers leaving a neighborhood Casa del Pueblo, killing two UGT workers and seriously wounding others. One day later two corpses were discovered outside the city. The first was identified as that of an eighteen-year-old student and son of a local businessman, not a Falangist but a friend of Falangists, who had evidently been held prisoner for several days and then shot. The second was that of a thirty-year-old retired infantry officer, either a member or sympathizer of the Falange, who had been kidnapped and stabbed thirty-three times. The government responded, as usual, not with a vigorous search for the perpetrators but with further arrests of Falangists, as though they were responsible for killing their own members and sympathizers. During the next three days it announced the arrests of 300 Falangists and rightists in Madrid province alone, though as usual no Socialists were arrested.[2] Any pretense of reconciliation had long since been abandoned, and the government's policy seemed to be to try to push the right ever further until the latter either surrendered completely or came out in a revolt that could be directly repressed.

The climactic events took place that weekend. At about 10:00 P.M. on Sunday, 12 July, the Assault Guard officer José del Castillo was shot and killed on a street in central Madrid en route to reporting for duty on the night shift. Castillo was a former army officer and ardent Socialist who had transferred to the Assault Guards and then been arrested for his mutinous participation in the insurrection of 1934, in which he was to have helped seize the Ministry of the Interior. The Azaña government had reassigned him to active service, and he had distinguished himself for his zeal in repressing rightists, having severely wounded a young Carlist during the mayhem of 16 April, as well as having engaged in various actions against Falangists. A militant of the UMRA and a leader in the Socialist militia, he apparently also helped to train the Communist MAOC on Sunday afternoons, and had for some time been a marked man.[3]

His killing immediately provoked intense reactions among his comrades in the UMRA, Assault Guards, and Socialist and Communist militias. Two months earlier, on 8 May in Madrid, Falangists had murdered Captain Carlos Faraudo, an army officer on active duty and also a leading figure in the UMRA and the Socialist militia. Though two Falangists had soon been arrested for Faraudo's killing, his UMRA comrades had vowed to exact vengeance if another of their comrades were killed, and had let it be known that they would not merely take the life of another Falangist, but would carry out a reprisal against a rightist political leader.[4] Soon after learning of Castillo's death, a group of Assault Guard officers went directly to the Ministry of the Interior to demand action. They were received by the left Republican undersecretary Bibiano Ossorio Tafall, who was being assiduously courted by the Communists and would later reveal himself to be a leading fellow traveler.[5] He quickly took them to see Juan Moles, who approved their demand that a further extensive list of Falangists be arrested. The Assault Guard officers refused to allow the arrests to be made by the armed police in the normal way and insisted on the right to make the arrests themselves, to which the minister feebly assented.

The Pontejos barracks of the Assault Guards, only a block behind the ministry, was dominated by leftist officers who had been specially selected by the government. That night it was frequented by a bizarre mix of Assault Guards (some not on official duty), some leftist Civil Guards, leftists from other kinds of police units, and various Socialist and Communist militiamen. It had generally been the government's policy to reinstate leftist police personnel irrespective of past behavior and to encourage politicization of police functions, including the intermittent inclusion of civilian political activists, such as the Socialist militia deputized as delegados in Cuenca and elsewhere. Thus when arrest orders were made up at the Pontejos barracks that night,[6] the Assault Guard squads that set out were made up of a lawless mixture of Assault Guards, Civil Guards, off-duty police from other units, and Socialist and Communist activists.[7]

The Dirección General de Seguridad had apparently made up lists of names of Falangists and rightists, but the insubordinate Assault Guard officers were not satisfied with these, and added names from other political lists, partly confected by the MAOC militia leader Manuel Tagüeña.[8] It was also decided to seize key rightist leaders such as Gil Robles and Calvo Sotelo, even though they enjoyed parliamentary immunity and such arrest was prohibited by the constitution, now a dead letter at least for these Republican police. Whether the police conspiracy by the revolutionaries planned from the beginning to murder the rightist leaders, as well, is something that can probably never be determined.

Gil Robles, as it turned out, was not in Madrid, but the squad that left to deal with Calvo Sotelo was a motley crew of Assault Guards, policemen, and Socialist activists, led by the Civil Guard captain Fernando Condés. Like the slain Castillo, Condés was a former army officer (decorated in the final Moroccan campaign) who had passed to the Civil Guards, where he was one of the minority of leftist officers. He had played a role in the abortive insurrection of 1934 in Madrid, for which he had been sentenced to life imprisonment and then reprieved by the Popular Front victory. His mutinous betrayal in 1934 had been so overt that even the left Republican government did not restore him to duty until 1 July, with promotion to captain as a reward for his earlier subversion. In the meantime he helped to train the Socialist militia of Prieto's "La Motorizada" unit and apparently still had not fully returned to Civil Guard service. He was dressed in civilian clothes when he led his mixed squad, containing four Socialist activists from "La Motorizada," to the home of Calvo Sotelo at about 2:00 A.M. on 13 July.

Calvo Sotelo remained in Madrid to participate in a major debate on the problem of public order scheduled to take place in the Cortes on the fourteenth. Though he had been given to understand that the army would soon rebel, neither he nor the other rightist leaders were part of the conspiracy itself. He had taken a bold position in parliament and had even publicly urged the army to intervene—albeit in slightly Aesopian language—because, as he said privately, the military needed to know that there were civilian groups that encouraged them and would support them. Calvo Sotelo saw no solution to Spain's problems other than the imposition of an authoritarian regime, and the fact that he was willing to espouse this position publicly made him the principal target of the left. Twice Communist and Socialist spokesmen in parliament had publicly referred to assassinating him, an action that had undoubtedly been discussed many times informally among revolutionary activists. The monarchist politician himself had a strong sense of patriotic duty and the need to fulfill what he saw as his responsibilities. Not long before, he had had the police authorities change the bodyguards assigned to protect him (as in the case of other major figures), when he had learned that their chief responsibility was surveillance more than protection, but really had no idea whether the new ones were more reliable. Beyond that, there was no special security. As of 12 July, neither Calvo Sotelo nor anyone else knew for sure what would happen in Spain. Despite reports he had received about the progress of the conspiracy, he could not be certain when the military would rebel, or indeed if they would rebel at all. Hence to that point he continued his normal political and personal life.[9]

The bodyguards at the entrance to the building accepted the professional identity cards of Condés and others, who proceeded unhindered to the apartment of the monarchist leader. Calvo Sotelo was shown Civil Guard identification by Condés and was able to verify through his window that a regular Assault Guard truck was waiting under a street light in front of his apartment building. Condés assured him that he was not being made subject to an illegal arrest but was simply being taken in the middle of the night to an emergency meeting in the Dirección General de Seguridad. Calvo Sotelo insisted on taking a small overnight case with him, should he be detained longer, but was in no position to resist once the squad of revolutionaries had gained entrance to his building.[10] The Assault Guard truck had proceeded only a few blocks when one of the Socialist militants, Luis Cuenca (an earlier police delegado in the corrupt Cuenca elections), abruptly shot the monarchist chief twice in the back of the head, killing him almost instantly. Some members of the squad would later allege that this had not been planned, but was a sort of "accident," though such testimony is not altogether credible, since the whole operation had been designed as an illegal act of revolutionary vengeance from the very beginning. The corpse was dumped at the door of the morgue of the Almudena, Madrid's main cemetery.

Within a short time the director general of security, José Alonso Mallol, was informed by Calvo Sotelo's family and friends of the illegal arrest—that is, kidnapping—which he denied ever having ordered (a claim that was undoubtedly true). A desultory investigation then began around 7:00 A.M., but the location of the corpse did not become known until midmorning. There was no response from the government except, as was often the case, from Martínez Barrio, president of the Cortes, who privately declared his solidarity with the slain leader's colleagues, and who spoke with the irresponsible Moles, minister of the interior, who had just presided over a disaster and seemed not to know what was going on.[11] Somewhat similarly, Felipe Sánchez Román, a friend of Azaña but a former classmate of Calvo Sotelo, is reported to have said that "the Republic has just dishonored itself forever" and left his card at the victim's home as a sign of condolence.[12]

Since the murder was led and executed by prietista Socialists, it was not surprising that leaders of the latter group were the first to be informed, apparently by the murderers themselves. Julián Zugazagoitia, director of *El Socialista,* later wrote that, on receiving the news at about 8:00 A.M., he immediately exclaimed, "This assassination means war!"[13] The Socialist leaders showed no concern to maintain Republican constitutionalism, now almost fatally broken. Consistent with the attitude that Prieto had taken for the past fortnight, they assumed major conflict—a military or rightist insurrection, or civil war, or both—was now inevitable and that the murder would serve as a catalyst. The assassins were told to go into hiding, and Condés moved into the home of the revolutionary Socialist Margarita Nelken,[14] who in the Cortes had publicly called for the expansion of violence and disorder.

Though it promised to investigate, the government made no effort to conciliate. It imposed immediate censorship to conceal the truth,[15] and prepared for armed confrontation by initiating yet another round of arrests of Falangists and rightists, as though they had been responsible for the murder. No effort was made to apprehend those directly responsible for the crime, though Calvo Sotelo's widow was able to identify Condés from police photographs that same day. The Casares Quiroga government had in effect already come very close to becoming a government of civil war, though it still recognized certain outward forms of constitutionality.

The principal exception to this policy, though only momentarily, was the work of the investigative judge Ursicino Gómez Carbajo, who recognized the seriousness of the crime and actively took up the case within just a few hours. By the following day he was beginning systematic interrogation of Assault Guard personnel when the government, with its customarily arbitrary procedure, took the case out of his hands, apparently out of concern that he was an honest and politically independent judge. Though a number of Assault Guards were arrested, Condés and Cuenca remained at liberty. A few days later, when the fighting began, the investigation came to an abrupt end, and those few who had been arrested were released. Both Condés and Cuenca were killed in combat in the mountains north of Madrid during the first days of the Civil War. Several Socialists involved in the assassination, such as Francisco Ordóñez and Santiago Garcés, later played major roles in the Republican forces.

The first political response came from leaders of the Communist Party, almost certainly pursuant to the standard Comintern instructions. They decided that very morning that this newest crisis provided a stimulus for advancing the long-announced agenda of forming the "new type of republic." The afternoon after the murder, Communist deputies submitted the following legislative draft, which immediately appeared in *Mundo Obrero,* to the other Popular Front groups:

> Article 1: All organizations of a fascist or reactionary nature, such as Falange Española, Renovación Española, CEDA, Derecha Regional Valenciana, and others with similar character-

istics, will be dissolved and their properties confiscated, as well as those of their leaders and inspirers.

Article 2: All persons known for their fascist, reactionary, or anti-Republican activities will be arrested and prosecuted without bond.

Article 3: The newspapers *El Debate, Ya, Informaciones,* and *ABC* and all the reactionary provincial press will be confiscated by the government.

This sweeping, totally unconstitutional proposal was a major feature of the plan to introduce the "new-type" all-leftist Republic, but the government's postponement of parliament—another of Casares Quiroga's arbitrary policies—made its formal presentation impossible before the fighting began, after which its provisions were carried out in a maximally violent and revolutionary manner in what would be termed the "Republican zone."

The council of ministers met twice on the thirteenth, agreed to suspend the next session of the Cortes, denounced the murder in a brief statement, and promised a full public investigation and prosecution, neither of which was ever carried out. Instead, the murderers would be promoted to positions of greater responsibility. Having sidestepped parliament, the council did nothing to reassure the ever-more-vulnerable opposition, but instead proceeded with its standard policy of blaming the victim. In the spirit of the new Communist proposal, it announced the decision to close the centers of the monarchist Renovación Española and of the CNT in Madrid, even though it was obvious that neither of these had been involved in the murder, and to arrest many more rightists. On the fifteenth the director general of security announced that another 185 provincial and local leaders of the Falange had been seized in recent days, in addition to the several thousand already in prison. On the morrow, in line with the government's new strategy of intensified polarization, all rightist centers in Barcelona were closed.

Meanwhile Marcelino Domingo had talked to Martínez Barrio, who agreed to urge Azaña to replace the Casares Quiroga administration with a more conciliatory and effective government. The president refused. While conceding that Casares would ultimately have to go, he alleged that to replace him immediately would be equivalent to making him responsible for the assassination.[16]

Whereas the UMRA saw the Castillo killing as one in a sequence of several murders of leftist officers, rightists had no doubt that the Calvo Sotelo assassination represented some sort of organized conspiracy, even though not necessarily by the Republican government itself. Many linked it with the two kidnap-murders by the left the preceding weekend as part of a new leftist tactic to sequester and then murder their victims. The slain monarchist was buried in a public funeral on the afternoon of the fourteenth, a ceremony attended by several thousand rightists, many of whom gave the fascist salute, a gesture that infuriated the police. Immediately afterward, hundreds of younger rightists decided to march back into the center of the city in a political demonstration. They were stopped by a police barricade, which searched each demonstrator to be sure that all were unarmed before permitting them to pass. As the unarmed group moved nearer the center of Madrid, Assault Guards and other police opened a general fusillade of gunfire to prevent them from proceeding further. Between two and five were killed, according to varying newspaper accounts, and many wounded.[17] Three Assault Guard officers who protested this deliberate police aggression against unarmed demonstrators were temporarily arrested, while some of the personnel in Castillo's own Pontejos barracks felt that the honor of their corps had been tarnished by the assassination and vigorously protested, demanding a fuller investigation on both the fourteenth and sixteenth. Several were briefly arrested before being released. At least two Assault Guard units seemed on the verge of mutiny against the government's arbitrary policies and could scarcely be controlled.[18] Meanwhile the government's action against the CNT encouraged further hostilities between the CNT and UGT, and in another affray in Madrid on the fourteenth a cenetista was killed.

The government could not avoid convening a meeting of the Diputación Permanente of the Cortes at 11:30 A.M. on 15 July. Though its nominal purpose was to approve another thirty-day extension of the state of alarm, this final session of a branch of the Republican parliament inevitably became a debate on the state of public order, the assassination, and its consequences. Debate was opened by the monarchist Conde de Vallellano, who charged: "This crime, without precedent in our political history, has been made possible by the atmosphere created by the incitements to violence and personal assault on the deputies of the right repeated daily in parliament. . . . We cannot coexist one moment longer with the facilitators and moral accomplices of this act." The rightist and centrist deputies pointed out that this was merely the most flagrant and decisive confirmation of their previous charges concerning the partisan and politicized administration of public order. Never before in the history of parliamentary regimes had a leader of the parliamentary opposition been kidnapped and murdered by a detachment of state police. They did not charge that the government itself had planned or ordered the murder, but they did assert that it had been responsible for encouraging the circumstances that made it possible.

Gil Robles presented another statistical résumé of disorders, which he said included sixty-one deaths from politically related acts between 16 June and 13 July. He observed that every day he read in leftist newspapers phrases such as "the enemy must be smashed" or one must "practice a policy of extermination." "I know that you are carrying out a policy of persecution, violence, and extermination against anything that is rightist. But you are profoundly mistaken: however great may be the violence, the reaction will be greater still. For everyone killed another combatant will rise up. . . . You who are today fostering violence will become the first victims of it. The phrase that revolutions, like Saturn, devour their own children is commonplace, but no less true for being so. Today you are complacent, because you see an adversary fall. But the day will come when the same violence that you have unleashed will be turned against you."

Portela Valladares declared that he would abstain from the vote on extending the state of alarm, since the Casares Quiroga government had shown that it lacked the honesty and objectivity to administer a state of constitutional exception. "The government has said that it is belligerent, and the extreme recourse to suspension of guarantees, which must be exercised with calm and measure, without passion and with equality, we cannot give to a government that declares itself belligerent." Juan Ventosa of the Lliga Catalana agreed with Portela and also declared his abstention, saying that the present government was completely unfit to deal with the crisis because of its self-avowed partisanship and refusal to apply the law equally to all, Casares Quiroga being "a man more likely to touch off civil war than to restore normalcy."

Prieto's response was very weak, emphasizing that Calvo Sotelo had been slain in revenge for the killing of Castillo. This merely repeated the feeble logic of the government's original statement two days earlier, which made the same point. Neither the government nor Prieto seemed to grasp that their argument placed the Republican state security forces on the same level as political assassins, thus virtually conceding the charges by the right.

Neither the government nor the prietista Socialists, intimately involved with the assassins, made any move to rectify the situation. Their policy had become one of armed civil conflict, which they believed inevitable and were confident of winning. On 14 July Prieto merely urged in *El Liberal* the union of the left rather than reconciliation with the right, whom he threatened with total destruction if they dared initiate any new violence of their own. As he put it, "It will be a battle to the death, because each side knows that if the enemy triumphs, he will give no quarter." This grim prophecy proved correct. Meanwhile Prieto personally shielded the assassins, and there is testimony that he intervened directly to prevent the government from going forward fully with appropriate arrests and investigation.[19] Since the killer was one of Prieto's own bodyguards, the Socialists considered it indispensable to veto any full investigation, which would inevitably expose the dominant role of the Socialists in the political violence in Spain.

The executive commission of the Socialist Party did call a meeting of its own members, of the Communist leaders, and of the JSU chiefs, all of whom signed a manifesto promising complete support for the government. This move was not, however, officially endorsed by the UGT, whose leaders did not recognize the legitimacy of the PSOE executive commission; but one UGT representative did attend the meeting and signed the manifesto as an individual.

For some time the caballerista strategy, like that of Mola, had been based on the need for a very brief civil war, which would be touched off by a military coup that would be quickly defeated by a revolutionary general strike of organized labor. The caballeristas had no direct plan to seize power themselves, a weakness of their strategy being that it left the initiative to the rightist military, but they held to the belief that a military revolt could not possibly be so strong that it could not be crushed by a general strike. Largo Caballero "believed blindly [*a pies juntillas*]"[20] that the combined effect of these two actions—military revolt and revolutionary general strike—would completely undermine the left Republican government, opening the way for the Socialists to take over. When Largo

Caballero returned from an international trade union meeting in London, *Claridad* complacently ranted on 15 July, "They don't like this government? Then let's substitute a leftist dictatorship for it. They don't like the state of alarm? Then let there be all-out civil war." The editors would very soon get more "all-out civil war" than they had bargained for.

On the following day *Claridad* published an article titled "Technique of the Counter–Coup d'état" to explain how to defeat the revolt that was not merely expected, but ardently desired and ceaselessly provoked, by the extreme left. This defeat could be readily accomplished, according to the article, by dissolving rebel military units and freeing their soldiers from military discipline, handing over arms en masse to "the people"—meaning not of course Spanish people in general but the organized revolutionary groups—and then combining the resulting revolutionary militia with loyal sectors of the army to defeat what was left of the rebellion.[21] The revolutionaries would then also replace what was left of the left Republican government.

One of the leading advocates of revolutionary civil war was Luis Araquistain, the editor of *Claridad*. Like Maurín, he had earlier opined that the left could easily win such a civil war and that the tense international situation precluded foreign counterrevolutionary intervention. After the killing of Calvo Sotelo, he wrote to his wife that an attempted armed revolt by the right was now likely, the result of which would be "either our dictatorship or theirs."[22] This assessment was correct. The democratic Republic had virtually, but not entirely, ceased to exist.

The executive commission of the Socialist Party called another meeting on 16 July of representatives of all the worker parties of the Popular Front to agree on a joint policy. This time the UGT did send official representatives, but at the meeting the latter declared that they could not agree to anything without first taking it back for consultation with the UGT leadership, and therefore abstained from the final decision. Representatives of the other Popular Front worker parties agreed to organize new committees throughout Spain to begin creation of an armed militia, and to petition the government for arms for such a militia and for a decisive purge of the military. They also agreed to offer a place for government representatives in the joint committees of all the political forces that supported the Casares Quiroga government, as a kind of armed soviet.

This proposal was too complicated and limiting for the caballeristas, who simply wanted arms to be handed directly to the worker syndicates, without any complex Popular Front structure. The UGT leaders therefore responded by asking who would guarantee the future political behavior of such multiparty militia committees, why such committees should take upon themselves military responsibility for fighting a rightist coup, how they could be sure that the government itself would not try to dissolve such committees, and why these should not rather be authorized by the government itself, which would guarantee that it would not subsequently try to disarm them.[23]

A situation had been reached in which the prietistas and Communists were now willing to form a multiparty militia to wage civil war, though theoretically in support of the government rather than as a direct rival, while the UGT proposed no initiative other than to receive power for such military committees from the government itself, awaiting the direct arming of the syndicates. Despite all their talk of Bolshevization, the revolutionary strategy of the caballeristas remained passive, first awaiting outbreak of the revolt, then waiting for the government to hand over to them a share of armed power, something that the Casares Quiroga government still refused to do. Its successor three days later would not be so squeamish.

The spectacle of preparation for civil war set alarm bells ringing at Comintern headquarters in Moscow. The Comintern bosses demanded stringent measures to disarm the right and avoid civil war, which they did not regard with the same complacency shown by Maurín, Araquistain, and other theorists. Not since 1919 had so favorable a situation existed for the extreme left in any European country as presently in Spain. The Popular Front formula had given the left almost total legal control of Spanish institutions. Such nominally legal power must be employed as vigorously as possible, and civil war averted. The Comintern leaders had had much more experience with revolutionary civil war than their Spanish counterparts, and did not want to see the present leftist domination in Spain placed at risk by a civil war that the left might not necessarily dominate so easily.

On 17 July, only a few hours before the military revolt would begin in the Moroccan Protectorate, Dimitrov and Manuilsky sent an urgent telegram to the PCE's politburo, insisting on immediate exceptional measures to thwart "the fascist conspiracy" and avoid the danger of civil war.

Communist leaders were ordered to encourage maximum unity of the Popular Front and to press ahead vigorously with their program of using government powers to arrest large numbers of rightists, purge the army, police, and administration, and suppress the rightist press altogether. In addition, they should press for introduction of a special "emergency tribunal" with revolutionary plenary powers to apply maximum penalties to rightists and confiscate their property, while the party should also move rapidly to form and expand worker-peasant alliance groups as active liaison units of the Popular Front.[24] These proposals, unconstitutional and revolutionary or prerevolutionary, were not at all part of the "moderate" program with which the Communists are often credited, but were fully consistent with the basic Comintern strategy of using government, as distinct from subversive or insurgent, powers to achieve total leftist domination. After the assassination, the last chance to avoid civil war had arrived. It could have been achieved in one of two ways. The first would have been immediately to adopt something like the Comintern proposal, which was not that far from Prieto's position at this time, though it would probably have had to have begun at a somewhat earlier date in order to be completely successful. The other would have been to announce an immediate reversal of course, a new policy of constitutional law and order, and a serious effort to conciliate the right. Indeed, Mariano Ansó, the Socialist who chaired the military affairs committee of parliament, received a visit immediately after the assassination from Lieutenant Colonel Tejero, an emissary of Mola, who told him that the general requested an immediate interview.[25] Ansó refused the request. On the assumption that his memory is correct, it may be conjectured that the head of the conspiracy sought to determine if the leftist leaders were finally willing to change course, or whether he must quickly go through with his long-planned but highly uncertain revolt.

The government adopted neither clear-cut alternative but continued with its policy of harassing the right, without the slightest gesture to rectify the situation. Portela Valladares would later charge in his memoirs that "Casares viewed the outbreak of military revolt with confident satisfaction, intending to present himself to parliament afterward to receive the victor's applause."[26] Santiago Carrillo, leader of the new Juventudes Socialistas Unificadas, has testified that he, Prieto, and the PCE secretary general José Díaz went to talk with Casares in these final days to urge him to give arms to the new worker committees being planned. According to Carrillo, "That frail, sickly man with feverish eyes tried to convince us that the government was in control of the situation and that the danger was not that great. He even said that he hoped for a revolt in order to crush them completely."[27]

This calculation might have been correct even as late as 12 July. Mola had continually encountered major obstacles in developing the conspiracy. Most officers did not really want to rebel, relations were strained with the Falangists, and even the Carlists refused to cooperate on Mola's terms. The projected date for revolt had been postponed several times, and on 9 July, after an apparently decisive rejection by the Carlists, Mola was in despair, lamenting to the Carlist leader Fal Conde that "we turned to you because in the barracks we have only men in uniforms who cannot really be called soldiers. . . . Of all those who have participated in this adventure, the only victim will be me."[28] At that moment he could foresee only a failed insurrection or perhaps none at all, followed by his own arrest and prosecution—or flight into exile.

The assassination had an electrifying effect on all the potential op-position, and proved to be the catalyst needed to transform a limping conspiracy into a powerful revolt that could set off a massive civil war, even though few of those involved anticipated the full extent of the great conflict that would result. The liberal officer Captain Jesús Pérez Salas, who would remain faithful to the Republican cause to the end, explained the effect this way:

> The catalyst sought by the right, which would guarantee a mili-
> tary revolt, finally arrived in the middle of July. That catalyst
> was the assassination of Calvo Sotelo. I do not know whose
> idea it was to commit such an outrage, but I will say that, even
> if they had been set up by the rebels themselves, those who did
> the deed could not have achieved a greater effect. It must have
> been planned by someone who really wanted to see the army
> rebel. . . . If the companions or allies of Lieutenant Castillo had
> applied the law of revenge and had shot down Calvo Sotelo in
> the street or wherever they found him, it would have been only
> one more act of terrorism, added to the many others that sum-
> mer. The impression this would have caused in the army would

THE ASSASSINATION OF CALVO SOTELO 333

of course have been deplorable, and consequently would have
constituted one more step toward a rebellion. Because of the
importance of Calvo Sotelo, an ex-minister of the dictatorship,
his death would have been exploited to demonstrate to military
officers the complete impotence of the government to prevent
such killings. But in no way would it have been the drop of
water that made the glass overflow. Such was the initial effect
of the news of the assassination, but after the details were
revealed and it was learned that the forces of public order had
themselves been involved, the reaction was tremendous. . . .
It is futile to try to deny the importance of this fact. If the forces
of public order, on whom the rights and security of citizens
depend, are capable of carrying out this kind of act, they effectively demonstrate their lack of discipline and obliviousness
to their sacred mission. . . . The resulting action of the army
might have been prevented by a rapid and energetic initiative
of the Republican government, punishing the guilty vigorously
and, above all, expelling from the security corps all contami-
nated elements, to demonstrate to the country that the government was determined to end terrorism, no matter where it
came from.[29]

Indeed, as noted above, there is some evidence that Casares would have
proceeded more energetically to arrest and prosecute the Assault Guards
involved, but was blocked by the veto of Prieto and the need always to rely
on the worker parties. By this point the Socialists preferred to encourage,
rather than discourage, the revolt, though Prieto was not at all as confident
as Largo Caballero of the final outcome.

As it was, the change in attitude was dramatic. For the first time it
seemed more dangerous not to rebel than to rebel. On 23 June Franco
had written to Casares Quiroga to assure him that the army was loyal but
urging him to change his policies, and as late as 12 July had sent word
to Mola that the time had not yet come and that he was not prepared to
join a rebellion. The first word of the assassination seems to have had
a decisive effect; on the thirteenth he dispatched a message that he was
now firmly committed and that the revolt must not be delayed.[30] Years
later, in a speech in 1960, Franco conjectured that the revolt would never

have developed adequate strength had it not been for the assassination.[31] Two days later, on 15 July, in view of the categorical insistence of the Navarrese Carlists, the Carlist leadership committed all its forces unreservedly to the rebellion,[32] and support for the insurrection hardened in many quarters.

Mola's final plan stipulated a rather bizarrely staggered schedule, with the revolt beginning in Morocco and several other places on the eighteenth, followed by the rest of the peninsular garrisons within the next forty-eight hours. It calculated that the rebels might not be strong enough to seize all the large cities immediately, but would be able to overwhelm them within just a few weeks, or else the revolt would probably fail. As it turned out, neither the one nor the other result obtained.

Premature disclosure precipitated the rebellion in Spanish Morocco just before 5:00 P.M. on Friday the seventeenth, and Casares Quiroga convened the council of ministers later that evening. According to most accounts, Casares admitted that it might be possible for the rebels to take over all the Moroccan Protectorate, but prophesied correctly that a loyal navy would prevent them from reaching the peninsula.[33] He seemed confident that any rebellion in the mainland could be put down by the government's own forces. Determined not to play Kerensky, he rejected any notion of "arming the people."

Socialist and Communist patrols had been seen occasionally in the streets of Madrid since the night of the fifteenth; the CNT had begun to send out patrols in Barcelona even earlier.[34] None of the worker movements had a major paramilitary militia, and had begun to face the practical issue of armed conflict only after the assassination, looking to the government for arms, though in Barcelona the FAI-CNT had begun a more serious search for weapons. It was only the Communists—in formal policy the most concerned to avoid civil war—who had made some preparation for it, having organized as many as 2,000 men in their MAOC, mostly in the Madrid area, while the chief organizer of the UMRA was a Communist officer on the General Staff of the army, Captain Eleuterio Díaz Tendero.

As the military revolt slowly spread on the eighteenth, the UGT declared a general strike, in accordance with a strategy already decided upon. Only forty-eight hours earlier Largo Caballero had announced the need for a revolutionary "red army," and by the afternoon of 18 July he and other revolutionary leaders began to demand that the government arm the workers, something already demanded by anarchist leaders in Barcelona. This Casares still refused to do, nor would Companys in Barcelona, for doing so would probably mean the end of the parliamentary Republic and the beginning of violent revolution. The prime minister has been quoted as stating that any officer found guilty of handing over arms would be shot.[35] Casares Quiroga convened an emergency meeting around 6:00 P.M., which was attended by, among others, Martínez Barrio, Prieto, and Largo Caballero, at which the latter once more demanded that arms be distributed. Yet again the prime minister refused, insisting that all Spaniards should instead rally round the forces loyal to the government. Nor is it clear that Prieto supported the demands of his Socialist rival, for he could appreciate the force of Casares' argument.[36]

Though the majority of military units did not join the revolt on the eighteenth, it began to expand through part of southern Spain, with some indication that other units were potentially poised to join. The gamble on a limited repetition of the sanjurjada seemed to be failing as a large rebellion unfolded, its full extent still unclear. About 10:00 P.M. that evening Casares Quiroga resigned, his government a failure on every front.

Azaña suddenly decided to reverse course and attempt a limited reconciliation, something that, had he done it five and a half days earlier, immediately after the assassination, might yet have retrieved the situation. He authorized Diego Martínez Barrio, leader of the small right wing of the Popular Front, to form a new and broader coalition of "all the Republican parties" of the left and center, excluding only the Communists and POUM on the left, the CEDA and other rightist groups, and in the center only the Lliga. Martínez Barrio had been the only major left Republican to grasp fully the significance of the assassination, and the only one who had reached out afterward in gestures of reconciliation toward the right. He received virtual carte blanche authorization to put down the rising and restore order. A Martínez Barrio government would implicitly break the Popular Front by including the antirevolutionary Republican center, but some such initiative, which ought to have been undertaken months earlier, was the only means by which the parliamentary Republic could have survived. Had such a government been formed in May, or even later, it might well have prevented the Civil War. The problem faced by Martínez Barrio on the night of 18–19 July was that, by definition, it is too late to prevent something from happening if action is delayed until after the event has already begun. Sánchez Román agreed to serve, and seems to have functioned as Martínez Barrio's chief adviser for the next few hours. Miguel Maura refused to participate, however, on the grounds that this was now too little too late, and Prieto also soon had to decline on instructions from his Socialist colleagues on the executive commission, though the latter apparently promised full support to the new government.[37]

Around 4:00 A.M. on the nineteenth Martínez Barrio began to contact district military commanders by telephone. Though he was not able to reach all of them, he found that several of those loyal to the regime had been virtually deposed by younger officers. Martínez Barrio was able to speak directly with Mola, and subsequently the main controversy about his abortive initiative would have to do with the terms of their conversation. Martínez Barrio has claimed that he merely assured Mola that the new government would restore order and asked him not to rebel.[38] Other sources claim that he went much further, even so far as to suggest a political deal with the military, who could name their own candidates for the Ministries of War, Navy, and Interior. The weight of evidence indicates that some sort of deal was discussed,[39] the irony being that a lesser compromise a week earlier might have averted the crisis. As it was, Mola replied that it was too late, for all the rebels had sworn not to be dissuaded by any political deals or compromises once the revolt had begun.

The great compromise had been attempted too late—the greatest of all Azaña's errors—though Martínez Barrio for the moment continued formation of his new left-center coalition, completed around 5:00 A.M. on 19 July. He was relying on Felipe Sánchez Román and Marcelino Domingo as his chief lieutenants, and his coalition included five members of his own Unión Republicana, three from Izquierda Republicana, three ministers from Sánchez Román's tiny Partido Nacional Republicano, one member from Esquerra Catalana, and a senior general, the pro-Republican José Miaja without party affiliation, in the Ministry of War. This coalition represented a shift toward the left-center, though it was not a coalition of the broad national-unity type.

The goal of the Martínez Barrio government was to maintain the constitutional regime, giving in to neither the rebels nor the revolutionaries. Its leaders probably did not know that at least two Madrid district military commanders had already begun to "arm the people."[40] Both Martínez

Barrio and Sánchez Román were firmly opposed to such a step, on the grounds that it would open the door to revolution and anarchy. Sánchez Román would later declare that he had told the new prime minister that this would be "ineffective militarily and pregnant with inconceivable dangers politically,"[41] yet another of his accurate prophecies. Martínez Barrio has been quoted as having insisted only a few days earlier that such a move was "madness. This would be to unleash anarchy. It is necessary to avoid that at any price."[42] His government represented the last chance to maintain the integrity of the regime, and still might have had a fighting chance to do so, since as of the early morning of the nineteenth the majority of military units, as well as Civil Guard and Assault Guard units, had not rebelled, and in fact about half would never do so. A responsible Republican government would still have had a chance to repress the revolt and restore order, avoiding a major civil war.

By dawn, however, the new government was being repudiated not merely by the caballeristas, ever insistent on arming the people, but also by some of the more radical leaders of Azaña's own party, who rejected the leadership of their chief rival, the more moderate Unión Republicana, and insisted on maintaining the unity of the Popular Front. The editor of *Política*, the official newspaper of Azaña's Izquierda Republicana, is sometimes given credit for organizing militants of the latter party to join Socialists in an early-morning street demonstration that demanded immediate resignation of the new government.[43] This was the last straw for Martínez Barrio, who had slept for only about one hour in the past forty-eight, and around 8:00 A.M. he abandoned his efforts, later charging that "the government of Martínez Barrio had died at the hands of the Socialists of Largo Caballero, the Communists, and also irresponsible Republicans."[44] Prieto apparently urged Martínez Barrio to stand fast,[45] but the opposition of militants of Izquierda Republicana was a graphic illustration of the Kerenskyist role assumed by Azaña's party.

His one tardy effort at compromise having collapsed, Azaña immediately returned to his already failed policy, appointing a new government headed by the physiology professor José Giral of Izquierda Republicana, basically a more leftist version of the Casares Quiroga ministry. The difference was that the Giral government, in view of the rapidly expanding military revolt, had none of its predecessor's reluctance to grant military power to revolutionaries and began the "arming of the people," thereby fostering revolutionary militias that would quickly gain de facto power in what was about to become known as the "Republican zone." The civil war had begun, and the constitutional life of the Republic had ended, replaced by what has varyingly been termed the "Third Republic,"[46] the "Spanish People's Republic,"[47] and the "revolutionary Republican confederation" of 1936–37.[48] In varying degrees, the wartime Republic was all of these, but not a continuation of the parliamentary regime of 1931–1936.

Conclusion

COULD THE BREAKDOWN HAVE BEEN AVOIDED?

THE MAMMOTH LITERATURE ON the Spanish Civil War has often obscured the fact that, to paraphrase Ortega,[1] the first and perhaps most important thing one needs to know about the Civil War is its origins, the reasons for the collapse of the democratic Republic. Common opinion has normally presented simplistic and reductionist explanations for the failure of the Republic, ranging from conspiracy theory—a plot by the revolutionary left or the radical right, or by the Axis powers or the Soviet Union, in concert with one of the former—to, at the more abstract end, the irresistible extremism of the left or right (or both), or to the weight of terrible social problems or general underdevelopment. While the alleged responsibility of foreign powers is a canard, the product of Civil War propaganda by both sides, the other standard explanations contain no more than an element of truth, which in every case falls short of a full and adequate explanation.[2]

The founding of the democratic Republic in Spain can be seen in broader perspective as the final and belated phase of the broad wave of liberalization following the end of World War I, which originally added ten new, in each case nominally liberal democratic, republics in central and eastern Europe (as well as the subsequent Irish Free State) to those already existing in France, Switzerland, and Portugal (though the Portuguese First Republic never became democratic). The chief reason that the new wave of democratization did not fully affect Spain earlier was its neutrality in the war, which gave the established regime a few more years of life than was the case elsewhere. Even the first impulses of postwar democratization had major repercussions in Spain, however, and contributed, together with the Moroccan débacle, to the downfall of the parliamentary system in 1923 and of the dictatorship that followed. The chronology of Spanish democratization was thus not totally distinct from the general European chronology, but rather proceeded in two phases, the second much more powerful than the first.

The initial major misfortunes took place in 1923–1926 and in 1930. The liberal regime of 1875–1923, despite distinct shortcomings, had been a major civic achievement. It made possible increasingly fair elections, growing access for the opposition, alternation in power, extensive institutional reform, and need not have ended in 1923. The old system experienced major difficulty in carrying out a transition to democracy, but was achieving steady progress. It is true that something of a genuine crisis developed in 1923, but if a temporary dictatorship was needed—as many liberals then thought—to effect change, restore order, and deal with the military challenge in Morocco, a strict time limit should have been placed on it. The achievements of the dictatorship, such as they were, had been completed by the end of 1925. At the very latest, 1926 should have brought new elections and a return to parliamentary government. Continuation of the dictatorship burned most bridges to the old regime and made it much more difficult to return to the constitutional system.

Even so, such a return might not have been impossible after Primo de Rivera's resignation in January 1930 had new elections been scheduled within ninety days. The final error of the old regime was to delay elections—just as the Provisional Government did in Russia in 1917. In Spain the delay was even longer, lasting more than a year, and when elections did take place a second error was made in beginning with municipal rather than national elections. The former always generated more leftist votes and had the effect of widening the institutional gap. National elections would probably not have resulted in an equivalent triumph for the left, and might have made possible a return to a reformed parliamentary monarchy.[3] The alternatives of 1923, 1926, or 1930 would in each case have probably been preferable to a drastic change of regime in 1931, which proved too radical a leap in the dark, eliminating the institutional continuity and moderating influence that might have made a democratic regime more viable.

As it was, peculiar Spanish conditions produced an artificial vacuum in 1931 that was filled by a rapidly and somewhat artificially expanded left, resulting in a new constituent process that did not fully reflect the political and cultural values of the citizenry as a whole, creating a new regime that existed in a permanent state of tension. Eventually, of course, nearly all the new representative or nominally democratic regimes established after the end of the war failed, with the exceptions only of Ireland, Czechoslovakia, and Finland (whose democratic regime was not new, but independent rather than merely autonomous). The 1930s were not a decade that favored the success of new democracies. Moreover, since all the other new systems in underdeveloped eastern and southern Europe gave way to more authoritarian regimes, the argument from social and economic backwardness is not to be dismissed lightly. Yet levels of development alone may not always be determinant, for democracy also failed in a much more modern Germany and more recently in other societies economically more advanced than was the Spain of 1936.[4] Conversely, the first liberal parliamentary systems were introduced and stabilized in countries then at a lower level of modernization than was the Spain of the Second Republic.

Detlev Peukert has described the drama of Weimar Germany as constituting the "crisis years of the classically modern,"[5] that is, the period in which the typical political, cultural, social, and economic forces of the early twentieth century came into full expression and direct conflict. Such a contention cannot be equally true of Spain, which was much less advanced, yet Spain was in fact not so backward as has often been supposed. Economic growth and social change during the 1920s had been among the most rapid in the world, literacy was increasing rapidly, and the agrarian sector of the labor force was falling below 50 percent. Moreover, Spain had a much longer history of modern liberal government than had Germany, though it possessed even less experience in direct democratization. The long course of constitutional government in Spain—however often honored only in the breach—had encouraged a bewildering panoply of parties and movements even more complicated, and offering even more different social and economic options, than those in Germany. To that extent the Second Republic constituted a distinctively Spanish version of the mass political and cultural "crisis of the classically modern," as all the major political and ideological forces of the twentieth century converged in Spain, albeit in a society less advanced in education and technological development than that of Germany. Movements such as traditionalism, neotraditionalism, anarchism, Trotskyism, Leninism (though not Stalinist Communism), and mass-mobilized micronationalism were all more strongly developed in Spain, though Spanish fascism was for some time quite weak.

Republican Spain was particularly rich, if that is the term, in leftist revolutionary, radical, and liberal reform projects. A minimal list would include the following:

- Moderate liberal democracy (the various center parties)
- Peripheral nationalism and autonomist movements (Esquerra Catalana, Partido Nacionalista Vasco, and many others)
- Moderate Republican left (Unión Republicana, Partido Nacional Republicano)
- Radical Republican left (Izquierda Republicana, Radical Socialists)
- Democratic evolutionary socialism (Besteiro)
- Radical social democracy (Prieto)
- Revolutionary socialism (Largo Caballero and the Socialist left)
- Leninism (BOC-POUM)
- Trotskyism (Izquierda Comunista)
- Stalinism (PCE)
- Syndicalism (Treintistas, Partido Sindicalista)
- Anarchosyndicalism (FAI-CNT)

This roster was particularly rich in revolutionary movements, indeed, the broadest such spectrum of any European country, creating a series of radical demands that could not have been met by any country in the world. Rather than concentrating on political democratization, the Second Republic instead opened a revolutionary process that ended in civil war.

Yet the extent and intensity of revolutionary mobilization under the Republic can also be misleading with regard to the character of Spanish society, for most citizens and voters remained moderate. Revolutionary and extremist parties, left or right, never gained more than a minority of votes, the CEDA outdistancing the radical right precisely because it was more moderate and legalistic. The country as a whole was not extremely radical or revolutionary, but contained large revolutionary minorities that enjoyed special opportunities in an unconsolidated new democratic system amid a time of economic crisis and of unprecedented political fragmentation.

The Second Republic also began with certain advantages over some of the new democratic regimes of, for example, eastern Europe. It was not necessary to build a newly united nation or construct a new state system from scratch, to reconstruct an economy devastated by World War I or absorb large numbers of refugees from irredentist territory, to face a mass populist monarchism or cope with a majoritarian peasant population (in the anthropological sense), even though the agrarian problems in parts of Spain were severe. And the proliferation and fragmentation of political parties were initially even more pronounced in an eastern European republic like that of Poland.[6]

In general, the main problems besetting the Republic may, for purposes of analysis, be divided into three categories: the structural, the conjunctural, and the more technically political. In each category grave deficiencies could be found. Social and economically structural problems were undoubtedly severe, the worst being the plight of the nearly two million landless farmworkers and their families, a plight made much more conflictive by the fact that Spain was now a rapidly modernizing country with democratic mass mobilization. The low wages, limited productivity, and poor living conditions of more than four million urban workers in industry and services were also a problem, even though not so acute in terms of social misery. Though industry and finance had expanded rapidly during the 1920s, the ability to sustain new expansion during the depression was problematic at best. A special kind of structural problem was the incomplete integration of the major regions, with their disparate rates of modernization, exacerbating cases of peripheral nationalism, which added horizontal political cleavage to the vertical sociopolitical divisions.

On the one hand, it would be difficult to demonstrate that these structural problems were in any way decisive by themselves, for some of them had been considerably worse a generation earlier. Rapid development between 1915 and 1930, however, had not yet overcome these difficulties, but had had the somewhat paradoxical effect of sharpening their political consequences. Recent economic improvements, together with the growth of literacy and expanding mobilization, had raised levels of consciousness and of expectations. A somewhat more modern, productive, politically conscious society demanded—or at least significant parts of it demanded—even more rapid change than had recently occurred or than was in fact possible. By 1930 Spain had begun to enter the full medium phase of expanding industrialization in which social conflicts were sharpest. It was a time when workers were sufficiently conscious and mobilized to demand much more, but also when the means to complete industrialization and achieve general prosperity were not yet at hand.

Another way in which social structure affected politics lay in the impact of demographics and age cohorts. The comparatively rapid growth of population meant that in Spain, as in Germany, there were many more young men in the 1930s than ever before, and this was the sector most liable to radicalization and confrontation. Moreover, even though the agrarian proportion of the labor force had declined rapidly during the 1920s, the growth of overall population meant that the number of farmworkers was in absolute terms greater than ever before, undoubtedly a factor in the agrarian radicalization.

The conjuncture was more negative yet, for the 1930s constituted the climax of the "long generation" of world war and intense sociopolitical conflict that stretched from 1914 to 1945. This was the period of the most extreme internal and external strife in modern history, provoked by the climax of European nationalism and imperialism, and by mass social and political struggles over issues of democracy, modernization, and equality. The depression years were scarcely propitious for new democratic experiments. In much of Europe they created conditions advantageous to the authoritarian right and to fascism, and such influences were felt in Spain from 1933 on. Yet it is also difficult to demonstrate that the historical conjuncture necessarily determined the course of events all by itself. Spain was for a long time remarkably immune to some of the major motivating forces of the great European conflict, such as intense nationalism (save for peripheral nationalism) and major imperialism, while generic fascism remained weak until the final weeks of the Republic. The impact of the depression was proportionately less than in some other lands, and much of the economy was recovering by 1935, proportionately more than in France or the United States.

Yet the conjuncture did have a powerful effect through the radicalizing impact of key developments abroad, in terms of both positive aspirations and negative apprehensions. The left was increasingly attracted by the mirage of revolution, in part as represented by the Bolshevik revolution and the Soviet Union. Though the anarchists marched to their own drummer, the Socialists and other Marxist groups were more and more drawn to the Leninist ideal (even if not capable of fully emulating it) and at the same time were sufficiently far from the Soviet Union's grim reality under Stalin not to become disenchanted. Equally important was the left's revulsion against the victories of fascism and the authoritarian right in central Europe during 1933–34, which had a strong negative demonstration effect and contributed to polarization in Spain.

All this occurred at a time when Spain was very little involved with foreign affairs. Unlike counterparts in some other continental countries, those active in Spanish politics had little to fear from any threat arising abroad. The concern rather was with imitation by domestic forces of authoritarian tendencies in other countries, but since there seemed to be no need to unite to face external challenges, domestic radicals on both left and right felt all the freer to indulge their own extreme preferences.

It can also be argued that the worst and most decisive problems stemmed from the specific dynamics of political leadership, policy choices, and party conflicts, rather than from the inevitable effect of structural problems or broader domestic and international conjunctural influences. Certainly the Republican political system suffered from impressively poor leadership in all major sectors, though it enjoyed no monopoly on this negative feature, equally evident in a more modern country like Germany.

The political problems began first of all with the founding Republicans themselves. Though they claimed to represent—and in some respects did indeed represent—a decisive break with the past, the left Republicans remained typical products of modern Spanish radicalism. They reflected the tenacious sectarianism and personalism of old-style nineteenth-century factional politics and the insistence on government as a kind of patrimony rather than as a broad representation of all the diverse national interests. As was the case with so many of the leaders of regime changes in the nineteenth century, they did not represent an effort to overcome the divisions of the past so much as the renewed zeal of a new group to impose its own values and take revenge on ousted predecessors.

This revival of nineteenth-century petit-bourgeois radicalism had been, of course, provoked by the Primo de Rivera dictatorship. Though

Primo de Rivera's regime constituted an unusually mild form of authoritarianism, it destroyed constitutional continuity, and its consequences lay like a dark shadow across the life of the Republic. It bore responsibility for initiating the new politics of polarization and repression, to which the left Republicans responded partly in kind, unable to transcend the original breakdown of liberalism in 1923.

The new Constitution of 1931, while codifying important principles, followed nearly all preceding Spanish constitutions in being the creation of one significant sector of political society to be imposed on other portions that did not share its values. In certain key respects it was no more the product of national consensus than its nineteenth-century predecessors (with the partial exception of the 1876 Constitution). Even worse, it turned out that those groups most responsible for writing the constitution were not themselves committed to all the rules that they had just set up. As soon as they lost the next election, they demanded an annulment and the opportunity to try again, for their concept of the Republic was "patrimonial," insofar as they would not tolerate its adoption of policies other than their own. In fact few sectors of Spanish politics were unreservedly loyal to the Republic as a democratic procedure; these existed only in the ever-narrowing center of the spectrum.[7] Lack of consensus about the basic rules of the game was a handicap from the beginning, and some later literature would suggest that basic agreement among elites is more important than sheer level of development in guaranteeing the stability of a new democracy.[8]

For key sectors of the founding Republican coalition, the new system did not represent a commitment to a set of constitutional rules so much as the decisive breakthrough and permanent hegemony of a leftist reformist process that involved not merely definitive political changes but also irreversible changes in church-state relations, education, culture, and the socioeconomic structure, together with the solution of key dilemmas in regional autonomy and military reform. Most of these reforms were salutary but should not have precluded equal respect for the democratic process, even at the cost of their partial or temporary reversal.

The question has frequently been asked if the original Republican leadership did not simply try to reform too much too fast, irremediably overloading the system. In terms of the way in which reforms were undertaken, the answer is undoubtedly yes, but it is not clear that this need have been the case with the substance of many of the reforms themselves. The country was greatly in need of continuing modernizing reform, and of a broad policy that concentrated on technical and practical reforms with obvious benefits—serious and inclusive educational development, military reform, regional autonomy, public works, improvement of labor conditions, and some measure of agrarian reform—were in most respects such obvious national needs that it might not necessarily have been impossible to have built a national coalition in support of them. The Republican achievements in education, regional autonomy, public works, and labor were in some respects fruitful. Military reform was long overdue and in key aspects positive, though subject to notable limitations. Nearly everyone agreed on the need for some sort of agrarian reform, though, as has been seen, the actual legislation was not well conceived in social and technical terms. There was also need for separation and reform in church-state relations, where much might have been achieved at minimal cost.

Conversely, the political introduction and style of the reforms was badly handled from the beginning, because of the sectarian rhetoric and procedures of the left Republican–Socialist coalition. On some issues an originally nonexistent opposition was stimulated gratuitously, because of the absence of any spirit of conciliation or desire for consensus among the reformers. A generally sensible military policy was converted by Azaña's lack of tact into what was perceived (with considerable exaggeration) as an antimilitary vendetta, generating hostility among army officers who were not originally hostile to the Republic. Worst of all, of course, were both the style and substance of the religious reforms, conceived as vengeance against religious interests—even though more Spaniards believed in Catholicism than in any other doctrine or political creed—instituting not merely separation of church and state but infringement of civil rights and persecution of religion. There seemed to be a determination to follow the extremist policies of Portugal and Mexico, though the former had already ended in failure and the latter was evolving into an uneasy truce.

There were also notable failures in economic policy. Fiscal reform was feebly addressed, and unnecessary amounts of money were consigned to replace the entire Catholic educational system, leaving all the less for stimulating employment, building necessary infrastructure, and encouraging economic expansion, not to speak of land reform. Most Republican leaders were too ignorant of—and also too uninterested in—economics to give it adequate attention, though this was such a common failing of that decade that there was nothing particularly Spanish or Republican about it.

The approach to some of these problems as a zero-sum game was especially counterproductive. Such an approach guaranteed that each new turn of the political wheel was used to exact vengeance on previous holders of power, establish retroactive new politicized jurisdictions, and discourage consensus. In this regard, the Republic, rather than being an improvement on the old parliamentary monarchy prior to 1923, in key respects represented a regression to the extreme factionalism of the mid-nineteenth century. This was what Ortega had in mind in 1932–33 when he lamented that Republican leaders, rather than addressing the most important new problems, embodied instead a return to certain fixations of the past.

One of the most destructive aspects of "patrimonial Republicanism" was that it blurred the realities of Spanish society to most of the new leaders. They ignored the extent of conservative interests and of popular Catholicism on the one hand and the potential of revolutionary extremism on the other,[9] while optimistically exaggerating the appeal of their own forms of Republican progressivism. This overconfidence was due to the initial effects of the rupture in 1931, when conservative interests remained too uncertain and disoriented to contest the first elections effectively, resulting in a parliament and a constitution not representative of the country as a whole.[10] Conversely, a more genuinely representative parliament would probably have produced a more moderate but still progressive constitution that might have made the Republic more acceptable to the majority of public opinion. Such a parliament would in certain respects have produced a more moderate social policy, alienating some workers even more rapidly than proved to be the case, but might have fostered a broader democratic liberalism among the middle classes, part of the agrarian population, and even among a minority of workers that might have generated more stable electoral majorities. There is no guarantee that such would have been the outcome—social antagonisms might have become so intense that no liberal democratic regime could have survived—but a more moderate strategy offered a potentially viable alternative to the politics of polarization.

The functioning of the Republic was further handicapped by a grossly defective electoral system and an extremely high rate of turnover in political personnel. The electoral system overcorrected the potential problem of multiparty proportionality, creating lopsided effects that translated any shift in public opinion or any major change in alliance strategies into massive polar swings in representation. Thus the political system suffered from both fragmentation and polarization at the same time, while the need to achieve majorities through multiparty lists sometimes gave disproportionate influence to minor parties. In this connection, failure to move toward electoral reform during 1935 was a major mistake, and here, at least, Alcalá Zamora was wiser than the party leaders.

The drastic turnover in political personnel was another destructive consequence of the dictatorship, which had eliminated the older political forces and then left a void not surprisingly filled with political novices. The drastic turnover in personnel that occurred in 1931 was repeated to a considerable degree in each of the two following elections, partly as a result of the exaggerated consequences of the electoral law, and constituted one of the major liabilities of the new regime. The most tolerant and conciliatory figures of the Republic were found among the minority of centrists and moderate conservatives who had already gained experience under the preceding regime, though they were greatly outnumbered by the radicalized novices who came to the fore after 1931.

Spanish economic interests behaved very much as major economic interests have done almost everywhere in similar circumstances, supporting the center-right and moderate right, though in some cases with movement toward the radical right. Mercedes Cabrera, the principal student of interest group politics in this period, concluded that they developed no real alternative of their own and hoped above all that a more stable and moderate Republican regime would preserve law and order. Large landowners constituted the principal sector more attracted by the radical right, yet even they as a whole played no corporate role in directly subverting the system.[11]

Openly subversive forces were at first neither numerous nor important, with the partial exception of the CNT. The latter was flanked on the extreme left by the Communists, while later the Republic would face the subversion of the monarchist radical right and the Falange. None of these were of any significance by themselves, again with the partial exception of the anarchists. The latter constituted a mass movement, but their libertarian insurrectionist tactics never seriously threatened to overthrow the regime. Perhaps the main consequence of anarchist extremism was to maintain pressure on the UGT that weakened the Socialist commitment to social democratic reformism.

Much more important and decisive were the stances of what Juan Linz has called the major "semiloyal" parties: the Socialists and the CEDA. The ambiguity of the CEDA was fundamental, though not by itself decisive. The party would never commit itself to "Republicanism" or to the democratic system *tout court*. The contribution of the CEDA was not to Republicanize the right, but to secure the commitment of the bulk of the Catholic electorate to legalistic and parliamentary procedures. This was of considerable importance to the Republic, yet it hardly solved the problem of the Republic's future, as the left incessantly pointed out. Though the CEDA, unlike the Socialists, refused to engage in political violence, it remained ambiguous about ultimate goals, which for many members clearly were to replace the Republic with a corporative and more authoritarian system. This ambiguity was, in turn, used by both the centrist president and the left to deny the CEDA normal parliamentary access to government.

The CEDA leadership was itself guilty of grave errors. More important even than the issue of ambiguity about ultimate aims was what the CEDA did in 1935. Its effort to pursue the repression proved counterproductive. Even though that effort was not in itself unreasonable, the determined opposition of the president and the ambivalence of the Radicals counseled a more prudent and conciliatory policy, for the CEDA could not enforce serious repression on its own. It failed to implement constructive reform, concentrating instead on a largely negative policy of undoing aspects of the previous legislation. Part of that reversal was necessary but was carried too far and never combined with adequate new constructive policy. The CEDA also failed to emphasize vital changes that were already within its grasp, such as electoral reform—strongly supported by the otherwise antagonistic Alcalá Zamora—though doing so would have required a major effort to overcome the peculiarly suicidal opposition of some of the smaller parties. And at the close of the year the exasperated and frustrated CEDA leaders adopted an arrogant and self-righteous policy that merely played into the hands of Alcalá Zamora's manipulations, a mistake compounded by their somewhat exclusivist approach to the elections that fragmented the opposition to the Popular Front.

Despite the party's failings, Alcalá Zamora's exclusionist policy against the CEDA must be seriously questioned. The CEDA was not some small party, or a violent revolutionary or fascist group that could simply be suppressed or ignored. It represented in fact the largest single specific political orientation found among Spanish citizens. Only in the imagination of the Spanish left was it possible for a democratic system to function without coming to terms with Catholic opinion, the orientation of a plurality if not a majority of the population. The question must therefore be raised whether or not the correct course in 1934–35 would simply have been to follow constitutional due process without manipulation, since a democracy cannot long function in any other way. It is not convincing to view Alcalá Zamora's initial decision to admit the CEDA to limited participation in 1934 as other than fully justified, and the violent reaction of the left as other than unjustified and disastrous. At that time both the president and the prime minister, together with the dominant coalition party, were all fully committed to parliamentary democracy. This commitment offered a reasonable opportunity to broaden the base of government, create a stable majority, and build a broader consensus, just as Lerroux planned. Subsequently, however, Alcalá Zamora refused to follow fully the logic of parliamentary democracy and allow the largest party to lead a government. Had he done so, a worst-case scenario would have ultimately led to a CEDA-dominated coalition, producing drastic constitutional reform in 1936–37. Had this development produced a semicorporative and more authoritarian system, it might have been the end of Republican democracy for a decade or so, but even that would have been much less disastrous than what actually happened. Such a scenario might have involved resistance and bloodshed, but less than the horrors of the Civil War and the early Franco regime. In hindsight, even the worst-case scenario for full CEDA inclusion or leadership would hardly have produced the worst outcome.

The Socialists on the left played a role somewhat similar to that of the CEDA on the right in their "semiloyalty." Their contribution to the coalition of the first biennium was noteworthy, marking a major step in the evolution, maturation, and expansion of the Socialist movement in Spain at a time when only in the more developed countries of Germany and northern Europe had Socialist parties advanced as far. Yet the PSOE lacked the maturity and unity of the German Social Democrats, its response to political adversity being the direct opposite of the latter.[12] Though it turned to government participation five years earlier than the French Socialists, its ambiguities more closely reflected those of the Austrian Social Democrats, whose "two and a half" position wavered somewhat between the Second and Third Internationals. The French Socialists eventually committed themselves to full social democratic collaboration just as caballerismo was in the ascendant in Spain.

Polarization crystallized not so much with the triumph of the CEDA in 1933 as with the insurrection of 1934, which revealed that the bulk of the worker left was committed to varying forms of revolutionary action. As seen earlier, the richness and diversity of revolutionism under the Republic have had few equals anywhere. Its extent and variety stemmed from the combination of a conflictive, underdeveloped social structure with a democratic, mobilized, and highly fragmented political system. Modern Spanish politics had regularly featured a unique conjunction of advanced political forms and institutions amid socioeconomic backwardness, a combination that prior to the 1920s had differentiated Spain from, for example, much of eastern Europe. The opportunity for mass mobilization and untrammeled democracy amid the depression,[13] following the unprecedented acceleration of modernization during the preceding generation, suddenly raised the classic "Spanish contradiction" to a new level that made revolutionary challenges very likely, though not at all irresistible.

This circumstance did not mean that Spain was merely "ripe" for revolution, as some theorists held, for in key respects the society had already become too complex for revolutionaries to conquer easily. If the urban and industrial labor force was proportionately much larger than that of Russia in 1917, so were the middle classes and the right in general. Moreover, in Spain there was a large landowning and conservative agrarian population, which was basically counterrevolutionary, something that had been almost nonexistent in Russia. Some of the key conditions that encouraged successful revolution in more backward societies, such as foreign economic and political domination or the absence of free institutions, did not obtain in Spain, whose circumstances were much more similar to those of Italy after 1919. But in Italy most of the worker left soon became more moderate and ended by trying to return to democracy. The case of Spain in 1934–1937 remains historically unprecedented as a major revolutionary revolt by the non-Communist worker left against an established democracy, and moreover one that occurred in peacetime, without major international complication or interference. In Italy the left soon succumbed to a rightist-Fascist coalition in some respects similar to the one that eventually won the Spanish Civil War, as moderates warned many times from 1934 into 1936. The Spanish left drew the wrong conclusions from foreign examples in every case, whether those of Russia, Italy, or central Europe. The political analyses carried out by the leaders and theorists of the revolutionary left, like many of those made by the left Republicans, had the effect more of masking than of illuminating key realities.

It is, nonetheless, beside the point to have expected those who rejected parliamentary democracy, whether on the left or right, to have somehow taken responsibility for safeguarding parliamentary institutions. The principal responsibility for safeguarding constitutional democracy lay with those primarily responsible for having created it in the first place—the liberal and left Republicans.

Of all the political sectors, only the centrist liberals—the forces of Alcalá Zamora, Maura, the Radicals, and the Lliga Catalana—took up positions primarily in defense of constitutional democracy and the rules of the game. Small parties such as those of Maura, Sánchez Román, and even the somewhat larger Lliga lacked the strength to influence the situation decisively, however, so that the major roles in the center were played by Alcalá Zamora and by Lerroux and his Radicals. If the Second Republic was to achieve stability in the form of parliamentary democracy like the Third Republic in France, it would probably have been necessary for the moderate, middle-class Radicals to play much the same stabilizing role as their French homonyms and counterparts, and this they certainly attempted to do during 1933–1935. The Radicals obviously failed, though their sins were more of omission than commission. That is, they did not commit major mistakes that violated the letter and spirit of democratic practice, as did most of the other major parties, but they lacked strong organization and sometimes also lacked effective policies. The Radicals quickly became the sole major representative in Spain of what was much more common in established democracies elsewhere—a sizable political sector devoted to pork-barrel politics and a tolerant liberal philosophy of live-and-let-live. In the supercharged Spanish atmosphere, such an approach had only limited appeal and was denounced as an absence of morality and purpose. Leadership was also lacking, Lerroux being too old and low in energy, and other party luminaries lacking in vision or ability.

Thus the Radicals failed for not being more than they were; yet if they had possessed significant counterparts, constitutional democracy might have endured.

In an increasingly polarized situation in which most major actors had limited or no commitment to democracy, President Alcalá Zamora saw himself as the ultimate guarantor of the liberal Republic. This stance was, of course, technically correct, and there was no doubt of the president's sincerity, yet he himself quickly became a major problem. Though Alcalá Zamora was a genuine liberal and constitutionalist, and a distinguished jurist, he was also a product of the nineteenth-century liberal tradition and culture. This was an essentially elitist and oligarchic political culture populated by localist and party notables. It represented a form of transition from the traditional culture that had been based in good measure on status and concepts of honor. Thus it had difficulty in overcoming a profound elitism and personalism, an obsession with status, and egocentric concerns.

For whatever reasons—some of them objectively grounded fears concerning the strength of antidemocratic forces of the left and right—Alcalá Zamora came to perceive his role as that of an independent *poder moderador* (moderating power) in an almost royalist manner. This attitude stemmed not from any lust for power, but from the defective Republican constitution, which created a system of "double confidence" in which the prime minister and his council of ministers had to have the confidence of both the president and the parliament.[14] Thus he himself came to interfere more overtly with the normal functioning of constitutional government than had the much-criticized Alfonso XIII. As soon as the initial strength of the Azaña coalition began to wane slightly, the president set to work, relieving the left Republican leader of power even before his parliamentary majority had disappeared. Yet his interference with Azaña's government was much less overt and high-handed than his role with the second Cortes, during whose mandate he constantly acted to thwart the possibility of normal parliamentary government, making and unmaking minority or less than fully representative cabinets at will. In the process, he inevitably earned the hatred of both right and left, each of whom aimed at removing him from office as soon as possible.

In certain respects it is perfectly understandable that the president felt the need to try to maintain some sort of balance vis-à-vis both the left and the right. More dubious was his apparent willingness to help destroy the existing structure of the center—Lerroux and the Radicals—in order to try to reconstruct it in a new form subordinated indirectly to his own leadership. This was the sheerest folly and not surprisingly ended in disaster. That Alcalá Zamora could seriously expect to rebuild a new center from the fulcrum of state power indicates the extent to which he remained culturally and psychologically a liberal of the old regime, and failed fully to understand the character and force of the new political institutions and society that he was helping to build under the Republic.

The greatest mistake of all was to deny power to the CEDA in December 1935 and recklessly to insist on calling new elections in a dangerously polarized situation. At that point the existing parliament still had two years of life, a perfectly workable majority, and a full legislative agenda. Wantonly to have destroyed this opportunity was the height of irresponsibility. Alcalá Zamora had no serious possibility of creating a newly manipulated center that could hold the balance of power in new elections. Instead, the new contest became a sort of plebiscite between the revolutionary process opened in 1934 and the counterrevolution, which the former won by a narrow but decisive margin, as the ship of state careened wildly from right-center to the left. The outcome was fully foreseeable and destructive in the extreme. Had the Cortes of 1933 been permitted to live out its normal constitutional life span, with elections held at the close of 1937, significant new reforms could have been enacted and polarization somewhat reduced, producing a different electoral outcome in 1937 that could have avoided civil war. Such a result was not just a vague possibility but a probability.

The only other Republican leader who enjoyed responsibility equivalent to that of Alcalá Zamora was Manuel Azaña, the only politician to have held roughly equivalent powers and initiative over as long a period. Azaña had publicly stressed at the beginning of the Republic that he was "sectarian" and "radical," not a "liberal." He was forthright throughout that Republican constitutionalism would have to be interpreted by essentially partisan rules in order to achieve his goals, but he did not understand until too late that such an approach in fact made a democratic Republic impossible. He himself occasionally recognized the extent of his pride and arrogance but had such faith in his own powers of judgment that he became convinced of his own indispensability. His rejection of a more tolerant liberal democracy in favor of radicalism and polarization coincided with a mass mobilization that greatly magnified the consequences of sectarianism. When the principal leaders of Republican politics in practice rejected the rules of the game they themselves had created, the polity could not long endure.

Though determined to represent a new politics, Azaña sometimes described himself privately as the "most traditionalist" man in Spanish public life. He was in fact much more a product of the old elitist and sectarian culture of the nineteenth century than he realized. A linear descendant of the exaltados of 1820, Azaña represented the old as much as the new. He was the last in a long line of nineteenth-century sectarian bourgeois politicians and might with little exaggeration be called the last great figure of traditional Castilian arrogance in the history of Spain.

Azaña's petit-bourgeois radical utopia rested on the voting support of no more than 15–20 percent of the population. In order to impose it, Azaña took the high-risk gamble of relying on the support of the Socialists, despite their growing revolutionism, hoping that a further period of leftist domination and socioeconomic reforms would dilute their radicalism to the point where they would return to social democracy. There remains the question of whether, had the right simply submitted to the massive abuses of the Popular Front, that indeed would have been the case. Certainly there is no reason to think so, at least anywhere in the short term. The establishment of an even more complete system of leftist dominance would more likely have produced a more extreme leftist government, eventually led by the Socialists, as occurred early in the Civil War. There was no likely way that the peculiar petit-bourgeois radical utopia of Azaña could be realized, since it enjoyed such limited electoral support. Reliance on the Socialists gave the latter the deciding voice, and made an autonomous policy of Azaña not more possible—as he thought—but in fact impossible, so that, as happened in the Civil War, a left Republican government could lead only to a Socialist government.

The Spanish failure was only the most dramatic and sanguinary of the many European failures in democratization during those years. Roughly speaking, in western European countries a key variable in success or failure was the ability to come to terms with organized labor. In northern and northwestern Europe, as well as in Czechoslovakia, organized labor was social democratic and played a key role in stabilizing democracy. Conversely, the revolutionary zeal of the labor movements in Italy and Spain, and of the large Communist movement in Germany, played central roles in the failure of democracy in those lands.[15]

Political violence, well before the Civil War, obviously played a major role in the life of the Second Republic, being proportionately more extensive overall than in any other central or western European regime of the period. Beginning with election day on 16 February 1936, there was a rapid reescalation of violence, culminating in the events of 12–13 July. The government, publicly interested only in minimizing the seriousness of the situation, had no interest in collecting and releasing political "crime statistics," and thus the only global data presented in the spring and summer of 1936 were those given by rightist leaders, especially Gil Robles, in parliamentary speeches—not subject to the broad censorship—denouncing the expanding chaos. Leaving aside the numerous instances of arson and property destruction, religious and secular, rightist sources claimed to have counted 204 political killings between 16 February and the middle of May, 65 more in the next month, and another 61 between mid-June and 13 July.[16] Though these figures were largely rejected by the government at the time, they were accepted in later years by some historians and even by leftist writers as an approximately accurate reflection of the general state of affairs.[17]

The only detailed statistical study of political violence in these months (or for any other period of the Republic) is that made by Edward E. Malefakis, further elaborated by Ramiro Cibrián.[18] In the absence of official records, this study relied on the leading Spanish newspaper of those years, *El Sol*, supplemented by the extensive coverage of Spanish affairs in *La Nación* and *La Prensa* of Buenos Aires, to compensate for the limitations imposed by censorship in Spain. The research yielded a grand total of 273 political killings from 31 January to 17 July 1936. These figures are slightly smaller than those of Gil Robles, but are also obviously incomplete, listing only 3 for Barcelona as compared with 15 in the research of Getman-Eraso. Gil Robles' data thus seem largely substantiated by subsequent research.

In general, these data indicate two periods of peak violence, near the beginning and the end of this final period of the Republic. The initial wave of lethal incidents in the first weeks following the elections declined after the outlawing of the Falange in mid-March. The volume of incidents began to increase once more after mid-April, reaching a second high point around 25 May and continuing until the final breakdown. These data disprove the contention of the American historian Gabriel Jackson that a relative decline had set in during the last weeks before the Civil War.[19]

The killings were centered in several major cities, led by Madrid and followed by Barcelona, Seville, and Málaga. There was also a high rate of disorder in certain parts of Old Castile, led by Logroño. Conversely, there was no correlation between the incidence of violence in 1936 and the revolutionary insurrection of 1934. Of the main centers involved in the latter, Asturias registered only a middling index of violent incidents in 1936, while the Basque Country was among the most peaceful regions. The two regions exhibiting the highest concentrations of radical farm-worker activity, Extremadura and Andalusia, had high incidences of arson, property destruction, and property seizures, but registered high incidences of violence against persons in only a few cities such as Seville, Málaga, and Granada. On the other hand, the geographic concentration of leftist violence in these months largely correlates with the highest incidence of political executions in the Republican zone during the Civil War.

Cibrián has formulated a theory to account for the regional distribution of violence in 1936, combining the three variables of Socialist strength, political polarization, and political radicalization. Socialist strength is measured by the Socialist Party vote in the February elections, polarization by adding the combined votes of all the parties clearly on the right or left, and radicalization by the combined number of candidates presented in a given district by Communists and Falangists. The combined measurements produced by these factors generally correlate loosely with the different regional levels of violence.[20]

Juan Linz has noted that the approximate total of 300 political killings in Spain within five and a half months in 1936 contrasts unfavorably with the volume of 207 political killings reported in Italy during the first four and a half months of 1921,[21] possibly the high point of violence there. Since Italy had a population nearly 50 percent greater, the Italian rate of violence was distinctly lower.

Tentative totals for political killings during the five years of the Republic are presented in table 7. The violence in Spain was proportionately more severe than that which occurred prior to the breakdown of democracy in Italy, Germany,[22] and Austria,[23] with the exception of the first months of quasi–civil war of the Weimar Republic in 1918–19.[24] The

Table 7

Total Political Killings

YEAR	MONTH	OCCURRENCE	NUMBER OF DEATHS
1931	April	Anarchist killings in Barcelona	22
	May	*Quema de conventos*	3
	May	San Sebastián	8
	July	Seville general strike	20
	Sept.	Barcelona general strike	6
	Sept.–Dec.	Various incidents	12
	Dec.	Castlblanco	5
1932	Jan.	Arnedo and other incidents	16
	Jan.	Anarchist insurrection	30
	Feb.	Various incidents	6
	March–April	"	7
	May–July	"	24
	Aug.	Sanjurjada	10
	Sept.–Dec.	Various incidents	9
1933	Jan.	Anarchist insurrection	80
	Feb.–May	Various incidents	23
	June–Sept.	"	4
	Oct.–Nov.	Electoral campaign and Madrid strike	9
	Dec.	Anarchist insurrection	89
1934	Nov.–June	Falangists killed by left	9
	June–Dec.	Slain by Falangists	5
	June	National farm strike	13
	Oct.	Revolutionary insurrection	1,700
1935		Executions	2
		Various incidents	43
1936		Numerous incidents	300
Total			**2,455**

Sources: Numerous newspapers, monographs, and other works.

sweeping powers exercised by the various Republican governments, the semimilitarization of the police and, after 1934, of the justice system, and the trigger-happy policies of the Civil Guard and Assault Guard were, even all taken together, inadequate to control the situation, amounting, as the Socialist Vidarte has said, to *palos de ciego* (flailings of a blind man).

The extent of violence was much less during the first three years of the Republic and did not then threaten to destabilize the regime. Truly serious violence developed only in 1934. The shift by the Socialists to violence and insurrectionary tactics created much more severe polarization in Spain than ever developed in the other three countries, where the Socialists and even the Communists followed more moderate tactics (though in the case of the latter, only after 1923). The character of violence in Spain also differed, the bulk of it stemming from one major revolutionary insurrection. The kind of *Zusammenstösse* (clashes between rival groups) so common in Germany and Italy were much less frequent in Spain, because of the numerical weakness of Spanish fascists and the reluctance of the nonfascist right to engage in organized street violence. As Paul Preston has said, violence from the right was carried on by "isolated pistoleros rather than squads of Blackshirts or Stormtroopers,"[25] and to some extent this was true of the left as well.

But Socialist strategy in 1936 differed from that of 1934. All four anarchist and Socialist attempts at revolutionary insurrection between 1932 and 1934 had failed, and no revolutionary movement was planning an imminent insurrection to seize power at any time in 1936. Given leftist control of institutions, this was not a priority, and neither of the large movements considered itself strong enough to try to seize power at that moment. Though all the revolutionary movements without exception foresaw the final stage of political struggle as leading to their own revolutionary dictatorship, in every case this was being postponed until a later phase.

Socialist strategy during 1936 was based on an *estrategia del desgaste*—a "wearing down" or fundamental weakening of capitalist and clerical power through strikes, violence, and seizure of property. What was taking place in Spain was not the revolution but the prerevolution. Moreover, the Socialists were divided. Prieto personally would have preferred to ally directly with the government and postpone or avoid prerevolutionary activity, but could not always control his own followers, who were sometimes as violent and destructive as the caballeristas. Though he expressed disgust and apprehension that the reckless strategy of the left would fail, as he put it, "for senselessness" or "for stupidity," he was unable to change it, and after the beginning of July he almost gave up trying. By that point the policy of all the left—including the government—was to promote the final confrontation, though as usual there was complete disagreement over how to go about it.

Only the Communists (and perhaps the POUM) had a clear revolutionary policy, though the Communist strategy was tactically less extreme than that of the other revolutionary groups. The Popular Front policy adopted by the Comintern rejected the previous program of revolutionary insurrectionism and adopted a variant of the "fascist strategy" for seizing power—in the name of "antifascism." Mussolini and Hitler had grasped that they could come to power only through legal means, with assistance from allies, and the new Communist strategy emphasized large coalitions that would be able to win elections and hand power legally to the left. This policy was consistently followed by the Spanish Communist Party during the spring of 1936 and indeed throughout the Civil War, and was more coherent than the strategy of any of the other revolutionary parties. Consistent with this policy, the Communists were more concerned than any of the other revolutionary parties to avoid civil war. As has been seen, their program was nominally legalistic but hardly "moderate."

Though the final spiral of violence in 1936 was extreme, certain other polities have undergone almost equal violence or disorder as occurred during those months without breaking down. Crucial to the final events of the Republic was the character of government policy. From 1931 to 1935, varying Republican administrations had taken a strong stand against any major violence, whether from right or left. Yet in 1936 the Azaña–Casares Quiroga governments feared to adopt strong measures against all violence, because their own policy remained predicated on alliance with revolutionaries. In this regard, they did not even pursue a thoroughly and consistently partisan policy, for their only measures—directed mainly against the right—were too limited to repress effectively either Falangist activists or military conspirators. In its own confused and contradictory manner, the government sought to preserve some semblance of the democratic Republic, and fell between two stools.

The final and climactic blow was the assassination of Calvo Sotelo by insubordinate leftist state police and Socialist activists. This killing was the functional equivalent in Spain of the Matteotti affair in Italy in 1924. The latter resulted in a crisis that precipitated full dictatorship; the former was the final precipitant of civil war. That Matteotti was killed by Fascists and Calvo Sotelo by a Socialist reflected the differences in the key source of violence within the two systems. There were, however, other equally important differences between the situations in Italy and Spain. In the former, the Fascist government had encouraged violence against the leftist opposition even though it may not have ordered the killing of Matteotti, and its own followers forced it finally to take responsibility for the murder. In Spain, the left Republican government had never directly encouraged violence but refused to take an effective stand against it and then proved unwilling to arrest and prosecute those responsible.

The question may be asked why violence under the Republic played so great a role in undermining the system when a continued high rate of deaths from terrorism completely failed to have such an effect on the democratic monarchy after 1975. One answer is simply that the proportionate number of deaths from terrorism after 1975, high though it was, never reached the proportionate totals of the Republican years. Equally or even more important was the refusal of the left Republican government to make a serious effort to repress disorder on both sides, all the while relying on the major source of the violence, the Socialists, to keep it in power. The governments of the democratic monarchy after 1975 made energetic efforts to maintain civil rights for all and to repress and prosecute political violence from all sources, bar none, while all the major political parties—with the partial exception of the Basque nationalists—categorically repudiated violence. Thus under the democratic monarchy, political violence, though extensive, has been confined to small terrorist groups acting in secret. Though approximately 1,000 political killings (the vast bulk of them by the Basque terrorist movement ETA) have taken place since 1975, this figure bears no comparison with the more than 2,400 deaths under the Republic in little more than five years, including a major insurrection and the involvement of some of the main political forces.

The character and extent of the breakdown of public order under the left Republican government in 1936 had no historical precedent of such proportions in western Europe, being equaled (and in fact exceeded) only by the situation in 1917 in Russia, where there was no effective government at all. The list of abuses is staggering:

- The great strike wave, featuring many strikes without practical economic goals but seeking instead to dominate private property, often accompanied by violence and destruction of property.
- Illegal seizures of property, especially in the southern provinces, sometimes legalized ex post facto by the government under the pressure of the revolutionary movements. Between illegal seizures and the acceleration of the agrarian reform, Tuñón de Lara has calculated that approximately 5 percent of all agrarian property in Spain changed hands within five months. The economic effects were in large part destructive, since they did not encourage modernization and productivity but the redistribution of poverty without capital or technological development.
- A wave of arson and property destruction, especially in the south.
- Seizure of churches and church properties in the south and east and some other parts of the country.
- Closure of Catholic schools, provoking a crisis in Spanish education, and in a number of localities the suppression of Catholic religious activities as well, accompanied by the expulsion of priests.
- Major economic decline, which has never been studied in detail, with a severe stock market decline, the flight of capital, and in some provinces of the south the abandonment of cultivation, since the costs of the harvest would be greater than its market value. Thus several southern Socialist mayors proposed the "penalty of remaining" for proprietors, rather than the penalty of exile.
- Broad extension of censorship, with severe limitations on freedom of expression and of assembly.
- Many hundreds—indeed several thousand—arbitrary political arrests of members of rightist parties, culminating in the kidnapping of Calvo Sotelo.
- Impunity of criminal action for members of Popular Front parties, who were rarely arrested. Occasionally anarchists were detained, since they were not members of the Popular Front.
- The politicization of justice through new legislation and policies, in order to facilitate arbitrary political arrests and prosecution and to place the rightist parties outside the law. In spite of the four violent insurrections of leftist parties against the Republic—which had no counterpart among the rightist parties—none of them was charged

with illegal actions, since justice had become completely politicized, in keeping with the Popular Front program.

- Official dissolution of rightist groups, beginning with the Falangists in March and the Catholic trade unions in May, and moving toward the monarchist Renovación Española on the eve of the Civil War. The process of institutional illegalization was designed to create conditions of political monopoly for the leftist organizations, first achieved in the trade union groups.
- Use of coercion in the new elections of May in Cuenca and Granada, with the arbitrary detention of rightist activists and the restriction of rightist activity.
- Subversion of the security forces through reappointment of revolutionary police officers earlier prosecuted for their violent and subversive actions. One of these commanded the squad that murdered Calvo Sotelo. Equally notable was the addition of what were called *delegados de policía*, normally activists of the Socialist and Communist parties named ad hoc as deputy police, though they were not regular members of the security forces. This practice followed the precedent of the Hitler government in appointing violent and subversive SA and SS activists as *Hilfspolizei* in Germany in 1933.
- The growth of political violence, though its extension was very unequal in different parts of the country. Some provinces experienced relative calm, while in others there was extensive violence, especially in the capital cities. Some 300 people died within five and a half months.

Edward E. Malefakis has evaluated the situation in the following terms:

> In 1934, prior to the Socialist rebellion, there was no change in the fundamental institutions of the government and no wholesale annulment of the legislation of the Constituent Cortes. In 1936, by contrast, the legislative innovations of the previous two years were immediately undone. At the same time the basic institutions of the Republic were threatened as thousands of municipalities were replaced by "executive committees," the President of the Republic was ousted by legal trickery, the leading politician of the opposition, Calvo Sotelo, was assassinated

by a group which included off-duty state police, and legislation was introduced by the Communists to ban most parties opposed to the Popular Front on the grounds that they were "fascist." As to the comparative personal plight of the millions of followers of the Right and Left, who is to say that the psychological terrors experienced by the former in the spring of 1936 were less legitimate a cause for rebellion than had been the economic hardships through which the latter had passed prior to October 1934?[26]

What did the government's many critics demand in 1936? Their basic demand was simply to apply the law, to enforce the Republican Constitution. In that sense the demands of the millions of critics were more "Republican" in 1936 than was the policy of the left, which refused to pay the slightest serious attention. Only a small minority of the radical right actively sought to overthrow the government through insurrection; that was why Mola had such difficulty organizing his conspiracy. The radical right were few in number and for some time partially isolated, and it was of course in the government's interest to keep things that way. But by refusing to enforce the law equally and by intensifying its policy of harassment of the right, the time would come when many moderate conservatives would be willing to ally themselves with the radical right. The Socialist policy of desgaste did not so much erode capitalism as push a large part of the lower middle classes into the arms of the rightist insurrectionists. Only much later did Manuel Azaña come to realize that what the left was facing was not some restricted *militarada* supported by a minority of wealthy landowners but a much broader middle-class reaction.[27]

Since it was impossible for the opposition to obtain honest government and equal enforcement of the law, the opposition was left with two alternatives: armed revolt or Christian resignation to the tyranny of the left. Since armed revolt might mean a horrendous civil war, while most of the opposition was Catholic, serious moral teaching might have counseled Christian resignation to the demands of arbitrary government.

Had the right responded with Christian resignation—which seems, paradoxically, to have been the demand of the violently anticlerical revolutionists—rather than armed force, what might have been the future of Spain? Counterfactual questions can be answered only with speculations.

Had the right simply submitted to the left, the government would probably have become more leftist yet, eventually with some sort of Socialist regime, as during the Civil War. The result might have been something more like a Latin American system than a Communist "people's republic," with a chaotic economy. Nonetheless, this economy might have been no worse than the one that Spain actually experienced between 1936 and 1950, though much worse than the one Spain enjoyed after 1950. The loss of freedom might not have been any greater. Given the profound differences among the left, the result of an all-leftist regime might well have been a different kind of civil war, an intraleftist conflict (as in fact occurred twice between 1937 and 1939), though this would have been a less extreme and destructive civil war than the one that took place. A further issue would have been the fate of such a regime in World War II, when it might have suffered an invasion from Nazi Germany, with incalculable effects on the course of the greater war.

A prerevolutionary implosion such as the one suffered by Spain was unprecedented in European countries during peacetime. It has some-times been suggested that the nearest analogy lay in the Chile of Salvador Allende in 1970–1973. Any such comparison, however, must be quite limited.

The only major similarity between Spain and Chile had to do with the pursuit of a revolutionary process through legal, or at least semilegal, channels. Beyond that comparison, almost everything was different. Salvador Allende won a plurality (though overall a distinct minority) of votes in the triangulated Chilean presidential election of 1970 as leader of Unidad Popular, a revolutionary coalition of Socialists, Communists, and several smaller parties. Though he enjoyed no parliamentary majority, as did the Spanish Popular Front, Allende was able to exercise broad power because of the presidential character of the Chilean government. As a revolutionary Socialist with ties to the Soviet Union and to Cuba, Allende stood far to the left of Azaña. His government sought to carry out the socialization of the economy through presidential and state power. Over a period of three years some 35 percent of all cultivated land was seized, 30 percent of industrial production was nationalized (to add to nearly 50 percent of all industrial production already in state hands), and most of the banking system was taken under state control. The left Republican government of Spain rejected socialism and pursued a radical policy only in the revised agrarian reform. By mid-1973 Chile was suffering from runaway inflation and a steep decline in economic production. Its economic crisis was severe, whereas in Spain in July 1936 the economic crisis had only just begun and was much less serious.

Yet in Chile national institutions still preserved much of their integrity. Both the parliament and the judiciary remained independent and opposed to the executive, while the military retained more institutional autonomy than in Spain. In Chile there was somewhat less political violence before the military coup in 1973, and no fraudulent or coercive elections as in Spain. Denial of civil rights was limited primarily to economic rights, though in this area oppression was severe. Government forces murdered no opposition leaders, nor was there religious persecution, and in Chile the Church played a moderating role.

The Allende government was nonetheless arbitrary to the point of tyranny. It ignored numerous judicial verdicts and parliament votes, making use of the Chilean constitutional provision that a unanimous vote by cabinet members could override parliament. Its own followers and the revolutionary militia of the MIR (Movimiento de la Izquierda Revolucionaria), which did not participate in the government, stockpiled arms on a significant scale, something that was not done by any of the Spanish revolutionary movements. Certain districts in the capital, Santiago, and in small parts of the countryside were under de facto revolutionary occupation and outside the rule of law. The government maintained a special relationship with Cuba and with the elaborately staffed Soviet embassy in Santiago, whereas the Spanish Republic had no relations at all with the Soviet Union. Though the Azaña–Casares Quiroga administrations permitted certain conditions of coercion, they did not at all engage in the kind of elaborate and arbitrary revolutionary activities that formed the core of Allende's administration. Only in the areas of violence, electoral coercion, and attacks on Church property were conditions more extreme in Spain. A further difference was that in 1973 the Chilean parliament by a clear majority vote detailed all the abuses of what it termed the incipiently "totalitarian" government of Allende, and asked the military to act—without specifying what kind of action—to restore the rule of law. The subsequent military coup may have been the only one in history to have been indirectly requested by parliamentary vote.

One partial similarity, however, lay in the extent of subsequent counterrevolutionary violence. Shortly before the coup, when the army was called out to repress a minor revolt, and complaints were heard about the twenty-two people killed, the new chief of staff, General Augusto Pinochet, was quoted as saying, "When the army comes out, it is to kill."[28] And so it had been in Spain. The counterrevolution is sometimes more lethal than the revolution. There was no civil war in Chile because the small Chilean military forces were united and acted in concert. Similar military unity in Spain would probably have prevented a long civil war.

There has never been a revolutionary process that has not been met with counterrevolutionary resistance, though sometimes such resistance has failed. One of the worst problems with such situations is that, as Joseph De Maistre first pointed out, a counterrevolution is not the opposite of a revolution, but often becomes a sort of opposing revolution. Clausewitz referred to what he called the effect of *Wechselwirkung*, of reciprocal action, and reciprocal transformation or radicalization, in major conflicts. This was the case in the Spanish Civil War, in which Franco's movement soon moved far beyond the political goals of Mola's original conspiracy to embrace a radical and semifascistic "national revolution." Such dialectical antitheses are not uncommon in history, but Spain experienced double jeopardy. The left destroyed much of democracy before July 1936, but the counterrevolution created an opposing radicalism that was violent in the extreme, at least in its early years, and sustained authoritarian rule for nearly four decades. The price of the revolutionary process was high indeed.

NOTES

INTRODUCTION

1. C. Dardé, *La aceptación del adversario: Política y políticos de la Restauración, 1875–1900* (Madrid, 2003).
2. The bibliography on Cánovas and the Restoration is extensive. For an introduction, see the papers presented at the conference on the centenary of his death: A. Bullón de Mendoza and L. Togores, eds., *Cánovas y su época* (Madrid, 1999), 2 vols. See also C. Seco Serrano, *De los tiempos de Cánovas* (Madrid, 2004); and J. Andrés-Gallego, *Un "98" distinto (Restauración, desastre, regeneracionismo)* (Madrid, 1998).
3. J. Maluquer de Motes, *España en la crisis de 1898: De la Gran Depresión a la modernización económica del siglo XX* (Barcelona, 1999).
4. On the political crisis of the reign of Alfonso XIII, see J. Tusell and G. G. Queipo de Llano, *Alfonso XIII: El Rey polémico* (Madrid, 2001); and the works of C. Seco Serrano, *Alfonso XIII y la crisis de la Restauración* (Barcelona, 1969), *Alfonso XIII* (Madrid, 2001), and *Estudios sobre el reinado de Alfonso XIII* (Madrid, 1998).
5. See the suggestive essay by Fernando del Rey Reguillo, "¿Qué habría pasado si Alfonso XIII hubiera rechazado el golpe de Primo de Rivera en 1923?," in N. Townson, ed., *Historia virtual de España (1870–2004): ¿Qué hubiera pasado si . . . ?* (Madrid, 2004), 93–137.

CHAPTER 1. THE REPUBLICAN PROJECT

1. *Estadísticas históricas de España siglos XIX–XX* (Madrid, 1989), 79.
2. For other aspects of the transformation of Spanish life, see A. Aguado and

M. D. Ramos, *La modernización de España (1917–1939). Cultura y vida cotidiana* (Madrid, 2002).

3. N. Townson, *The Crisis of Democracy in Spain: Centrist Politics under the Second Republic, 1931–1936* (Brighton, 2000), 349.

4. J. M. Macarro Vera, *La utopía revolucionaria: Sevilla en la Segunda República* (Seville, 1985), 479.

5. R. Ramos, book review, *Luso-Brazilian Review*, 38:2 (Winter 2001), 144.

6. There has been much more historical writing about Azaña than about any other two or three figures of the left combined, though no serious critical scholarly biography—a genre still very weak in Spain—has ever been done. The first biographies were F. Sedwick, *The Tragedy of Manuel Azaña and the Fate of the Spanish Republic* (Athens, Ohio, 1963); and E. Aguado, *Don Manuel Azaña* (Barcelona, 1972); but the fullest political account is S. Juliá, *Manuel Azaña, una biografía política* (Madrid, 1990), though its treatment ends abruptly in the spring of 1936. C. de Rivas Cherif, *Retrato de un desconocido* (Barcelona, 1980), is a fond portrait by his brother-in-law and best friend and the best source for intimate details. J. M. Marco, *La inteligencia republicana: Manuel Azaña, 1897–1930* (Madrid, 1988), is good on his early years. J. Montero, *El drama de la verdad en Manuel Azaña* (Seville, 1979), treats his intellectual life; and M. Muela, *Azaña, estadista* (Madrid, 1983), his political goals and projects. Also important are Juan Marichal's prologue to the four volumes of Azaña's *Obras completas* (Mexico City, 1965–1968) and Marichal's *La vocación de Manuel Azaña* (Madrid, 1968). Books about Azaña continue to appear regularly, and Spanish historiography is not known for its originality.

7. M. Maura, *Así cayó Alfonso XIII* (Barcelona, 1968), 223–25.

8. Ibid., 230.

9. See R. Rémond, *L'anticlericalisme en France. De 1815 à nos jours* (Brussels, 1985).

10. There is a growing literature on Spanish anticlericalism in the nineteenth and early twentieth centuries. For an overview, see E. La Parra López and M. Suárez Cortina, eds., *El anticlericalismo español contemporáneo* (Madrid, 1998). There is also a growing literature on anticlericalism at the regional level, such as the lucid study by M. P. Salomón Chéliz, *Anticlericalismo en Aragón: Protesta popular y movilización política (1890–1939)* (Zaragoza, 2002). The most recent and in many ways the best study of anticlerical politics under the Second Republic is M. Alvarez Tardío, *Anticlericalismo y libertad de conciencia: Política y religion en la Segunda República española (1931–1936)* (Madrid, 2002).

11. On the origins of anarchist violence, see R. Núñez Florencio, *El terrorismo anarquista (1888–1909)* (Madrid, 1983); and, more broadly, E. González Calleja, *El máuser y el sufragio: Orden público, subversión y violencia política en la crisis de la Restauración (1917–1931)* (Madrid, 1999); J. Aróstegui, ed., *Violencia política en España (Ayer, 13)* (Madrid, 1994); J. Romero Maura, *La Romana del diablo: Ensayos sobre la violencia política en España (1900–1950)*

(Madrid, 2000); and *La militarización de la política durante la II República* (*Historia Contemporánea*, 11, 1994).

12. Unless specified otherwise, quotations from remarks in the Cortes are taken from the *Diario de las Sesiones* for the date indicated.

13. The most extensive study of the CEDA is J. R. Montero, *La CEDA* (Madrid, 1977), 2 vols. R. A. H. Robinson has presented the most scholarly positive evaluation of the CEDA in *The Origins of Franco's Spain* (London, 1970), and Paul Preston the most searing indictment in *The Coming of the Spanish Civil War* (London, 1978). See also J. Tusell, *La historia de la democracia cristiana en España. Los antecedentes. La CEDA y la II República* (Madrid, 1974).

CHAPTER 2. THE TURNING POINT OF THE REPUBLIC

1. J. J. Linz, M. Jerez, and S. Corzo, "Ministers and Regimes in Spain: From the First to the Second Restoration, 1874–2002," *South European Society and Politics*, 7:2 (Autumn 2002), 62.

2. The best analysis of Azaña's position in June 1933 is found in S. Juliá, *Manuel Azaña, una biografía política. Del Ateneo al Palacio Nacional* (Madrid, 1990), 263–70.

3. *XIII Congreso del PSOE* (Madrid, 1932), 561–62.

4. *El Socialista*, 13 October 1932, cited in M. Contreras, *EL PSOE en la II República* (Madrid, 1981), 245.

5. According to J. Avilés Farré, *La izquierda burguesa en la II República* (Madrid, 1985), 187, a total of 22,670 of the approximately 35,000 settlements negotiated by the jurados during 1933 were categorized by official statistics as favorable to workers. There remained the significant minority won by employers and the effects of increasing unemployment.

6. P. Moa, *Los orígenes de la Guerra Civil Española* (Madrid, 1999), 164.

7. See the detailed study by S. Juliá, *Madrid 1931–1934. De la fiesta popular a la lucha de clases* (Madrid, 1984); and his summary, "Economic Crisis, Social Conflict and the Popular Front: Madrid, 1931–1936," in Paul Preston, ed., *Revolution and War in Spain, 1931–1939* (London, 1984), 137–58.

8. *El Socialista*, 25 July 1933.

9. Ibid., 4 July 1933.

10. Quoted in P. Preston, *The Coming of the Spanish Civil War* (London, 1978), 78.

11. *El Socialista*, 16 August 1933. Largo's principal speeches during this period are collected in his *Discursos a los trabajadores* (Madrid, 1934).

12. A. de Blas Guerrero presents a succinct panorama of the radicalization process within Spanish Socialism in his *El socialismo radical en la II República* (Madrid, 1978). The principal Soviet account is S. P. Pozharskaya, "Taktika Ispanskoi Sotsialisticheskoi Rabochei Partii v pervye gody burzhuazno-demokraticheskoi revoliutsii (1931–1933 gg.)," in Institut Istorii Akademiya Nauk SSSR, *Iz istorii osvoboditelnoi borby ispanskogo naroda* (Moscow, 1959), 263–307.

13. See the argument made in this regard by Nigel Townson, "¿Qué hubiera pasado si los partidos republicanos se hubieran presentado unidos en las

elecciones de 1933?," in N. Townson, ed., *Historia virtual de España (1870–2004): ¿Qué hubiera pasado si . . . ?* (Madrid, 2004), 139–73.

14. A. Alcalá Galve, *Alcalá-Zamora y la agonía de la República* (Seville, 2002), 247.

15. M. Azaña, *Obras completas* (Mexico City, 1965–1968), 3:464.

16. See F. Martínez Roda, *Valencia y las Valencias: Su historia contemporánea (1800–1975)* (Valencia, 1998), 415–16.

17. The only good study is W. J. Irwin, *The 1933 Cortes Elections* (New York, 1991).

18. J. J. Linz, "Continuidad y discontinuidad en la elite política española," in *Estudios de Ciencia Política y Sociología (Homenaje al profesor Carlos Ollero)* (Madrid, 1972), 362–94.

19. See J. M. Macarro Vera, *Socialismo, República y revolución en Andalucía (1931–1936)* (Seville, 2000), 303.

20. N. Alcalá Zamora, *Memorias* (Barcelona, 1977), 258–59.

21. D. Martínez Barrio, *Memorias* (Barcelona, 1983), 212–13, presents the text of the letter. Cf. Alcalá Zamora, *Memorias*, 260; and C. Seco Serrano, "De la democracia a la Guerra Civil," in *Historia general de España y América* (Madrid, 1986), 17:xxii–xxiii. In his *Manuel Azaña*, Santos Juliá rationalizes the subversive policy of his hero by arguing that Azaña was willing to dispense with the constitution in order to save "democracy," presenting a bizarre definition of the latter.

22. Alcalá Zamora, *Memorias*, 260–61.

23. Zaragoza was the national headquarters of the FAI, the hard-core anarchist federation. See G. Kelsey, "Anarchism in Aragon during the Second Republic: The Emergence of a Mass Movement," in M. Blinkhorn, ed., *Spain in Conflict, 1931–1939* (London, 1986), 60–82; E. Montañés, *Anarcosindicalismo y cambio politico: Zaragoza 1930–1936* (Zaragoza, 1989); and, more broadly, J. Casanova, *De la calle al frente: El anarcosindicalismo en España (1931–1939)* (Barcelona, 1997).

24. For synopses of these events, J. Brademas, *Anarco-sindicalismo y revolución en España* (Madrid, 1974); R. W. Kern, *Red Years, Black Years* (Philadelphia, 1978), 123–25; and J. Arrarás, ed., *Historia de la Segunda República española* (Madrid, 1956–1963), 2:250–56.

25. For a complete list of all periods of constitutional exceptionalism under the Republic, see J. J. Linz, J. R. Montero, and A. M. Ruiz, *Elecciones y política* (in press), cuadro A.51.

26. This was especially the goal of Luis Lucia and most of the Derecha Regional Valenciana, a key component of the CEDA. See V. Comes Iglesia, *En el filo de la navaja: Biografía política de Luis Lucía Lucía* (Madrid, 2002). Angel Herrera, editor of *El Debate,* Spain's leading Catholic newspaper and one of the best in the country, also sought a democratic movement rather like the Catholic Center Party in Germany, but was thwarted by the more rightist inclinations of most of the CEDA. J. M. García Escudero, *Conversaciones sobre Angel Herrera* (Madrid, 1986) and *De periodista a cardenal: Vida de Ángel Herrera* (Madrid, 1998).

27. J. Pabón, *Palabras en la oposición* (Seville, 1965), 196.
28. There are two good studies of the Radicals: N. Townson, *The Crisis of Democracy in Spain: Centrist Politics under the Second Republic, 1931–1936* (Brighton, 2000); and O. Ruiz Manjón, *El Partido Republicano Radical 1908–1936* (Madrid, 1976). See also A. de Blas Guerrero, "El Partido Radical en la política española de la Segunda República," *Revista de Estudios Políticos*, 31–32 (January–April 1983), 137–64.
29. See M. Cuber, *Melquiades Álvarez* (Madrid, 1935); the work of the same name by M. García Venero (Madrid, 1974); and E. E. Gingold, "Melquiades Álvarez and the Reformist Party, 1901–1936" (Ph.D. diss., University of Wisconsin, 1973).
30. As Preston observes, *Coming of the Spanish Civil War*, 107.
31. On the Radical Party in Valencia, see S. Lynam, "Moderate Conservatism and the Second Republic: The Case of Valencia," in Blinkhorn, *Spain in Conflict*, 133–59; and L. Aguiló Lucia, "El sistema de partidos en el País Valenciano durante la Segunda República," in M. Tuñón de Lara, ed., *La crisis del Estado español* (Madrid, 1978), 505–16.
32. The most complete study is I. Saz, *Mussolini contra la II República* (Valencia, 1986), 66–85. For a memoir by one of the participants, see A. de Lizarza Iribarren, *Memorias de la conspiración* (Pamplona, 1969), 34–36.
33. J. F. Coverdale, *Italian Intervention in the Spanish Civil War* (Princeton, 1975), 64.
34. The most notable was by the canon Aniceto de Castro Albarrán, *El derecho a la rebeldía* (Madrid, 1934), while E. Vegas Latapié, *Catolicismo y República* (Madrid, 1934), included an appendix on "Insurrección" that sought to legitimize the concept.
35. Alcalá Zamora presented his version of this crisis in his *Memorias*, 271–74; that of Lerroux is in his *La pequeña historia* (Madrid, 1963), 248–52.

CHAPTER 3. THE REVOLUTIONARY INSURRECTION OF 1934

1. One of the best analyses is found in J. M. Macarro Vera, "Causas de la radicalización socialista en la II República," *Revista de Historia Contemporánea*, 1 (December 1982), 21–44. J. Merino, *Los socialistas rompen las urnas: 1933* (Barcelona, 1986), adds details.
2. S. Juliá, in N. Townson, ed., *El republicanismo en España (1830–1977)* (Madrid, 1994), 181.
3. S. Juliá, *Historia del socialismo español (1931–1939)*, vol. 3 of M. Tuñón de Lara, ed., *Historia del socialismo español* (Barcelona, 1989), 79.
4. *Boletín del Ministerio de Trabajo*, January 1935, in P. Preston, *The Coming of the Spanish Civil War* (London, 1978), 219.
5. According to Preston, ibid., 100.
6. Quoted in Juliá, *Historia del socialismo español*, 85.
7. Quoted in P. Moa, *Los orígenes de la Guerra Civil Española* (Madrid, 1999), 220. This speech was not published in *El Socialista*.
8. M. Azaña, *Obras completas* (Mexico City, 1965–1968), 2:951–52.

9. The text of both projects may be found in D. Ibárruri et al., *Guerra y revolución en España* (Moscow, 1967), 1:52–57; that of the party is given in Juliá, *Historia del socialismo español*, 347–49.

10. Amaro del Rosal has published a large part of the discussions held there and at other leadership levels of the UGT during the two preceding months. See his *1934: Movimiento revolucionario de octubre* (Madrid, 1983), 34–204.

11. On the Madrid section, see A. Pastor Ugeña, *La Agrupación Socialista Madrileña durante la Segunda República* (Madrid, 1985), 2 vols.

12. From the text of the instructions for insurrection in S. Juliá, ed., *Largo Caballero: Escritos de la República*, quoted in Moa, *Los orígenes*, 404–14.

13. Quoted in Moa, ibid., 271.

14. See Juliá, *Historia del socialismo español*, 101–06.

15. On the USC, see A. Balcells, *Ideari de Rafael Campalans* (Barcelona, 1973).

16. According to Maurín, the BOC had grown from approximately 3,000 in 1931 to 5,000 by 1934, with notable membership outside Catalonia only in Castellón and Valencia (response to a questionnaire of 24 February 1968). There is no fully adequate study of Maurín, the best being Y. Riottot, *Joaquín Maurín de l'anarcho-syndicalisme au communisme (1919–1936)* (Paris, 1997). See also A. Monreal, *El pensamiento político de Joaquín Maurín* (Barcelona, 1984); M. Sánchez, *Maurín, gran enigma de la guerra y otros recuerdos* (Madrid, 1976); and V. Alba, *Dos revolucionarios: Andreu Nin / Joaquín Maurín* (Madrid, 1975). The history of the BOC has been well studied in A. C. Durgan, *BOC 1930–1936: El Bloque Obrero y Campesino* (Barcelona, 1996). A good analysis of the ideological maneuvers involved may be found in P. Heywood, "The Development of Marxist Theory in Spain and the Frente Popular," in M. S. Alexander and H. Graham, eds., *The French and Spanish Popular Fronts* (Cambridge, 1989), 116–30. For the Socialist Party in Barcelona during the Republic, see A. Balcells, "El socialismo en Cataluña durante la Segunda República (1931–1936)," in *Sociedad, política y cultura en la España de los siglos XIX–XX* (Madrid, 1973), 177–213.

17. A. Shubert, *The Road to Revolution in Spain* (Urbana, 1987), 141–62; Juliá, *Historia del socialismo español*, 115–16.

18. See J. M. Macarro Vera, "Octubre, un error de cálculo y perspectiva," in G. Ojeda, ed., *Octubre 1934* (Madrid, 1985), 269–82.

19. R. Salazar Alonso, *Bajo el signo de la revolución* (Madrid, 1935), 75–77, 122–28.

20. Preston, *Coming of the Spanish Civil War*, 114–15; and E. E. Malefakis, *Agrarian Reform and Peasant Revolution in Spain* (New Haven, 1970), 317–42. G. A. Collier, *Socialists of Rural Andalusia: Unacknowledged Revolutionaries of the Second Republic* (Stanford, 1987), presents an anthropological study of a small town containing 1,000 farmworkers in the sierra of northern Huelva province. There the Socialists won the municipal elections of April 1933 and ran the district until October 1934. They seem to have had little interest in collectivization and socialism per se, but instead sought radical changes in labor relations. They were fueled by a revolution of rising expectations, enormously stimulated by their apparent success.

21. Malefakis, *Agrarian Reform*, 337.
22. The best accounts of the strike are ibid., 338–42; and M. Tuñón de Lara, *Tres claves de la Segunda República* (Madrid, 1985), 130–53.
23. Articles dealing with the role of political militias and violence in six organizations appear in the special section under that title in *Historia Contemporánea*, 11 (1994), 13–179.
24. See C. M. Winston, *Workers and the Right in Spain, 1900–1936* (Princeton, 1985), 290–92.
25. A. Balcells, *Crisis económica y agitación social en Cataluña de 1930 a 1936* (Barcelona, 1974), 20.
26. See my *Fascism in Spain, 1923–1977* (Madison, 1999), 102–14; and the well-researched, highly detailed, but nonetheless incomplete tabulation in F. de A. de la Vega Gonzalo, *Aniquilar la Falange. Cronología persecutoria del Nacionalsindicalismo* (Oviedo, 2001), 35–48.
27. *ABC* (Madrid), 13 February 1934. As the former Socialist (later Communist) militia leader Manuel Tagüeña, who helped organize some of these attacks on the Falangists, would later put it: "There were some reprisals . . . but, in the beginning, the Falangists got the worst of it"; *Testimonio de dos guerras* (Mexico City, 1973), 53–54.
28. I. Prieto, *Discursos en América* (Mexico City, 1944), 106. Or, as Largo Caballero later commented of the Socialist Youth, "They did whatever they felt like." *Mis recuerdos* (Mexico City, 1950), 141.
29. Preston, *Coming of the Spanish Civil War*, 117.
30. *Boletín de la UGT*, August 1934, in ibid., 118.
31. The splintering of left Catalanism is treated in E. Ucelay da Cal, "Estat Català" (Ph.D. diss., Columbia University, 1979), 495–549; and M. D. Ivern i Salvà, *Esquerra Republicana de Catalunya (1931–36)* (Montserrat, 1988), 1:265–428.
32. See the long quotation from Dencàs in J. Miravitlles, *Crítica del 6 d'octubre* (Barcelona, 1935), 117.
33. The first biography was A. Ossorio y Gallardo, *Vida y sacrificio de Companys* (Buenos Aires, 1943); but J. M. Poblet, *Vida i mort de Lluis Companys* (Barcelona, 1976), is a fuller account.
34. The basic study is A. Balcells, *El problema agrari a Catalunya (1890–1936): La qüestió rabassaire* (Barcelona, 1968).
35. The case was argued for the Generalitat by Amadeu Hurtado, as he recounts in his memoir *Quaranta anys d'advocat* (Esplugues de Llobregat, 1967), 2:256–98. On the technical issues, see A. Lubac, *Le Tribunal Espagnol des Garanties Constitutionelles* (Montpellier, 1936).
36. Azaña, *Obras completas*, 2:977–82.
37. Quoted in J. Pabón, *Cambó* (Barcelona, 1969), 2, pt. 2:356–58.
38. During the preceding year Dencàs had served effectively as councilor of sanitation and social assistance, and deserved some of the credit for the government's achievements in health services. His Escamots had first appeared in their green shirts in a mass parade at Barcelona's Montjuich stadium in

October 1933. While their opponents talked of a "Catalan fascism," the Escamots sometimes referred to themselves as a "Catalan liberation army." J. M. Morreres Boix, "El Enigma de Joseph Dencàs," *Historia Nueva*, 21 (October 1978), 94–104.

39. Quoted in J. Arrarás, ed., *Historia de la Segunda República española* (Madrid, 1956–1963), 2:395–96.

40. N. Alcalá Zamora, *Discursos* (Madrid, 1979), 638–45.

41. Idem, *Memorias* (Barcelona, 1977), 279–84.

42. Preston, *Coming of the Spanish Civil War*, 127.

43. Quoted in A. de Blas, *El socialismo radical en la II República* (Madrid, 1978), 118.

44. L. Shevtsova, *Putin's Russia* (Washington, D.C., 2003).

45. J. Avilés Farré, *La izquierda burguesa en la II República* (Madrid, 1985), 232–36. This movement toward the left by Izquierda Republicana may be compared with the "New Radical Movement" in the French Radical Party between 1926 and 1932. The differences were, of course, that the French Radicals were a much stronger, more broadly based group and in the long run were not won over by the new leftism. See M. Schlesinger, "The Development of the Radical Party in the Third Republic: The New Radical Movement, 1926–1932," *Journal of Modern History*, 46:3 (September 1974), 476–501.

46. Avilés Farré, *Izquierda burguesa*, 243–44.

47. On this schism, see ibid., 239–40; and especially N. Townson, *The Crisis of Democracy in Spain: Centrist Politics under the Second Republic, 1931–1936* (Brighton, 2000), 227–41.

48. Or so Martínez Barrio later told Azaña during the Civil War. Azaña, *Obras completas*, 4:717–18.

49. Cf. S. Juliá, *Manuel Azaña, una biografía política* (Madrid, 1990), 331.

50. M. Azaña, *Mi rebelión en Barcelona* (Madrid, 1935), 35; *El Socialista*, 3 July 1935.

51. J. Pérez Salas, *Guerra en España* (Mexico City, 1947), 67–68. See also Moa, *Los orígenes*, 335–36.

52. F. Largo Caballero, *Escritos de la República* (Madrid, 1985), 111–16.

53. D. Martínez Barrio, *Memorias* (Barcelona, 1983), 331–32.

54. Alcalá Zamora, *Memorias*, 277–78.

55. Juliá, *Manuel Azaña*, 338; Largo Caballero, *Escritos*, 116.

56. Arrarás, *Segunda República*, 2:410.

57. Years later Prieto gave his version of this episode in "Mi escapatoria de 1934," *El Socialista* (Toulouse), 5 July 1951. His inconsistencies as a Socialist leader have been denounced by Victor Alba, *Los sepultureros de la República* (Barcelona, 1977), 105–95. The fullest reconstruction of the *Turquesa* incident is found in P. I. Taibo II, *Asturias 1934* (Gijón, 1984), 1:81–96.

58. *El Sol*, 18 September 1934.

59. For a brief survey of the early years of the PCE, see my *The Spanish Civil War, the Soviet Union, and Communism* (New Haven, 2004), 1–50, which contains references to the pertinent bibliography.

60. R. Cruz, *El Partido Comunista de España en la Segunda República* (Madrid, 1987), 184–86.

61. Quoted in N. Greene, *Crisis and Decline: The French Socialist Party in the Popular Front Era* (Ithaca, 1969), 4–39.

62. See R. Cruz, *El arte que inflama: La creación de una literatura bolchevique en España, 1931–1936* (Madrid, 1999); and A. Elorza and M. Bizcarrondo, *Queridos camaradas: La Internacional Comunista y España, 1919–1939* (Barcelona, 1999), 193–206.

63. Elorza and Bizcarrondo, *Queridos camaradas,* 60–61.

64. Cruz, *El Partido Comunista,* 188–89.

65. Elorza and Bizcarrondo, *Queridos camaradas,* 215–16.

66. Ibid., 216–20; Cruz, *El Partido Comunista,* 193–94.

67. J. M. Gil Robles, *No fue posible la paz* (Barcelona, 1968), 161; Salazar Alonso, *Bajo el signo,* 319–20.

68. Interviews with Eloy Vaquero, New York City, May–June 1958.

69. Azaña, *Obras completas,* 2:983–98.

70. Alcalá Zamora, *Memorias,* 286–87.

71. Moa, *Los orígenes,* 288. According to the official report by the Dirección General de Seguridad, the total number of weapons confiscated by the authorities after defeat of the insurrection amounted to 90,000 rifles and 30,000 pistols, though some of these weapons may have been counted twice. Ibid., 287. Whatever the exact number, most of them had been acquired before the insurrection, since only about 21,000 were seized from the Oviedo arms factory.

72. In Prieto's *El Liberal* (Bilbao), 23 January 1936.

73. A. Lerroux, *La pequeña historia* (Madrid, 1963), 302.

74. E. López et al., *Diego Hidalgo* (Madrid, 1986); and C. Muñoz Tinoco, *Diego Hidalgo* (Badajoz, 1986), are brief accounts. Hidalgo published an instant memoir of his experience as minister of war, *¿Por qué fui lanzado desde el Ministerio de la Guerra?* (Madrid, 1935).

75. J. Pérez Salas, *Guerra en España* (Mexico City, 1947), 67–68; Moa, *Los orígenes,* 335–36.

76. The original Catalan text may be found in L. Aymamí i Baudina, *El 6 d'octubre tal com jo l'he vist* (Barcelona, 1935), 249–51.

77. There are several contemporary accounts of the farcical drama in Barcelona: L. Aymamí i Baudina, *El d d'octubre tal com jo l'he vist* (Barcelona, 1935); E. de Angulo, *Diez horas de Estat Català* (Madrid, 1935); F. Gómez Hidalgo, *Cataluña-Companys* (Madrid, 1935); A. Estivill, *6 d'octubre: L'ensulsiada dels jacobins* (Barcelona, 1935); J. Miravitlles, *Crítica del d d'octubre* (Barcelona, 1935); and, more recently, M. Cruells, *El 6 d'octubre a Catalunya* (Barcelona, 1970); and J. Tarín-Iglesias, *La rebelión de la Generalidad* (Barcelona, 1988).

78. S. Campos i Terre, *El 6 d'octubre a les comarques* (1935; reprint, Tortosa, 1987). There were also a few scattered disorders in the Catalan countryside during the weeks that followed. See R. Vinyes i Ribes, *La Catalunya internacional: El front populisme en l'exemple cátala* (Barcelona, 1983), 98–120.

79. Azaña's memoir is *Mi rebelión en Barcelona* (Madrid, 1935), reprinted in vol. 3 of his *Obras completas*. He reported that he was told by Catalanist leaders that a revolt would be used as no more than a bargaining chip (pp. 74–76). The nineteenth-century pronunciamiento quality of all this is doubly ironic in Azaña's case. He would never have endorsed revolutionary violence per se but would obviously have wanted the illegal pronunciamiento to succeed— an indication that some of his political instincts were not very different from those of the traditional Spanish military men for whom he expressed such supercilious disdain.

80. Cf. J. D. Carrión Iñíguez, *La insurrección de 1934 en la provincia de Albacete* (Albacete, 1990).

81. The best brief treatment of the revolt in the Basque provinces is J. P. Fusi, "Nacionalismo y revolución: Octobre de 1934 en el País Vasco," in G. Jackson et al., *Octubre 1934* (Madrid, 1980), 177–96.

82. Cf. L. Paramio, "Revolución y conciencia preindustrial en octubre del 34," in ibid., 301–15.

83. The Asturian background is explained in Adrian Shubert's *The Road to Revolution in Spain: The Coal Miners of Asturias 1860–1934* (Urbana, 1987). He concludes that mining per se did not necessarily produce a more united or radical labor force than other sectors of industrial employment. Shubert instead emphasizes the historical and economic context in Asturias. Asturian coal, though relatively abundant, is of low quality, and the industry was never adequately capitalized or efficient to achieve high productivity. Both the dictatorship and the Republic had tried and failed to provide a remedy, when the only true solution was development or diversification, virtually impossible during the depression. On the CNT in the region, see A. Barrio Alonso, *Anarquismo y anarcosindicalismo en Asturias (1890–1936)* (Madrid, 1988).

84. The use of Moroccan as well as elite Legion troops from the protectorate was much criticized by the left, but Azaña had called in both the Tercio and the Regulares against the anarchists in 1932.

85. On the role of the Communists in Asturias, see M. Grossi, *La insurrección de Asturias* (Madrid, 1978), 86–98; and "J. Canel" (pseud.), *Octubre rojo en Asturias* (Madrid, 1935), 153–54.

86. According to Yagüe's remarks, quoted in J. Arrarás, ed., *Historia de la Cruzada española* (Madrid, 1940), 7:259.

87. Some of the most precise estimates are found in A. de Llano Roza de Ampudia, *Pequeños anales de quince días* (Oviedo, 1935), the best of the contemporary accounts; and in B. Díaz Nosty, *La comuna asturiana* (Madrid, 1972), 503.

88. A government report of 30 October 1934 claimed 220 officers and troops killed and 43 missing, for a total of 263. The Civil Guard apparently suffered 111 fatalities, and other police a total of 81. See E. Barco Teruel, *El "golpe" socialista del 6 de octubre de 1934* (Madrid, 1984), 258; and F. Aguado Sánchez, *La revolución de octubre de 1934* (Madrid, 1972), 503. For the extensive bibliography pertaining to the insurrection, see my *Spain's First Democracy: The Second Republic, 1931–1936* (Madison, 1993), 430–31.

89. Doval had lost his commission because of his involvement in the sanjurjada but had been readmitted to the Civil Guard after the amnesty. This reappointment, like the much larger number of reappointments of revolutionary subversives carried out by the left Republican government after February 1936, was unconscionable under constitutional government. Such deliberate subversive politicization of the police played a key role in sparking the final catalyst to civil war.

90. The total prison population by the beginning of 1935 was approximately 30,000, compared with a normal total of common criminals of less than 15,000. The left conveniently cited Spain's total prison population, thus nearly doubling the actual number of imprisoned revolutionaries.

91. G. Jackson, *The Spanish Republic and the Civil War, 1931–1939* (Princeton, 1965), 166, estimates about forty. The principal study of the assaults on the clergy is A. Garralda, *La persecución del clero en Asturias (1934 y 1936–1937)* (Avilés, 1977), 2 vols. See also ACNP de Oviedo, *Asturias roja: Sacerdotes y religiosos perseguidos y martirizados* (Oviedo, 1935); and the hagiographic *Los mártires de Turón* (Madrid, 1935). Amid a violent revolution, a number of common crimes (murder, rape, theft) occurred under the cover of revolutionary turmoil. The government's report, *En servicio a la República: La revolución de octubre en octubre* (Madrid, 1935), mentioned three women raped and killed by revolutionaries.

92. One of the fullest statements is "Ignotus" (Manuel Villar), *La represión de octubre* (Barcelona, 1936). Even after the Popular Front victory in 1936, however, no systematic investigation was completed, so that no reliable statistics are available.

93. Jackson, *Spanish Republic*, 167.

94. R. Ledesma Ramos, *¿Fascismo en España?* (Madrid, 1935), 38.

95. S. de Madariaga, *Spain: A Modern History* (New York, 1958), 434–35.

96. E. Malefakis, in R. Carr, ed., *The Republic and the Civil War in Spain* (London, 1971), 34; R. Carr in ibid., 10.

97. R. A. H. Robinson, *The Origins of Franco's Spain* (London, 1970), 106.

98. I. Prieto, *Discursos en América* (Mexico City, 1944), 102.

CHAPTER 4. A CONSERVATIVE REPUBLIC?

1. Federico Escofet has published a biographical note, *De una derrota a una victoria* (Barcelona, 1984), 69–143.

2. N. Alcalá Zamora, *Los defectos de la Constitución de 1931* (Madrid, 1936), 190–91.

3. J. M. Gil Robles, *No fue posible la paz* (Barcelona, 1968), 145–48.

4. Two accounts of the repression, different but not entirely incongruent, are found in G. Jackson, *The Spanish Republic and the Civil War, 1931–1939* (Princeton, 1965), 159–64; and R. de la Cierva, *Historia de la Guerra Civil española*, vol. 1: *Perspectivas y antecedentes* (Madrid, 1969), 435–56.

5. A total of 1,116 out of 8,436, according to R. Salazar Alonso, *Bajo el signo de la revolución* (Madrid, 1935), 116–29.

6. N. Alcalá Zamora, *Memorias* (Barcelona, 1977), 299. During the Civil War a newspaper in Valencia published extracts from a draft of the memoirs seized by revolutionaries. In it the former president referred to a meeting with Lerroux and Martínez Barrio in which the latter said that during a luncheon before the insurrection Azaña had informed him of his dealings with the revolutionaries. On 7 August 1937 Azaña got Martínez Barrio to "remember" that such a luncheon had never taken place. M. Azaña, *Obras completas* (Mexico City, 1965–1968), 4:725, as noted by A. Alcalá Galve, *Alcalá-Zamora y la agonía de la República* (Seville, 2002), 534.

7. Teodomiro Menéndez had suffered greatly in jail and had attempted to commit suicide, though it was not clear whether he had suffered physical torture.

8. Lerroux's brief report appeared in his *La pequeña historia* (Madrid, 1935), 373–74.

9. On the terms of repression in the rural zone of Catalonia during 1935, see Unió de Rabassaires, *Els desnonaments rustics a Catalunya* (Barcelona, 1935); and R. Vinyes i Ribes, *La Catalunya internacional: El frontpopulisme en l'exemple català* (Barcelona, 1983), 98–138.

10. Quoted in J. Arrarás, ed., *Historia de la Segunda República española* (Madrid, 1956–1963), 3:161. Cambó, as usual, made the most astute observation about the phenomenon of huge mass meetings: "the excitement of the masses is the indispensable prerequisite for a fascist coup or a proletarian revolution. . . . These mass rallies can never be used by a party that wants to maintain a center position." Quoted in J. Pabón, *Cambó* (Barcelona, 1969), 2:433.

11. Lerroux's attitude was most graphically symbolized by a military parade and joint banquet that he and Gil Robles attended in the arch-CEDA city of Salamanca. He later wrote of this occasion: "I had reached the following conclusion: in order for the Republic to gain its balance and survive, it had to move from its sad experience of two years of demagogy with Azaña to the experience of two more years of balanced and moderate government that would in turn facilitate subsequent progressive and stable center governments. The second experience requires power in the hands of the CEDA. Let it so [enjoy power], so that the party may lose doctrinaire rigidity, learn to compromise, unify and organize itself, and cleave to the Republic, however rightist it may be. Afterward the political pendulum will resume its synchronic swing." Lerroux, *La pequeña historia*, 393. This apparent harmony led wits to speak of a "Pact of Salamanca" that had supposedly replaced the 1930 Pact of San Sebastián.

12. E. E. Malefakis, *Agrarian Reform and Peasant Revolution in Spain* (New Haven, 1970), 343–55. See also J. Tusell and J. Calvo, *Giménez Fernández, precursor de la democracia española* (Seville, 1990), 70–100.

13. Malefakis, *Agrarian Reform*, 362.

14. De la Cierva, *Historia*, 1:487.

15. R. A. H. Robinson, *The Origins of Franco's Spain: The Right, the Republic and Revolution, 1931–1936* (London, 1970), 226–27.

16. The most succinct study is found in an essay by C. Boyd in *Historia general*

de España y América (Madrid, 1986), 17:162–69; and the most thorough in M. Aguilar Olivencia, *El Ejército español durante la Segunda República* (Madrid, 1986), 365–468.

17. *Documents on German Foreign Policy* (Washington, D.C., 1950), series C, vol. 4, docs. 303, 330, and 445, cited in P. Preston, *The Coming of the Spanish Civil War* (London, 1978), 159.

18. A. Rodriguez de las Heras, *Filiberto Villalobos: Su obra social y política (1900–1936)* (Salamanca, 1985), 177–272, offers a detailed account of his work under the Samper and fourth Lerroux governments.

19. These were elaborated by D. Niceto in a small book, *Los defectos de la Constitución de 1931* (Madrid, 1936). In his *Memorias,* he claimed that Azaña himself admitted that these and even more defects existed, but that since reform had become a polarizing issue between right and left, he, Azaña, would have to oppose reform. The first weeks of 1935 saw the appearance of *Jerarquía o anarquía,* a new book by Madariaga on the question of popular representation. It proposed to combine limited direct voting with representation that was partially indirect and corporative. The fact that it coincided in part with the critique commonly made by the moderate right was quickly noted.

20. See F. Carreras, "Los intentos de reforma electoral durante la Segunda República," *Revista de Estudios Políticos,* 31–32 (January–April 1983), 165–97.

21. In various weekly articles appearing in the journal *JAP* from November 1934 to March 1935.

22. Robinson, *Origins of Franco's Spain,* 208–15.

23. Calvo Sotelo, who astutely favored greater deficit spending, which might have eased some of the social problems, observed that the Republic had had one budget of twelve months, another of nine months, two of six months, and five three-month prorogations.

24. Quoted in Arrarás, *Segunda República,* 3:148.

25. J. Chapaprieta, *La paz fue posible* (Barcelona, 1983), 165–201. See also M. Ramírez Jiménez, "Las reformas tributarias en la II República española," in *Las reformas de la II República* (Madrid, 1977), 185–98; and J. Gil Pecharromán, "La opinión pública ante las reformas hacendísticas de Joaquín Chapaprieta," *Hispania,* 47:167 (1987), 1001–26.

CHAPTER 5. FRUSTRATION OF THE PARLIAMENTARY SYSTEM

1. See the analysis by Carlos Seco Serrano in his prologue to J. Chapaprieta, *La paz fue posible* (Barcelona, 1983), 58–59.

2. "Straperlo" was a neologism that combined the names of its two promoters, Strauss and Perle. The term quickly passed into common usage as *estraperlo* and became the national term for black-market dealing after the Civil War. The Strauss wheel differed from conventional roulette in that it was not based on chance but followed complex yet regular procedures that might be calculated by nimble players (though the operator had the means of further manipulating the outcome if he chose, to throw off a winning calculation).

This arrangement theoretically created a new game of "skill" rather than one of pure chance.

3. Chapaprieta, *La paz fue posible*, 267–68; O. Ruiz Manjón, *El Partido Republicano Radical 1908–1936* (Madrid, 1976), 503–04; N. Townson, *The Crisis of Democracy in Spain: Centrist Politics under the Second Republic, 1931–1936* (Brighton, 2000), 315–17; N. Alcalá Zamora, *Memorias* (Barcelona, 1977), 312.

4. See the frank observations by the journalist and sometime Radical minister César Jalón in his *Memorias políticas* (Madrid, 1973), 214–18.

5. Chapaprieta, *La paz fue posible*, 256–60.

6. Jalón, who felt great respect and admiration for Lerroux, referred to the adopted son and his *camarilla* (personal circle) as "the Aurelio clan" and as "the customs house." *Memorias*, 223.

7. See particularly the extensive coverage in *El Debate*, 26 October 1935 and days following.

8. See Ruiz Manjón, *El Partido*, 500–27; and Townson, *The Crisis*, 319–25.

9. Alcalá Zamora, *Memorias*, 311, where the former president affirms that the cancellation had been due to simple nonperformance of services, a claim that seems accurate.

10. Chapaprieta, *La paz fue posible*, 307–09; Lerroux, *La pequeña historia*, 394–400.

11. The internal collapse is examined in Ruiz Manjón, *El Partido*, 529–59; and in Townson, *The Crisis*, 330–46. This may be compared with the much different situation in Spain in 1990, when a more strongly organized Socialist Party with a bare parliamentary majority was nonetheless able to ride out the most severe financial scandals in Spanish history, and even increase its vote in Andalusian regional elections.

12. Chapaprieta, *La paz fue posible*, 82.

13. Quoted in J. Arrarás, ed., *Historia de la Segunda República española* (Madrid, 1956–1963), 3:267.

14. The version of Gil Robles appears in ibid., 361–64. Alcalá Zamora later justified his veto on the grounds of Gil Robles' inability or refusal to restrain the authoritarian "fascist" elements of his party, especially the JAP. He claimed that Gil Robles sought to justify his permissive policy with this sector by alleging that such elements were less dangerous in the CEDA, where he could control them, than if they passed to the Falange. *Memorias*, 341, 343.

15. J. M. Gil Robles, *No fue posible la paz* (Barcelona, 1968), 363.

16. Over a year later, Franco—by then head of the Nationalist rebel regime— sent a personal letter to Gil Robles to quash rumors that the CEDA had blocked a coup proposed by Franco. His missive of 4 February 1937 declared: "Neither out of duty nor because of the situation of Spain, then difficult but not yet in immediate danger, nor in terms of the appropriateness with which you had proceeded throughout your work in the ministry, which would not have authorized such a step, could I have proposed to you something which at that moment would have lacked adequate justification or even the means

of being carried out, since the Army—which can take action when so sacred a cause as that of the Fatherland is in imminent danger—cannot normally become the arbiter of partisan politics." This letter first appeared in *El Correo de Andalucía*, 6 April 1937; a facsimile is reproduced in Gil Robles, *No fue posible*, 377–78.

17. *El Sol*, 14 December 1935.
18. A. Alcalá Galve, *Alcalá-Zamora y la agonía de la República* (Seville, 2002), 575.
19. The president's principal biographer comes to the roughly similar conclusion that allowing Gil Robles to become prime minister in 1935 would have given the Republic greater stability. Ibid., 677–86.
20. The best analysis of these alternatives is J. J. Linz, "From Great Hopes to Civil War: The Breakdown of Democracy in Spain," in Linz and A. Stepan, eds., *The Breakdown of Democratic Regimes: Europe* (Baltimore, 1978), 142–215.
21. Lerroux recognized the eclectic composition of his party under the Republic, emphasizing that it was doing a service by the incorporation of diverse elements into Republican democracy, and speculating about its ultimate disappearance after a truly democratic Republic had become consolidated. Evaluations of the Radicals may be found in O. Ruiz Manjón, *El Partido Republicano Radical 1908–1936* (Madrid, 1976), 677–85; and in Townson, *The Crisis*, 347–59.

CHAPTER 6. TOWARD THE POPULAR FRONT

1. M. Portela Valladares, *Memorias* (Madrid, 1988), 160–61.
2. J. Chapaprieta, *La paz fue posible* (Barcelona, 1983), 353–60.
3. J. M. Gil Robles, *No fue posible la paz* (Barcelona, 1968), 386–90.
4. Quoted in J. Arrarás, ed., *Historia de la Segunda República española* (Madrid, 1956–1963), 3:293.
5. The most detailed analysis of the Socialist radicalization is S. Juliá, *La izquierda del PSOE 1935–1936* (Madrid, 1977); but see also A. de Blas Guerrero, *El socialismo radical en II República* (Madrid, 1978). Useful brief treatments are in P. Preston, *The Coming of the Spanish Civil War* (London, 1978), 131–50; and in his "The Struggle against Fascism in Spain: *Leviatán* and the Contradictions of the Socialist Left, 1934–6," in M. Blinkhorn, ed., *Spain in Conflict, 1931–1939* (London, 1986), 40–59. The broadest short overview is H. Graham, "The Eclipse of the Socialist Left, 1934–1937," in F. Lannon and P. Preston, eds., *Elites and Power in Twentieth-Century Spain* (Oxford, 1990), 127–51.
6. The quotations in the preceding paragraphs are from K. McDermott and J. Agnew, *The Comintern: A History of International Communism from Lenin to Stalin* (Houndmills, 1996), 130–32, 155–59.
7. A. Elorza and M. Bizcarrondo, *Queridos camaradas: La Internacional Comunista y España, 1919–1939* (Barcelona, 1999), 250.
8. McDermott and Agnew, *The Comintern*, 132.
9. Elorza and Bizcarrondo, *Queridos camaradas*, 223–25.

10. Ibid., 225–26.
11. R. Cruz, *El Partido Comunista de España en la II República* (Madrid, 1987), 229.
12. Elorza and Bizcarrondo, *Queridos camaradas,* 232.
13. As outlined in a report by the Romanskii Lendersekretariat (Romance Language Countries Secretariat) of 8 February 1935. Rossiiskaya Akademiya Nauk, *Komintern i grazhdanskaya voina v Ispanii* (Moscow, 2001), 99–101.
14. Elorza and Bizcarrondo, *Queridos camaradas,* 230–34.
15. José Díaz, *Tres años de lucha* (Barcelona, 1978), 1:43.
16. On the founding of the POUM, see A. C. Durgan, *BOC 1930–1936: El Bloque Obrero y Campesino* (Barcelona, 1996), 350–59; Y. Riottot, *Joaquín Maurín de l'anarcho-syndicalisme au communisme (1919–1936)* (Paris, 1997), 301–19; V. Alba, *El marxisme a Catalunya* (Barcelona, 1974), vol. 1; and V. Alba and S. Schwartz, *Spanish Marxism versus Soviet Communism: A History of the POUM* (New Brunswick, N.J., 1988), 87–110.
17. *La Libertad* (Madrid), 13 April 1935; D. Martínez Barrio, *Orígenes del Frente Popular* (Buenos Aires, 1943), 24–31.
18. The key study is S. Juliá, *Los orígenes del Frente Popular en España (1934–1936)* (Madrid, 1979), 27–41.
19. The text soon appeared in a polemical denunciation by a left Socialist, Carlos de Baráibar, *Las falsas "posiciones socialistas" de Indalecio Prieto* (Madrid, 1935), 139–45.
20. *La Libertad,* 30 March 1935. See also J. S. Vidarte, *El bienio negro y la insurrección de Asturias* (Barcelona, 1978), 387–98.
21. A. del Rosal, *1934: El movimiento revolucionario de octubre* (Madrid, 1983), 263.
22. On the campaign and the mobilization of memory, see B. D. Bunk, "'Your Comrades Will Not Forget': Revolutionary Memory and the Breakdown of the Spanish Republic," *History and Memory,* 14:1–2 (Fall 2002), 65–92.
23. Juliá, *Los orígenes del Frente Popular,* 47–48.
24. J. Besteiro, *Marxismo y antimarxismo* (Madrid, 1935). Preston notes that "his insinuations that the violence of the Socialist left was hardly distinguishable from fascism did not endear him to the Caballerists." P. Preston, *The Coming of the Spanish Civil War* (London, 1978), 138. The besteiristas published their own weekly, *Democracia,* from June to December 1935. A true Socialist "right," such as Déat's Neosocialism in France or De Man's "Planism" in Belgium, did not exist in Spain. *Besteirismo* was essentially a return to Kautskyism.
25. The three principal speeches of Azaña in 1935 were published as *Discursos en campo abierto* (Madrid, 1936). The great meeting at Comillas was described by an eyewitness, Henry Buckley, in his *The Life and Death of the Spanish Republic* (London, 1940), 179–88; and by F. Sedwick, *The Tragedy of Manuel Azaña and the Fate of the Spanish Republic* (Athens, Ohio, 1963), 15–50.
26. Cruz, *El Partido Comunista,* 228.
27. J. Díaz, *Nuestra bandera del Frente Popular* (Madrid, 1936), 31, 57.

28. Cruz, *El Partido Comunista*, 235–39.
29. Ibid., 245–46.
30. Elorza and Bizcarrondo, *Queridos camaradas*, 255.
31. Varying accounts of this meeting and the split are found in *Claridad*, 23 December 1935; *El Socialista*, 20–25 December 1935; F. Largo Caballero, *Mis recuerdos* (Mexico City, 1954), 146–48; Vidarte, *El bienio negro*, 26; and G. Mario de Coca, *Anti-Caballero* (Madrid, 1936), 193–98.
32. The clearest discussion of these negotiations remains Juliá, *Los orígenes del Frente Popular*, 70–149.
33. Félix Gordón Ordás, now a leader of the Partido de Unión Republicana, would later declare that both he and Sánchez Román had done all they could to exclude the Communists, but failed. Gordón Ordás, *Mi política en España* (Mexico City, 1951), 2:519.
34. Cited in P. Moa, *El derrumbe de la Segunda República y la Guerra Civil* (Madrid, 2001), 251.
35. S. Juliá, *Manuel Azaña, una biografía política* (Madrid, 1990), 441.
36. Cruz, *El Partido Comunista*, 249–50.
37. This manifesto appeared in the press on 16 January 1936.
38. Quoted in Juliá, *Manuel Azaña*, 444.
39. For a comparison of the two Popular Fronts, see G.-R. Horn, *European Socialists Respond to Fascism: Ideology, Activism and Contingency in the 1930s* (New York, 1996); M. S. Alexander and H. Graham, eds., *The French and Spanish Popular Fronts: Comparative Perspectives* (Cambridge, Mass., 1989); and H. Graham and P. Preston, eds., *The Popular Front in Europe* (London, 1987). On the French Popular Front, G. Lefranc, *Histoire du Front Populaire, 1934–1938* (Paris, 1965); J. Jackson, *The Popular Front in France: Defending Democracy, 1934–1938* (Cambridge, 1984); J. Kergoat, *La France du Front Populaire* (Paris, 1986); and K. H. Harr Jr., *The Genesis and Effect of the Popular Front in France* (Lanham, Md., 1987).
40. Juliá, *Los orígenes del Frente Popular*, 134–49. According to Gordón Ordás, the Popular Front tried to include a Communist on the list for Gordón's home ticket in León, where there were no Communist voters. He threatened to resign and gained removal of the Communist candidacy. *Mi política en España*, 2:519.
41. A. Shubert, "A Reinterpretation of the Spanish Popular Front: The Case of Asturias," in Alexander and Graham, *The French and Spanish Popular Fronts*, 213–25. See also J. Getman Eraso, "Rethinking the Revolution: Utopia and Pragmatism in Catalan Anarchosyndicalism, 1930–1936" (Ph.D. diss., University of Wisconsin–Madison, 2001); D. Abad de Santillán, *Por qué perdimos la guerra* (Buenos Aires, 1940), 36; and C. M. Lorenzo, *Les anarchistes espagnols et le pouvoir 1868–1939* (Paris, 1969), 89–92.
42. *El Sol*, 14 January 1936.
43. *Claridad*, 25 January 1936.
44. Elorza and Bizcarrondo, *Queridos camaradas*, 263–64.
45. Ibid., 267.

46. *Mundo Obrero*, 23 January 1936.
47. Elorza and Bizcarrondo, *Queridos camaradas*, 261, 496–97.
48. Díaz, *Tres años de lucha*, 2:97–98.
49. Cruz, *El Partido Comunista*, 254–55.
50. The prison population of Spain officially listed for 15 February 1936 was 34,526. The average before mid-1934 had been approximately 20,000, and thus the number of new prisoners dating from the insurrection was presumably in the neighborhood of 15,000. Benito Pabón, one of the two deputies elected by Pestaña's Partido Sindicalista, admitted as much in the Cortes on 2 July 1936.

CHAPTER 7. THE ELECTIONS OF FEBRUARY 1936

1. M. Portela Valladares, *Memorias: Dentro del drama español* (Madrid, 1988), 167–68.
2. Ibid., 168.
3. Portela indicates that a more indirect understanding was also reached with Martínez Barrio in Seville. Ibid., 166.
4. Though in Badajoz province Portela was able to make a deal with the Socialists, as J. S. Vidarte explains in *Todos fuimos culpables* (Barcelona, 1977), 1:38–41.
5. According to J. Chapaprieta, *La paz fue posible* (Barcelona, 1981), 390–96.
6. O. Ruiz Manjón, *El Partido Republicano Radical 1908–1936* (Madrid, 1976), 559–72; N. Townson, *The Crisis of Democracy in Spain: Centrist Politics under the Second Republic, 1931–1936* (Brighton, 2000), 339–43.
7. Cf. A. Alcalá Galve, *Alcalá-Zamora y la agonía de la República* (Seville, 2002), 618.
8. R. A. H. Robinson, *The Origins of Franco's Spain: The Right, the Republic, and Revolution, 1931–1936* (Pittsburgh, 1970), 243–44.
9. *JAP*, 14 February 1936, cited in S. Lowe, "The Juventud de Acción Popular and the 'Failure' of 'Fascism' in Spain, 1932–1936" (M.A. thesis, University of Sheffield, 2000), 75.
10. *El Debate*, 31 January 1936; reprinted in R. de la Cierva, ed., *Media nación no se resigna a morir: Los documentos perdidos del Frente Popular* (Madrid, 2002), 104–19. See the discussion in M. Álvarez Tardío, *Anticlericalismo y libertad de conciencia: Política y religión en la Segunda República española (1931–1936)* (Madrid, 2002), 346–48.
11. The best description of the campaign of the right is found in Robinson, *The Origins of Franco's Spain*, 241–47.
12. *La Publicidad* (Granada), 23 January 1936, in M. Pertíñez Díaz, *Granada 1936: Elecciones a Cortes* (Granada, 1987), 46.
13. The only study of the latter is in Pertíñez Díaz, ibid., limited primarily to citations of mutually hostile partisan local newspapers.
14. Javier Tusell has found that, of the major historical accounts, the one nearest the correct figures was the highly rightist *Historia de la Cruzada española* (Madrid, 1940), edited by Joaquín Arrarás. Estimates by various writers are

given in J. Tusell Gómez et al., *Las elecciones del Frente Popular en España* (Madrid, 1971), 2:15.

15. This investigation is the nearest to a definitive study that we shall probably ever have and computes totals for each district in terms of the highest number of votes for the leading candidate on each list (presumably the absolute total number of voters voting that particular list in that district), with some correction when one ticket gained both the majority and the minority seats in a given district.

16. R. Salas Larrazábal, *Los datos exactos de la Guerra Civil* (Madrid, 1980), 42, 256–57.

17. J. J. Linz and J. de Miguel, "Hacia un análisis regional de las elecciones de 1936 en España," *Revista Española de la Opinión Pública*, no. 48 (April–June 1977), 27–67.

18. Following the breakdown in ibid.

19. Ruiz Manjón, *El Partido Republican Radical*, 572–88.

20. J. M. Macarro Vera, *Socialismo, República y revolución en Andalucía (1931–1936)* (Seville, 2000), 400–01.

21. In Badajoz, where in 1933 the Socialists had drawn 139,000 votes compared with 8,000 for Azaña's party, the left Republicans had been given four of ten places on the Popular Front ticket in order to deny representation to the besteiristas, according to P. Preston, *The Coming of the Spanish Civil War* (London, 1978), 148. A. Shubert, in "A Reinterpretation," in M. S. Alexander and H. Graham, eds., *The French and Spanish Popular Fronts: Comparative Perspectives* (Cambridge, Mass., 1989), 221, states that in Asturias "each candidate given the Republicans represented 8,552 votes, while each Socialist place represented 12,775."

22. The main differences after the start of the Civil War would be found in New Castile and in Galicia, both of which reversed identities. New Castile had mostly voted for the right but was held in the Republican zone by the pull of Madrid and its military strength, while Galicia, which returned more Popular Front candidates than any other region, was won by the insurgents. The popular vote in Galicia was in fact distinctly more triangulated than in most regions, and the outcome was therefore heavily influenced by the alliance system, so that the actual Popular Front plurality there was considerably smaller than the number of deputies elected made it seem.

23. J. M. Gil Robles, *No fue posible la paz* (Barcelona, 1968), 491–92.

24. According to Portela, *Memorias*, 174.

25. Portela's version is in ibid., 175–82; that of Gil Robles in *No fue posible*, 492–97.

26. Franco's version is presented in J. Arrarás, ed., *Historia de la Segunda República española* (Madrid, 1956–1963), 4:50–51.

27. Portela Valladares, *Memorias*, 182–84.

28. Ibid., 184–85.

29. Arrarás, *Segunda República*, 4:57–58.

30. Portela Valladares, *Memorias*, 186–87.

31. Ibid., 188–90. A different perspective is found in Vidarte, *Todos fuimos culpables,* 1:40–50.

32. He adds somewhat cryptically, after narrating Franco's offer to bring in the elite units: "In this [Franco] was correct. The most recent reports reaching the ministry only provided abundant confirmation of those received earlier," presumably referring to the expansion of disorder. Portela Valladares, *Memorias,* 192.

33. As might be expected, there is some variance between the lengthy version of Portela, ibid., 192–96, and the terser account of Alcalá Zamora, *Memorias* (Barcelona, 1977), 347–48, who called this brief section of his narrative "The Resignation-Flight of Portela." Alcalá Zamora claimed that until the last minute Portela was convinced that his centrist electoral maneuver would succeed, but that his nerves totally collapsed on the evening of the sixteenth. He contended that Portela was most concerned about leftist riots the next day, became increasingly alarmed over military pressures on the eighteenth, and was finally panicked by more leftist disorders into immediate resignation on the nineteenth.

34. Alcalá Zamora has been quoted as claiming a month later in private conversation that Portela "failed me in everything; he became terrified and, in his desertion, in spite of my efforts, allowed the revolutionary front to carry off undeservedly sixty seats with their postelectoral abuses." J. Tusell and J. Calvo, *Giménez Fernández, precursor de la democracia española* (Seville, 1990), 201.

CHAPTER 8. THE LEFT RETURNS TO POWER

1. M. Azaña, *Obras completas* (Mexico City, 1965–1968), 4:564. Concerning Azaña's virtual fear of victory and of heading a new government, see Marichal's introduction to vol. 3, pp. xxvii–xxix.

2. Azaña noted that the tone of the speech "had been agreed upon in the Council to calm the disordered surge of the Popular Front and urge calm for everyone." Ibid., 4:566.

3. *El Sol,* 21 February 1936.

4. Cf. the remarks of Portela Valladares in his *Memorias* (Madrid, 1988), 197–98.

5. *El Socialista* announced on 18 February that some Popular Front groups had already managed to open a number of prisons the day before, and similar announcements were made in several other leftist newspapers.

6. *El Sol,* 26 February 1936.

7. See J. M. Macarro Vera, *Socialismo, República y revolución en Andalucía (1931–1936)* (Seville, 2000), 408–09.

8. Catalonia under the Popular Front is treated in R. Vinyes, *La Catalunya internacional: El frontpopulisme en l'exemple català* (Barcelona, 1983).

9. It was typical of the distance between leaders of left and right that Azaña could record in his diary that he had personally met Giménez Fernández for the first time on 20 February, adding that the latter "assures me that nothing

separates him from me but religious policy. I have never heard him speak or read anything of his. I have no idea if he is any good. . . . He seems to me a utopian conservative, fit only for speeches at the floral games." When Giménez Fernández complained to him of violent assaults on CEDA centers and newspapers, Azaña as usual merely shrugged off any violence by the left, telling him: "'you must understand,' I say to him laughing, 'that the right-wing of the Republic is me, while you are simply wayward apprentices.'" *Obras completas*, 4:570, 572. Azaña would soon learn to stop laughing.

10. *El Debate*, 6 March 1936; J. M. Gil Robles, *No fue posible la paz* (Barcelona, 1968), 575.
11. Gil Robles, *No fue posible*, 576.
12. Quoted from the Giménez Fernández archive in Macarro Vera, *Socialismo, República y revolución*, 441.
13. Ibid., 414. See also M. Pertíñez Díaz, *Granada 1936: Elecciones a Cortes* (Granada, 1987), 102–06; and the lurid propaganda piece by A. Gollonet and J. Morales, *Rojo y azul en Granada* (Granada, 1937).
14. Macarro Vera, *Socialismo, República y revolución*, 415.
15. Many but far from all of these incidents can be reconstructed from the partially censored press. Lengthy narratives may be found in J. Pla, *Historia de la Segunda República española* (Barcelona, 1940), vol. 4; J. Arrarás, *Historia de la Segunda República española* (Madrid, 1968), vol. 4; and F. Rivas, *El Frente Popular* (Madrid, 1976).
16. F. de A. de la Vega Gonzalo, *Aniquilar la Falange: Cronología persecutoria del Nacionalsindicalismo* (Oviedo, n. d.), 162–70.
17. D. Jato, *La rebelión de los estudiantes* (Madrid, 1967), 285–89, narrates these incidents from the Falangist viewpoint. J. A. Ansaldo, *¿Para qué . . . ?* (Buenos Aires, 1953), 119, recounts flying the Falangist gunmen to Biarritz.
18. Perhaps the only historian of the Republic to place this in objective perspective is L. Romero, *Por qué y cómo mataron a Calvo Sotelo* (Barcelona, 1982), 40–42.
19. According to Rivas, *El Frente Popular*, 122.
20. On Falange during the final months of the Republic, see my *Fascism in Spain, 1923–1977* (Madison, 1999), 185–208.
21. Quoted in C. Rivas Cherif, *Retrato de un desconocido: Vida de Manuel Azaña* (Barcelona, 1980), 666–67.
22. As Luis Romero says of the many leftists committing violent acts: "The police never arrested them." *Historia 16*, 9:100 (August 1984), 55.
23. L. Romero, *Por qué y cómo*, 56–58.
24. Ibid., 59; though Azaña himself derived no personal satisfaction from the anticlerical outbursts. The most spectacular case of arson in March, aside from the riots in Granada, occurred in the town of Yecla, where fourteen churches and other religious buildings were torched in one day. The large-scale arson and disorder provoked the temporary flight of part of the local population, but prompted the Communist *Mundo Obrero* to inquire rhetorically on 21 March how many churches and other religious buildings there

were to be burnt in all Spain, if so many could be torched in one comparatively small town.

25. Quoted in Rivas Cherif, *Retrato*, 672.

26. E. E. Malefakis, *Agrarian Reform and Peasant Revolution in Spain* (New
Haven, 1970), 392.

27. C. Sánchez Albornoz, *De mi anecdotario político* (Buenos Aires, 1972), 116.

28. *Mundo Obrero*, 2 March 36.

29. Rivas, *El Frente Popular*, 149-51.

30. Quoted in Arrarás, *Segunda República*, 4:87-88.

31. A. Cacho Zabalza, *La Unión Militar Española* (Alicante, 1940), is not an
entirely reliable account.

32. J. S. Vidarte, *Todos fuimos culpables* (Barcelona, 1977), 1:50-51. On the small
leftist minority in the officer corps, see the first part of the memoirs of
A. Cordón, *Trayectorias* (Barcelona, 1977).

33. Of the eight generals attending, only two held active commands and five
were retired. Two monarchist colonels (Ángel Galarza and José Enrique
Varela) were also present.

34. See F. Olaya Morales, *La conspiración contra la República* (Barcelona, 1979),
314-23; and D. Sueiro, "Sublevación contra la República," pt. 2, *Historia 16*,
8:90 (October 1983), 21-32.

35. On Basque Socialists in this phase, see R. Miralles, *El socialismo vasco durante
la II República* (Bilbao, 1988); and his article "La crisis del movimiento socialista en el País Vasco, 1935-1936," *Estudios de Historia Social*, 3-4 (1987),
275-87.

36. ECCI Directive of 21 February 1936. Rossiiskaya Akademiya Nauk, *Komin-
tern i grazhdanskaya voina v Ispanii* (Moscow, 2001), 104-07. Cf. the British
Intelligence decrypt quoted by G. Roberts in C. Leitz and D. J. Dunthorn,
Spain in an International Context, 1936-1959 (New York, 1999), 102 n. 42.

37. A. Elorza and M. Bizcarrondo, *Queridos camaradas: La Internacional Comunista y España 1919-1939* (Barcelona, 1999), 267-68.

38. Ibid., 269-70.

39. Ibid., 279.

40. *El Socialista*, 12 February 1936.

41. This was the front-page demand of *Mundo Obrero*, 7 March 1936.

42. *Claridad*, 11 February 1936. On Araquistain, see M. Bizcarrondo, *Araquistain
y la crisis socialista en la II República: Leviatán (1934-1936)* (Madrid, 1975);
and the anthology edited by P. Preston, *Leviatán* (Madrid, 1976); as well as
S. Juliá, *La izquierda del PSOE 1935-1936* (Madrid, 1977); and A. de Blas
Guerrero, *El socialismo radical en la II República* (Madrid, 1978).

43. Elorza and Bizcarrondo, *Queridos camaradas*, 272-77. For the background of
Carrillo and of the JS, see R. Viñas, *La formación de las Juventudes Socialistas
Unificadas (1934-1936)* (Madrid, 1978); and M. E. Yagüe, *Santiago Carrillo*
(Madrid, 1978).

44. According to the veteran PCE leader Fernando Claudín, *Santiago Carrillo
(Crónica de un secretario general)* (Barcelona, 1983), 31-39, Manuilsky ex-

plained the need for the Spanish party to proceed with the hammer and sickle in one hand and the cross in the other.

45. This lengthy document was widely publicized and appeared not merely in *Mundo Obrero* but also, at least in part, in other newspapers.

46. *Claridad,* 25 January 1936.

47. G. Mario de Coca, *Anti-Caballero: Crítica marxista de la bolchevización del Partido Socialista* (Madrid, 1936), 207, 211.

48. Viñas, *Formación de las Juventudes Socialistas Unificadas.* The memoir by the former Socialist Youth activist Angel Merino Galán, *Mi guerra empezó antes* (Madrid, 1976), 73–99, emphasizes that the unification was carried out exclusively by the top leadership without consulting the lower echelons.

49. *Solidaridad Obrera,* 15 April 1936.

50. Ibid., 24 April 1936.

51. Many of these incidents were not recorded in the *Diario de las Sesiones,* though they were sometimes picked up by the press.

52. *Mundo Obrero* presented its list on 19 February.

53. C. Seco Serrano in L. Pericot García, ed., *Historia de España* (Barcelona, 1968), 6:158.

54. S. de Madariaga, *España* (Buenos Aires, 1964), 359–60.

55. Macarro Vera, *Socialismo, República y revolución,* 415.

56. See P. Preston, *The Coming of the Spanish Civil War* (London, 1978), 175.

57. The most pertinent treatment is that of Pertíñez Díaz, *Granada 1936,* 106–22.

58. The right certainly had more money to try to corrupt the electoral process in several areas than did the left, but, with the exception of Granada, the principal interference probably came from the machinations of the Ministry of the Interior, favoring the center, though often without success.

59. See Prieto's prologue to L. Solano Palacio, *Vísperas de la guerra de España* (Mexico City, n. d.), 6–7.

60. J. Tusell Gómez et al., *Las elecciones del Frente Popular en España* (Madrid, 1971), 2:190.

61. N. Alcalá Zamora, *Memorias* (Barcelona, 1977), 351.

CHAPTER 9. THE LEFT CONSOLIDATES POWER

1. S. Juliá, *Manuel Azaña, una biografía política* (Madrid, 1990), 418.

2. *Boletín del Ministerio de Trabajo,* in P. Preston, *The Coming of the Spanish Civil War* (London, 1978), 178.

3. E. E. Malefakis, *Agrarian Reform and Peasant Revolution in Spain* (New Haven, 1970), 367–68.

4. Cited in M. Cabrera, *La patronal ante la II República* (Madrid, 1983), 293.

5. Malefakis, *Agrarian Reform,* 369.

6. J. M. Macarro Vera, *Socialismo, República y revolución en Andalucía (1931–1936)* (Seville, 2000), 428.

7. Ibid., 373.

8. *El Sol,* 23 June 1936.

9. For a good brief treatment of the economic policy of the last Republican government, see J. M. Macarro Vera, "Social and Economic Policies of the Spanish Left in Theory and Practice," in M. S. Alexander and H. Graham, eds., *The French and Spanish Popular Fronts* (Cambridge, 1989), 171–84.

10. On restoration of the jurados mixtos and the problem of labor costs, see J. Montero, *Los Tribunales de Trabajo (1908–1938): Jurisdicciones especiales y movimiento obrero* (Valencia, 1976), 193–98, which is very critical of the form in which they were reestablished.

11. M. Perez Galán, *La enseñanza en la Segunda República española* (Madrid, 1975), 309–22; M. De Puelles Benítez, *Educación e ideología en la España contemporánea (1767–1975)* (Barcelona, 1980), 345–47.

12. S. de Madariaga, *España* (Buenos Aires, 1964), 409.

13. Ibid., 452–53.

14. One province where landowners became aggressive was Guadalajara. See A. R. Díez Torres, "Guadalajara 1936: La primera crisis del caciquismo," *Estudios de Historia Social*, 3–4 (1987), 289–305.

15. Most of this was described in the press. The lengthiest accounts are in F. Rivas, *El Frente Popular* (Madrid, 1976), 172–90; and in I. Gibson, *La noche en que mataron a Calvo Sotelo* (Madrid, 1982), 250–53. Madrid police authorities endeavored to behave responsibly, arresting numerous workers as suspects in firing on the procession, and even briefly detaining for interrogation the Assault Guard lieutenant and militant Socialist José Castillo, who was aggressive in repressing the demonstration, shooting point-blank and seriously wounding one of its participants.

16. On the afternoon of 16 April Azaña remarked angrily to the Socialist Vidarte, "With your jeering at the Civil Guard, as you did on the fourteenth, you Socialists turn them against the Republic." J. S. Vidarte, *Todos fuimos culpables* (Barcelona, 1977), 1:90–91.

17. Ibid., 103.

18. L. Romero, *Por qué y cómo mataron a Calvo Sotelo* (Barcelona, 1982), 87.

19. A. Ramos Oliveira, *Historia de España* (Mexico City, 1952), 3:244.

20. N. Alcalá Zamora, *Memorias* (Barcelona, 1977), 353.

21. According to his letters to his brother-in-law, Cipriano de Rivas Cherif, quoted in the latter's *Retrato de un desconocido* (Barcelona, 1980), 667–72.

22. Alcalá Zamora, *Memorias*, 352.

23. Ibid., 357.

24. Ibid.

25. Ibid., 358.

26. Ibid., 359.

27. A. Alcalá Galve, *Alcalá-Zamora y la agonía de la República* (Seville, 2002), 642.

28. J. Chapaprieta, *La paz fue posible* (Barcelona, 1971), 407–12.

29. Alcalá Zamora, *Memorias*, 359–60.

30. Juliá, *Manuel Azaña*, 471.

31. Alcalá Galve, *Alcalá-Zamora*, 628–31.

32. J. M. García Escudero, *Historia política de las dos Españas* (Madrid, 1976), 3:1065.

33. Chapaprieta, *La paz fue possible*, 414, makes the disdainful observation that "Azaña spoke of economic problems with his customary ignorance of them." See the critique by Juan Velarde Fuertes, "Azaña, o haciendo la República sin conocer la economía," in F. Morán and Velarde Fuertes, *Manuel Azaña* (Barcelona, 2003), 121–210.

34. The fullest account of the constitutional problems involved and of the session of 3 April is found in J. T. Villarroya, *La destitución de Alcalá Zamora* (Valencia, 1988), 85–106.

35. Azaña to Rivas Cherif, in *Retrato*, 676.

36. Chapaprieta, *La paz fue posible*, 406–11.

37. Alcalá Galve, *Alcalá-Zamora*, 663.

38. Madariaga, *España*, 454. Vidarte, *Todos fuimos culpables*, 1:75, quotes Julián Besteiro as having told the Socialist parliamentary delegation: "It seems to me that we are the ones least entitled to say that the CEDA Cortes was not properly dissolved, since in meetings, in the press, and on every hand we never stopped asking for that very thing."

39. M. Tuñón de Lara et al., *Historia de España* (Valladolid, 1999), 588.

40. J. Tusell, *Historia de España en el siglo XX* (Madrid, 1998), 224.

41. Alcalá Zamora, *Memorias*, 360–73.

42. Ibid., 372.

43. J. M. Gil Robles, *No fue posible la paz* (Barcelona, 1968), 559–60.

44. Macarro Vera, *Socialismo, República y revolución*, 450.

45. This episode has been explained in different ways by Franco's brother-in-law and go-between, Ramón Serrano Suñer, in his *Memorias* (Barcelona, 1977), 56–58; J. Gutiérrez Ravé, *Gil Robles, caudillo frustrado* (Madrid, 1967), 165; and Gil Robles, *No fue posible*, 563–67.

46. The organized armed force of Madrid Socialists was known as "La Motorizada" from their habit of traveling about by car, bus, or truck. Its membership was largely drawn from the UGT syndicate of Artes Blancas (composed especially of bakers) and also from some members of the JSU. Organized around the first of March, its members seem to have been as much beholden to Prieto as to Largo Caballero, indicating how simplistic it is to attribute all direct activism to caballeristas.

   Communists in the Madrid area had organized their own Milicias Antifascistas Obreras y Campesinas (Worker-Peasant Antifascist Militias; MAOC), which, though small, was more overtly paramilitary and received some weekend instructions from officers of the UMRA. Cf. E. Líster, *Memorias de un luchador* (Madrid, 1977), 67.

47. R. García, *Yo he sido marxista* (Madrid, 1953), 115, is an account by the sometime Socialist daughter of one of the principal victims.

48. I. Prieto, *Cartas a un escultor* (Buenos Aires, 1961), 94.

49. J. Pla, *Historia de la Segunda República española* (Barcelona, 1940), 4:437–38. Prieto subsequently considered this one of the most important speeches of

his career, having it reprinted twice during the Civil War and citing it numerous times in later writings. But its message was vehemently rejected by *Claridad* on 4 May, which declared that the most fundamental need was for greater intensification of the class struggle. The existing disorder must continue until eventually it led to the revolutionary seizure of power.

50. Romero, *Por qué y cómo*, 100.
51. J. A. Primo de Rivera, *Obras completas* (Madrid, 1952), 919–23.
52. "The pallor of Azaña's face was cadaverous, and his nervousness impressed us all. . . . In spite of his extraordinary facility of speech, he stumbled several times in repeating the brief oath of loyalty to the Republic." *No fue posible*, 605.
53. See Marichal's introduction to vol. 3 of Azaña's *Obras completas* (Mexico City, 1965–1968), xxxi–xxxii.
54. E. g., Vidarte, *Todos fuimos culpables*, 1:74–80; J. Zugazagoitia, *Guerra y vicisitudes de los españoles* (Paris, 1968), 1:20; and even F. Largo Caballero, *Mis recuerdos* (Mexico City, 1954), 155.
55. C. Sánchez Albornoz, *De mi anecdotario* (Buenos Aires, 1972), 127.
56. Though Azaña has left no documentation on this point, his brother-in-law and confidant Cipriano de Rivas Cherif asserts that he seriously backed the Prieto option. *Retrato*, 328.
57. Though this proposal was scarcely plausible, in a letter to the author of 30 October 1959 Prieto expressed nostalgic regret that he had not made a stronger effort to reach an understanding with the more broad-minded elements far to the right of the Socialists.
58. Preston, *Coming of the Spanish Civil War*, 178.
59. Ibid.
60. Largo Caballero, *Mis recuerdos*, 145.
61. According to José Larraz, the emissary. *ABC*, 16 June 1965.
62. Vidarte, *Todos fuimos culpables*, 1:117–26; I. Prieto, *Convulsiones de España* (Mexico City, 1967), 1:164 and 3:135–36; A. del Rosal, *Historia de la U. G. T. de España 1901–1939* (Barcelona, 1977), 1:479.
63. Azaña, *Obras completas*, 4:570–71.
64. D. Marínez Barrio, *Memorias* (Barcelona, 1983), 329. See also J. Carabias, *Azaña: Los que le llamábamos don Manuel* (Barcelona, 1980), 230–33.
65. Rivas Cherif, *Retrato*, 328–29.
66. See the observations of the financially austere Alcalá Zamora, in his *Memorias* (Barcelona, 1977), 378.

CHAPTER 10. BREAKING DOWN

1. The left Republican Mariano Ansó would write years later that Casares' stance declaring himself "in a state of war against part of the national polity" was something "totally unprecedented in a leader of government." *Yo fui ministro de Negrín* (Barcelona, 1976), 118. In the same vein see F. Gordón Ordás, *Mi política en España* (Mexico City, 1962), 2:526.
2. Quoted by Carlos Seco Serrano in his prologue to J. Tusell Gómez et al., *Las elecciones del Frente Popular en España* (Madrid, 1971), 1:xvii–xviii.

3. J. M. Gil Robles, *No fue posible la paz* (Barcelona, 1968), 618–19; J. Arrarás, *Historia de la Segunda República española* (Madrid, 1956–1963), 4:275; J. S. Vidarte, *Todos fuimos culpables* (Barcelona, 1977), 1:135–36; and J. Avilés Farré, *La izquierda burguesa en la II República* (Madrid, 1985), 305.

4. R. A. H. Robinson, *The Origins of Franco's Spain* (London, 1970), 226–27. This policy was consummated by fiat after the Civil War began, all Catholic schools being taken over by a decree of 28 July.

5. E. E. Malefakis, *Agrarian Reform and Peasant Revolution in Spain* (New Haven, 1970), 374.

6. Cf. A. Balcells, *Crisis económica y agitación social en Cataluña de 1930 a 1936* (Esplugues de Llobregat, 1971), 233–34.

7. Again, see the discussion by J. M. Macarro Vera, "Social and Economic Policies of the Spanish Left in Theory and in Practice," in M. S. Alexander and H. Graham, eds., *The French and Spanish Popular Fronts* (Cambridge, 1989), 171–84.

8. At the end of 1935 various Catholic labor groups had come together in a Frente Nacional Unido de Trabajo (United National Labor Front), claiming 276,389 members, at that moment nearly 15 percent of organized labor in Spain. In June 1936 their Madrid headquarters was closed by the government because of alleged "provocations."

9. J. M. Macarro Vera, *Socialismo, República y revolución en Andalucía (1931–1936)* (Seville, 2000), 426.

10. *El Sol,* 26 May 1936.

11. Macarro Vera, *Socialismo, República y revolución,* 426–27.

12. *Información,* 14 May 1936, in M. Cabrera, *La patronal ante la II República* (Madrid, 1983), 303–04.

13. M. Cabrera, "Las organizaciones patronales ante la II República," *Arbor* (1981), 168, cited in Macarro Vera, *Socialismo, República y revolución,* 427.

14. F. Sanchez Perez, "La huelga de la construcción en Madrid (junio–julio, 1936)," *Historia 16,* 14:154 (February 1989), 21–26.

15. Macarro Vera, *Socialismo, República y revolución,* 424–25.

16. Malefakis, *Agrarian Reform,* 372.

17. The best account of these problems is found in Macarro Vera, *Socialismo, República y revolución,* 431–35.

18. Cabrera, *La patronal,* 291.

19. *Hoy* (Badajoz), 27 May 1936, in F. Rosique Navarro, *La reforma agraria en Badajoz durante la IIa República* (Badajoz, 1988), 304.

20. M. Pérez Yruela, *La conflictividad campesina en la provincia de Córdoba 1931–1936* (Madrid, 1979), 204.

21. According to the figures corrected by L. Garrido and F. Sigler, in Andalusia about 100,000 hectares had been expropriated for 12,000 new proprietors, or about 8 hectares each. These ranged from an average of 16 in Cádiz to 12 in Jaén to 4 in Huelva, while in Extremadura they averaged only 2.5 hectares per yuntero. Macarro Vera, *Socialismo, República y revolución,* 430.

22. Malefakis, *Agrarian Reform,* 371–72.

23. Macarro Vera, *Socialismo, República y revolución*, 426.
24. As in the terms of 26 June established by the jurado mixto of Cordoba, studied in M. Pérez Yruela, *La conflictividad campesina en la provincia de Córdoba* (Madrid, 1979), 412–29.
25. Malefakis, *Agrarian Reform*, 384.
26. Ibid., 383. B. Diaz de Entresotos, *Seis meses de anarquía en Extremadura* (Cáceres, 1937), is a melodramatic account published after the Civil War began, but the reality was serious enough.
27. M. Tuñón de Lara, *Tres claves de la Segunda República* (Madrid, 1985), 194–95.
28. Almost all the forms of radical agrarian activity attending the Russian revolution of 1905, as detailed by T. Shanin, *Russia, 1905–07: Revolution as a Moment of Truth* (New Haven, 1986), 84–90, found expression in southern Spain during the spring and early summer of 1936. This is not an indication that conditions were generally equivalent in the two countries as a whole, but there were some clear parallels between the earlier situation in Russia and the agrarian unrest in the south.
29. Macarro Vera, *Socialismo, República y revolución*, 435–36.
30. Ibid., 442–43.
31. A. Lazo, *Retrato del fascismo rural en Sevilla* (Seville, 1998), 25–34, 98–107.
32. R. Quirosa-Cheyrouze, *Católicos, monárquicos y fascistas en Almería durante la Segunda República* (Almería, 1998), 66–74, cited in Macarro Vera, *Socialismo, República y revolución*, 449.
33. Malefakis, *Agrarian Reform*, 382.
34. Macarro Vera, "Social and Economic Policies of the Spanish Left," 184.
35. See M. Requena Gallego, *Los sucesos de Yeste* (Albacete, 1983); and R. M. Sepúlveda Losa, "La primavera conflictiva de 1936 en Albacete," *Pasado y memoria*, 2 (2003), 221–40. F. Rivas, *El Frente Popular* (Madrid, 1976), 275–80, gives the version of the Guardia Civil.
36. F. Manuel, *The Politics of Modern Spain* (New York, 1938), 168.
37. J. Arrarás, *Historia de la Segunda República española* (Madrid, 1956–63), 4:280.
38. H. de la Torre Gómez, *A relação peninsular na antecâmara da guerra civil de Espanha (1931–1939)* (Lisbon, 1998), 85–101; C. Oliveira, *Portugal y la Segunda República española 1931–1936* (Madrid, 1986), 169–87; A. P. Vicente, "O cerco à embaixada da República Española em Lisboa (Maio a Outubro de 1936)," in F. Rosas, ed., *Portugal e a Guerra Civil de Espanha* (Lisbon, 1998), 3–105; and C. Sánchez Albornoz, *Mi testamento histórico-político* (Barcelona, 1975), 195–99; idem, *Anecdotario político* (Barcelona, 1976), 196–245.
39. De la Torre Gómez, *A relação peninsular*, 93–94.
40. D. Little, "Red Scare, 1936: Anti-Bolshevism and the Origins of British Non-Intervention in the Spanish Civil War," *Journal of Contemporary History*, 23 (1988), 291–311; and E. Moradiellos, "The Origins of British Non-Intervention in the Spanish Civil War: Anglo-Spanish Relations in Early 1936," *European History Quarterly*, 21 (1991), 339–64.
41. See A. Ossorio y Gallardo, *Vida y sacrificio de Companys* (Buenos Aires, 1943),

148–55; M. D. Ivern i Salvà, *Ezquerra Republicana de Catalunya (1931–1936)* (Montserrat, 1988), 2:177–210; J. Pabón, *Cambó* (Barcelona, 1969), 2:486–89; and M. García Venero, *Historia del nacionalismo catalán* (Madrid, 1967), 2:417–19.

42. These and other data later in this section are taken from J. Getman Eraso, "Rethinking the Revolution: Utopia and Pragmatism in Catalan Anarchosyndicalism, 1930–1936" (Ph.D. diss., University of Wisconsin–Madison, 2001), chap. 8, which treats the five months February–July 1936. In the chapter "L'oasi català: Un miratge" of his *La Catalunya internacional* (Barcelona, 1983), 303–35, Ricard Vinyes i Ribes similarly dissents from the metaphor, as has E. Ucelay da Cal, *La catalunya populista: Imatge, cultura i política en l'etapa republicana (1931–1939)* (Barcelona, 1982), 271–73.

43. *Caspe: Un estastuto de autonomía* (Zaragoza, 1977); L. Germán Zubero, *Aragón en la II República* (Zaragoza, 1984), 189–206; and R. Sainz de Varanda, "La autonomía de Aragón en el período del Frente Popular," in M. Tuñón de Lara, ed., *La crisis del Estado español* (Madrid, 1978), 517–33.

44. For a broad treatment of the autonomy process under the Republic, see J. Beramendi and R. Maíz, eds., *Los nacionalismos en la España de la II República* (Madrid, 1991); and, more briefly, J. Beramendi, "Nacionalismos, regionalismos y autonomía en la Segunda República," *Pasado y memoria*, 2 (2002), 53–82.

45. X. Vilas Nogueira, *O Estatuto Galego* (Pontevedra, 1975); A. Bozzo, *Los partidos políticos y la autonomía de Galicia* (Madrid, 1976); X. Castro, *O galeguismo na encrucillada republicana* (Orense, 1985); B. Maíz, *Galicia na IIa República e baixo o franquismo* (Vigo, 1987); A. Hernández Lafuente, *Autonomía e integración en la Segunda República* (Madrid, 1980), 386–90.

CHAPTER 11. COMPETING UTOPIAS

1. *El Congreso confederal de Zaragoza (mayo, 1936)* (Toulouse, 1955). CNT figures for 1 May 1936 showed little more than 30 percent of Catalan industrial workers in their syndicates, compared with more than 60 percent at the end of 1931. A. Balcells, *Crisis económica y agitación social en Cataluña de 1930 a 1936* (Esplugues de Llobregat, 1971), 198.

2. *Solidaridad Obrera*, 11 May 1936. See the commentary in J. Brademas, *Anarcosindicalismo y revolución en España (1930–1937)* (Esplugues de Llobregat, 1974), 168–70.

3. *Solidaridad Obrera*, 13 May 1936.

4. *La Vanguardia*, 5 June 1936, in J. Getman Eraso, "Rethinking the Revolution: Utopia and Pragmatism in Catalan Anarchosyndicalism, 1930–1936" (Ph.D. diss., University of Wisconsin–Madison, 2001), 311. The latter is the key study of the Catalan CNT on the eve of the Civil War.

5. S. Juliá, *La izquierda del PSOE (1935–1936)* (Madrid, 1977), 105–07.

6. J. M. Macarro Vera, *Socialismo, República y revolución en Andalucía 1931–1936* (Seville, 2000), 409, 455–56.

7. *New York Times*, 26 June 1936.

8. *El Socialista*, 15 July 1936. I am grateful to an unpublished study by Juan Linz for additional data on the Socialist elections.

9. *El Socialista*, 1 July 1936; and J. S. Vidarte, *Todos fuimos culpables* (Barcelona, 1977), 1:195–208. Vidarte maintains that he also invalidated some of the votes from his native Badajoz for the same reasons.

10. Linz MS, 148–49.

11. *Claridad*, 10 July 1936.

12. Ibid., 13 July 1936.

13. A. Elorza and M. Bizcarrondo, *Queridos camaradas: La Internacional Comunista y España, 1919–1939* (Barcelona, 1999), 280.

14. Ibid., 282.

15. J. Díaz, *Tres años de lucha* (Barcelona, 1978), 1:165.

16. Elorza and Bizcarrondo, *Queridos camaradas*, 282.

17. Ibid., 282–83.

18. J. Díaz, *Tres años*, 165.

19. G. Dimitrov, "The United Front of the Struggle for Peace," *Communist International*, 13:5 (May 1936), 290–93.

20. Elorza and Bizcarrondo, *Queridos camaradas*, 285.

21. M. V. Novikov, *SSSR, Komintern i grazhdanskaya voina v Ispanii 1936–1939 gg.* (Yaroslavl, 1995), 2:76.

22. Elorza and Bizcarrondo, *Queridos camaradas*, 285–86.

23. Ibid., 287.

24. Figures for the earlier dates are from R. Cruz, *El Partido Comunista de España en la II República* (Madrid, 1987), 57, who calculates (p. 60) that by 18 July membership may have reached 83,867, though this is uncertain. B. Bolloten, *The Spanish Civil War: Revolution and Counterrevolution* (Chapel Hill, 1991), 83, cites an article by Manuel Delicado of the party's central committee that appeared in *La Correspondencia Internacional*, 23 July 1939, giving a figure of approximately 40,000 on the eve of the Civil War.

25. A. C. Durgan, *BOC 1930–1936: El Bloque Obrero y Campesino* (Barcelona, 1996), 526.

26. Ibid., 411–16; Y. Riottot, *Joaquín Maurín de l'anarcho-syndicalisme au communisme (1919–1936)* (Paris, 1997), 335–38.

27. Quoted in Durgan, *BOC*, 418.

28. J. L. Martin i Ramos, *Els orígens del PSUC* (Barcelona, 1977); L. V. Ponomariova, *La formació del Partit Socialist Unificat de Catalunya* (Barcelona, 1977); M. Caminal, *Joan Comorera: Catalanisme i socialisme (1913–1936)* (Barcelona, 1984); and R. Alcaraz i González, *La Unió Socialista de Catalunya* (Barcelona, 1987).

29. Durgan, *BOC*, 428–29.

30. Riottot, *Joaquín Maurín*, 216–22; Durgan, *BOC*, 432–44.

31. L. Trotsky, *The Spanish Revolution* (New York, 1972), 207–10, 215–24.

32. Durgan, *BOC*, 435–36.

33. Ibid., 477–79.

34. Ibid., 480–84.
35. See G. Lefranc, *Le mouvement socialiste sous la Troisième République* (Paris, 1963) and *Histoire du Front Populaire* (Paris, 1965); J. Colton, *Léon Blum, Humanist in Politics* (New York, 1967); Colloquium: *Léon Blum, chef de gouvernement* (Paris, 1968); G. Ziebura, *Léon Blum: Theorie und Praxis einer sozialistischen Politik* (Berlin, 1963); I. M. Perrot and A. Kriegel, *Le Socialisme français et le pouvoir* (Paris, 1966); and A. Prost, *La CGT à l'époque du Front Populaire* (Paris, 1964). There is a good brief treatment in I. Wall, "French Socialism and the Popular Front," *Journal of Contemporary History,* 5:3 (1970), 5–20. M. Seidman, *Workers against Work: Labor in Paris and Barcelona during the Popular Fronts* (Berkeley, 1991), presents a penetrating and reliable account of the evolution of labor attitudes and behavior in two major cities.

CHAPTER 12. THE FINAL PHASE

1. C. Sánchez Albornoz, *Anecdotario político* (Barcelona, 1976), 196–97.
2. M. García Venero, *Historia de las Internacionales en España* (Madrid, 1958), 3:106–08. Apparently this document was never published by the PNR, but García Venero testified to having seen the original and had "no doubt of its authenticity."
3. Sánchez Román had never been reluctant to criticize the failings of Azaña's policies when he thought it necessary. At the time when he had become a critic of Azaña's first government in June 1933, Azaña had written: "Sánchez Román is in great fashion among the opposition. Since he possesses greater understanding and ability than almost all the other deputies opposed to the government, each time that he speaks, they listen to him with rapture, since he gives them what they most lack: ideas and arguments." *Diarios 1932–1933* (Barcelona, 1997), 372.
4. J. Aviles Farré, *La izquierda burguesa en la II República* (Madrid, 1985), 306–07; J. M. Gil Robles, *No fue posible la paz* (Barcelona, 1968), 680.
5. Vicente Cárcel Ortí reports:

> According to official data collected by the Ministry of the Interior, supplemented with other data from the diocesan clergy, during the five months of government by the Popular Front before the beginning of the war:
> - Several hundred church buildings were burned, pillaged, or variously attacked;
> - Some were illegally seized by civil authorities and illegally occupied by municipal governments;
> - Dozens of priests were threatened and forced to abandon their parishes, while others were forcibly expelled in a violent manner;
> - A number of rectories were burned and looted, while others were taken over by local authorities;
> - The same thing happened to certain Catholic centers and to numerous religious communities;

- In various towns in a number of provinces religious services either were not permitted or were restricted, with the ringing of church bells, the procession of the viaticum and other practices prohibited;
- A number of cemeteries and tombs were also profaned. . . ;
- Theft of the holy sacrament and the destruction of sacred forms was also frequent;
- Sacrilegious carnivals were conducted as parodies in Badajoz and Málaga;
- Assassination attempts were made against a number of priests;
- Everywhere the authors of these deeds went unpunished.

Historia de la Iglesia en la España contemporánea (siglos XIX y XX) (Madrid, 2002), 163–64.

6. N. Alcalá Zamora, *Memorias* (Barcelona, 1977), 376–78, recalled that he was forced to hand over money twice. Salvador de Madariaga also refers to the highway extortions.

7. J. Zugazagoitia, *Historia de la guerra de España* (Buenos Aires, 1940), 9.

8. E.g., *La Libertad*, 28 June 1936.

9. *Le Petit Journal* (Paris), 2 July 1936, quoted in Gil Robles, *No fue posible*, 681.

10. *Ahora*, 30 June 1936.

11. L. Romero, *Por qué y cómo mataron a Calvo Sotelo* (Barcelona, 1982), 165–66.

12. Cf. C. Vidal, *Checas de Madrid: Las cárceles republicanas al descubierto* (Barcelona, 2003).

13. Mije's remarks in Badajoz on May 18 as quoted in *Claridad*, 19 May 1936.

14. *Mundo Obrero*, 13 June 1936.

15. *Claridad*, 3 July 1936.

16. *Mundo Obrero*, 10 July 1936.

17. *Material de discusión para el Congreso Provincial del Partido Comunista que se celebrará en Madrid durante los días 20, 21 y 22 de junio de 1936* (Madrid, 1936).

18. D. Ibárruri et al., *Guerra y revolución en España, 1936–1939* (Moscow, 1967), 1:66; J. Modesto, *Soy del Quinto Regimiento* (Barcelona, 1978), 63–67.

19. In Seville the city councilmen of Unión Republicana resigned on 10 July because the Socialists and Communists had not supported their candidate for deputy mayor. On the tensions within the Popular Front in Andalusia, see J. M. Macarro Vera, *Socialismo, República y revolución en Andalucía (1931–1936)* (Seville, 2000), 466–67.

CHAPTER 13. THE MILITARY CONSPIRACY

1. The serious historiography is much smaller, but nonetheless detailed. The broadest account is F. Olaya Morales, *La conspiración contra la República* (Barcelona, 1979), though vitiated by being a partisan account from the opposite perspective. The best treatment is still R. de la Cierva, *Historia de la Guerra Civil española*, vol. 1: *Antecedentes* (Madrid, 1969), 735–816. There are briefer accounts in my *Politics and the Military in Modern Spain*

(Stanford, 1967), 314–40, and *The Franco Regime, 1936–1975* (Madison, 1987), 78–100.

2. On the revival of Carlism, see M. Blinkhorn, *Carlism and Crisis in Spain, 1931–1939* (London, 1975), 1–206. A Carlist narrative is found in L. Redondo and J. Zavala, *El Requeté* (Barcelona, 1957), 225–310.

3. P. C. González Cuevas, *Acción Española: Teología política y nacionalismo autoritario en España (1913–1936)* (Madrid, 1998), is the most thorough ideological study; but see R. Morodo, *Orígenes ideológicos del franquismo* (Madrid, 1985).

4. On monarchist politics under the Republic, see J. Gil Pecharromán, *Conservadores subversivos: La derecha autoritaria alfonsina (1913–1936)* (Madrid, 1994); and J. L. Rodríguez Jiménez, *La extrema derecha en España en el siglo XX* (Madrid, 1997), 118–33.

5. Relations with Italy are treated in I. Saz, *Mussolini contra la II República (1931–1936)* (Valencia, 1986).

6. The best general treatment of the politics of the modern military is C. Seco Serrano, *Militarismo y civilismo en la España contemporánea* (Madrid, 1984). See also G. Cardona, *El poder militar en la España contemporánea* (Madrid, 1984).

7. For the early twentieth century, see C. Boyd, *Pretorian Politics in Liberal Spain* (Chapel Hill, 1979).

8. On the feeble Falangist plans for insurrection in 1935, see my *Fascism in Spain, 1923–1977* (Madison, 1999), 170–75.

9. Ibid., 185–208.

10. As mentioned in *Claridad* on 6 April and 10 May 1936, noted in P. Preston, *The Coming of the Spanish Civil War* (London, 1978), 174.

11. It has recently been claimed that Sanjurjo hoped to lead a new military government that would hold a national plebiscite on the issue of monarchy versus republic for Spain, something that signally had not been done in 1931. This is the thesis of E. Sacanell Ruiz de Apodaca, *El general Sanjurjo, héroe y víctima: El militar que pudo evitar la dictadura franquista* (Madrid, 2004), which makes use of the general's surviving papers, but in such a limited and disorganized way that no clear new conclusions can be reached.

12. This document has been published several times. See La Cierva, *Historia*, 769–71.

13. Quoted in J. Arrarás, ed., *Historia de la Cruzada española* (Madrid, 1940), 3:49.

14. Gil Robles has written that the CEDA provided a subsidy "shortly before" the revolt, but that he himself had no contacts with the leading military conspirators. Though this claim sounds disingenuous, it may be technically correct in a narrow sense. Gil Robles did, however, encourage the Carlists and others to cooperate with the military; the instructions he gave to party members were "for everyone to act according to his conscience, without compromising the party; to establish direct contact with the military, not forming independent militias; and, above all, to wait for concrete orders for the beginning of the movement." *No fue posible la paz* (Barcelona, 1968), 730, 798.

15. In June the secretary of the Valencian section, the DRV, allegedly promised Mola 1,250 militia volunteers at the beginning of a revolt and 50,000 after five days. La Cierva, *Historia,* 743–44. In most cases, however, the CEDA and JAP could not convincingly make such promises.

16. Cf. L. Romero, *Por qué y cómo mataron a Calvo Sotelo* (Barcelona, 1982), 238; R. Garriga, *Los validos de Franco* (Barcelona, 1981), 25; and R. Serrano Suñer, *Memorias* (Barcelona, 1977), 52–60. In later years Franco would always emphasize his reluctance to rebel. He observed on 29 June 1965, "I always told my companions, 'As long as there is any hope that the Republican regime can put a halt to the anarchy and does not hand over power to Moscow, one must support the Republic, which was first accepted by the king, then by the monarchist government, and finally by the army.'" F. Franco Salgado-Araujo, *Mis conversaciones privadas con Franco* (Barcelona, 1979), 452. He repeated this position in his limited memoirs: "Our duty must be to see the Republic triumph . . . serving it without hesitation, and if unfortunately it fails, that should not be because of us." F. Franco, *Apuntes personales del Generalísimo sobre la República y la Guerra Civil* (Madrid, 1987), 16, 21–22. Thus hard-core conspirators in Pamplona had come to refer to Franco derisively as "Miss Canary Islands of 1936" for his "coquetry."

17. R. A. Friedlander, "The July 1936 Military Rebellion in Spain: Background and Beginnings" (Ph.D. diss., Northwestern University, 1963), 100–03.

18. For Churchill's dark view of the situation in Spain, which he thought was heading toward Communism, see his *The Gathering Storm* (Boston, 1948), 212–13.

19. For further discussion, see V. Palacio Atard, "El Gobierno ante la conspiración de 1936," in his *Aproximación histórica a la guerra de España* (Madrid, 1970), 133–65.

20. Gil Robles, *No fue posible,* 608.

21. Juan Marichal, in his introduction to vol. 3 of Azaña's *Obras completas* (Mexico City, 1963–1968), xxxii.

22. J. Zugazagoitia, *Historia de la guerra de España* (Buenos Aires, 1940), 5–6; I. Prieto, *Convulsiones de España* (Mexico City, 1967), 1:163, 3:143–44; J. S. Vidarte, *Todos fuimos culpables* (Barcelona, 1977), 1:146–47, 190–92; F. Largo Caballero, *Mis memorias* (Mexico City, 1950), 161–63.

23. Vidarte, *Todos fuimos culpables,* 1:151–52.

24. Ibid., 192.

25. Quoted in F. Ayala Vicente, *La violencia política en la provincia de Cáceres durante la Segunda República* (Brenes, 2003), 157.

26. Ibid., 158.

27. Vidarte, *Todos fuimos culpables,* 1:252–55.

CHAPTER 14. THE ASSASSINATION OF CALVO SOTELO

1. C. Santacana and X. Pujadas, *L'altra olimpiada: Barcelona '36* (Badalona, 1990).

2. All these events were reported in the Madrid press. Summaries may be

found in L. Romero, *Por qué y cómo mataron a Calvo Sotelo* (Barcelona, 1982), 167–70; and F. Rivas, *El Frente Popular* (Madrid, 1976), 350–51.

3. It has usually been assumed that Falangist gunmen shot Castillo, a natural assumption in that the former were responsible for nearly all killings of Socialists in the Madrid area. The most objective study, however, Ian Gibson's *La noche en que mataron a Calvo Sotelo* (Madrid, 1982), uncovered evidence indicating that the deed may have been done by Carlists in revenge for the shooting on 16 April (pp. 204–14).

4. R. Fraser, *Recuérdalo tú y recuérdalo a otros: Historia oral de la guerra civil española* (Barcelona, 1979), 1:133–34.

5. The suspicions of more moderate left Republicans, such as his Galicianist party leader Emilio González López, later fell on Ossorio for his role in this affair. Interview with González López, New York City, 10 June 1958. Three years later, in the attempted Negrinist-Communist takeover of much of the Republican army command, Ossorio would be named political commissar-in-chief of the Republican army.

6. The most detailed reconstruction of these events is Gibson, *La noche*. Many valid details, along with much interpretation and some distortion, are found in *Comisión sobre la ilegitimidad de los poderes actuantes en 18 de julio de 1936* (Barcelona, 1939), app. 1; and *Causa General: La dominación roja en España* (Madrid, 1943), both prepared by special commissions of the Franco regime.

7. At least one Communist militia leader has admitted participating in the organization of the arrest assignments, yet more evidence of the breakdown of police procedure. J. Tagüeña, *Testimonio de dos guerras* (Barcelona, 1978), 72.

8. Ibid., 99–100.

9. Calvo Sotelo's activities in the days leading up to his assassination are carefully detailed in A. Bullón de Mendoza y Gómez de Valugera, *José Calvo Sotelo* (Barcelona, 2004), 661–77. This outstanding study is one of the few major scholarly biographies of a significant figure in contemporary Spanish history that bear comparison with major biographies elsewhere.

10. The only detailed eyewitness account is that of Calvo Sotelo's daughter, Enriqueta, quoted in ibid., 677–81.

11. Ibid., 682–85.

12. Ibid., 691.

13. J. Zugazagoitia, *Guerra y vicisitudes de los españoles* (Barcelona, 1977), 1:28–31.

14. According to the Socialist leaders themselves: J. S. Vidarte, *Todos fuimos culpables* (Barcelona, 1977), 1:213–17; I. Prieto, *Convulsiones de España* (Mexico City, 1967), 1:162.

15. That day the rightist newspapers *Ya* and *La Época* published what little information was available, and were therefore immediately suspended by the authorities. The latter, which had been one of Spain's leading newspapers for nearly a century, would never reappear.

16. J. Avilés Farré, *La izquierda burguesa en la II República* (Madrid, 1985), 311.

17. See the testimony in Bullón de Mendoza, *Calvo Sotelo*, 694–95.

18. Ibid., 695–96; Romero, *Por qué y cómo*, 252.
19. Bullón de Mendoza, *Calvo Sotelo*, 704–05; and Gibson, *La noche*, 198. Cf. P. Moa, *El derrumbe de la Segunda República y la Guerra Civil* (Madrid, 2000), 323.
20. According to Santos Juliá in N. Townson, ed., *Historia virtual de España (1870–2004): ¿Qué hubiera pasado si . . . ?* (Madrid, 2004), 186. Cf. J. Zugazagoitia, *Historia de la guerra de España* (Buenos Aires, 1940), 5.
21. Juliá, in Townson, *Historia virtual*, 196.
22. Quoted in J. Tusell, "La recuperación de la democracia. El último Araquistain (1933–1959). Política y vida de un escritor socialista," his introduction to Araquistain's *Sobre la guerra civil y la emigración* (Madrid, 1983), 11–128.
23. Cf. the discussion in J. M. Macarro Vera, *Socialismo, República y revolución en Andalucía (1931–1936)* (Seville, 2000), 467.
24. A. Elorza and M. Bizcarrondo, *Queridos camaradas: La Internacional Comunista y España, 1919–1939* (Barcelona, 1999), 291–92.
25. M. Ansó, *Yo fui Ministro de Negrín* (Barcelona, 1976), 126, cited in Bullón de Mendoza, *Calvo Sotelo*, 705–06.
26. M. Portela Valladares, *Memorias* (Barcelona, 1988), 223.
27. S. Carrillo, *Memorias* (Barcelona, 1993), 168, quoted in Bullón de Mendoza, *Calvo Sotelo*, 706.
28. Quoted in Melchor Ferrer's unpublished manuscript, "La conspiración militar de 1936 y los carlistas," 28.
29. J. Pérez Salas, *Guerra en España (1936 a 1939)* (Mexico City, 1947), 82–83.
30. B. Félix Maíz, *Alzamiento en España. De un diario de la conspiración* (Pamplona, 1952), 277; F. Franco Salgado-Araujo, *Mi vida junta a Franco* (Barcelona, 1977), 150; P. Preston, *Franco* (London, 1993), 136–38.
31. *ABC*, 14 July 1960, quoted in Bullón de Mendoza, *Calvo Sotelo*, 703.
32. A. Lizarza Iribarren, *Memorias de la conspuiración* (Pamplona, 1969); T. Echevarría, *Cómo se preparó el alzamiento: El General Mola y los carlistas* (Madrid, 1985); the introductory study of Julio Aróstegui in his *Los combatientes carlistas en la guerra civil española* (Madrid, 1989), vol. 1; and the lucid summary in J. C. Peñas Bernaldo de Quirós, *El carlismo, la República y la guerra civil (1936–1937): De la conspiración a la unificación* (Madrid, 1996), 17–43.
33. Vidarte, *Todos fuimos culpables*, 1:255–56; D. Martínez Barrio, *Memorias* (Barcelona, 1983), 358–59.
34. J. Getman Eraso, "Rethinking the Revolution: Utopia and Pragmatism in Catalan Anarchosyndicalism, 1930–1936" (Ph.D. diss., University of Wisconsin–Madison, 2001), 335–40.
35. Zugazagoitia, *Historia de la guerra*, 40.
36. Martínez Barrio, *Hoy* (Mexico City), 20 April, 1940, cited in B. Bolloten, *The Spanish Civil War: Revolution and Counterrevolution* (Chapel Hill, 1991), 40. As Bolloten notes, in his only commentary on this meeting Prieto failed to clarify the position he had taken on that occasion.

　　Of all the major characters in this tragedy, Prieto played the most complex and ambiguous role. During the spring he had largely advocated a constructive and responsible, though extremely leftist, policy, seeking to encourage a stronger, more coherent leftist government, even though his followers often played violent and repressive roles. By early July he had apparently moved to encouraging leftist unity and preparation for armed conflict, which he apparently believed could no longer be avoided. At first he made no effort to palliate the magnicide of Calvo Sotelo, in effect maintaining in the Diputación Permanente that Republican police forces had an equal right to engage in terrorism, and working to thwart the judicial investigation and shelter the murderers, who were his own personal followers.

But by 16 July he was again taking a more nuanced position, trying to encourage discipline and responsibility on the part of the left, for he believed that either anarchy or violent revolution would ruin Spain. Thus he published the following warning in his Bilbao newspaper *El Liberal* on the morning of 17 July, only hours before the revolt began:

> Citizens of a civilized country have a right to tranquility, and the state has the duty to assure that. For some time—why deceive ourselves?—citizens of Spain have been deprived of that right because the state cannot fulfill its duty of guaranteeing that. . . .
>
> In the same way that history can justify peasant revolts, it can approve military insurrections when the one and the other put an end to situations that, for whatever reason, have become incompatible with the political, economic or social progress required by the people.

Prieto, like everyone else, expected a military revolt, and had earlier sought to arm the left, but as soon as the revolt began he tacked toward moderation, supporting the efforts to develop a moderate and effective government response on 18–19 July.

37. Martínez Barrio, *Memorias,* 361–63; M. Azaña, *Obras completas* (Mexico City, 1964–1968), 4:714–15. There is some disagreement between these principal sources on the breadth of the proposed coalition: Azaña says it was to have extended "from the Republican right to the Communists," while Martínez Barrio contradicts himself in this respect in other statements.

38. Martínez Barrio, *Memorias,* 363–64; and A. Alonso Baño, *Homenaje a Diego Martínez Barrio* (Paris, 1978), 67–107.

39. Vidarte, *Todos fuimos culpables,* 1:236–38, 252–53, 280–84, confirms this version according to the reports of government monitors who listened in on the conversations, as did Sánchez Román (who had been in the room with Martínez Barrio at the time) to a third party, cited in J. M. Gil Robles, *No fue posible la paz* (Barcelona, 1968), 791. An edition of *El Pensamiento Navarro* (Pamplona) later that day claimed that Mola had been offered the Ministry of War. Further references may be found in Bolloten, *The Spanish Civil War.* See also J. M. Iribarren, *Con el general Mola* (Madrid, 1945), 102–03; Zugazagoitia, *Historia de la guerra,* 58–65; L. Romero, *Tres días de julio* (Barcelona, 1967), 158, 193; M. García Venero, *El general Fanjul* (Madrid, 1970), 287–90;

F. Largo Caballero, *Mis memorias* (Mexico City, 1950), 156–57; and J. Pérez de Madrigal, *Memorias de un converso* (Madrid, 1943–1951), 7:65–68.

40. It has been claimed that Azaña's former personal military secretary, Lieutenant Colonel Juan Hernández Saravia (who had just been transferred to the War Ministry), authorized the initial release of arms. E. de Mateo Sousa, "La sublevación en Madrid," *Historia 16*, 15:165 (January 1990), 111–16. Better documented is the initiative of Lieutenant Colonel Rodrigo Gil, commander of the Artillery Park in Madrid. See the numerous sources cited in Bolloten, *Spanish Civil War*, 754 n. 31.

41. In an interview with Burnett Bolloten, *Spanish Civil War*, 40.

42. Clara Campoamor, *La Révolution espagnole vue par une républicaine* (Paris, 1937), 2, quoted in R. A. Friedlander, "The July 1936 Military Rebellion in Spain: Background and Beginnings" (Ph.D. diss., Northwestern University, 1963), 181.

43. Zugazagoitia, *Historia de la guerra*, 46; M. Domingo, *España ante el mundo* (Mexico City, 1947), 233.

44. In a letter to Madariaga, first quoted in the prologue to the fourth edition of the latter's *España* (Buenos Aires, 1944), Martínez Barrio wrote that in striving to form the new coalition he felt that "the military rebellion was not our worst enemy. The most serious lay within our own ranks, due to irresolution, disorientation, and fear of heroic decisions." *Memorias*, 361.

45. According to Martínez Barrio, *Hoy*, 27 April 1940. This was confirmed by Sánchez Román to Burnett Bolloten, *The Spanish Civil War*, 756, and, as Bolloten notes, was further corroborated by Largo Caballero, *Mis recuerdos* (Mexico City, 1950), 167. Prieto also confirmed this in a letter to Robert Friedlander, 19 September 1961, in Friedlander, "The July 1936 Military Rebellion," 185. Prieto claimed that even after the resignation of the Martínez Barrio government, he attempted to bring its leaders into close association with the succeeding Giral government, to give the latter greater strength and coherence, but was unable to do so.

46. The term coined by Burnett Bolloten, the third chapter of his *The Spanish Civil War* being titled "The Revolution and the Rise of the Third Republic."

47. The standard Comintern title, first employed with regard to the Mongolian regime of 1924 and used by PCE leaders throughout the Civil War and for many years thereafter. For a discussion of this model as applied to the wartime Republic, see my *The Spanish Civil War, the Soviet Union, and Communism* (New Haven, 2004), 298–306.

48. The term coined for the first year of the Civil War by C. M. Rama, *La crisis española del siglo XX* (Mexico City, 1960).

CONCLUSION

1. As Ortega put it in the "Epílogo para ingleses" of the later editions of *La rebelión de las masas*, "The Englishman or American has every right to his opinion about what has happened and ought to happen in Spain, but that right is offensive if he does not accept a corresponding obligation: that of

being well informed about the reality of the Spanish Civil War, whose first and most important chapter is its origins, the causes that produced it."

2. The most searching discussion of the causes of the breakdown of the Republic is found in the chapter by Juan J. Linz, "From Great Hopes to Civil War: The Breakdown of Democracy in Spain," in Linz and A. Stepan, *The Breakdown of Democratic Regimes: Europe* (Baltimore, 1978), 142–215.

3. See the discussion in J. Tusell and G. García Queipo de Llano, *Alfonso XIII: El rey polémico* (Madrid, 2001), 588–633; and the key works by C. Seco Serrano, *Alfonso XIII y la crisis de la Restauración* (Madrid, 1969), *Estudios sobre el reinado de Alfonso XIII* (Madrid, 1998), and *La España de Alfonso XIII* (Madrid, 2002).

4. The extent to which, for example, the more advanced and stable French Third Republic was endangered in the 1930s is still debated. See P. Bernard and H. Dubief, *The Decline of the Third Republic, 1914–1938* (Cambridge, 1988).

5. D. Peukert, *Die Weimarer Republik: Krisenjahre der klassischen Moderne* (Frankfurt, 1987), 5.

6. In this regard, see the cogent remarks by Edward Malefakis, "La Segunda República española: Algunas observaciones personales en su 50 aniversario," *La IIa República española* (Barcelona, 1983), 97–109.

7. Conversely, it might be argued that the judiciary constituted an element of strength, for the court system remained largely free of overt politicization, in the process drawing criticism from both left and right. It did not discriminate on behalf of those guilty of political crimes of violence either on the left or (as in Weimar Germany) on the right. The pressing concern of the left in 1936 to pass new legislation for the political purging of the judiciary indicated that the latter had remained largely free of the new partisan leftist hegemony.

8. Dankwart Rustow has emphasized the crucial importance of agreement among political elites at the outset of a new system, since the "hardest struggles are against the birth defects of the political community." "Transitions to Democracy: Toward a Dynamic Model," *Comparative Politics,* 2 (April 1970), 337–63. Cf. H. J. Spiro, *Government by Constitution* (New York, 1959), 361–83; R. A. Dahl, *Polyarchy: Participation and Oppression* (New Haven, 1971), 71; S. P. Huntington, "Will More Countries Become Democratic?" *Political Science Quarterly,* 99 (Summer 1984), 193–218; and J. Higley and R. Gunther, *Elites and Democratic Consolidation in Latin America and Southern Europe* (Cambridge, 1992).

9. Both left Republicans and Socialists initially tended to confuse the middle-class leftist intelligentsia and small progressive sectors with broad bourgeois interests generally, a massive sociopolitical miscalculation that recapitulated at a surprisingly late date and admittedly in a different form the same confusion found in Russia in 1905. Cf. T. Shanin, *Russia, 1905–1907: Revolution as a Moment of Truth* (New Haven, 1986), 73 and passim.

10. In Germany, for example, the Weimar constitution was created by a coalition

of moderate Socialists, middle-class democrats, and the Catholic center (Catholicism, always minoritarian in Germany, was more liberal and progressive there than in Spain).

11. M. Cabrera, *La patronal ante la II República* (Madrid, 1983), 307–12.

12. See H. A. Winkler, "Choosing the Lesser Evil: The German Social Democrats and the Fall of the Weimar Republic," *Journal of Contemporary History*, 25:2–3 (May–June 1990), 205–07; and idem, *Der Weg in die Katastrophe: Arbeiter und Arbeiterbewegung in der Weimarer Republik 1930–1933* (Berlin, 1990).

13. As Sydney Tarrow has observed of a later period of conflict in Italy, crises tend to develop as "social conflict is transparent and political opportunities are expanding," rather than in times of restricted political rights and opportunities. *Democracy and Disorder: Protest and Politics in Italy, 1965–1975* (New York, 1989), 48–49.

14. For a lucid discussion of this problem in comparative perspective, see J. J. Linz and A. Valenzuela, eds., *Las crisis del presidencialismo* (Madrid, 1997).

15. For a sophisticated and intriguing comparative analysis, even if not always fully convincing, see G. M. Luebbert, *Liberalism, Fascism, or Social Democracy: Social Classes and the Political Origins of Regimes in Interwar Europe* (New York, 1991).

16. In the speeches of Gil Robles and Calvo Sotelo, frequently cited above and elsewhere, and reproduced extensively in the longer historical accounts, and most recently in R. de la Cierva, *Media nación no se resigna a morir: Los documentos perdidos del Frente Popular* (Madrid, 2002).

17. Cf. J. Peirats, *La C. N. T, en la revolución española* (Toulouse, 1951), 1:121.

18. R. Cibrián, "Violencia política y crisis democrática: España en 1936," *Revista de Estudios Políticos*, 6 (November–December 1978), 81–115.

19. G. Jackson, *The Spanish Republic and the Civil War, 1931–1939* (Princeton, 1965), 222.

20. Cibrián, "Violencia política."

21. Reported in R. De Felice, *Mussolini il fascista: La conquista del potere* (Turin, 1966), 35–39, 87.

22. For data on the Weimar Republic, see E. Rosenhaft, *Beating the Fascists? The German Communists and Political Violence, 1919–1933* (Cambridge, 1983); and R. Bissel, *Political Violence and the Rise of Nazism: The Storm Troopers in Eastern Germany, 1925–1934* (London, 1984).

23. G. Botz, *Gewalt in der Politik: Attentäte, Zusammenstösse, Putschversuche: Unruhen in Österreich*, 2nd ed. (Vienna, 1983).

24. H. W. Koch, *Der deutsche Bürgerkrieg: Eine Geschichte der deutschen und österreichischen Freikorps 1918–1923* (Berlin, 1978); the anonymous account *Die Münchner Tragödie. Verlauf und Zusammenbruch der Räterepublik* (Berlin, 1919); H. Hillmayr, *Roter und Weisser Terror in Bayern nach 1918* (Munich, 1974); and H. A. Winkler, *Arbeiter und Arbeiterbewegung in der Weimarer Republik 1918 bis 1924* (Berlin, 1984).

25. P. Preston, *The Spanish Right under the Second Republic* (Reading, U.K., 1971), 6.

26. E. E. Malefakis, *Agrarian Reform and Peasant Revolution in Spain* (New Haven, 1970), 390 n. 3.

27. Cf. the remarks of M. A. Egido León, *Manuel Azaña entre el mito y la leyenda* (Valladolid, 1998), 358–59.

28. Quoted in P. E. Sigmund, *The Overthrow of Allende and the Politics of Chile, 1964–1976* (Pittsburgh, 1977), 215. This remains perhaps the best study. See also A. Valenzuela, *The Breakdown of Democratic Regimes: Chile* (Baltimore, 1978); R. Moss, *Chile's Marxist Experiment* (London, 1973); C. Huneeus, *El regimen de Pinochet* (Santiago de Chile, 2001), 77–87; and F. G. Gil et al., eds., *Chile at the Turning Point: Lessons of the Socialist Years, 1970–1973* (Philadelphia, 1969), especially the comparison between Spain and Chile written by Juan J. Linz and Henry A. Landsberger, 399–438.

Alcalá Zamora, Niceto: and Republican center-right, 11, 39; as president, 26, 129–30; and coalitions, 27, 104–5, 106; and Azaña, 28–29, 30, 35, 50, 75, 76, 103, 224–25, 230–31, 354, 380n6; and Martínez Barrio, 36, 74, 85; and elections of *1933*, 37, 41, 42; and electoral law, 38, 54, 115, 130, 138, 349, 350; and CEDA, 44–45, 130, 131–34, 141, 224, 225, 230, 350–51, 355; and Gil Robles, 44–45, 131–34, 137, 382n14, 383n19; and rule by minority government, 44–51, 83; and December crisis, 50, 51, 131–34, 137; and Samper, 62; and Catalonia, 67; and economic conditions, 70–71; and repression of revolutionaries, 97, 100; and constitutional reform, 114–15, 130, 131, 157, 381n19; and government reorganization of September *1935*, 117, 118–19; and corruption scandals, 121–25, 126, 127; and Portela Valladares, 133, 140–43, 184, 232, 388nn33, 34; personalistic style of, 136–37, 225, 354; and budget, 141, 142; and elections of *1936*, 170, 173, 178, 182, 212–14, 355; impeach-ment of, 224–33, 243, 250; and Azaña's *1936* government, 225–28, 231, 232; and extortion on high-ways, 298, 400n6; and constitu-tional democracy, 353, 354–55

Alianza Obrera (AO), 59–60, 66, 72–73, 80–82, 85–89, 151, 207, 209

Araquistain, Luis, 71, 73, 144, 151, 153, 157, 205–6, 242, 279–81, 329–30

Azaña, Manuel: and Acción Republi-cana, 12; leadership style of, 14–15, 24–25, 132, 137, 191, 310; rhetoric of, 14, 15, 229, 231, 234, 236; and anticlericalism, 17–18, 197, 389n24; and military, 18, 20, 112–13, 197, 199, 200–201, 247, 309–11, 315–17, 320, 347; and press censorship, 24; and Casas Viejas executions, 26–27; and Alcalá Zamora, 28–29, 30, 35, 75, 76, 103, 224–25, 230–31, 354, 380n6; and municipal elections, 31, 196, 226–27, 228, 236; government of *1931–1933*, 35–37, 309; and Social-ists, 35–36, 55, 73, 75–76, 83–84, 104, 144, 157–58, 187, 202, 356; and Martínez Barrio, 36, 76, 185, 246, 325, 380n6; and electoral law,

Azaña, Manuel (*continued*)
    39; and elections of *1933*, 41–42,
    181, 372n21; and crisis of *1934*,
    50–51; and land distribution, 61,
    110; and labor relations, 63; and
    Catalonia, 68–69, 75; and republi-
    canism, 74–75; and alternative left-
    center government, 75–76, 86–87;
    and radicalism, 75, 197, 215, 355–
    56; and arms discovery, 77; and
    revolutionary insurrection of *1934*,
    88, 276, 378n79; prosecution of,
    101, 103–4; political rallies of, 106,
    107, 120, 151, 157; and government
    reorganization, 118; and corruption
    scandals, 121, 122; and leftist alli-
    ance, 154, 155, 157–58, 161–66, 231;
    and Spanish Popular Front, 160,
    162, 163, 185, 193, 283, 296, 316;
    and elections of *1936*, 180, 185, 213,
    240, 387n21; and Portela Valla-
    dares, 183, 185; Republican Left
    government under, 185–86; and
    Sánchez Román, 185–86, 242, 250,
    294, 296, 399n3; government of
    1936, 186–97, 198, 202–4, 215,
    219–21, 223–24, 227–29, 233–37,
    251–52, 310–11, 388–89n9, 393n33;
    and revolutionary left, 193–94,
    196, 197, 201, 316, 317, 361; as presi-
    dent, 241–47, 294; and conspira-
    cies, 311, 316; and Goded, 314; and
    military conspiracy/revolt of *1936*,
    316–18, 335, 365; and civil war pre-
    vention, 335–37; Allende compared
    to, 367; historical writing on,
    370n6; and constitutional reform,
    381n19

Basque Nationalists, 19, 64, 66, 68–70,
    171–72, 176, 179, 189, 207, 211, 271,
    358, 362
Besteiro, Julián, 32–34, 39, 55–57, 71,
    86, 95, 118, 156, 180, 205, 208, 219,
    243, 250, 263, 384n24, 393n38

Calvo Sotelo, José: return to Spain, 50;
    and Socialists, 98, 249; and civil
    rights, 100–101; and Cambó, 103;
    and state of alarm, 106; and mili-
    tary, 112, 174; and Gil Robles, 116;
    and Alcalá Zamora, 119; and mon-
    archist coalition, 172; and authori-
    tarianism, 174; and elections of
    1936, 211, 213, 241; assassination of,
    224, 315, 322–28, 331, 332, 333–34,
    361–65; and Azaña's *1936* govern-
    ment, 234; and jailing of right,
    266–67; and regional autonomy,
    272; and violence, 297–98, 299;
    and Galarza, 302; and military
    conspiracy/revolt of *1936*, 307, 311,
    322; and Assault Guard, 321–24,
    326, 333; and budget, 381n23
Casares Quiroga, Santiago: and anti-
    clericalism, 18; and elections of
    1933, 42; and municipal councils,
    62; and elections of *1936*, 211, 241;
    as prime minister, 246, 248–49,
    251; and agrarian reform, 249, 252,
    260; and economic conditions,
    249, 252, 253; and violence, 265,
    361; and Civil Guard, 269, 317;
    and Socialists, 270, 279, 280, 290,
    330; and CNT, 277; and Sánchez
    Román, 297; and Calvo Sotelo,
    298, 299, 324, 325, 333; and Mar-
    tínez Barrio, 302; and conspiracies,
    311, 316; and Franco, 314, 333; and
    military, 316–17; and military con-
    spiracy/revolt of *1936*, 317–18, 331–
    32, 334, 335; criticism of, 327; and
    Spanish Popular Front, 329; resig-
    nation of, 335; Allende compared
    to, 367
Catalonia, 19, 21–22, 40, 43, 58–60,
    66–69, 78, 87–88, 94, 99–100,
    158, 168, 171–72, 188, 207, 233,
    253, 270–71, 278–79, 288–89
Catholic Church: Catholic opinion, 11,
    18, 25, 36–37, 64, 107, 174, 178,
    351, 365–66; Catholic education,
    12, 18, 47, 114, 129, 134, 189, 220–
    21, 238, 251–52, 347, 363; and
    Republican left, 16, 195, 348; and
    civil rights, 17, 20, 38, 136, 347;

anti-Catholicism, 22, 114; Catholic corporatism, 25, 45; and elections of 1936, 173. *See also* Confederación Española de Derechas Autónomas

Chapaprieta, Joaquín, 74, 116–17, 119–20, 122, 125–34, 141–42, 172, 220–21, 227, 231, 393n33

Civil War of 1936, 10, 33, 37, 92–94, 111, 151, 180, 235–36, 247, 275, 303, 329–32, 335–39, 353, 362, 387n22, 405n39, 406n44

Comintern: and Spanish Communist Party, 23, 79–82, 164, 167–68, 202, 204–6, 284–85; and revolutionary insurrection of 1934, 57–58, 100, 144, 145–46; and fascism, 79, 80, 145–46, 148, 158; and France, 80–81, 145, 146, 150, 158–59, 291; and Popular Front, 145–46, 154, 158, 159–60, 164; and Maurín, 152; and leftist alliance, 162; and Spanish Popular Front, 167, 168, 203, 285, 291, 303, 361; and right, 173; and revolutionary movements of 1936, 283–87, 288; and Marxist parties in Catalonia, 288–89; and POUM, 290; and assassination of Calvo Sotelo, 324; and preparations for civil war, 330; and leftist domination, 331

Companys, Lluís, 67, 87–88, 106, 187–88, 270, 278, 335

Confederación Española de Derechas Autónomas (Spanish Confederation of Autonomous Rightist Groups; CEDA): rise of, 25, 52; and violence, 25, 195, 235, 267; and electoral law, 39; and elections of 1933, 40, 41; and Alcalá Zamora, 44–45, 130, 131–34, 141, 224, 225, 230, 350–51, 355; coalition with Radical Republican Party, 46, 105, 106, 107, 118, 380n11; and Catholic education, 47, 189, 221, 251; power of, 47, 165, 342; and center-right coalition, 48, 141, 172; and Lerroux, 50, 53, 105, 351; and labor and land norms, 55; and revolutionary insur-

rection of 1934, 71, 94, 98, 173; and fascism, 72, 93, 94, 136, 153, 301; and Azaña, 75, 83–84, 104, 189, 229, 234, 235; and minority government, 82–84; and military, 98–99, 112, 113, 200, 300, 307; and political rallies, 106–7, 120; and agrarian reform, 109; and constitutional reform, 114, 115, 172; and electoral reform, 115, 136, 138, 350; and Gil Robles, 116, 131; and budget, 117, 128, 129, 130, 131, 143; and corruption scandals, 124, 126, 127; and counterrevolutionary front, 142, 275; electoral operation of, 143; and Araquistain, 144; and elections of 1936, 172–73, 178, 181, 237, 238–39; and Comintern, 202; and Spanish Communist Party, 204; and Cortes, 209; and municipal elections, 227; and majoritarian government, 243, 251; and Socialists, 245; and regional autonomy, 271; and anticlericalism, 306; and conservatism, 309; and conspiracies, 311; and military conspiracy/revolt of 1936, 314, 401n14, 402n15

Confederación Nacional del Trabajo (National Confederation of Labor; CNT): and anarchosyndicalism, 5, 20, 270; and violence, 5, 64, 72, 105, 222, 257, 266, 277, 278; flexibility of, 22; repression of, 23; and Socialists, 32, 201; and elections of 1933, 43, 44; mini-insurrection of, 54; decline of, 56; and strikes, 58, 79, 209, 222, 254, 256–58, 261, 266, 268, 270, 276, 277, 278, 284; and UGT, 60, 89, 209, 268, 276–77, 278, 289, 326; and direct action, 66; and Escamots, 67; domination of, 79, 87; and Alianza Obrera, 89; and repression of revolutionaries, 101; and jurados representation, 108; and leftist alliance, 166; and elections of 1936, 178, 179, 180; goal of, 218; and agrarian reform, 258; division within, 276;

Confederación Nacional del Trabajo
(*continued*)
and revolutionary movements of
1936, 276–79; and libertarian communism, 281; and assassination of
Calvo Sotelo, 325; and military con-
spiracy/revolt of *1936*, 334; subversion of, 349

Díaz, José, 79, 81, 150, 158, 168, 203–4,
235, 283–84, 331

Economic depression, 19, 31–32, 52–53,
60–61, 89, 116, 130, 274, 343–44,
352
Economic development, 5, 8, 10–11,
55–56, 189, 205, 273–74, 339, 341,
343–44, 347–48
Economic recovery, 70, 121, 138, 216
Education, 12, 16–18, 20, 47, 113–14,
129, 134, 189, 220–21, 238, 251–52,
277, 346–47, 363
Elections of *1933*, 39–43, 154, 178, 181,
182, 372n21
Elections of *1936*: polarization in, 28,
137–38, 174, 179, 181; and Portela
Valladares, 160, 170–72, 173, 176,
178, 181–84, 213; and right, 170–81,
189, 211–12, 237–41, 310, 364; and
left, 173–81, 183–84, 189, 210–12,
237–39, 241–42; results of, 174–81,
184, 210, 387nn15, 21, 22; and
Azaña, 180, 185, 213, 240, 387n21;
and Franco, 182–84, 238–39, 310,
388n32; and Comisión de Actas,
210–14; and Cuenca, 211, 212, 236,
237–41, 251, 364; and Prieto, 238,
239–40, 393–94n49

Falange Española: closing down centers
of, 43; and Gil Robles, 47; militia
of, 64; and left, 65, 194; and Socialists, 76, 375n27; and violence, 82,
195, 221–23, 265, 267, 306, 310,
319–20; and agrarian reform, 111;
and elections of *1936*, 180, 237;
freeing of, 187; and Popular Front,
191–93; underground members

of, 200; and military, 201, 241,
310; and Spanish Communist
Party, 204; disarming of, 229;
growth in, 263, 266–67; arrests
of, 266, 316, 317–18, 320–21, 324,
325; and MAOC, 305; and military
conspiracy/revolt of *1936*, 314, 332;
subversion of, 349; official dissolution of, 364
France, 6, 9–10, 80–81, 101–2, 126–27,
145–46, 150, 158–59, 164–65, 253–
54, 268–69, 274, 284, 291–93,
339, 344, 352
Franco, Francisco: and revolutionary insurrection of *1934*, 86; and Yagüe,
91; and rumors of military regime,
97; repression of *1936*, 102; and Gil
Robles, 112, 132, 382–83n16; and
elections of *1936*, 182–84, 238–39,
310, 388n32; and Azaña, 186; and
Canary Islands, 198, 200, 311; and
rebellion of 18 July, 199; and military conspiracy/revolt of *1936*, 308,
314, 333–34, 368, 402n16; and assassination of Calvo Sotelo, 333–34;
early regime of, 351

Germany, 64–65, 78, 80–81, 84, 101–2,
142–43, 153–54, 269, 314, 341–42,
344–45, 351, 357–58, 360, 364,
407–8n10
Gil Robles, José Ma.: leadership of, 25;
and electoral law, 39; and Alcalá
Zamora, 44–45, 131–34, 137,
382n14, 383n19; legislative program of, 47; and Lerroux, 50, 122;
and fascism, 72, 94, 153, 173,
382n14; and minority government,
82, 83, 208; and military, 98, 104,
112–13, 132; as minister of war, 105,
119; and political rallies, 106–7,
380n11; and agrarian reform, 109;
and constitutional reform, 116, 131,
173; and center coalition, 118–19;
and corruption scandals, 126; and
taxation, 129; and budget, 131, 141–
42; and coup d'état, 132, 382–
83n16; and Chapaprieta, 141; and

elections of *1936*, 172, 181, 182, 183, 237; and Cortes, 231–32; and Azaña, 234–36, 242, 316, 394n52; and Prieto, 245; and law, 249; and majoritarian government, 250, 251; and Spanish Communist Party, 286; and violence, 297, 300, 327, 357; and Assault Guard, 321; and military conspiracy/revolt of *1936*, 401n14

Giménez Fernández, Manuel, 105, 109–10, 189–90, 211, 243–44, 250–51, 388–89n9

Hitler, Adolf, 39, 52, 59, 80–81, 212, 224, 240, 283, 361, 364

Italy, 20, 56, 65, 67, 84, 101, 153, 221, 269, 288, 309, 314, 352–53, 356, 358, 360, 362

Largo Caballero, Francisco: and revolution, 13–14, 54; and labor relations, 19, 53; and Republican left, 31, 75–76; and dictatorship of proletariat, 33, 34, 159; and fascism, 33, 71; on Communists, 55, 207; and ten-point program, 56; and UGT, 57, 279; and Maurín, 60; and revolutionary committee, 62, 88; and strikes, 63, 65–66; and violence, 94, 195; and revolutionary insurrection of *1934*, 144–45, 158, 282–83; and leftist alliance, 156, 157–58, 161, 166, 169; and Comintern, 159, 167; and Prieto, 160, 245; resignation of, 201; and Albornoz, 242; and Britain, 270; and CNT, 277; and Socialist split, 281, 282; and POUM, 288, 290; and military conspiracy/revolt of *1936*, 328–29, 333, 334–35

Lerroux, Alejandro: and Republican center-right, 11; political experience of, 14; and press censorship, 24, 106; and coalitions, 35–36, 119; and Radical Republican Party, 46–47, 83, 122, 383n21; and right, 47; and 97–98; and Martínez Barrio, 48, 74, 98; and amnesty legislation, 50; and CEDA, 50, 53, 105, 351; and Alcalá Zamora, 51, 75, 97, 103, 121, 127, 130, 355; and fascism, 53, 97; and municipal boundaries law, 54; and social reforms, 55; Samper compared to, 62; and Socialists, 77, 86; and revolutionary insurrection of *1934*, 90, 96; and repression of revolutionaries, 100, 104; and cedorradicals, 105, 107, 380n11; and labor relations, 107; and military, 112; and electoral reform, 115; and corruption scandals, 123–28; and agrarian reform, 134; and Spanish Communist Party, 286, 304; and constitutional democracy, 353

Madariaga, Salvador de, 38, 49–50, 94, 210, 221–22, 226, 232, 381n19

Malefakis, Edward, 94, 196–97, 252, 264, 357, 364–65

Manuilsky, Dimitri, 167, 203, 206, 284, 330, 390–91n44

Martínez Barrio, Diego: and Alcalá Zamora, 36, 74, 85; and Azaña, 36, 76, 185, 246, 325, 380n6; and electoral law, 41–42; and Lerroux, 48, 74, 98; and leftist alliance, 154, 157, 161, 166–67; and elections of *1933*, 182; and Portela Valladares, 183; as Cortes president, 210, 235; and elections of *1936*, 212; as acting president, 232; and majoritarian government, 250; and Socialists, 302; and assassination of Calvo Sotelo, 323, 335; and military conspiracy/revolt of *1936*, 335, 336; and prevention of civil war, 335–37, 405n39, 406n44; and revolutionary insurrection of *1934*, 380n6

Marxism, 20–21, 30, 32–34, 59–60, 68, 151, 153, 156, 158, 167, 196, 205, 208, 281, 288–89, 345

Marxism-Leninism, 23, 52, 60, 168, 204, 207, 209, 272

Maura, Miguel: and Republican center-right, 11, 39; on Azaña, 15; and elections of 1933, 41; and revolutionary insurrection of 1934, 85; and Lerroux, 98; and Alcalá Zamora, 132, 133, 232; and Portela Valladares government, 143; and elections of 1936, 179, 189; and majoritarian government, 243, 249, 250; and fascism, 300–301; and Martínez Barrio, 336; and constitutional democracy, 353

Maurín, Joaquín, 23, 58–60, 79, 151–54, 288–91, 299, 329–30

Milicias Antifascistas Obreras y Campesinas (Worker-Peasant Antifascist Militias; MAOC), 65, 80, 286, 290, 304–5, 320, 334, 393n46

Mola, Emilio, 112, 198, 199, 312–15, 317, 328, 331–34, 336, 365, 368

Ortega y Gasset, José, 27, 38, 105, 339, 348, 406–7n1

Partido de Izquierda Republicana. See Republican left

Partido Obrero de Unificación Marxista (Worker Party of Marxist Unification; POUM), 151, 153–54, 158, 161, 166, 205, 209, 272, 275, 280, 287–91, 361

Popular Front, 145–46, 154, 158–60, 164–65, 168, 253–54, 284, 291–93. See also Spanish Popular Front

Portela Valladares, Manuel: as governor general, 99; and Lerroux, 104, 106; and Alcalá Zamora, 133, 140–43, 184, 232, 388n33, 34; and elections of 1936, 160, 170–72, 173, 176, 178, 181–84, 213; resignation of, 181–84, 388nn32, 33, 34; and Prieto, 244; and state of alarm vote, 327; and military conspiracy/revolt of 1936, 331

Portugal, 2, 12–13, 25, 45, 153, 269, 313, 339, 347

Prieto, Indalecio: and Alcalá Zamora, 29; and coalitions, 33, 35–36; and Russia, 34; and amnesty legislation, 49; ten-point program of, 56; and military, 57; on Socialist Youth, 65; and Catalan conflict, 69; and Republican left, 75; and arms delivery, 77, 376n57; and revolutionary insurrection of 1934, 95, 166, 239; and Strauss, 121; and corruption scandals, 127; and leftist alliance, 155, 156, 161, 163, 165–66; and Largo Caballero, 160, 245; and press, 166, 249, 281–82, 300, 302, 305, 306–7, 328; and violence, 195, 239–40, 306, 360, 393–94n49; and executive commission of Socialists, 201; and bolshevization of Socialists, 208; resignation of, 212; and Azaña, 229, 230, 242, 243–44; on January dissolution of Cortes, 231–32; and elections of 1936, 238, 239–40, 393–94n49; and majoritarian government, 244–46, 249, 250, 251, 297; and strikes, 255; and regional autonomy, 271; and Socialist split, 281–82; and militia groups, 322; and assassination of Calvo Sotelo, 323, 327–28, 331, 333, 405n36; and military conspiracy/revolt of 1936, 333, 335, 404–5n36; and Martínez Barrio, 336, 337, 406n45

Primo de Rivera, José Antonio, 47, 64, 111, 124, 191, 193, 238, 240–41, 244, 309–10, 313–14

Radical Republican Party: and Republican center-right, 11, 39; and Republican coalition, 14, 29–30; and elections of 1933, 40; and Alcalá Zamora, 45–46, 104, 130, 133, 355; coalition with CEDA, 46, 105, 106, 107, 118, 380n11; diversity of, 46; and Lerroux, 46–47, 83, 122, 383n21; and Martínez Barrio, 48, 74; and Republican reforms, 49, 107; and Pich y Pon, 99; and military, 112; and education, 114; and electoral reform, 115; and corruption scandals, 121–28, 138; decline of, 130, 131; and democratization, 138, 383n21; and budget, 143; and elections of 1936, 171–72, 178, 179; and violence, 186; and land expropriation, 217; and constitutional democracy, 353–54

Radical Socialist Republican Party, 12, 14, 27, 35, 74, 93. *See also* Socialists

Republican left: and Republican coalition, 11, 12, 14, 26, 29, 35, 52, 96; and democratization, 12–13, 155; and radicalism, 12, 215, 275, 345–46; and social reforms, 12, 16–20, 26, 41, 52, 61, 62, 346–47; and anticlericalism, 16–18, 27, 195, 347; and Socialists, 31–34, 37, 39, 73, 83–84, 86, 94, 95, 141, 151, 155, 157, 160–61, 163, 201, 202, 243, 244, 280, 328, 337, 347; and elections of 1933, 40, 41–43, 154, 181; and electoral law, 54, 156; and Catalonia, 66; economic program of, 73–74, 76; fragmentation of, 74–75; and Azaña, 75, 76, 84–85, 185–86, 242, 246; governing role of, 93, 243; repression investigation of, 99–100; and Lerroux, 107; and agrarian reform, 111, 260, 262, 264, 366–67; and Alcalá Zamora, 118, 230–31; and Spanish Communist Party, 148, 165, 203–4; and leftist alliance, 154, 157, 164, 165–66; and Spanish Popular Front, 160, 161, 163–66, 195, 215, 303; and Portela Valladares, 171; and elections of 1936, 174, 175, 178, 180, 184, 185, 212, 213, 237, 387n21; and fascism, 194; and violence, 195–96, 268, 362–63; and municipal elections, 196; and military, 201, 316; and left, 215–16, 376n45; and education, 220–21; and international affairs, 221; and Republican government, 243, 247; and Prieto, 244; and Casares Quiroga, 248, 394n1; and economic conditions, 252–53, 264; and strikes, 257; and regional autonomy, 271; and revolutionary

movements of 1936, 293; and Sánchez Román, 297; and left-center coalition, 336, 337; and polarization, 346, 348

Revolutionary insurrection of 1934: and breakdown of Second Republic, 26; polarization of, 26, 309, 352; and Comintern, 57–58, 100, 144, 145–46; and Revolutionary Liaison Committee, 57–58, 62, 71, 77, 84, 88, 91; and Maurín, 58–60; and strikes, 62–63, 65, 77–78, 85–86, 88, 89; and Catalan conflict, 66–69, 78; and Basque conflict, 69–70; and political rivalries, 70–78; and arms, 76, 77, 85, 87, 89–92, 103, 104, 377n71; and Spanish Communist Party, 79–82, 145, 147, 150, 151; beginning of, 82–95; and violence, 90–93, 99, 162, 165, 173, 258, 358, 360; sumarísimo court-martial proceedings, 96–97; repression following, 97–103, 106, 121, 135, 151, 155, 157, 160, 168–69, 173, 197, 223, 239, 304; myth of, 156; and elections of 1936, 180; amnesty for prisoners of, 187, 197; purpose of, 282–83; and Castillo, 320; and Condés, 321

Revolutionary movements of 1936, 273–75, 307, 308, 311–18, 331–38, 352–53, 365

Russia, 7, 20–21, 34, 54, 73, 79, 85, 101, 144, 152–53, 167, 205–6, 270, 274, 290, 340, 352–53. *See also* Soviet Union

Samper, Ricardo, 50, 62, 68–70, 76–77, 83, 98, 123

Sánchez Román, Felipe: and coalitions, 54, 155, 157, 161–62, 165, 294–96, 385n33; and Martínez Barrio, 74, 336, 337; and revolutionary insurrection of 1934, 85; and elections of 1936, 179; and Azaña, 185–86, 242, 250, 294, 296, 399n3; and assassination of Calvo Sotelo, 323; and party strength, 353

Sanjurjo, José, 23, 51, 96, 112, 200, 308, 312, 316, 335, 379n89, 401n11
Socialists: and Republican coalition, 11, 13, 14, 26, 29–30, 35–36, 37, 39, 52; and trade unions, 13, 22; weakness of, 13; and social reform, 16, 32; and agrarian reform, 19, 258, 261, 263–64; and anarchosyndicalism, 21–22, 52, 218; role of, 25, 35–36; tactics of, 25, 37, 39, 360–61; ambivalence of, 30–34, 351–52; and Largo Caballero, 31, 54, 55; and Republican left, 31–34, 37, 39, 73, 75, 83–84, 86, 94, 95, 141, 151, 155, 157, 160–61, 163, 201, 202, 243, 244, 280, 328, 337, 347; Socialist Youth, 31, 33, 57–58, 63–65, 72, 76, 79–80, 82, 86, 91, 144, 155–57, 168, 192, 202, 206–9, 279–80, 288, 391n48; and Azaña, 35–36, 55, 73, 75–76, 83–84, 104, 144, 157–58, 187, 202, 356; and elections of 1933, 40, 42; policy shift during 1933–1934, 52, 59; radicalization of, 52–57, 144; revolutionary role of, 52–53, 93–95, 144–45, 151, 155, 258, 275, 276, 305, 360; and strikes, 53, 58, 60, 62–63, 85, 88, 89, 218, 257, 328, 360; and government support, 54, 328, 351–52; bolshevization of, 55, 144, 159, 164, 208, 287, 292, 330; militia groups of, 57, 121, 237, 238, 240, 320, 321, 322, 329–30, 364, 393n46; and Revolutionary Liaison Committee, 57–58, 62, 71, 77, 84, 88, 91, 155; and violence, 57, 64, 65, 71–73, 76, 93–95, 98, 135, 156, 195, 221, 265, 268, 304, 328, 358, 360, 362, 384n24; and arms discovery, 76, 77; and Spanish Communist Party, 80, 81, 144, 147, 147–51, 157, 159, 201–3, 204, 206, 206–9, 286, 304, 330; governing role of, 93, 94; and repression of revolutionaries, 99–100, 101; and Alcalá Zamora, 118; and political rallies, 120, 188; prietistas of, 143–44, 151, 155, 156, 160, 167, 196,

201–2, 208–9, 240, 245–46, 279, 281, 323, 328, 330; caballeristas of, 144, 150–51, 155–57, 160, 162, 164, 166, 180, 201–2, 204, 207–9, 244–45, 276, 279–82, 288–89, 304, 328–30, 337, 352; and democratization, 153, 155; and leftist alliance, 154, 157, 164, 165–66, 188, 197; besteiristas of, 156, 208, 384n24; differences among, 160, 201–2, 205, 208, 245, 249, 279–83, 360–61; and Spanish Popular Front, 160, 161, 163–66, 268, 280, 329–30; and Portela Valladares, 171; and elections of 1936, 173, 174, 178, 180, 213, 237, 238, 239, 387n21; and military, 200, 202, 280, 290, 328; and Cortes, 209–11; and majoritarian government, 243, 244; and Casares Quiroga, 270, 279, 280, 290, 330; and POUM, 288; and assassination of Calvo Sotelo, 322, 323, 324, 328, 361–62; and military conspiracy/revolt of 1936, 334; and Leninist ideal, 345. See also Radical Socialist Republican Party
Soviet Union, 34, 102, 153–54, 157, 167, 173, 203, 205–7, 226, 285, 289, 339, 345. See also Russia
Spanish Communist Party (Partido Comunista de España; PCE): and Comintern, 23, 79–82, 164, 167–68, 202, 204–6, 284–85; and elections of 1933, 40; role of, 52, 202–6; and Catalonia, 58–59, 168; and fascism, 64–65, 146–47, 286, 324–25; and revolutionary insurrection of 1934, 79–82, 145, 147, 150, 151; and Socialist Youth, 79, 80, 91, 168, 202, 206, 207–9, 279–80, 391n48; and Socialists, 80, 81, 144, 147–51, 157, 159, 201–3, 206–9, 286, 304, 330; and strikes, 80, 284, 285, 286; alliance tactics of, 148–49; thirteen-point program of, 149–50; propaganda of, 150–51, 161, 198, 205; and democratic re-

public, 152; and Spanish Popular Front, 161, 167, 168, 280, 286, 303, 361; and elections of *1936*, 180, 213, 237; and political rallies, 188, 287; and violence, 192, 195, 221, 360; and municipal elections, 196; and Worker Alliances, 202–3, 206, 283–86; militia groups of, 237, 320, 321, 330, 364, 393n46, 403n7; and agrarian reform, 261, 264, 286; and revolutionary movements of *1936*, 275, 283–87, 293; and POUM, 288, 290; and assassination of Calvo Sotelo, 315, 322, 324; and avoidance of civil war, 330–31, 334, 361

Spanish Popular Front: and Azaña, 160, 162, 163, 185, 193, 283, 296, 316; and Republican left, 160, 161, 163–66, 215, 303; and Socialists, 160, 161, 163–66, 268, 280, 329–30; and Prieto, 161, 166, 244; and Sánchez Román, 161–62, 165, 295; and Spanish Communist Party, 161, 167, 168, 280, 286, 303, 361; role of, 166, 168, 169, 196, 302; and Comintern, 167, 168, 203, 285, 291, 303, 361; and prison openings, 169, 388n5; and elections of *1936*, 171–73, 175–81, 189, 211, 212, 213–14, 230–31, 237, 240, 242, 288, 310; victory march of, 188; and fascism, 191, 221, 267, 303; contradictions within, 197, 234, 275; program of, 204, 208, 210, 215, 216, 233, 260, 299, 304; land distribution under, 219; and auxiliary police, 223–24; and Alcalá Zamora, 224, 232; and municipal elections, 228; and Giménez Fernández, 250; and economic conditions, 253, 255, 264; and regional autonomy, 271, 272; and CNT, 277, 278; and Trotsky, 290; militias of, 329; and avoidance of civil war, 330, 331; and military conspiracy/revolt of *1936*, 337; impunity of criminal action for, 363

Spanish Socialist Workers Party (PSOE). *See* Socialists

Unemployment, 19, 31, 53, 108–9, 131, 134, 216, 219–20, 233, 244, 252–55, 265

Unión General de Trabajadores (General Union of Workers; UGT): as mass movement, 13; role of, 21–22; and strikes, 32, 53, 58, 62, 63, 66, 77–78, 86, 107–8, 209, 254, 257–58, 261, 279, 284, 334–35; and Largo Caballero, 33, 57, 157, 160; and radicalization, 55; divisions within, 56–57; and BOC, 59; and CNT, 60, 89, 209, 268, 276–77, 278, 289, 326; and Republican left, 75; and Samper, 76–77; domination of, 79; closing of headquarters, 93; revolutionary class nature of, 156; and Comintern, 159; and leftist alliance, 161, 165; and elections of *1936*, 178; and left Socialists, 201; and Spanish Communist Party, 206, 207–8, 279; and land expropriation, 262; and agrarian reform, 263–64; and Socialist split, 279, 280, 350; and Spanish Popular Front, 280, 329–30; and Catalonia, 289; and Falangists, 319; and government support, 328

Unión Republicana, 74, 85, 154, 183, 185–86, 190, 195, 212, 242, 247, 255, 259, 268, 297, 302, 306, 336, 337

Violence: and CNT, 5, 64, 72, 105, 222, 257, 266, 277, 278; and martial law, 6; Azaña's aversion to, 15, 223, 392n16; and anarchosyndicalism, 22, 65, 135, 195, 304; and strikes, 24, 32, 221, 257, 264–65, 266, 270–71; and Largo Caballero, 33; rise of, 38, 306–7; and elections of *1933*, 39–40, 43; and Socialists, 57, 64, 65, 71–73, 76, 93–95, 98, 135, 156, 195, 221, 265, 268, 304, 328, 358, 360, 362, 384n24; and

Violence (*continued*)

  fascism, 64–65, 193, 195, 240; and
  Falange Española, 82, 195, 221–23,
  265, 267, 306, 310, 319–20; and
  left, 90, 93, 134, 136, 141, 183, 190–
  91, 193–94, 223, 238–39, 241, 249,
  265, 303–4, 326, 357–58; and revolutionary insurrection of *1934*, 90–
  93, 99, 162, 165, 173, 258, 358, 360;
  and right, 93, 186, 190–91, 194–
  95, 222–23, 357; and military
  courts, 106; and labor relations,
  111; decrease in, 120; and elections
  of *1936*, 181, 182–84, 239–40, 241,
  357; and Azaña's *1936* government,
  186, 190–95, 234, 235, 236–37; and
  anticlericalism, 194, 195, 221, 226,
  234, 238–39, 252, 297, 306, 389–
  90n24, 399–400n5; expansion of,
  221–24, 264–69, 357–58, 360, 361,
  364; and foreign embassies, 269–
  70; and Catalonia, 270–71, 278;
  totals for political killings, 358,
  359, 360; and counterrevolution,
  367–68

Worker Alliances, 147, 149–50, 156–59,
  167–68, 202–3, 206, 280, 283–86,
  288–91